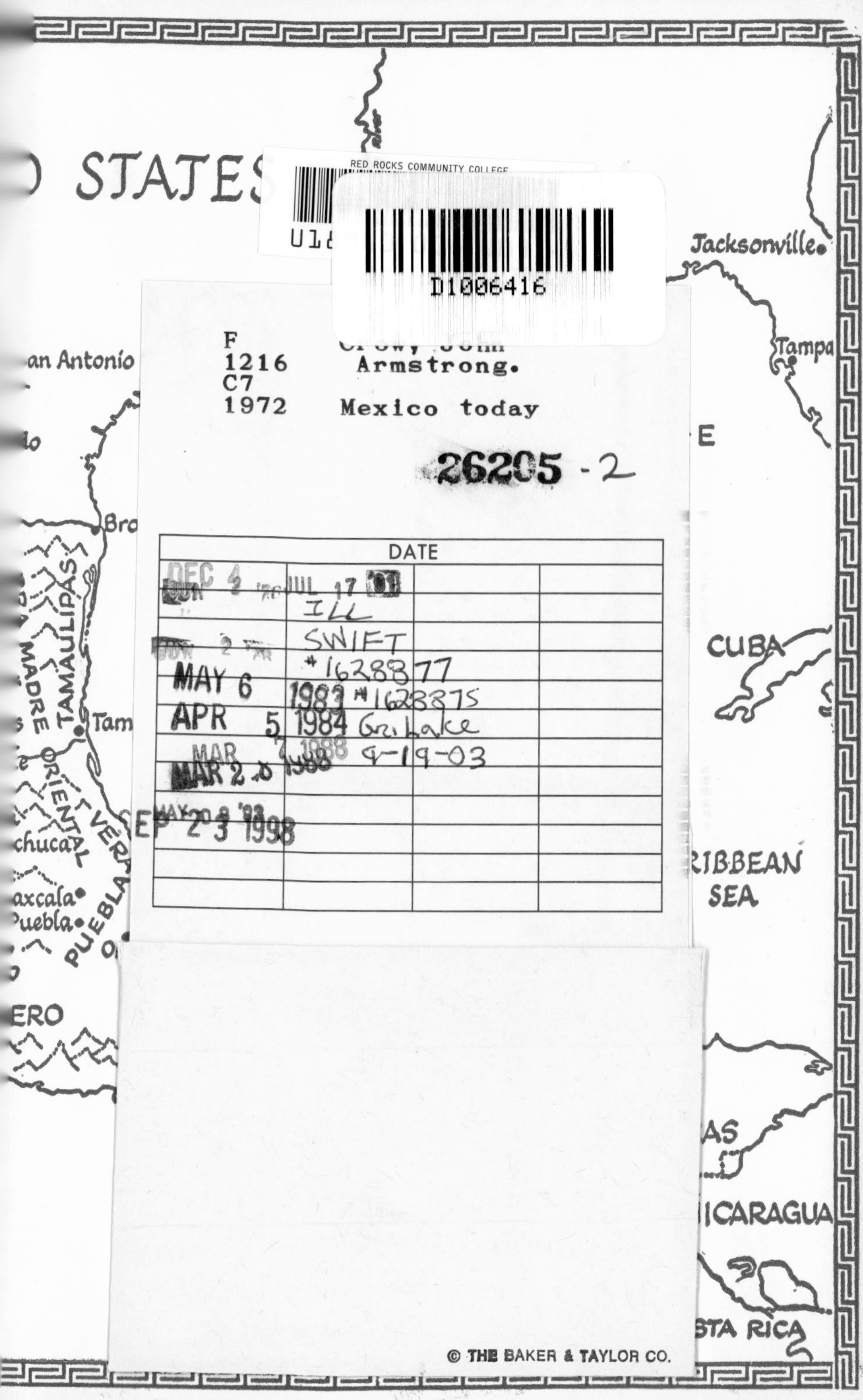

STATES
Jacksonville
Tampa
San Antonio
CUBA
TAMAULIPAS
MADRE
ORIENTAL
VERA
PUEBLA
Tlaxcala
Puebla
RIBBEAN
SEA
NICARAGUA
STA RICA

MEXICO TODAY

Other books by the same author

The Epic of Latin America

Panorama de las Américas

Spanish-American Life

Spain: The Root and the Flower

Italy: A Journey Through Time

Greece: The Magic Spring

MEXICO TODAY

Revised Edition

JOHN A. CROW

HARPER & ROW, PUBLISHERS

New York, Evanston, San Francisco, London

 For information address Harper & Row, Publishers, Inc., 49 East 33rd Street, New York, N.Y. 10016. Published simultaneously in Canada by Fitzhenry & Whiteside Limited, Toronto.

STANDARD BOOK NUMBER: 06-010923-8

LIBRARY OF CONGRESS CATALOG CARD NUMBER: 71-156517

To my wife Jo

CONTENTS

MEXICO
UNITED STATES
GULF OF MEXICO
PACIFIC OCEAN
CARIBBEAN SEA
N
S
E
W
San Diego
Mexicali
Nogales
Ciudad Juárez
El Paso
SONORA
Hermosillo
CHIHUAHUA
Chihuahua
LOWER CALIFORNIA
GULF OF CALIFORNIA
La Paz
SIERRA MADRE OCCIDENTAL
San Pedro
SINALOA
Culiacán
Mazatlán
Tres Marías Islands
DURANGO
Durango
COAHUILA
Nuevo Laredo
Laredo
San Antonio
Houston
Galveston
New Orleans
Mobile
Jacksonville
Tampa
Brownsville
Monterrey
Saltillo
NUEVO LEON
ZACATECAS
Zacatecas
SIERRA MADRE ORIENTAL
TAMAULIPAS
Tampica
SAN LUIS POTOSI
San Luis Potosí Valles
Tamazunchale
Tepic
Aguas Calientes
Guanajuato
Guadalajara
JALISCO
L. Chapala
Querétara
Pachuca
Morelia
MEXICO CITY
Colima
MICHOACAN
Tlaxcala
Puebla
PUEBLA
Cuernavaca
Taxco
Chilpancingo
GUERRERO
Acapulco
Jalapa
Vera Cruz
VERA CRUZ
Orizaba
Oaxaca
OAXACA
Villa Hermosa
TABASCO
Tuxtla
CHIAPAS
Campeche
CAMPECHE
YUCATÁN
Mérida
Chichen-Itzá
QUINTANA ROO
BRITISH HONDURAS
GUATEMALA
HONDURAS
EL SALVADOR
NICARAGUA
COSTA RICA
CUBA
0
100
200
300

ILLUSTRATIONS

Illustrations will be found following page 114:

Illustrations will be found following page 242:

ACKNOWLEDGMENTS

PHOTOGRAPHS from Fotos Hermanos Mayo, Mexico City, except plates 6, 8, 13, 14, 16, 17, 18, 22, 23, Films, C.A.P. de Mexico; 25, Mary Saint Albans; 26, Jack Howard; 27, 28, 29, 31, 32, Mexican National Tourist Council; 30, Ignacio Mariscal. Quotations have been taken from the following works, identified by the following numbers as they appear in the text: 1. Quotations from magazine *Arte Vivo Mexicano*, issue of July, 1955; 2. Henry Bruman, "The Culture History of Mexican Vanilla," which appeared in *Hispanic American Historical Review*, August, 1948; 3. Alfonso Caso, on "Pre-Spanish Art," in *Twenty Centuries of Mexican Art*, 1940; 4. Américo Castro and Raymond Willis, *Iberoamérica*, 1970; 5. Stuart Chase, *Mexico*, 1931; 6. Miguel Covarrubias, "Modern Art," in *Twenty Centuries of Mexican Art*, 1940; 7. Quotation from William Rex Crawford, *A Century of Latin American Thought*, 1961; 8. John A. Crow, *The Epic of Latin America*, 1971; 9. Bernal Díaz, *Architecture in Mexico*, 1947; 29. William Spratling, in "The Color of Silver Is White," in *Mexico This Month* magazine, June, 1956; 30. Frances Toor, *A Treasury of Mexican Folkways*, 1947; 31. Manuel Toussaint, "Colonial Art," in *Twenty Centuries of Mexican Art*, 1940; 32. George C. Vaillant, *The Aztecs of Mexico*, 1966; 33. José Vasconcelos, *Breve Historia de México*, 1937; 34. Antonio Vázquez de Espinosa, *Compendium and Description of the West Indies*, 1612 (Washington, Smithsonian Institution, 1942); 35. Daniel Cosío Villegas, in *Extremos de América*, Mexico, 1949; 36. Hutton Webster, *History of Mankind*, 1928; 37. James W. Wilkie and Edna Monzón de Wilkie, *México Visto en el Siglo Veinte*, interviews with famous Mexicans, Instituto Mexicano de Investigaciones Económicas, Mexico, 1969; data used is from statements made by Jesús Silva Herzog; 38. Octavio Paz, *The Labyrinth of Solitude*, 1962; 39. Juan Rulfo, *Pedro Páramo*, 1959; 40. Agustín Yáñez, *The Edge of the Storm*, 1964; 41. Carlos Fuentes, *The Death of Artemio Cruz*, 1964; 42. Carlos Fuentes, *Where the Air Is Clear*, 1960; 43. Luis Harss and Barbara Dohmann, *Into the Mainstream*, 1967; 44. Banco Nacional de México, *Statistical Data for 1969*, an economic report; 45. Francis M. Foland, "Agrarian Reform in Latin America," in *Foreign Affairs*, October, 1969; 46. Robert W. Northrop,

"Archeological Map of Middle America," with appended data and with the collaboration of Ignacio Bernal, Director of Mexico's National Museum of Anthropology, October, 1968, issue of *The National Geographic;* 47. John Womock, Jr., "The Spoils of the Mexican Revolution," in *Foreign Affairs,* July, 1970; 48. Stan Steiner, "Chicano Power," in *The New Republic,* June 20, 1970; 49. "Informe al Pueblo," the "State of the Union Address" by retiring President Gustavo Díaz Ordaz, Sept. 2, 1970, issue of *Cultura y Ciencia Política,* Mexico City; 50. "A Decade of Economic Strategy," a report made by Antonio Ortiz Mena, Mexico's Secretary of the Treasury, in *Mexico This Month,* issue of August, 1970; 51. Gordon Ragle, "Rodolfo Usigli and his Mexican Scene," in *Hispania,* May, 1963.

PREFACE

You cross the border and enter another world, more foreign than Europe. The visitor to Europe, beneath the quality of strangeness, will feel that he is at the source of a culture that belongs to him. He can at least look and see his own roots. The visitor to Mexico will feel no such bond; he will stand perplexed. If he is the superficial sort, he may spout forth a few clichés about the quaintly picturesque. If he is of a business turn of mind, he will undoubtedly see opportunities by the dozen. But if he has any sincere wish to understand Mexico and her people, he will at first feel plainly bewildered.

This book, it is hoped, may help to bring some clarity to that confusion. At present many millions of Americans visit Mexico every year. They spend more than a billion dollars there annually. The total of these visitors to Mexico comes close to the total number of Americans who visit all the European countries combined. Geography does not argue; Mexico is our nearest foreign neighbor.

Most educated Mexicans now speak English, and many of them have been to school in the United States. But Mexico is not a Western country. It is a crucible, far more than the United States, which invented the term. While we have been blending the members of one family, Mexico has been welding opposites. She is a crucible of two races and of three cultures, unique, highly colored, with an inordinate pride and a tremendous drive now riding the surge of a forward motion which is at its crest.

The races are Indian and white. The cultures are Indian, Hispanic (itself a fusion of Moorish-Roman-Iberian), and Anglo-Saxon. Many Mexicans would object to the inclusion of the Anglo-Saxon, but its influence is so omnipresent and so inescapable that it now permeates the Mexican techniques supporting life, which in turn will at least partly determine the Mexican culture of tomorrow.

Mexico now, after many years of upheaval and oppression, is a peaceful and progressive country. The beauty of its land, its cities, and its villages is a marvel to behold. There is an intensely pictorial quality to the country to which the foreigner never becomes wholly accustomed.

It is the primary intention of this book to present the main currents in the ebb and flow of Mexican life. You will not find any lists of all the Mexican viceroys or presidents, nor any detailed accounting of every article in the constitutions of Mexico. This book is not a history, but an interpretation. Histories usually emphasize political development. My intention is to emphasize the underlying feelings which cause this development.

Yet, there are facts and figures in abundance which prove the dynamic quality of Mexico today. If you are interested only in statistics and in contemporary progress, skip the first half of the book. But one who does so will fall into the category of the American who goes to a foreign country without knowing a word of the language, yet expects to understand fully and to be fully understood. He will, in a word, expect the impossible.

I did not interview the public leaders of Mexico in order to write this book, but rather drew on a lifetime of study and teaching in the field of Latin-American civilization. My contacts in Mexico have been with the ordinary people that anyone can meet. Workers and schoolteachers in all parts of the republic went out of their way to encourage and help me. I only hope that a Mexican visitor to the United States might receive such generous and warm attention. There are only three persons I would like to single out for particular mention: Anita Brenner, editor of the magazine *Mexico This Month*, who along with her fine staff has given me great aid in this project; also Professor Manuel Agraz Aranda, Director of the Escuela Urbana Federal "Licenciado Benito Juárez," in Yahualica, Jalisco, who is symbolic of the best spirit of teaching in Mexico today; and finally, my good friend, Gilberto Alcalá, of Mexico City, who has patiently obtained for me hard-to-find statistics in many areas. No one but myself, however, is in any way responsible for any statement made in this book.

John A. Crow
University of California
Los Angeles

I

THE LAND

It was all for their love of the land, which is man's true navel cord.

—Ciro Alegría

Take the train, the automobile, the plane, or try it on burro or afoot, it would be the same. Go south from Brownsville to Mexico City, or from Laredo, or El Paso, or Nogales. You would see in Mexico first a replica of the Southwestern United States. Mountains and desert. More mountains than in the United States. More desert. At least, more uncultivated desert. Where dams have been built, and irrigation is under way, there are oases, green jewels in the midst of an alkaline aridity of gray-white. The higher mountains, too, are green—green and occasionally timbered.

As one travels south the mountains thicken, reach higher, and the green also spreads out over the slopes. Finally, you swoop up over the crest and are among the Central Highlands. Now emerald valleys are surrounded by lofty peaks and dissected by gorges so deep the eye and brain get dizzy plumbing the depths. Drop a big stone and wait an eternity for it to hit bottom. After the gray desert and rocky piles of northern Mexico the greenery here is more intense; the lifted crags baying out in rim on rim, sierra after sierra, are mightier and more imposing. This is a land where the mountain is King. Volcanic cones, covered with snow, heave upward like Sheba's Breast. Scattered among them, in the level valleys, cornfields everywhere. Cornfields also along the slopes, cornfields even on ledges and steep escarpments. Villages too, perched precariously and picturesquely in pockets placed incredibly among rocky and timbered sierras. This is the land where the Toltecs roamed, where the Aztecs later ruled an empire, where Cortés, the Fair God from across the seas, came to conquer them in the year One Reed, or *Ce Acatl*, according to the ancient Indian prophecies. It is a red man's world, despite the great city that is the nation's capital, despite the towering skyscrapers, despite the beautiful metropolitan airport which surpasses our best.

South of the metropolis, still more Indian country. More mountains, then finally an end of mountains, and at their end tropical jungles, a riotous rain forest in which are buried so many of the ancient Maya settlements. Scattered mounds still dot the countryside, hiding the glories of their ancient pageantry. Many of them have never been visited, much less excavated by the white man.

Mexico City, with a population approaching six million, is the heart of a country that is more Indian than European, more European than North American, yet so Americanized that steel-girdered skyscrapers now rise steadily from the marshy lake bed of the ancient Aztec capital. It is a city of bustle and great wealth, a city of parks and flowers, a city of teeming business where the lavish Continental Hilton lifts its curved height from the Paseo de la Reforma, one among many luxurious hostelries catering to the tourist from the north, with a service that is modern and decorations that are steeped in the colorful Indian past of Mexico.

Mexico is color and contrast. Even in the cool capital, 7,486 feet above the sea, are all the colors of tropical birds—in the great murals, in the stone mosaics at University City, in the bright tones of the fabulous homes in the Gardens of the Pedregal. And a stone's throw from all this modernity and all this wealth, beggars living in shacks on vacant lots, urchins in rags, poverty that is hopeless, diseased, and overwhelming.

Climb high enough in a plane or a balloon, and with a magic pair of binoculars one could see the entire land of Mexico, a land whose geographic contours are the astonishment of travelers and the bane of those overzealous reformers who would overnight catapult their country into the industrial world of tomorrow.

When Cortés appeared before the king and was asked to describe what Mexico was like, he took a sheet of paper, crumpled it in his hand, then dropped it on the table. "Like that, your Majesty," he said. And he was very right.

Mexico is a country of mountains. Whether you are traveling in the north or in the south, in the east or in the west, you are seldom out of sight of the mountains except on the wide limestone plain of Yucatán. To be more exact still, two-thirds of Mexico is mountainous, ranging in altitude from three to eighteen thousand feet. Of the one-third that is level, a great part is arid desert. The writer who described the country as one great mountain was not far from wrong. Mexico does lift itself in a mighty heave from the two oceans, with its apex of towering volcanic cones just south of the capital in the Central Highlands.

However, Mexico is not one but many mountains. Some of them rise almost sheer from the plains "lone as God and white as a winter moon." Others are piled one against the other in fantastic crags that line or crisscross every rail and highway. Within this mountainous wonderland are all landforms, all contours, and almost every climate known to man.

Mexico is shaped like a horn, its wider open end bordering the United States. Along this border Mexico is over a thousand miles in width. At its other end, where the horn narrows into the Isthmus of Tehuantepec, the country is hardly more than a hundred miles wide. Below the isthmus is the wider mouthpiece which juts out into the Gulf. This is the peninsula of Yucatán.

On each side of the horn is a long coastal plain. This is Mexico's hot country. And just a few miles inland from each of these coastal plains is a long range of mountains, one in the east, the other in the west. Those in the west are higher. Lying between these two mountain ranges is a vast tableland, wide in the north, narrow in the south. This is where most of the Mexican people live.

The mountains of the east are called the Sierra Madre Oriental ("Mother Range of the East"), while those of the west are called Sierra Madre Occidental ("Mother Range of the West"). They are probably called "Mother" ranges because they cradle the Mexican heartland, which lies between them. A few miles south of Mexico City the two ranges join in a colossal jumble of mountains watched over by Popocatépetl, the "Mountain that Smokes," and Ixtaccíhuatl, the "Sleeping Lady." Both rise from the maguey- and cornfields above which their snow-crested peaks seem to float like two white wraiths. By day they stand upon a gray-blue haze, but at the setting of the sun their summits and the sky are mingled in shades of delicate pink and lilac.

Between the long east and west ranges are transverse mountains that block easy passage across the tableland, and divide the country into a checkerboard of valleys, basins, and pockets. The population of Mexico, clustered in these walled-off valleys, lives in isolated communities, each with its own distinct customs and pattern of life largely unchanged with the passage of centuries. The people of Mexico are largely a mountain people. The mountains surround them and give them life. The mountains have kept them, as one writer says, "from becoming Hispanized, westernized, mechanized or Americanized." It is an overstatement, but bears a large grain of truth. The mountains have kept them poor, but have made the obliteration of their blood and of their indigenous culture impossible.

Alexander Humboldt, in his celebrated book on Mexico, gave this sociological interpretation of geography.

"The physical contours of a country, the way in which the mountains are grouped, the extension of the plains, the elevation which determines temperatures, in short, everything that constitutes the structure of the earth, bears the closest relationship with the progress of the population and the welfare of the people. Geographic structure influences the state of agriculture, which varies according to the different climates; it influences also the facilities for trade, the communications which are favored or not favored by the terrain, and finally, it influences strongly the national defence on which the security of the colony depends."

The issue could not be more clearly stated. Mexico's life has depended upon her geography, and her people have naturally grouped themselves in the Central Highlands, which have for centuries been the corn basket of the nation. As that region has gone, so has gone the nation, for the region of corn cultivation is the blood, bone, and sinew of the Mexican people.

Let us put on a pair of magic binoculars and view the horn of Mexico from a great height. These are the distinctive geographic parts of the country that we would see:

The Tableland of the North. Is a vast plateau ranging in altitude from 3,500 to 4,000 feet. It is dry and arid, and in appearance resembles the country around El Paso, or the southern portions of the states of Arizona, New Mexico, and California. This area is not at all like the great plains of central Texas, a flat unbroken prairie of tremendous fertility, but is heavily encrusted with desert mountain ranges that jut upward from the arid land in great rocky piles. Rainfall is slight, only 10 to 20 inches yearly, so irrigation is necessary for farming. The major part of the northern tableland is cattle country, particularly the state of Chihuahua. There is only a scattered population in this area, and very few cities, the largest being the industrial center Monterrey. And yet, despite the scarcity of people and the aridity of the soil, this is the most progressive part of Mexico. At least it is the part that is most like the United States.

The East and West Ranges. These two long sierras that cradle the tableland are not of equal height. The eastern chain is lower, the higher range lies along the west. Both ranges drop down to the coastal plains in steep escarpments, dissected by deep gorges. Therefore, nearly all the highways and railways of Mexico run north and south on the tableland, rather than east and west across it, for crossing these mountains and their escarpments is extremely difficult and costly. From Ciudad Juarez, just across the river from El Paso, clear down to Guadalajara, 1,000 miles south, a single spectacular mountain road leads over the higher western mountains. It connects Durango with tropical Mazatlán. On the western side, despite an abrupt descent, the mountains in many sectors bear a lush cover of forest and grass before they die out in the narrow coastal plain which borders the Pacific.

The Central Highlands. This is the area surrounding Mexico City. It is not a single valley, but a series of valleys and basins, ringed with Mexico's highest mountains. The basins themselves range from 4,500 to 8,000 feet in elevation. The capital occupies one valley at an altitude of 7,486 feet. Cuernavaca, only a short drive away, lies in another only 4,500 feet high. Puebla occupies a third valley, and Guadalajara, Mexico's second largest city, is located in still another.

These Central Highlands make up the third highest plateau land of comparable size in the world. Only the cold, bleak plateaus of Tibet and Bolivia are higher. Rainfall in this part of Mexico is sufficient for agriculture, and the climate is pleasantly mild throughout most of the year. Mexico City, which lies hundreds of miles to the south, is cooler in summer and warmer in winter than Chicago or New York. Little wonder that in these highlands most of the people live.

South of these highlands lies Mexico's volcanic axis, one of the greatest chains of volcanic cones in the world. Here is where the long east and west ranges of the country meet and mingle. Still farther south are other mountains and other valleys, of which Oaxaca is the largest. Then tropical jungle.

The Peninsula of Yucatán. It sticks out of Mexico's horn like a great thumb, and is the country's only true unbroken plain. Its shallow soil rests on a great flat limestone base. Rainfall is moderate on the north side, increases toward the south. Vegetation, hence, is scrubby on the upper part of the pennisula, while the lower half is beautifully forested.

Yucatán is an island on the land. Until recently there were no overland connections with the rest of the country. The inhabitants of this area for many years hardly considered themselves Mexicans. They were Yucatecs, a proud and admirable lot whose roots dipped back into the fabled Maya past. Northern Yucatán is the big hemp-producing area of Mexico, while in the south lie the famous ruins of Chichén-Itzá in a land of untilled forests.

The differences between the urban nuclei and the rural population of Mexico are far greater than in Western Europe or in the United States. Only during the past couple of decades has communication among the various Mexican states become relatively easy, with the advent of airlines and the extension of highways. But even these are merely trunk lines that link Mexico's cities, passing by her hundreds of rural villages. Consequently, Mexico has one foot in the past, the other in the present. There is an abyss between.

In Mexican geography "up and down" are more important than "north and south." Altitude largely determines the climate. There are three main climatic zones. The "hot country," or *tierra caliente,* of Mexico is low, mostly along the coasts. The "temperate land," or *tierra templada,* is higher up, ranging from three to six thousand feet in elevation. Above six thousand feet lies the *tierra fría,* or "cold country."

Climate in Mexico is vertical, and wet or dry. The terms "summer" and "winter" do not take on the importance they have in the United States. In the central area the rainy season covers the months of June, July, August, and September, during which months it rains a great deal, with daily showers a frequent occurrence. These showers almost invariably come in the late afternoon or night. The mornings are generally clear, but before long the sky is overcast with a heavy covering of cumulus clouds which blacken and empty. These clouds and rain are so frequent during the summer months in the Central Highlands that the hottest month is generally May, rather than July or August.

During the summer, consequently, the earth is green, while in the winter it takes on a dry and brownish hue. On the other hand, the winter months are rain-free and clear, with a crystal loveliness of air and sky which brightens the most sluggish heart and makes the most despondent traveler feel primevally alive. Artists and architects revel in the silver light. Bright colors are natural under such a brilliant sun.

The summer rains extend to the northern tableland, in the midst of which lies the industrial city of Monterrey. But here there is a desert aridity that defies the water. The only greenery is at the end of a hose, or alongside an irrigation ditch. Yet Monterrey, despite its alkaline desert and despite its being so many hundreds of miles farther south, is much cooler in summer than the plains of Texas or Kansas. Again, the climate is vertical. Monterrey lies at an elevation of 1,624 feet at the foot of the mountains.

In many parts of Mexico one can, within a few miles, pass from a land of pine forests to the tropical jungle, from the high cold stands of conifers to the banana plantations, wild orchids, and vanilla trees of the lowlands. Of course, it is hard to cultivate the mountains, and it is hard to farm in the jungles.

But what of the one-third of Mexico that is fairly level? The two biggest areas are the shallow, limestone plain of Yucatán, and the arid desert lands of northern Mexico, just across the U.S. border. These two areas are not suitable for general agriculture. The north is too dry and arid. Yucatán's shallow limestone soil is too quickly exhausted. The other level areas are found in the smaller basins and valleys among the mountains of the Central Mexican Highlands. Here the climate is better, the rainfall more dependable, the soil richer.

In the utilization of the soil the great Mexican crop is corn. The ancient Indian cultures were based on corn, the colonial population of Mexico lived on corn, and today's Indianist rural population still subsists on a diet of corn. Fifty per cent of all Mexican farm land is devoted to the cultivation of this one crop. Without corn half the people of Mexico would soon starve to death. Since the beginning of Mexican history it has been the mainstay of their lives and of their sustenance.

Corn will grow almost anywhere. It does not require much rain. It can stand a lot of heat and it can stand cold. It does not require a rich soil. New seed strains have greatly increased productivity in the last decade, but the poor farmer who tills only two or three acres, all planted in corn, is barely able to subsist, a constant sore spot in the economy.

Much of this corn farm land could more efficiently be used as pasturage for cattle or as dairy country. It could also, under irrigation, be used to produce a great variety of crops more efficiently than corn. Corn could be grown more efficiently in the tropical parts of Mexico, but so far this has not been attempted on any sizable scale. In any case, the corn economy of Mexico is a subsistence economy. The Mexican farmer grows corn to eat, not to sell. He is not a meat eater and he doesn't drink milk.

The traditional corn belt is in the Central Highlands. Here climate is propitious and water is abundant for concentrated settlement. Protected by high mountain barriers, the successive waves of native cultures came, conquered, were absorbed, resided. Here, still today, among these Central Highlands, are clustered the majority of the people of Mexico, just as they were when the Spaniards arrived over four hundred years ago.

The Mexican landscape is spectacularly beautiful for the tourist. But only one acre in twenty is good farm land, and over 46 per cent of the working population are farmers. (The U.S. percentage is only 15.) They subsist on a soil that is certainly not ideal for farming and they grow a crop that is certainly not ideal for the soil they do possess. No one can blame the land itself for this. It is a question of history and of tradition, today's residue from the Indian past of Mexico. From this tradition springs the deeply rooted poverty of the Mexican people, a poverty which only now is being attacked with all the vigor of a virile leadership.

II

THE FLOWER: ANCIENT INDIAN CULTURES

The Indian in Mexico is a subtle reality. All Mexicans carry some portion of that reality within themselves.

—Moisés Sáenz

Mexico is overwhelmingly Indian. Out of a total population of some 50 million, at least 60 per cent follow a life that is more Indianist than Western. About 30 per cent are pure Indian. Another 30 per cent are mostly Indian. Probably not more than 10 per cent are mostly Caucasian. The roots of Mexico are red. They reach back into the templed past, into mountain valley and jungle, onto the limestone plains, and penetrate deep, very deep into the Mexican earth. Mexico today, with all its progress, can never forget them.

At the time of the conquest the Indian population of Mexico was probably between five and seven million. Compare this with the one million Indians estimated to have been living in the entire territory of the United States when the first colonists arrived. Although Mexico is only one-third as large as the United States, at the time of the discovery it had five to seven times as many inhabitants, or, let us say, a concentration of Indians around fifteen times as great. Little wonder that the Indian element has not disappeared from Mexico today. In fact, there are undoubtedly more pure Indians in Mexico now than there were in 1492, and about twice that number of mestizos, who also are mostly Indian.

The heartland of the United States is the great central prairie, sparsely inhabited by red men, into which streamed the covered wagons when our westward expansion began. The population gaps left on the eastern seaboard were filled up by immigrants who poured in from Europe by the millions.

Mexico's heartland is the Central Highlands. In this small area of cool green valleys, rimmed with some of the most magnificent mountain scenery in the world, lived most of the ancient Mexicans. The Spaniards who settled here were but a drop in the bucket, their pale color soon lost in that great mass of Indian blood. The conquest itself would not have been possible had not hatreds among the native races given the Spaniards as many Indian soldiers as there were fighting in the army of their enemies.

Even in the dark beginning the white man's most powerful weapons were sex, to break down the pure Indian; faith, to destroy the native's belief in his own gods and in himself; and knowledge, of superior weapons and of superior (or at least easier) techniques of supporting life.

The red man in Mexico was conquered, his cities were destroyed, his idols toppled. He became the vassal of his Spanish landlord. He was beaten, he was crushed, he was twisted. But his roots were strong. Like the roots of a tropical rain forest that has received the blows of fire and ax, after a spell he grew again. The new growth received pollen from across the seas; the hybrid was stronger.

Who were these red men of Mexico whose culture amazed the Spaniards? Where did they come from, and how, and why, and when? What was the nature of their culture, so much of which survives in Mexico today?

Twenty-five thousand years ago Mexico was probably uninhabited by man. Only the cries of wild beasts and birds and the sound of volcanoes disturbed her sleep of centuries. Twenty-five thousand years is but a moment in the dark fabric of time. Mexico, then (indeed all of the Western Hemisphere), is an infant in terms of human history, for man has inhabited the earth for an estimated 500,000 years.

The first inhabitants of our hemisphere probably crossed the Bering Strait around fifteen to twenty thousand years ago. Successive waves of Orientals followed as the centuries passed, and slowly pushed toward the south. They reached the Valley of Mexico perhaps ten thousand years ago, and continued southward, crossing the isthmus of Central America and fanning out in the Andean area of South America.

Any observer who has seen groups of both Mexican and Japanese soldiers will note the striking similarity between them. The same brown hue, the same cast of figure and face, the same peculiar shuffle as they walk. Mexican Indians in their own tribal garb may not suggest Orientals. We are accustomed to a certain picturesqueness which we call Indian. But put them in uniform, dress them all alike, walk them down the street, and the conclusion is inescapable. Mexicans are Orientals.

The early waves of migration from Northeastern Asia must have ceased around 8000 B.C. The Spaniards "were struck by many strange deficiencies in even the highest civilizations." There were no domesticated animals in Mexico except the dog and several kinds of fowls. There were no beasts of burden, no cattle, horses, pigs, goats, or sheep. There were no burros. The many plants and animals that Neolithic man domesticated after the year 8000 B.C. were all completely lacking in America. If the earliest Indians had known them, they certainly would have brought them along, and if later waves of migrants continued to flow into the New World without happening to bring these things, they would surely have sent back for them. Hence, the time for the end of the period of migration can be fairly accurately fixed at around 8000 B.C.

What the red man achieved in America, therefore, was achieved isolated and alone; there was no contact with or fertilization from other world cultures. This fact makes the early Indian civilizations a fascinating study, and as more than one archaeologist has remarked, the early Americans can often give a sounder insight into man and his accomplishments than any other people. This and its closely woven social fabric are the principal glories of the American Indian cultures.

The early Mexicans were, of course, nomadic. They hunted, they fished, they ate roots and whatever fruits and berries grew wild, and when they had cleared one place of its food supply they simply moved on to another. Then something happened which changed the entire course of Indian history. It was the discovery of corn. Archaeologists do not know exactly when this discovery took place, but let us guess that it was five or six thousand years ago.

The Indian noticed a wild plant growing in the fertile valley. It was *teocintl*, a stalk that bore a tiny cornlike ear. It was edible. The Indian ate it and liked it. He dropped a few seeds around his dwelling. They grew without any care, and the ears that they produced he ate with more than usual relish. He did not have to stray so far to seek his food. The next step in the process of Indian civilization is obvious. Soon the red man was planting corn, and growing his own food. It became the staff of Indian life, just as wheat had been the staff of life in Europe, and rice the mainstay of the Asiatic peoples.

Corn was easy to grow, and the Indian no longer had to wander. Indeed, he had to stop wandering if he wanted to reap the benefits of his meager labors of clearing the fields and sowing his seeds. So he built himself a better house, and settled down in more or less permanent communities. Then commenced the process of accumulation. This was the beginning of Indian civilization.

The next step was to notice that at certain times of the year, when there was an assured amount of rain, the corn grew better. This led to a critical observation of weather phenomena and eventually to a study of the astral bodies. How many moons did the dry season last? How many moons made up the rainy season? How many moons passed before the corn was ripe? Where were the bright morning and evening stars when the seasons changed? Where was the sun during these seasons? Where were the constellations?

In order to answer these questions the Indian took up astronomy. In order to observe the heavenly bodies more clearly he erected pyramids. Before long his wise men were performing certain pagan rites so that the corn gods might smile upon his people. There were corn myths, corn dances, corn symbols, and almost, we might say, a corn religion, with weather and corn as members of the new pantheon. For on these two elements the red man thrived or perished.

The next step was to decorate the pyramids, in order to make them worthy of the new gods. Architecture and painting were born, and the fine art of Indian mosaics. From the gradual development of corn culture, plus a study of the stars, plus architecture, ritual and belief, with its pantheon of telluric gods and its almighty priesthood, emerged the whole culture substance of ancient Indian life.

Around 1000 B.C. the Olmecs developed the earliest Indian culture of Mexico along the rain-drenched Gulf Coast south of today's Veracruz. The main site was at a place called La Venta. The Olmecs are noted for their colossal stone heads, which weigh from 10 to 20 tons, and for their man-jaguar god, the creator-destroyer, a kind of Indian Dionysus. Olmec religion and art influenced all of Middle America. The Olmecs also built pyramids and created a form of writing out of which may have evolved the later, more refined glyphs of the Mayas. The first Maya centers were in Guatemala and Honduras, but later centers were established in Chiapas and Yucatán.[46] *

Amateur archaeologists began to study the Maya ruins back in the 1840's. The American John Stephens and his friend Catherwood, an English artist, spent many months in Maya country during that decade and came back to publish one of the most delightful works imaginable: *Incidents of Travel in Central America, Chiapas, and Yucatán*. The book was illustrated with beautiful engravings of the Maya buildings and sculpture.

* These numerals refer to books listed in the Acknowledgments, p. xi.

After Stephens there were many others, Thompson, Spinden, Hewett, Gamio, Caso, and their archaeology gradually became more scientific. Finally came Samuel Griswold Morley, a trained archaeologist who devoted his entire life to a study of Maya lore. His work, *The Ancient Maya,* is the classic interpretation of that culture. Professor George Brainerd of U.C.L.A. has recently brought Morley's masterpiece up to date. None of the earlier archaeologists were certain of their Maya chronology. They learned how to read the Maya time symbols and could tell how long it was between different Maya dates, but they could not with certainty correlate these dates with our own calendar. Hence, all kinds of wild guesses were made as to how far back the Maya culture went into the past. Some said 2000 B.C. Others said A.D. 300. Nobody was certain.

Within the past few years a new way of finding out the age of old ruins and pottery has been discovered. It is the formula of Carbon 14, calculated by the amount of radiation given off by the material over a period of time. Anything that has lived (wood, bones will do) will radiate and lose carbon content. Calculate the radiation and you can find out how long ago the item was alive. Anything else in the same heap or layer must be of approximately the same age.

According to Carbon 14, the Old Period of Maya culture, the period of its finest flower in Guatemala and Chiapas, Mexico, may be dated from A.D. 300 to 900. The later Maya renaissance in Yucatán came around A.D. 900–1400.

A North American archaeologoist, Spinden, called these periods Old Empire and New Empire, respectively. Other archaeologists have objected to the terms, saying that there was no empire among the Mayas. Indeed, some of them affirm that there was no civilization, but only a culture. No tightly organized political economy, but only a flourishing of the arts, a procession of barbaric pageantry.

But whether or not there was any Maya "empire," and certainly the facts all seem to refute it, there were clearly different periods of Maya culture development. These may very conveniently be reduced to three, and Maya chronology, then, runs something like this:

Formative Period	2000 B.C. to A.D. 300 Guatemala
Early Maya (Classic)	A.D. 300 to 900 Guatemala and Chiapas, Mexico
Late Maya (Toltec)	A.D. 900 to 1400 Yucatán

Each of the above periods reached into the next. During the Formative Period the Mayas began to migrate into southern Mexico, and during the Classic Period, as early as A.D. 400, they began to migrate into Yucatán. It was a constant expansion, which at last turned into a mass flight into Yucatán, around the year A.D. 900.

Why this great wandering across the trackless jungles? Some archaeologists have suggested epidemics, others have said defeat in war, but Morley, who has studied the problem most acutely, says that the Mayas had to migrate because of what they did to the land. Like all the early Indian cultures of America, they grew corn. Their only farm tools were rude stone axes and a pointed wooden plow. First, they hacked and burned the area that was to be cultivated. Then they planted their crops. During the first few years the corn grew well. But, as time passed, tough-rooted grasses began to take over the fields, and the Maya farmers, with their rude tools, could not get rid of them. So they moved on to another spot. And thus the expansion continued, prodded on, no doubt, by both war and pestilence.

Around the year A.D. 300 the Mayas began to build in stone. Their civilization leaped forward. Within another two or three centuries they were erecting the exquisite pyramid-temples which made up the ceremonial centers of Copán, Tikal, Palenque, Bonampak, and many others.

This was the so-called Classic Period (A.D. 300 to 900), during which Maya culture reached its zenith. Indeed, it attained a height which, for all-around artistic development, was undoubtedly the high point of Indian culture on the American continent. Some archaeologists divide this period of Maya culture into two parts: Early Classic, A.D. 327 to 600, and Late Classic, A.D. 600 to 900.

After the mass flight into Yucatán, around the year 900, the old centers were abandoned and the new centers were given a new lease on life. Chichén-Itzá and Uxmal are the two most accessible and best known of these new centers. They are both easily reached on paved highways out of Mérida. There are hostelries at both places, so that the visitor may remain and examine the ruins at his leisure.

This is the Late Maya-Toltec Period, and is not pure Maya. Warriors from the Mexican Highlands also streamed into these new centers and overcame them. Before long the two cultures were blended, and there emerged a style of architecture of which the feathered serpent columns and serpent decorative motifs are characteristic. There was a great renaissance of all the arts. The new culture was Maya-Toltec, and lasted until shortly after the year 1400, when Chichén-Itzá and Uxmal were abandoned to the forest. When the Spaniards arrived, the

Maya civilization was hardly more than a legend. The Aztecs, those tougher warriors of the Mexican Plateau, were now running Mexico from their great capital of Tenochtitlán, today's Mexico City.

Judge a culture by its art, and the Mayas stand high in the pages of ancient history. Remember that all they accomplished was achieved alone, without contact or borrowing from any other source, and one is amazed at their accomplishment. At a time when King Alfred was herding his barbaric warriors across England, when the European Continent was sunk in its Darkest Ages, long before Charlemagne, the Mayas were undoubtedly among the most highly civilized people of the Western world.

The Mayas knew all about solar and lunar eclipses, they knew of the solstices, the equinoxes, they followed the course of Venus, Lord Big Eye, across the skies, they knew the progress and positions of the moon and sun. Many of their pyramid-temples were oriented toward certain clusters of stars, for example, the Pleiades, or were so placed that the sun crossed fixed temple markers at the time of the solstices or equinoxes.

Out of their astronomical knowledge the Mayas developed a calendar which was considerably more accurate than any developed by Greece or Rome. They followed the lunar months, and their year, like our own, was of 365 days. There was no possible confusion of a day in over 300,000 years.

The Mayas developed the most refined architecture of the New World. The best-known centers of their Early Period were Copán in Honduras, Tikal in Guatemala, and above all Bonampak and Palenque (*circa* A.D. 700) in the state of Chiapas, Mexico. These were not really cities in the European sense, but were huge ceremonial centers, where the Mayas assembled to worship and to build for their priests and for their gods. The ordinary Maya citizen of those days, like the rural Maya of today, lived in a small but neat square house with adobe walls, of a single room, and with a high-pitched roof of thatch.

The early Maya ceremonial centers were of stucco and stone. They contained temples of many sizes and shapes, some of them mounted on tall pyramids, others rising nobly from lower bases. They towered above the meager dwellings of the ordinary Maya in the same way that the Gothic cathedrals had stood so magnificently over the squalor of medieval villages. Many of them had tall crests or roof combs, narrow and delicately designed. The façades frequently had beautifully stylized carvings and sculpturing in which were outlined perfectly proportioned figures of Maya warriors and priests. The feathered serpent design also was frequently used as an artistic as well as a religious symbol.

The Maya architects did not know how to use the keystone or the arch, hence their buildings could not support a wide roof. The walls were thick, very thick, and the interiors were cramped and dark. Their structures were almost invariably more lovely on the outside than they were within. Many of the buildings contained colored murals and the façades of others were brightened with pigments of various hues. However, in all the excavated centers these had been scratched off or had faded out due either to weather or to improper restoration, and not a single good example or Maya mural art was known until the jungle-hidden ruins of Bonampak were discovered in 1946. The large figures here, performing some kind of religious ritual, are so placed and so well proportioned that they bear comparison with those of the Early Italian Renaissance.

Omitting Bonampak, which is rarely visited because of its inaccessibility in the matted jungle, the three best-known Maya centers of Mexico are Palenque, in northern Chiapas, which belongs to the early Classic Period, and Uxmal and Chichén-Itzá in Yucatán, which belong to the Late Maya epoch.

Palenque is situated in the foothills overlooking a fertile valley. Here the forest is thick, but not impenetrable. The ruins are not easily accessible but may be reached by train. Maya architecture at Palenque is beautifully proportioned and exquisitely decorated. The human figures carved and formed in relief in stucco and stone are worthy of being ranked with the world's best art. Many think this center marks the highest point of Indian civilization in preconquest America. It reached its peak around A.D. 700.

Until recent excavations at Palenque it was believed that Maya pyramids were merely bases for the religious temples. But at Palenque in the Temple of Inscriptions, there has been discovered the magnificent tomb of a Maya priest-king. A colossal and beautifully carved stone tablet sealed off the crypt. Within the tomb lay the body of the priest-king dressed in full regalia and wearing an elaborate jade-mosaic mask. The garments have crumbled, and so has the mask, but from carvings on the walls archaeologists have been able to reconstruct them, and at the Museum of Anthropology and History in Mexico (if one does not wish to visit Palenque) can be seen a reconstruction of the entire tomb.

Uxmal, about fifty miles west of Mérida, is a later center. It falls between the Old and New Periods, but is not deeply influenced by

Plateau Mexican culture, as is the case at Chichén-Itzá. There is now an inn near the ruins, and an excellent highway connects these with Mérida. At Uxmal is a graceful quadrangle of buildings, now in an excellent state of reconstruction, and a towering pyramid (underneath it is a still older one), still in its ruined state. The quadrangle gives the visitor an impressive idea of the fine proportions of Maya architecture, and most particularly of the decorative mosaic façade work which contrasts vividly with the narrow and dingy interiors.

Chichén-Itzá, about seventy-five miles southeast of Mérida, also reached by a good paved highway, is larger than Uxmal. At least the excavated portions of these ruins give it that appearance. Here is located the famous pyramid-temple of Kukulkan (the Maya name for Quetzalcoatl), which the Spaniards called El Castillo (the Castle), because they placed a small fortress on top.

Take a close look at this temple, or at any good photograph of it, and proof of Maya ingenuity in linking astronomical and calendric data with architecture and art becomes quickly evident. On each side of the pyramid is a stairway containing 91 steps. Four times 91 equals 364, and plus the landing on top adds up to 365 days. To the left and right of these stairways are 26 indented surfaces, that is, 52 such surfaces on each of the four sides of the pyramid. This figure (52 years) is the Maya "century." Again, to the left and to the right of each stairway are 9 ledges as one examines the ascent, or, 18 ledges on each of the four complete sides. This figure is the number of Maya months in the year. Markings on the temple go into even more calendric detail, but the above facts are enough to prove our point.

Other structures at Chichén-Itzá are the so-called Nun's House, the Temple of the Warriors, the Temple of the Tigers, the huge ball court where the Mayas played a kind of basketball by knocking a rubber ball through a large stone ring, and El Caracol (the Snail), a round building capping a large base often referred to as the astronomical observatory.

The buildings are all beautifully decorated with carvings or projecting pieces of statuary, many of them calendric symbols. The structural material is limestone, of which almost the entire Yucatán peninsula consists. This gives rise to a very shallow soil, easily exhausted; hence, the Mayas of earlier days, and also those of today, use a plot of ground for a couple of years, then give it a long rest, while they move on to another.

The limestone basis of the plain also makes surface water extremely scarce, except in time of rain. Limestone is very porous and the waters quickly disappear beneath. The Mayas sometimes caught their drinking water in cisterns, but their main centers were located near openings in the limestone cap which exposed the undersurface water. These *cenotes*, or limestone wells, go deep into the earth. There is a huge one in Mérida itself, now used as a place for picnics and parties, and the sacred well at Chichén-Itzá is another.

In many of the Early Maya centers the Mayas left tall stone columns called stelae, which were beautifully carved with Indian faces and chronological glyphs. These were time markers, but their picture writing was so exquisite that they are also works of art. Morley says that the Mayas were at the point of developing a phonetic alphabet at the time of their decline, but their written language was largely pictorial.

Not only did they write in stone and stucco, but the Mayas also drew up dozens of codex scrolls, which folded much like those of the Orient. These contained graceful glyphs so beautifully colored that they are the equal of the lovely illuminated manuscripts of the Middle Ages. These scrolls were on parchment or maguey paper. When the Spaniards reached Yucatán one of their bishops, Diego de Landa, ordered all Maya codices to be placed in a great pile and burned as the instruments of a heretical religion. Only three manuscripts survived the holocaust.

The Mayas discovered the zero symbol many years before it was discovered in India, from whence it reached the Arabs and through them was introduced into Europe. This gave them a basis of mathematical calculations much easier to handle than the clumsy numerals of the Romans. They used the vigesimal (by twenties) rather than the decimal system in their calculations.

The pantheon of Maya gods and goddesses runs the gamut of the earth forces: rain, wind, sun, and stars. They also made a god of the red jaguar, who drove the deer from their cornfields. (There is a large statue of this animal in the old temple buried under the huge El Castillo pyramid in Chichén-Itzá.) They also seemed to believe that man originally was made from corn, the god of life turning that golden food into human form. In Chichén-Itzá there are also obvious evidence of phallic worship, for here are several large stone carvings of man's reproductive organ.

One of my fondest memories of Mexico is the time spent at Mayaland Lodge among the ruins of Chichén-Itzá, where every room, all of them neat as a pin, are replicas of the ancient Maya dwellings. Here one can really enjoy a bit of amateur archaeology in comfort. After an invigorating swim in the pool, it is sheer magic to stroll among the miles of ruins or sit relaxed upon the porch against whose open end the circular *caracol,* or astronomical observatory, stands out in bold relief against the soft sky and illumined trees.

This part of Yucatán receives more rain than the northern coast, and is covered with a beautiful forest. Not too thick, not too open and slender. It is the land of the pheasant and of the deer, a forest primeval as enchanting as any in the wide world. Little wonder that both the Mayas of the south and the Plateau Mexicans streamed into this sylvan paradise a thousand or more years ago.

Bonampak, with its brilliant murals which almost no traveler sees, because they are still hidden in the jungle, Palenque, with its delicate architecture and graceful carvings, Uxmal, with its perfectly proportion quadrangle and its beautiful mosaic façades, Chichén-Itzá, with its Temple of the Warriors and its pyramid to Kukulkan (El Castillo) —these are but a handful among the dozens of ruins left by the ancient Mayas. But even these four are enough to prove the unique achievements of that mysterious race. They were indeed the great creators among the Indian cultures of America, hence Morley calls them "The Greeks of the New World." It is a characterization they richly deserve.

In the Central Valley of Mexico, where today's great metropolis stands, the other great branch of Mexican Indian culture put down its roots. The time was around the birth of Christ, nearly two thousand years ago. Several successive waves of invaders swept over the cool valley, each adding or subtracting its fragment, until finally the warlike Aztecs achieved dominance. They still ruled far and wide when the Spaniards arrived. Even on the Gulf coast subject tribes mentioned their name with fear and referred to their great capital in tones of awe.

The Valley of Mexico was green and beautiful. The natives called it Anahuac, "the land on the edge of the water." It was, and is, a wonderful place to live. Over seven thousand feet above sea level, a ring of magnificent mountains "walled in a fertile valley in which lay a great salt lake, Texcoco, fed at the south by two fresh water lagoons, at the northwest by two more, and at the northeast by a sluggish stream, the Acolman River, which drained the fertile Valley of Teotihuacán." A Mexican writer, Alfonso Reyes, added this: "Traveler, you have reached the most transparent region of the air."

The slopes were covered with great stands of cedar, long since used up by the Spanish settlers who left these lovely mountains as bare as the hills of their own Castile, where, as the saying goes, "even a bird can hardly find a branch on which to light." There was a vast array of volcanic cones, lava beds, eroded stumps of long-dead volcanoes, hot springs, cinder cones, and ash beds. Many of the basins were blocked by volcanic flow and contained shallow lakes. On their marshy shores was an abundance of wild fowl, and the thickly wooded slopes teemed with deer. Thick alluvial deposits were washed down along the lake shores, making them ideal for primitive agriculture.

Here in this valley once thrived a culture that could rival that of the Mayas in its refinement. This, let us be at pains to point out, was long before the Aztecs began their sway over the neighboring tribes.

The early culture of the Valley of Anahuac began before the birth of Christ. Its tremendous ceremonial center, often referred to as "the pyramids of San Juan Teotihuacán," was probably constructed early in the Christian era by a group known as the Teotihuacanos. Some archaeologists believe this is the mother culture from which the Maya germinated. Others turn the statement around. Manuel Gamio, who has studied the ruins carefully, states simply that the Mayas built them. Using the Carbon 14 formula samples dug from the center of the great pyramid have been dated at 31 B.C.

It was the custom of all the Indian pyramid builders to heap up great mounds of earth and rubble, and over this to place their pyramid staircases leading to a temple on the summit. The dated rubble, therefore, might well be a few years older than the great pyramid facing. A further element of confusion is that one Indian culture group often built right on top of what a preceding group had left behind. Thus, one pyramid frequently contained another smaller and older one inside.

The Pyramid of the Sun at Teotihuacán covers a greater ground area than the largest pyramid in Egypt. At the base it measures nearly 700 feet on each side, and reaches a height of over 200 feet, about that of a 20-story skyscraper. Atop this colossal structure once stood a temple, of which no vestige remains. The walling of the sides of the pyramid is faced with stone and plaster, and at regular intervals along the ascent are recessed terraces encircling the entire structure. To the ancient spectators of Indian pageantry a procession of priests in their splendid regalia mounting these stairs, suddenly (at each terrace) disappearing into space, then appearing again to continue their heavenly ascent, must indeed have been a majestic sight.

Teotihuacán is still an imposing sight. Located only 35 miles northeast of Mexico City, and readily accessible by car or bus, the ceremonial area occupies a space 3½ miles long and 2 miles wide. The entire precincts have been paved with plaster many times by the successive waves of settlers. The early inhabitants of the place, the original builders, are called simply the Teotihuanacos. By A.D. 100 their great pyramid-temples were completed, and for five or six centuries their classic culture flourished and influenced all of Middle America. Around A.D. 700 Teotihuacán fell to Chichimec barbarians from the north, and was abandoned. There were three centuries of darkness in the Valley of Mexico. Around A.D. 950 the Toltecs, also from the north, occupied Teotihuacán and established their own great center at Tula. Toltec culture lasted in the Valley until Tula succumbed to another Chichimec onslaught in A.D. 1160. Soon after this, circa A.D. 1200, the Aztecs arrived, but by this time the area of Teotihuacán was regarded as a "City of the Dead."[46]

The architecture at Teotihuacán is certainly not comparable to that of the Mayas in artistic refinement, delicacy, or sinuous grace. The great Temple of Quetzalcoatl, decorated with giant stone serpent heads with open jaws, obsidian eyes, and enormous teeth, is the nearest approach to a Maya building.

Everywhere in the pre-Columbian history of the Mexican Indian the plumed serpent, Quetzalcoatl, is present. The Mayas used feathered serpent decorative motifs in some of their earliest pyramids in Central America, and centuries later at Chichén-Itzá the feathered serpent stone column, foreshortened, with head on the ground and tail lifted upward, supported many of their buildings.

Quetzalcoatl was also an Indian deity. The most lavish temple of the builders of Teotihuacán bore his name, and the famous Maya pyramid at Chichén-Itzá was dedicated to his cult. The Maya name for this god was Kukulkan, but it is the Toltec-Aztec name *Quetzal-coatl* (quetzal: bird-serpent) that is most widely used. He was reputed to have been the bringer of the arts of civilization, and legend has it that he was driven out of the country. The god-man prophesied that in the year *Ce Acatl*, or One Reed, strange white men from across that sea would conquer his people; then he headed for the Gulf. There he mounted a raft of coiled serpents that bore him across the sea. That is why the great Montezuma shuddered when the news of Cortés' arrival reached him.

The feathered serpent was, therefore, not only the basic artistic motif of the early Mexican Indian cultures, but was also one of their greatest gods, the god who symbolized both cultural progression and the life principle. In some of the Maya representations there are huge serpent jaws opened wide, with the head of a man emerging from the monster's maw. The inference is obvious: creativity and man's progress.

But the bird-serpent was more than a cult, more even than a god. To the Indian it represented the deific union of earth and sky, the parallel wonders of creation, the two planes of being.

To the Indian everything in the earth or the sky was, and is, part of this creativity: the twig on the aspen tree, the cry of the wild boar, the shimmering gold of the sunflower, and first gray flecks of dawn. A part of it is the stately motion of the antlered stag, the silent flow of the jaguar's feet, the wistful eyes of the fawn, or the white foam of swirling waters. All this is alive, all this is creativity. And to the Indian it is all spirit, earth spirit, sky spirit or water spirit, or spirit in cloud or foam or sunset. It is all one great deific presence, one poematic being. Like all things alive it is responsive, and like a sounding river it is forever in motion. The Indian sees it walk and hears it speak. He feels its presence, he hears it whisper, he warms in its embrace.

The Indian speaks to this creativity when he is troubled. To its varied language he answers in his own dark, formless, but deeply rooted tongue. He does not pray as civilized man can pray, nor does he make sweet music as he dances or as he bends.

He is troubled and he needs rain, his land is fallow and he needs corn. Into the bottomless well of the past he sends his cry to the elements, for they will answer. Have you heard a siren go by and listened to the dogs of a neighborhood all howl in unison? The Indian, too, howls or moans or croaks or mutters darkly when he tries to address the elements. Like a dog's, his ears are sharper than ours. He has heard the siren cry of rock or cloud or clod or tree, and he has answered. He does not really try to sing. He merely calls on the names of the deific presence; he makes sounds, he beats rhythms, he wails or cries, he croaks and howls and stutters. But every sound comes from deep in the bloodroots. It is not music. There is no harmony to what is said or sung. It is more like a pack of dogs, all howling, moaning in unison. But this is Indian music, and these are Indian prayers.

The white man hates the sound. It is not his dimension. It makes his own blood ring with dark hatreds, with deep dark panic, with bitter revolt. This is not civilization. He cringes away from the sound the way he would cringe away from a pack of wolves on the hunt. Despite all the sloppy sentimentalities of the romantics, the two worlds can meet but never truly blend. Here lies the dichotomy of the mestizo, the race that looks this way or that, but feels its bloodroots seething darkly without security or nutriment, without bedrock, without a belonging.

The last of the great Indian cultures of Mexico was that of the Aztecs, which was at its zenith when the Spaniards arrived. The early chroniclers who accompanied the first expeditions witnessed and recorded for posterity their firsthand impressions of Aztec culture. It is, therefore, by far the most thoroughly recorded of all the indigenous civilizations of Mexico. Unfortunately, despite the colorful barbaric pageantry and wide political extension of their regime, the Aztecs represented a regression, and not an advance, in the evolution of Mexican culture history.

The story of the conquest itself, with many fascinating comments on the Aztecs, is superbly told by one of the lieutenants of Cortés, Bernal Díaz del Castillo. His work is called *A True History of the Discovery and Conquest of New Spain.* What this chronicle lacks in lofty rhetoric it more than makes up in straightforward charm and colorful details. All the great historians of Mexico have relied heavily on Bernal Díaz, among them William Robertson (1776), W. H. Prescott (1843), Antonio Solís, H. H. Bancroft, and dozens of others.

Bernal Díaz did not write his history during the time of the conquest, but many years later when he was living on his estate in Guatemala as a retired soldier. The story is that he had gotten hold of another history of the conquest by Cortés' chaplain, López de Gómara, which he did not believe did justice to the common soldier. Bernal Díaz proceeded to balance the tables. His memory was prodigious. There was hardly a horse whose name and color he could not remember, and the details of every battle, the gist of every conversation also seemed permanently etched in his mind. Besides this he had a photographic memory for scenes that he had witnessed.

In the preface of his *True History*, Bernal Díaz wrote: "I am now an old man, over eighty-four years of age, and I have lost my sight and hearing, and as luck would have it, I have gained nothing of value to leave my children and descendants but this my true story, and they will presently find out what a wonderful story it is." [9]

Let us move back in time to the year 1519 when, after many weeks of fighting and marching across inhospitable terrain, the small Spanish contingent rounded the last mountain barrier and entered the Valley of Mexico. There before them stood Tenochtitlán, the great capital of the Aztecs. The Spaniards were struck with awe and wonder. The causeway that led into the city, despite its width of eight paces, was so crowded with brightly dressed Indians that there was hardly room for them all. The towers and pyramids also were flooded with people, and the lake was teeming with canoes bearing more curious observers, none of whom had ever before seen either white man, musket, or horse.

Let Bernal Díaz describe the sight:

> During the morning, we arrived at a broad Causeway and continued our march, and when we saw so many cities and villages built in the water and other great towns on dry land, and that straight Causeway going towards Mexico City, we were amazed and said that it was like the enchantments they tell of in the legend of Amadís, on account of the great towers and temples and buildings rising from the water, all built of masonry. And some of our soldiers even asked whether the things we saw were not a dream. It is not to be wondered at that I write it down here in this manner, for there is so much to think over that I do not know how to describe it, seeing things as we did that had never been heard of or seen before, nor even dreamed of.

The city was built in the middle of the huge Lake of Mexico and passage to and fro was either by canoe or along the narrow walks bordering the canals. The larger buildings were of stone. Many of the houses of the chieftains were of soft pink volcanic *tezontle*. The majestic pyramid-temples were colored with brilliant hues and adorned with serpents. The "palaces" were spacious and many of them "were coated with shining cement and swept and garlanded." Inside were beams and rafters of cedar and other aromatic woods, while over the open spaces were canopies of cotton cloth. Outside the city were orchards and floating gardens, and the canals were teeming with boats carrying supplies into the city. The main temple plaza measured about 1,085 feet by 930 feet, and here stood the great twin-temple to the tribal god, Huitzilopochtli, whose thirst for human blood so sickened the Spaniards.

The city was cleaner than those of Spain, and the Spaniards noted that it was possible to walk along any of the streets without stepping into something. Boats were tied up at strategic intervals along the thoroughfares as public toilets, and a horde of street sweepers kept the avenues clean. Owing to the lack of extensive farm land in the volcanic valley, every available plot was put to use, and human fertilizer was carefully hoarded and applied to the fields in order to increase the harvest. (This is still one of the great banes of food production in Mexico and the other Indianist parts of Latin America. The visitor must take every care not to eat unpeeled fruit or unwashed vegetables. Amoebic dysentery and acute diarrhea are the scourges of the foreigner in the Indianist lands.)

Sweet water was brought into the city from the springs of Chapultepec down a long and well-constructed aqueduct. Along the eastern rim of the city rose a long dike which protected it from the occasional heavy rains. This great work was 16 kilometers long. It "was constructed of stone and clay and crowned with a wall of rubble masonry, and was protected on both sides by a strong stockade which broke the force of the waves."

This dike divided the valley lake into two parts, Lake Texcoco on the east, on whose borders rose the city of that name, and the Lake of Mexico on the west. Lake Texcoco, lacking a proper outlet, had become so saline that not even fishes could live in it. The waters of this lake also sterilized the soil and made it impossible to grow corn along the shores. The Lake of Mexico, on the other hand, received the waters drained from so many other nearby lakes and rivulets that its waters remained fresh. Both fish and aquatic fowls abounded in its vicinity. This also made possible the flowering orchards around the City of Mexico mentioned by the chroniclers.

During the colonial period, in order to prevent further floods, all these lakes with the exception of Lake Texcoco were drained. It was also thought that their beds would provide further tillable land, but so briny were the waters that this has not been so. (Lake Texcoco today is a shallow and ugly mud-colored stretch of water which enlarges and recedes depending on the rainfall. Viewed from the air, with the Indians poking across its surface in long sharp canoes, it gives the impression of a vast flooded mud flat. Xochimilco, the "floating gardens," still make up the truck garden area for Mexico City. However, of late the city has actually had to spend money to pump water into this area to keep it from shrinking away.)

The great staple of the Aztecs was, of course, corn. This, together with beans, squash, tropical fruits, and wild game, provided a nutritious if somewhat unvaried diet. Huge tortillas, "measuring a good foot in diameter," were made out of ground corn. The child of three "received half a tortilla a day; at four and five his ration was doubled; from six to twelve a tortilla and a half were prescribed, and at thirteen the allotment was two."

Montezuma's fare, of course, was considerably more appetizing. Bernal Díaz describes the royal victuals in the following way: "I have heard it said that they were wont to cook for him the flesh of young boys, but as he had a variety of dishes, made of so many things, we could not succeed in seeing if they were of human flesh or of other things, for they daily cooked fowls, turkeys, pheasants, native partridges, quail, tame and wild ducks, venison, wild boar, reed birds, pigeons, hares and rabbits, and many sorts of birds and other things which are bred in this country, and they are so numerous that I cannot finish naming them in a hurry; so we had no insight into it, but I know for certain that after our captain censured the sacrifice of human beings, and the eating of their flesh, he ordered that such food should not be prepared for him thenceforth."

From this paragraph it is clearly brought out that the Aztecs were cannibals. However, their cannibalism was generally limited to religious sacrifices and to feasts on human flesh after victory in battle. Frequent mention is made of these gorgings in the early Spanish chroniclers. The Aztecs also ate the flesh of small dogs which were especially raised for this purpose.

Corn, beans, and the potato of the Peruvian Highlands (now known as the Irish potato) were the great domesticated plants of the Indians. The cacao bean, from which chocolate was made, was another delicacy of the Aztec larder. Its richness amazed the Spaniards, and Cortés wrote back to the emperor that "a cup of this drink is enough to keep a man going all day." Cacao, vanilla, and pineapples were brought from Veracruz. Tomatoes, chile, red and green peppers, avocados, and sweet potatoes also were cultivated by the Aztecs and their neighbors. No plant cultivated by the American Indians was known elsewhere in the world prior to the conquest. "The introduction of these plants," writes George Vaillant in his *Aztecs of Mexico*, "more than doubled the food supply of the older continents." Certainly their addition to the diet of the poor of so many lands was worth far more than all the gold and silver from Mexico and Peru.

The indispensable maguey, a sharp-leaved cactus, yielded a juice from which the Aztecs fermented pulque, a sickly grayish alcoholic drink which is the national drink among the lower classes in Mexico today. The maguey also furnished the fiber from which the writing scrolls were made; thread, cord, pins, and even sandals were made from the leaves, as were the walls and roofs of the poorer dwellings.

The Aztecs and many other Indian tribes of Middle America also used cacao beans as a kind of currency. One of the storehouses of

Montezuma contained forty thousand loads of these, packed in bales so large they could hardly be lifted by six men, according to the historian Juan de Torquemada. This was probably the chieftain's greatest treasure chest. The historian Oviedo points out that a rabbit was worth ten cacao beans, a slave was worth a hundred, and a native prostitute charged her customers from eight to ten beans. This was in the area to the south of Montezuma's domain. An order of the viceroy, dated January 11, 1576, stated that common laborers in Acatlán were to be paid thirty cacao beans per day, instead of twenty.

The early Spaniards did not particularly care for Mexican chocolate, for it was prepared without sugar, and generally without vanilla, hence had a bitter oily taste. Oftentimes red pepper and corn meal were used by the Indians to give it flavor. In Nicaragua it was colored red to look like blood (which the natives also liked). Father Sahagún lists nine ways to make cacao beverages, in only one of which the use of vanilla is specified. The drink was widely popular among the chieftains but was beyond the means of most of the common people. The flavor which we in this country associate with chocolate is that of the vanilla, not of the cacao. It was only toward the end of the sixteenth century, when widespread use of vanilla, sugar, and cinnamon in the chocolate drinks made them more palatable to the European taste, that these became popular among the Spaniards. Thomas Gage, who was in southern Mexico, in Chiapas, frequently mentions the tremendous consumption of hot chocolate in that region in the early seventeenth century. One of his most entertaining stories concerns the custom the women of Chiapas had of ordering hot chocolate to be served to them in church in order to fortify themselves against the tedium of lengthy sermons. When the clergy tried to put a stop to this practice, the ladies rose up en masse and refused to budge an inch.[2] The English word *chocolate* is from the Aztec (or Nahua) *chocolatl;* so is our word for *tomato* (*tomatl*).

Vanilla itself was strictly American in origin. In Mexico it was principally raised in the tropical lowlands of the Gulf coast area in the vicinity of Veracruz. In the eighteenth century the Totonac Indians around the town of Papantla (who had grown vanilla for the Aztecs) began to cultivate it more widely, and it is this area which still produces most of Mexico's vanilla. Indeed, this crop is the principal cause of the Totonacs' relative prosperity among the native Mexican groups today. At its best their vanilla has a quality that is unequaled elsewhere in the world.

According to the Mendoza Codex, which traces their peregrinations in some detail with little odd-shaped human glyphs, the Aztecs came from the north and reached the Valley of Mexico in the year A.D. 1325. There in the middle of a lake they saw a tunal cactus growing out of a rock, where an eagle had made its home. Scattered about on the earth were the bony remains of its prey. This was considered a good omen, so the Aztecs established themselves on the mudbank, which must have resembled the later floating gardens. They called their city Tenochtitlán, which means "tunal growing from a rock."

Another story tells that when they arrived at the lake they saw an eagle on a tunal bush, with a large serpent in its mouth. This union of bird and serpent was taken as a favorable sign, and so the Aztecs settled at the site. This latter tale is reflected in the official Mexican seal of today.

The Aztecs were a nation of warriors, and quickly extended their realm and increased their city. In order to protect the food supply they fished up vast quantities of mud from the lake bottom, slapped it onto wattles and aquatic plants, and made small gardens on the lake's surface. Held together by roots and tendrils, these eventually became so large that there was room and strength on top for a hut to shelter a caretaker and his family. Thus began today's Xochimilco, the floating gardens.

As in all warrior nations, the women soon outnumbered the men, and polygamy prevailed in the social life. Both concubinage and prostitution were sanctioned, and a man could even divorce his wife "if she were sterile, were subject to prolonged ill temper or neglected the household duty."

Aztec "picture writing" was definitely at a lower stage than that of the Mayas. The little misshapen bodies of men performing various kinds of actions resemble hordes of ants running up and down the maguey scrolls or parchments on which they were painted. Many Aztec codices have survived, and these have been read and recorded by antiquarians, for when the Spaniards conquered Mexico there were many natives who could interpret the glyphs, and this knowledge has been preserved. No such key has ever been found to open up the mysteries of the Maya glyphs.

Aztec writing was done by trained scribes who could quickly read or write the glyph scrolls, and a considerable number of such manuscripts (some say hundreds) had accumulated by the time of the conquest. Most of them were destroyed by overzealous Spaniards, but the story that the first bishop of Mexico, Juan Zumárraga, burned the marvelous library of Texcoco, is distinctly apocryphal and incorrect. No writer of these days even makes mention of such a library, yet the story of the destruction is still widely told.

The Aztecs were good astronomers, and developed their own calendar, inferior to that of the Mayas. The famous Calendar Stone, a huge block of black porphyry, with carvings representing the four cycles of creation, or "the four suns," as the Aztecs called them, is now in the Museum in Mexico City. Formerly it was placed in front of the Temple of the Sun and probably served as an altar on which human sacrifices were made. In 1560 the archibishop had it buried, fearing that its presence might revive the old pagan practices. It was rediscovered at the end of the eighteenth century.

Aztec religion was the most bloodthirsty of any produced on the American continents. Spanish chroniclers refer to "thousands of skulls" on the rack of the main temple enclosure, and Aztec glyphs take these sacrifices as a matter of course. Bernal Díaz and his companions entered the "holy of holies" in Tenochtitlán and saw on the altar three smoking human hearts, the day's offering to the Aztec god.

To perform the sacrifice priests grasped the sacrificial victim, held his arms and legs in a firm grip, and with a flint knife cut out his palpitating heart. This was held aloft to the sun, then cast upon the altar. The Aztecs firmly believed that this offering of man's greatest boon, life itself, was the gift most acceptable to the gods. The stench and filth that pervaded these temple precincts was almost unendurable, and contrasted sharply with the cleanliness of the rest of the city. As a result of these wholesale sacrifices the Aztecs did learn more about human anatomy and the circulatory system than was known in Europe at that time.

The arts and crafts of the Aztecs were on a higher level. Their examples of mosaic work, exquisite pottery, beautiful dyed cloths of cotton and rabbit hair, carved jade, and ornaments of gold and silver all amazed the Spaniards, who claimed that nothing in their own country was superior. Two huge plates, "large as carriage wheels," one of gold and one of silver, both richly carved with plants and animals, were sent to Cortés as a gift by Montezuma. These and hundreds of other priceless objects of art were melted down in Spain. The Aztecs also excelled in featherwork. Cloaks and draperies were made of brilliant feathers pasted onto a webbing of cotton. Gold and silver were not highly regarded; the most precious of all things to the Aztecs was jade.

One of the outstanding expressions of Aztec civilization, indeed of Indian culture everywhere, was the market. Every village had its market day, and nearly everybody in and around town showed up before the day was ended. The Spaniards were dumfounded by the size of the great marketplace in Mexico City, and by the profusion of its wares. Bernal Díaz describes it thus:

> Each kind of merchandise was kept by itself and had its fixed place marked out. Let us begin with the dealers in gold, silver and precious stones, feathers, mantles, and embroidered goods. Then there were other wares consisting of Indian slaves, both men and women; and I say that they bring as many of them to that great market for sale as the Portuguese bring negroes from Guinea; and they brought them tied to long poles, with collars round their necks so that they could not escape, and others they left free. Next there were traders who sold great pieces of cloth and cotton, and articles of twisted thread, and there were *cacahuateros* who sold cacao. In this way one could see every sort of merchandise that is to be found in the whole of New Spain. There were those who sold cloths of henequen and ropes and the sandals with which they are shod, which are made of the same plant, and sweet cooked roots, and other tubers which they get from this plant. All these things were kept in one part of the market in the place assigned to them. In another, there were skins of tigers and lions, of otters and jackals, deer and other animals and badgers and mountain cats, some tanned and others untanned, and other classes of merchandise.
>
> Let us go on and speak of those who sold beans and sage and other vegetables and herbs in another place, and to those who sold fowls, cocks with wattles, rabbits, hares, deer, mallards, young dogs and other things of that sort in their part of the market, and let us also mention the fruiterers, and the women who sold cooked food, dough and tripe in their own part of the market; then every sort of pottery made in a thousand different forms from great water jars to little jugs, these also had a place to themselves; then those who sold honey and honey paste and other dainties like nut paste, and those who sold lumber, boards, cradles, beams, blocks and benches, each article by itself, and the vendors of *ocote* pitch-pine for torches, and things of a similar nature. But why do I waste so many words in recounting what they sell in that great market?—for I shall never finish if I tell it all in detail.
>
> Paper, which in this country is called *amal*, and reeds scented with *liquidambar*, and full of tobacco, and yellow ointments and things of that sort are sold by themselves, and much cochineal is sold under the arcades which are in the great market place, and there are many vendors of herbs and other sorts of trades. There are also buildings where three magistrates sit in judgment, and there are executive officers like *alguaciles* who inspect the merchandise. I am forgetting those who sell salt, and those who make the stone knives, and how they split them off the stone itself; and the fisher women and others who sell small cakes made from a sort of ooze which they get out of the great lake, which curdles, and from this they

make a bread having a flavor something like cheese. There are for sale axes of brass and copper and tin, and gourds and gaily painted jars made of wood. I wish I could finish telling of all the things which are sold there, but they are so numerous and of such different quality, and the great market place with its surrounding arcades was so crowded with people, that one would not have been able to see and inquire about it all in two days.

Ah, well, Bernal Díaz, you've done a fairly respectable job of presenting the case!

The Aztecs, of course, did not originate the Indian market. In fact, they originated very little in Mexican culture history. They were the organizers, the warriors; or, we might say, the Romans of Mexico.

From all the records their capital itself was the outstanding achievement of the Aztecs. No chronicler mentions less than sixty thousand dwellings, which would mean a city of at least three hundred thousand inhabitants. Even if the estimates were high, which is quite probable, Tenochtitlán would still be, in 1519, one of the largest cities in the world. When the Spaniards, after bein ejected, finally overran the city block by block, they were at pains to destroy every building, filling in the canals with the rubble. Bernal Díaz, many years later, recalls the great capital nostalgically, and laments its destruction. "Of all these wonders that I then beheld," he writes, "today all is overthrown and lost, nothing is left standing."

The Mexican archaeologist, Ignacio Marquina, in his book on pre-Columbian Indian architecture, has reconstructed the city as it was in 1519. His picture of the great temples, with friezes of bright yellow, green, red, and blue, is indeed an imposing sight. The ruins of Teotihuacán give us an idea of the size but not of the dazzling colors that were so typical of Aztec Tenochtitlán, a city which now exists merely in a few museum pieces and a small section or two of a buried pyramid unearthed during the construction of modern Mexico City.

Perhaps the Aztecs had it coming to them. War was their way of life; their religion was based on human sacrifices and their tax collectors roamed far and wide collecting from the subject tribes. It was this combination of hateful ingredients which turned the tide in the Spaniards' favor. Thousands joined the invaders, willing to risk everything on a chance of getting even with their hated oppressors.

The substance of Indian culture was strong and whole in pre-Columbian America. This culture expressed itself in Maya, Toltec, Aztec, Zapotec, and dozens of other periodic and regional manifestations. When Cortés landed in Mexico at least fifty different languages were spoken in that area. But there undoubtedly existed one great mother culture from which all these emerged and grew in the way that branches grow and flower upon the same tree.

Indian culture was a closely knitted, firmly integrated thing, its roots deep in the earth, its hopes in the sky. In this culture every man had his place. There was no outsider, no one who did not belong. When there was work to be done, all joined in and worked. When there was loss or death, all lamented together. When there was worshiping, all participated in the great dreaming. When there was music, song, or dance, everyone had a part. No one was a spectator in Indian life. Participation was the great catharsis. The naked isolation of the individual in today's world would have been incomprehensible to an Indian. Neuroses growing out of loneliness or maladjustment were non-existent.

Art existed in every home. Use separated from beauty was almost unthinkable. The meanest kitchen jar was shaped and colored with loving care and was meant to delight the eye and heart as well as the stomach. The undying human urge to create was expressed fully and freely in every art and craft and in every cultural expression. Creativity, participation, a sense of belonging to the group, a sense of being an integral part of something larger than oneself, this was the core and heart of Indian culture. It is only in modern civilization that philosophers and artists have begun to lament the alienation of man.

Certain ideas and feelings are basic in any interpretation of pre-Spanish art. First, and foremost, is the strong religious instinct, expressed in design and symbol. Second, is the "naturalistic development of separate details, although the whole may be a purely imaginary conception." And, third, is the use of decorative motifs "whose fundamental mode of expression is rhythmic repetition; hence the need for symmetry and the desire to cover with decoration all available space without leaving any large plain surfaces." [3] Last of all, there is color, the live telluric colors of tropical nature, the brightness of the jungle, the startling clarity of the high plateau. Unite all these, and the true characteristics of Mexican art begin to fall into focus.

The communal folk feeling which is such an integral part of Mexican Indian culture was strongly rooted in the attitude toward the earth itself. Not only was the earth man's source of life (i.e., land rather than the sea, or capital, or even labor), but land itself was an almost holy thing, just as the air above it or the waters below. Land was not privately owned. It belonged to the clan or tribe; only its produce belonged to the individual. The tribe apportioned it to heads of families, but its use was contingent upon proper cultivation. "The tribal council divided the land among the clans, and the leaders of each, in turn, apportioned its share among the heads of families justly and equitably. Sections were also reserved for the maintenance of the chief and the temple staff, for war supplies and the payment of tribute; these were worked communally." [32]

The produce of those lands that were individually tilled belonged to the families. Hence, a man who was an efficient farmer (or a fine craftsman, or wily hunter) rose in the estimation of the tribe. He might become a clan chieftain or a member of the tribal council and could thus wield a considerable power in the direction of village life and the policy of the group.

Since there was only a limited amount of arable land available in Mexico, this community control was a matter of life and death to the Indian villages. The Spanish conquest, with its principle of private ownership, uprooted the communal land tradition. The acquisition of large areas by the more successful conquistadores led to the development of the *latifundium,* or hacienda, system. The native population of these areas went along with the land, and wherever the white man settled there rapidly emerged a society of landlords and day laborers. The Indian, lacking control of the land, which was man's umbilical cord, lacked everything. The Spaniard who controlled the land controlled everything. Land, therefore, became synonymous with oppression, with liberty.

However, in the outlying villages which managed to escape the thrall of the conquistador, the old traditions continued throughout the colonial epoch. In the late nineteenth century Porfirio Díaz dealt them devastating blows, and the big hacienda became a way of life, but after the Mexican Revolution of 1910 the national government reversed this policy and rested its case upon a revival of communal landownership in the widespread *ejido* villages. This restitution of land to the landless has done more to restore a pride in race and country than all the paper patriotism in Mexico's history.

III

BANNER OF THE CROSS: THE CONQUEST

I came to get gold, not to till the soil like a peasant.

—Hernán Cortés

Cortés also said, "Doubt not that the Almighty will shield you, for your cause is just, and you are fighting under the Banner of the Cross." *Glory*, *gold*, and *gospel*—this was the trinity of the Spanish conquest in Mexico, and in all Spanish America. Spain was ready for the conquest; the other countries of Europe were not. For nearly eight centuries the Christian soldiers of the peninsula had been struggling to drive the Moors from Spanish soil. War and religion were the two great poles of medieval life, and in Spain these had been fused in one: religious war. The Moors were not only foreign invaders, they were infidels. Therefore, the struggle against them naturally took on a deep religious significance. It became almost a crusade, but unlike the crusades of the other European countries in Palestine, this crusade was successful. A Spanish writer, Américo Castro, points out that the Moors were superior to the Spaniards in all ways but one, epic faith. And this faith won out over every adversity. It was in no wise a Hellenic intellectual expression, but one of pure feeling, of belief, of the soul (*del alma*). It was a certitude of destiny.

By some miracle of coincidence final victory against the Moors came in the year 1492. The cross was planted on Alhambra's hill, and Spain was flushed with the dark powers of victory. In 1492, also, a Spaniard, Alexander Borgia, was selected as the Pope of Rome. In 1492, another Spaniard, Antonio Nebrija, published his *Gramática castellana*, the first grammar of a modern European tongue. In its preface he pointed out that language was the ideal weapon of empire. In 1492 the Jews, the only other peninsular minority, were driven from Spanish soil. And, of course, everyone knows that Columbus discovered America in 1492. It was a year of epic proportions such as had never before been known in the history of mankind.

Spain was at her flood; in 1492 no power on earth could stop her. Every nation has its day in the sun, and this was the day for Spain.

In the year 1000 she would have been incapable of the conquest, and in the year 1900 she would have been equally impotent. But in the early sixteenth century Spain was the only European nation which combined the cultural unity of the Middle Ages with the political unity of the Renaissance. There was no Reformation on the horizon in Spain, and the long centuries of warfare against the Moors had welded her peoples into a nation. Spain was unified as never before or afterward, in power, in language, in religion, in drive to expansion. She was invincible.

In the Middle Ages the center of the universe was God, and the lives and paths of all men led to Him. Sharp Gothic spires, arches, windows of stained glass shaped like hands in prayer, reached up to eternal life. Dreary lives were ennobled by consecration to these great cathedrals of heaven on earth. They were the collective expression of an epoch. What did it matter that life in this world was a misery, if life everlasting, in the world to come, would make all men gloriously equal?

With the Renaissance the center of the universe became man. Greek and Roman antiquities spread the aura of their pagan spirit over the approach to life, humanizing its values. They freed it from the oneness of medieval religion, projected it like a catapult into the individualism of a new outlook. This multiplication of Man, this glorification of the individual and his prowess, caused many men to grasp higher than they could reach, but those who reached highest equaled the best of the Age of Athens.

However, the masses of little men, torn loose from the tenets of their old religion, were made ready to follow the reformers of the Protestant schisms in droves. In Spain alone there never arose a single Protestant church. The state simply seized on the church as its weapon and would not relinquish it. Uniformity was not exactly forced on the Spaniards, though the Council of Trent and the Counter Reformation did tighten the screws. But the eight-century-long struggle against the Moors had already made this single-mindedness an integral part of their being, an expression of the collective will. Hence, Spain was the only European nation immediately ready to undertake the conquest of America, in which a unified home front was of the first importance.

The reconquest of Spain from the Moors welded Spanish church and state inseparably in union. The war was as much for the Cross as it was for the land and for political dominion. Priests went into battle and fought as bravely as any soldier. When victory finally came there was no longer any possibility of a division between the powers of church and government. A new kind of absolutism emerged in European history, the *iglesia-estado*, or church-state. This was carried to America as the culmination of the last and greatest of all crusades, and was firmly implanted in the colonies. In Mexico it was outstandingly successful.

"The discovery of America represents the greatest revolution ever effected in the history of mankind. It shifted completely the center of gravity of the known world, turned the eyes of civilization from the Crusades of the East toward the conquest of the West, marked the end of the Middle Ages and the beginning of the modern era, and above all altered and broadened the entire nature of man's thinking." [8]

The epic of Cortés in Mexico has undergone many tellings. We could not hope to duplicate it here. Suffice it to say that Cortés was undoubtedly the greatest of the conquistadores. He was the one who opened the way; he set the pace of those who followed. It is always easier to move along a path which someone else has cut. Cortés entered Mexico City with four hundred men, and with a force never exceeding fifteen hundred Spanish soldiers he conquered a nation of several millions. True, he carried many of the trumps, but it took a great leader to know how to use them. Firearms, horses, the legend of white men who would come from beyond the seas to conquer Mexico, Montezuma's indecision, the widespread hatred of the Aztecs among the subject peoples, a horde of Indian allies, a superior faith, and a group of hard-hitting shock troops whose stoicism and bravery are unexcelled in history—all these things aided Cortés greatly. No one of them should be minimized in the victory that followed.

But the force that welded them together, the force that gave them drive and function, was the dynamic personality of the leader without which each of the above elements would have existed singly, like amputated members, without profit or body. Cortés wanted gold and slaves, and gold and slaves he found in vast abundance, after taking a nation.

Cortés began his adult life as a typical small-time *caballero*. He was a fighter and he was a great chaser of women. At the age of seventeen he had enlisted in one of the early expeditions to the New World, but on the night prior to the departure he scaled a high wall in order to keep a clandestine rendezvous, a rock broke loose, and the young swain fell in a battered heap below. He was unable to leave on the morrow. When he did reach Santo Domingo a couple of years later he continued his pursuit of the fair sex, and fought several duels. These episodes salted his seven years as an island settler.

But Cortés was not merely a Lothario. He was popular among the men as well as among women, he was strong, he was a good soldier. Most of all, he possessed the magic alchemy of leadership. When Governor Velásquez of the island was entrusted with the task of subjugating Cuba (1511), Cortés went along and distinguished himself in the campaign. He was made the governor's secretary and the King's treasurer. When Velásquez decided to send an expedition to the mainland, from whence had come reports of a wealthy empire, Cortés was appointed as leader. He began to spruce up, put on a velvet jacket, donned a plumed hat, and went about preparing the great enterprise. At the last moment news reached his ears that he was about to be replaced. With the same power of decision that characterized his later life, he simply took off for Mexico and left the Governor disconsolate. The year was 1519.

His landing on the mainland, his many battles, his march into the Valley of Mexico, and his victory over the Aztecs need only a recapitulation. One early episode, however, must be mentioned and recorded. After the defeat of the coastal Tabascans the native chieftain presented the Spaniards with twenty maidens, among them the famous Malinche, or, as she was known in Spanish, Doña Marina. This young woman knew both Maya and Aztec, and by way of a Spanish soldier who had previously been shipwrecked on the coast and had learned Maya, it was now possible for Malinche to act as interpreter. Before long she also acted as Cortés' mistress, and soon the language of love had turned her into a loyal adviser. She quickly learned Spanish and bore Cortés a son. Linked to her own people by blood and by tradition, Malinche did all that was humanly possible to mitigate the conquest, but never on any occasion did she waver in loyalty to her white lover. Without her the conquest of Mexico would have been vastly more difficult, perhaps impossible.

The Valley of Mexico lies almost three hundred miles inland. In order to reach it the Spaniards had to cross the marshy tropical lowlands, where their horses were mired down "clear to the belly," and then climb the high mountain barrier which separates the Central Valley from the coast. The soldiers slept in their armor regardless of the weather, sweltering it out in the jungle, chilled to the marrow on the mountain slopes. They swatted insects, they were struck down with tropical fever, or from exertion and illness at the higher altitudes they often spit blood. On occasion their skin stuck to the steel and on being pulled loose left raw and painful wounds. They endured it all "with stoic Iberian adaptability," cursing profusely as they marched, but always marching.

One of the historians writes that Cortés informed Montezuma that the Spaniards were afflicted with a disease of the heart for which gold was a specific remedy. Another tells of a gilt helmet that was sent to the Aztec chieftain with the suggestion that it be returned filled with gold. Unfortunately for the Aztecs, this was done, and in so doing Montezuma signed not only his own death warrant but that of his people.

Many Indian warriors joined ranks with the Spaniards because they hated the Aztecs. They hauled the cannon and acted as guides, scouts, and porters. The fierce mountain warriors of Tlaxcala at first opposed the Spaniards, but after being defeated in several pitched battles became their stanchest allies, a veritable fulcrum with which to pound away at the proud capital.

Bernal Díaz makes immoderate attempts to minimize the number of these Indian allies, but Cortés himself refers to "a tremendous number," "countless soldiers," and estimates those who fought alongside him in the final conquest of the city at "more than one hundred and fifty thousand men." These statistics must all be taken with a grain of salt, for any number above ten thousand was probably "an infinite number" to these Spaniards unversed in the intricacies of higher calculations.

At last, on a wintry day toward the end of October, 1519, the expedition reached the Valley of Mexico and a vista of surprising loveliness was spread out before the weary Spaniards. The valley was covered with green fields, lakes, canals, giant causeways, and sprinkled with towns and villages which shone brightly under the clear sunlight. A forest of giant cedars and conifers extended down the mountainsides, and brilliant flowers colored the valley. The Queen City of Anahuac, with its dazzling stone palaces and the enormous mass of its great pyramid-temple, shone like a fairy city across the lake waters. There were flowers, flowers everywhere, even on the rooftops of the stone and adobe houses. The causeways were lined with great crowds; canoes were teeming on the lake. No wonder the Spaniards thought it was a dream from some romance of chivalry.

Bernal Díaz wrote: "Gazing on such wonderful sights, we did not know what to say, or whether what appeared before us was real, for on one side, on the land, there were great cities, and in the lake were so many more, and the lake itself was crowded with canoes, and in the

Causeway were many bridges at intervals, and in front of us stood the great City of Mexico, and we—we did not even number four hundred soldiers!"

Montezuma came out to receive them. He had prayed to his gods, and they had answered with fearsome omens. The great chieftain was paralyzed with indecision, so he came forth as a friend and took his enemies into the city. On this fateful day of their first meeting Montezuma was carried in a litter and above his head attendants held a canopy of green feathers. He wore a blue mantle, embossed with threads of gold. Sweepers brushed clean the ground before him. Cortés advanced and the two men spoke briefly. Two worlds met in that encounter, so different in their conceptions that they might as easily have been from two different planets.

The Spaniards entered the city as guests and settled down to the long weeks of impatient waiting. They lived like potentates. Montezuma gave them gifts of gold and silver, and they were waited on, hand and foot. He also gave them women, and the soldiers reveled in their concubines, "who knew very well how to keep them warm in the dark."

Bernal Díaz gives a vivid description of the Indian Chieftain in the following words:

> The Great Montezuma was about forty years old, of good height and well proportioned, slender and spare of flesh, not very swarthy, but of the natural color and shade of an Indian. He did not wear his hair long, but so as just to cover his ears; his scanty black beard was well shaped and thin. His face was somewhat long, but cheerful, and he had good eyes and showed in his appearance and manner both tenderness, and, when necessary, gravity. He was very neat and clean, and bathed once every day in the afternoon. He had many women as mistresses, daughters of Chieftains, and he had two great Cacicas as his legitimate wives. He was free from unnatural offences. The clothes that he wore one day, he did not put on again until four days later. He had over two hundred Chieftains in his guard, in other rooms close to his own, not that all were meant to converse with him, but only with one another, and when they did go to speak with him they were obliged to take off their rich mantles and put on others of little worth, but they had to be clean, and they had to enter barefoot with their eyes lowered to the ground, and not to look up in his face.

The Spaniards were most anxious to penetrate the Aztec sanctuaries, to see how their religion functioned, and to put a stop, if possible, to their bloodthirsty rite of human sacrifices. In order to reach the main temple they had to pass through a spacious enclosure "larger than the plaza of Salamanca, with two walls of masonry surrounding it, and the court itself all paved with very smooth and very white flagstones. And where there were not these stones it was cemented and burnished and all very clean, so that one could not find any dust or straw in the whole place." One day they ascended the great temple and saw the "cursed idols," and inside the place of sacrifice there was so much clotted blood and such a foul stench that all were anxious to return to the open air again.

From the summit they looked out over the great City of Mexico and saw the three causeways that led into it, and the fresh water that came from Chapultepec which supplied the city, and the bridges on the three causeways, placed at regular intervals, under which the waters of the lake flowed from one side to the other. There was a huge multitude of canoes, "some coming with supplies of food, and others returning loaded with cargoes of merchandise; and we saw that from every house of that great city, and of all the other cities that were built in the water, it was impossible to pass from house to house, except by draw-bridges which were made of wood or in canoes; and we saw in all the cities temples and oratories like towers and fortresses and all gleaming white, and it was a wonderful thing to behold."

Cortés attempted to speak to Montezuma of the religion of the Cross, but met with a cold reception. Then they all descended. "And as the steps numbered one hundred and fourteen, and as some of our soldiers were suffering from tumors and abscesses, their legs were tired by the descent." They returned to their quarters and put in more time of anxious waiting.

Many writers have pitilessly criticized Montezuma for being such a weak and vacillating monarch. Why did he not take immediate action against the Spaniards, before additional soldiers arrived? In the first place, Montezuma was no monarch at all in the European sense. This term of king or emperor, which the Spaniards so often applied to him, was merely a matter of semantics, not of fact. They used the word which signified the ruler of a great state in Europe, but it did not fit the case. Montezuma was merely the head chieftain; he held no autocratic power. He could not wage a military campaign without getting the consent of all the clans. Besides, the Spaniards had arrived at the end of summer, during the harvest season. Thousands of warriors were in the fields, gathering the crops, and to draw them away was a risky business which might mean the loss of the harvest, and consequent famine. Then, too, there was that legend, the story of the Fair God who in the year of *Ce Acatl,* which was the exact year that Cortés landed in Mexico (1519), with strange white men from beyond the seas would come to conquer his people.

No, Montezuma was no weakling. He was merely a prisoner of his beliefs and of his epoch. So he temporized, and waited. He came bearing gifts, but he was no Greek. The Spaniards soon were chafing at the bit. They were anxious to grab *all that gold* and get out of the country. Then came the fatal "incident."

The Spanish garrison that had been left on the coast was attacked and several soldiers were slain. Montezuma was blamed for it. He was "visited" by a small guard (of whom Bernal Díaz was one) and taken prisoner. His face turned white when he knew what the Spaniards wanted of him, but he was told that if he so much as made a false gesture he would die in his tracks. Reluctantly, he accompanied the Spaniards back to their quarters. He was treated well, and many of the soldiers came to like him.

News reached Mexico City that a large body of Spanish soldiers had landed on the coast under Pánfilo de Narváez, who was to replace Cortés as leader. The captain himself left for the coast posthaste in order to head this off. He arrived with gold and more golden promises, and after a brief sharp encounter with a few of the diehards, these soldiers were persuaded to join him. With nearly a thousand additional men Cortés returned to the capital, where the Aztecs were seething with hatred and rebellion.

Alvarado, left in charge while the Captain was away, had seen a large group of Indians assemble in order to celebrate the feast of their god Huitzilopochtli, and without taking time to check the facts he scented trouble and fell upon the Indians and slew them all. The city was incensed, and rose up as a single man against the invaders. However, "the structural weakness of the Indian government became bitterly evident when the chiefs permitted Cortés and his reinforcements to join the beleaguered Alvarado." It was not within the Aztec concept of military strategy to split the adversary's army, and then destroy its separate parts.

Back in the city Cortés encountered a bedlam. The inhabitants attacked en masse, hurling arrows and missiles. The Spaniards could not maneuver on the narrow footpaths along the canals and were forced to retreat to their quarters. Montezuma attempted to speak to his people, and was met with a barrage of stones. He died shortly thereafter, either as a result of his wounds or, as two excellent authorities state (Sahagún and Durán), he was strangled by the Spaniards. After a week in the palace, Cortés saw that he would have to run for it. The Spaniards tried to sneak out before dawn, but a woman getting water from the canal saw them and gave the alarm.

Now began the death battle. The Aztecs tore up the bridges along the causeway, assailed the flanks in canoes, and kept up a constant pressure against the rear. Many Spaniards, burdened with gold and with the weight of their armor, fell into the water and either sank or were clubbed to death. The retreat turned into a flight. Cannons, muskets, even gold was dumped into the lake so that the flight could be speeded up. The Aztecs constantly taunted the invaders:

"Not a Spaniard will leave this valley alive!"

It came near to being a prophecy. But not quite. Three-quarters of the Spanish army was lost before the remnants reached the sanctuary of the open fields, and all the rest were wounded. This was the famous *Noche triste* (sad night), on which Cortés sat under the great cypress tree and wept. Yet somehow these soldiers kept their flight from becoming a rout, and once on the open plains they immediately fell into a disciplined formation, regrouped their staggering forces, and on the Vale of Otumba repulsed every attack of the natives. For the Spaniards this was their finest hour. The Tlaxcalans stood by them bravely against all odds, and with their aid the battered soldiers retreated in a more orderly fashion to the Valley of Tlaxcala in order to lick their wounds. The most decisive battle in the history of Mexico was ended.

Again the Aztecs had failed dismally to follow up their advantage; they might have pursued the invaders relentlessly, night and day, until they were annihilated. It could probably have been done. But this was simply not the way the Indians fought their battles. Their attacks were always massed assaults, and they could only bring a small fraction of their forces into play at any given moment. If these were routed, the rest were confused and milled about aimlessly. They were warriors, but they were not soldiers in the European sense. They knew no formations, no planned strategy. They followed their chieftains, who were symbols of the tribal spirit, not just military leaders; hence, if these fell, the "army" disintegrated. In the history of their people defeat had always been only an incident, not a catastrophe. They could not envisage its meaning the extinction of their civilization. This was how they had always fought other Indians. They knew no different plan of battle. Any well-trained, properly led European expeditionary force might have defeated them. "Properly led" is a big order, but it is no unique miracle of achievement.

The Spaniards rested in Tlaxcala and awaited reinforcements. Then they "pacified" the surrounding country, town by town, until the way was clear for an all-out attack on Tenochtitlán. This time the inhabitants of the lake city of Texcoco, who had formerly fought against them, came over to their side. This gave the Spaniards a beachhead from which to launch their assault.

The Spaniards made thirteen brigantines, brought them over the mountains and put them on the lake, mounted them with firearms, and thus kept the canoes from swarming. Carefully they surrounded the capital. Then street by street and building by building they advanced into the city, battering, slaying, demolishing, leaving not one stone upon another. The rubble was cast into the canals, making the passage easier. Every causeway was sealed off, and it was impossible to bring food into the city. The siege lasted for seventy-five days, then, realizing that the jig was up, the pitiful remnants of the proud Aztec Confederation, their faces pinched and blackened from disease and famine, came forth from their final hiding places and attempted to escape. Their chieftain, Cuautemoc, shot across the lake in the royal canoe, his pennon proudly waving. He was quickly captured. Tenochtitlán was level with the dust. It was the thirteenth of August, 1521. Later the Spaniards strangled Cuautemoc, for they were afraid to harbor a living symbol among them. So ends the tragic conquest of Mexico.

Bernal Díaz, the old soldier of eighty, remembers the conquest as if it lay just before him, and puts it all in his *True History*. When he writes of his companions who had fallen or who had been sacrificed to the Aztec gods, he sagely adds that "they died in the service of God and his Majesty, and to give light to those who sat in darkness, and also to acquire that wealth which most men covet." No truer characterization of the Spanish conquest was ever stated.

At the head of the Paseo de la Reforma in Mexico City there stands a giant black statue of Cuautemoc, his raised hand clasping a lance. He wears a feather plume, and his features are regal, almost Roman. He hardly resembles an Indian. In the history of Mexico he has come to typify the ideal man of those days of conquest, the man of the Renaissance, the embodiment of every cultural aspiration. With this difference: here in Mexico the aspiration was Indian. Despite the victory of the Spaniards, despite the three centuries of colonial empire, it was still Aztec Indian when the Revolution overthrew Porfirio Díaz (1911).

Cortés, on the other hand, has frequently been vilified by the historians, particularly by the Mexican historians. For years there was no statue to him in all of Mexico. Yet Cortés was the epitome of the

Spanish Renaissance, not Cuautemoc. While other European countries were making of the Renaissance a period of artistic flowering, a rebirth of interest in classic antiquity, Spain made of it a period of conquest and expansion, and the conquistador, not the man of art, was her proudest achievement. Beyond any doubt the name of Cortés stands in first place among those of the conquistadores. In him the "epic faith" and certitude of destiny were incarnate. The Spanish writer Américo Castro says that Cortés is therefore the equal of any da Vinci. It is the typical Spanish point of view, pride in the age of Spain's glory. Take it or leave it.

The balance sheet of Cortés versus Cuautemoc has undergone many alterings in Mexico. One contemporary Mexican historian, José Vasconcelos, decries the apotheosis of the Indian. He writes:

"The myth of Cuautemoc was invented by Prescott and other North American historians and is defended by all the indirect agents of Protestantism who wish to erase every trace of Spain in America. The sentimentalism which surrounds Cuautemoc is like that expressed today by those unconsciously influenced by British imperialism in favor of the Negus of Abyssinia. . . . Cortés, on the other hand, the most human of the conquistadores, is spiritually joined with the vanquished Indians when he forced them to the faith, and his action leaves us the legacy of a real nation." [33]

The Spanish historian Salvador de Madariaga echoes these sentiments:

> How could he ever have guessed that the day would come when they would have to conceal his ashes, buried in Mexico at his own express wish, from the fury of the masses whose nation he had founded, who rose in destructive fury against the very man to whose vision they owed their country? How could he have foreseen that the Mexico created by him would some day erect a statue to Cuautemoc, not to honor Cuautemoc, but to insult *him;* that a painter of that race for which he had done so much to ennoble and set free from horrible practices, would one day adorn the walls of his palace in Cuernavaca with slanderous scenes of the conquest, about which even the said painter is innocent, since they burst forth out of the unfathomable abyss of racial feelings? [19]

And so the scales will tip first one way, then the other, while the work of Cortés and the symbol of Cuautemoc spin out together the measure of Mexico's destiny, which is a mestizo destiny, neither Indian nor Spanish, that lies between them. Amoeba-like the Indian heritage and the brown faces recoiled at the first sharp encounters, but amoeba-like also they continued to move and flow like some live liquid until finally they engulfed, then swallowed the invader.

IV

RED GOLD: LANDS AND INDIAN LABOR

The ducks are hatched in the bulrushes, and throw themselves into the water without having been taught how to swim. The butterfly bursts through its wrappings and wings freely into the sky. The snake comes into being and glides through the weeds with death in its mouth. . . . We were like that too, and that is why the tribe has been able to survive its sufferings. It is not strange that the child knows how to swim without having been taught. . . . What has happened to us is that under the domination of another race, we have begun to lose faith in our instincts.

—López y Fuentes, in *El indio*

We might call this chapter "from *encomienda* to hacienda," with a few side reflections on America in the Renaissance. To the Spaniards who came to Mexico hoping to find gold, and who did not find it (and these were certainly in the great majority), land and Indians became a very acceptable substitute. Land gave them a title and a definite social stature. The Indians either paid them tribute or worked the land and made it pay.

The story did not have a violent beginning. When the first Spaniards arrived in the islands of the Antilles they encountered a gentle population who followed one of the most idyllic economies on earth. They fished, they picked the abundant tropical fruits, they walked naked in the sun, unashamed of their bodies and having no need of clothes. Columbus wrote: "They are so guileless and generous with all that they possess, that no one would believe it who has not seen it. Anything they have, if it be asked of them, they never refuse; on the contrary, they offer it and show as much love as if they would give their hearts." Of Cuba, he said it was "the fairest land that human eyes have ever seen." The land was "as green as April in Andalusia. The singing of the birds is so beautiful that one wishes never to leave. There are thousands of trees, all with their delicious fruits."

But Spanish greed quickly put an end to the utopian life. The men with Columbus saw a few baubles of gold, and that did it. They promptly went berserk, demanding a Midas treasure. The Indians were forced to dig in the earth or stand in the streams and pan the waters until they dropped. A gentle population was turned into violent enemies.

These Indians had followed an idyllic economy. Work was not in their vocabulary or in their temperament. Yet without them the Spanish colonization, postulated as it was on a basis of large groups of manual laborers, was doomed to failure. No Spaniard came to the New World in order to continue at the same menial task he had performed in the Old. And so the *encomienda* system was revived by the crown, ostensibly to protect the Indians, actually to make them work.

The word *encomienda* means *trusteeship* and refers to a setup that goes back to feudal times, when the peasants often "commended" themselves to the lord of the nearest manor and received his protection in return for certain specified personal services.

The *encomienda,* therefore, was a feudal fief. It did not include ownership of the land itself, but it gave the trustee or *encomendero* the right to demand certain services (labor in the fields and household work) and the right to collect tribute. Many of the trustees did receive outright grants of land, however, and soon the *encomienda* and landownership became inseparably woven together. They constituted a little closed-off world in which the pattern of lord and vassal was intrinsic. This was the birth of the hacienda system. Like the Roman *latifundium* of old it meant the perpetuation of landownership in the hands of a chosen few and the growth of uprooted landless masses, who, deprived of their birthright, became mere serfs in the hands of a civilization they did not understand.

In the Antilles the *encomienda* system was an unmitigated disaster. Unaccustomed to rigorous labor of any kind, the natives died like flies at the end of the lash and of the white man's diseases. In 1492 the island of Santo Domingo had an estimated population of 100,000; but by 1550 only 5,000 Indians survived. On the other hand, in Mexico, where the natives were a "hardy agrarian people, long inured to the exacting labors of the field and to the primitive feudalism of the native overlords," the *encomienda* was a resounding success.

Success? At least it worked, and yielded a profit to the overlords, and by such a measure would any feudal arrangement be judged. To the underdogs it was like a dry rot that slowly ate away the substance of native culture, but the underdogs of Mexico did not die.

This is why today's visitor to Havana will never see an Indian, or even anyone resembling an Indian, while the visitor to Mexico City will be positively overwhelmed with the myriads of brown faces. In the islands of the Antilles, and to an only slightly lesser extent in Argentina and Uruguay, the native populations were much like the Indians of the United States. They died rather than live as bondsmen. There was no superior courage or bravery involved. The Mexican Indian was as brave as any man. But unfortunately the Indians of Mexico had already become accustomed to working for their own "top brass" and a change of governments was primarily a change of masters. To the Indians of the Antilles (and of Argentina and of the United States) such a life was unthinkable, hence impossible. So they were either herded off to reservations or annihilated.

The *encomienda*, or trusteeship, was first established in the Antilles in the year 1503, after repeated violence had already destroyed the last vestige of respect for the white man on the part of the natives. Temporarily things took a turn for the better, but this did not last. There were too few upright and honorable men in the high places.

It soon became apparent to the crown that the Spaniards in the New World were abusing the native population, and many laws were passed for the "good treatment and preservation of the Indians." They came too late. The islands of the Antilles were already a lost cause; and later in Mexico the pressure of public opinion among the colonists for Indian labor was so strong that no power on earth could snatch away their control over the natives.

Cortés did not approve of this way of "paying off" the soldiers, and neither did the king. But against the best judgment of both, and contrary to the express wishes of the crown, the more powerful soldiers simply took *encomiendas* for themselves right and left, and before long an accomplished fact rendered impotent even the best efforts of regal legislation. Cortés himself was always a realist of the first water, and when he saw how the wind was blowing he took the largest concession of all for himself. It consisted of 22 towns, 23,000 heads of families, and a total population of approximately 115,000. The area that fell under his jurisdiction amounted to about 25,000 square miles, in the states of Morelos, Oaxaca, Puebla, Mexico, and Veracruz. It included some of the richest farm land in all Mexico. Cortés was to have "complete civil and criminal jurisdiction over the inhabitants," and also all "woods, pastures, and all water, both running and stagnant."

All these original possessions, plus those acquired subsequently, were in 1535 converted into an entailed estate known in Spanish as the *mayorazgo,* so that it might pass on undivided and inalienably to his heirs. At the beginning of the nineteenth century this vast estate was still largely intact, consisting of 15 villas, 157 pueblos, 89 haciendas, 119 ranchos, 5 *estancias,* with a total population of about 150,000.

Others among the conquistadores received grants only slightly less imposing. Pedro de Alvarado received the rich farming area of Xochimilco with its 30,000 Indians. Another of his lieutenants received 10,000 square miles of land in the state of Guanajuato. And so it went.

Most of the conquered area of Mexico was held in *encomienda* by the end of the first half century, and G. M. McBride, in *The Land Systems of Mexico,* states that by 1572 at least 507 *encomiendas* had been granted to private individuals. These embraced the best arable land of the country. At first it was not intended that these grants should be made permanent, but they were extended from generation to generation until soon possession was a fact, legalities notwithstanding. Furthermore, by means of the entailed estate, or *mayorazgo,* accumulation went on constantly; division was practically impossible. When the *encomienda* was finally abolished in 1720 (legally abolished, of course, not abolished in fact), it had simply been replaced by the *hacienda.* Nothing now could uproot the owner from his land, or from his vassals. Well, almost nothing. The bloody Revolution of 1910 was the volcano that eventually did it.

Private individuals were not the only holders of vast haciendas. The Church was the greatest landlord of all. Many branches of the Church organization and a considerable number of individual prelates were granted *encomiendas.* In addition, the royal treasury furnished half the money for the construction of most religious buildings, the resident Spanish population furnished the other half, and the Indians performed the labor without remuneration. Ecclesiastical capital was almost always free from taxation, and the clergy were able to increase this constantly through tithes, fees, first fruits, bequests, gifts, alms, and so forth. Members of the clergy also frequently operated grocery stores and meat markets and engaged in commerce of all kinds. They received considerable sums from legal practice in both civil and ecclesiastical courts. They were the bankers of the colonial epoch.

From the outset they had the economic advantage over even the richest *encomenderos,* who had to build their own houses and provide their own working capital, and had not the sources of income that the clergy had. So, with the immense prestige of the Church behind them, it is not surprising that the clergy dominated the colonial era economically and politically. Nor is it strange that, as the years went on, the early missionary fervor tended to give place to complacent well-being and easy acceptance of priority thrust upon them; that adventurers were to be found in the ranks of the clergy as in all walks of life; that this easy means of acquiring an honorable position and a comfortable livelihood attracted such large numbers that in 1644 the town council of Mexico City implored Philip IV to send no more monks, as more than six thousand were without employment, living on the fat of the land.[24]

The Mexican historian Lucas Alamán, a partisan of the clergy, estimates that at the end of the colonial epoch the Church owned or controlled at least half of the real property and capital of Mexico.

A North American economist concludes that "the hacienda was the major contribution of Spain to the organic life of Mexico." Other writers disagree, and point to the city, the Church, or to the pattern of Hispanic cultural attitudes imposed on the native population. In any case, the hacienda was a symbol of the Spanish land system as developed in Mexico. It takes the place of the small American farm of early colonial days, but bears comparison with the southern plantation of a later epoch.

However, the hacienda was not the only manifestation of the Spanish land pattern. The other side of the medallion, not so obvious to the casual eye, was the "free" villages with their communal lands, that is, the villages not included in *encomiendas*. The crown issued numberless decrees in an effort to protect these villages against the encroachments of the haciendas. Special officials were appointed and special courts were set up for this express purpose. With such legal support a few indigenous communities actually increased their holdings, for colonial laws allowed the Indians to establish new pueblos, even on private property, and officials were obliged to give these communities one square league of land. Some of the native chieftains quickly picked up the sharp practices of the Spaniards and pulled every trick in the book in order to shield their holdings. These villages were by no means in the majority, but they were the ones which most nearly continued the preconquest land system of the native population. They were symbolic of a deep-rooted feeling for the land, whose spiritual and even political strength far exceeded its economic importance. The War for Independence and the Revolution of 1910 were both largely inspired by the desire of the dispossessed natives to recover their beloved land.

This public ownership of village lands had its counterpart in medieval Spain, where hundreds of communities owned similar village commons.

These consisted of agricultural terrain, woodlands, pasture, and the uncultivated public *ejido*, used for a variety of purposes, such as the threshing floor, the slaughterhouse, space for beehives, a village dump, perhaps a playground. In Spain, as in Mexico, these lands were inalienable. Approximately 12,500 towns and villages in Spain participated in this form of public ownership which saved them from landless serfdom.

When the Spaniards established a pueblo in Mexico they invariably assigned to the new village, in its corporate capacity, a large plot of publicly owned land, and so before long both the old "free" Indian villages and the newly founded Spanish pueblos were following a parallel course in their land patterns. The *ejido*, therefore, was characteristic of the Spanish, the Indian, and the mestizo agricultural economy.

The word *ejido*, which has become such a common term in Mexican agrarian revolution and reform, is the Spanish derivation of Latin *exitus* (English: *exit*), which means "on the way out." The *ejido* lands were generally located near one of the exits from the village. In Spain the *ejido* referred only to a limited portion of the communal and public lands, as defined above. In Mexico it came quickly to include all the village lands that were held in common.

We have spoken so much of the "Indian" way of living that the phrase must be clarified and some kind of balance struck. An American economist, Stuart Chase, in his book on Mexico, strives to prove that the Indian handicraft economy holds many advantages over the machine economy, and that in Mexico the handicraft economy is still very much alive despite four centuries of Hispanic "civilization." Chase concludes that a better world could be achieved were we to blend our industrial society with the best elements of that of the Mexican Indian. Chase was writing in 1931.[5] In the intervening years Mexico herself has followed this pattern of blending more than any other nation on earth. Perhaps she alone of all contemporary nations is best adapted by history and temperament to achieve such blending. In any case, Mexico, for this reason, is now unique among modern nations.

But before going into today's Mexico, which is quite another story, let us offer a contrast between the handicraft society and our industrial economy.

They of the handicraft society live on an island. Their market is the village plaza. We live in the world, and the world is our emporium. Their horizon is the farthest rim of hills. Ours is the farthest-flung airstrip across the seas. They have the necessities of life and do subsist, *if they survive*. Among us only a small fraction fails to survive, and a vast majority of those who do fare better than mere subsistence. They live slowly, advance like the snail, and literacy is the privilege of the chosen few. We leap across the barriers of knowledge. They are never without work, never without activity. We suffer depressions, unemployment, extremes of poverty and wealth. They belong to a society in which mental complexes are unknown, and all have a part both in the creation and in the performance of their forms of art. We are divided from the fruits of our labors. By and large we do not participate either in an individual or in a group creativity. We are a nation of spectators.

We possess much. They possess nothing but a full and busy life. We are vastly superior in all the techniques of supporting life. They are superior in the wholeness and integration of their culture in which the individual is not tossed about between aspiration, nothingness, and despair. Does this mean that we might profitably learn a few things from the Indian way of life? In our country this is a philosophical possibility, but is highly improbable. In Mexico, however, it is one outstanding fact of the country's dynamic personality today.

V

AN INTERLUDE: SOME DIFFERENCES BETWEEN US

One of our poles lies in Europe, the other in the United States. We receive inspiration from both. Our Utopian constitutions combine the political philosophy of France with the federalism under a president of the United States. The sirens of Europe and the sirens of the United States woo us at the same time. By and large, the mind of our America (without denying the affinities between it and the most select spirits of the other America) seems to find in Europe a more universal vision of human problems, more basic, more in keeping with its own feelings. Aside from historic misgivings, fortunately ever less justified and needing no mention here, we are not in sympathy with the tendency toward race distinctions. It displeases us to regard any human type as a mere curiosity or an interesting exotic case, for this is not the basis of real moral sympathy. The first preceptors of our America, the missionaries, lambs with the hearts of lions, terrible in their independence, embraced the Indians with love, promising them the same heaven which had been promised themselves. The first conquerors established the principle of equality in the delights of miscegenation.

—Alfonso Reyes, dean of Mexican letters in our time

Canada and Mexico both border the United States. One is almost a replica of our own society, the other is almost as foreign as China. These differences make Mexico a fascinating place to visit. They also make her tremendously difficult to understand. The traveler who becomes enmeshed in the "picturesque" aspects of Mexican life, without much knowledge of its language and less still of its history, is very like the fish who gulps the colorful fly that is cast before him and is thus irrevocably removed from his element. Somehow the grotesque struggles of many Americans to make themselves understood and liked in Mexico remind me of these flailing fishes.

Take, for example, the most obvious medium of communication, language.

The Spanish language is rich with generous phrases, which are the mark of good manners but are not to be taken at face value. There is a resonant floridity to it which is reflected readily in the eloquent pattern of politeness. The Mexican is a master of the hyperbole, and will offer you the shirt off his back with a generosity that is often insistent and overwhelming. You have but to admire something that belongs to him, and he will say "it is yours." Of course, this too is courtesy, and only the misguided will take it. The foreigner must be on his guard in mentioning things that he admires. Say to the Mexican "I think those flowers are simply beautiful," and he will take it to mean very plainly "I would certainly like to have a nice bouquet of those flowers." And he will insist that you take them. If you do accept them, you will have commited two faux pas instead of one. The country and village Mexican is even more insistent than his city counterpart. Once you have conversed with him in his own house he will invariably press some gift upon you. This merely means that he has enjoyed your visit. But do not take it, unless you have some gift to return. There is no such thing in the Mexican pattern as accepting something that has been offered merely in order not to offend, as is so frequently the American pattern.

Beware, too, of the exaggerated compliment. Sputter a few words in Spanish and almost any Mexican will tell you, "You speak fluently. You talk like a native. You speak divinely." The American traveler will feel himself all puffed up at this compliment, which merely means "You have said something and I have been able to understand you. This is no mean feat for an American." The older and wiser foreigner would thoroughly dislike such an exaggerated compliment. Why should a Mexican go out of his way to make any comment whatsoever concerning one's Spanish unless it is notably bad and so evokes the need for a monumental courtesy.

Language is a means of communication. When communication is smooth, there is no need for remarks about accent or fluency. Only when the going is rough does there arise the demand for a verbal nicety.

One often hears of the North American who spent six months in

Mexico (or six weeks)and came back speaking like a native. You meet dozens of them after every summer. But how much is this visitor able to say like a native? "Sí, señor. No, señorita." Is this what you call conversation? I'd love to hear him rattle off a few unbroken sentences, without errors, without hesitation, and still sound like a native. Show me a person who can speak like that and I'll show you the baldest liar, if he claims to have learned it in less than five to ten years of concentrated study. Americans all think that a foreign language is something you can pick up in a few weeks or months abroad, or in a couple of years of classroom study. No European would so deceive himself. In Europe, foreign language study is a serious matter, continued unbroken for many years, and at the proper age level for learning a foreign tongue, so that a final mastery of it is no miracle of the curriculum. Americans who take two or three years of Spanish or French in high school or college and expect to be able to converse fluently in the language might as well expect a two-year course in law or medicine (shortened to one hour a day of class work) to produce a lawyer or a doctor.

The differences between the United States and Mexico, of course, are not limited to the linguistic. So many of them go back to the time of the conquest, and to the time before the conquest, that any intelligent effort to understand Mexico must begin with a little history.

The Spanish conquest was characterized by a search for gold and slaves, and a desire to convert the natives. The Spanish colonists, mostly priests and soldiers, who came to the New World without their wives and families epitomized Spain and wished to create in America a replica of the homeland. They were not minority groups or religious dissidents. In Mexico and Peru they encountered Indian civilizations at a relatively high level of achievement. They defeated these well-organized regimes in a few pitched battles, and the campaign was won. Used to consorting with the Moors, they quickly found Indian mistresses. Then they took over a going concern: trained workers, tilled fields, mines, a whole economy that was already functioning, and in which they merely replaced the upper echelons of the ruling caste. They created a caste society of landlords and day laborers. They found gold and silver and established a mining economy on top of a subsistence agriculture. They occupied an immense territory, incorporated the Indian into their society, and established a one-church regime.

The English were religious refugees who came to America seeking a new life. They brought their wives and families and established their homes in the new land. They did not consort with the Indians. Pocahontas is famous because she was unique. They found neither gold nor silver, and they settled down on a narrow strip of coastal territory as farmers and artisans. The nomadic tribes they encountered could not be defeated in a few pitched battles nor could they be turned into laborers. The English knew what self-government was, and immediately set about to achieve it.

In brief, the Spaniards colonized in the Roman sense, imposing their will, their culture, and their language upon a vast territory and a vast number of foreign peoples. The English colonized in the Greek sense, establishing small coastal settlements which were miniature "Englands" in a foreign land, except that the new communities did represent a desire for religious and political freedom not typical of the homeland.

Adam Smith, the father of modern economy, in his *Wealth of Nations,* refers to the discovery of America and the opening of the new sea routes of global communication as the greatest event in the history of mankind. And Karl Marx in *Das Kapital* points out that the discovery of gold and silver in America, the addition of this great wealth to the European economies, and the enslavement of the native populations, "signalized the rosy dawn of the era of capitalist expansion."

The discovery of America changed the focus of world civilization from the Mediterranean to the Atlantic. This focus had moved from Persia and Babylonia to Egypt and Greece, thence westward to Rome, and after the decline and fall of the Roman Empire the headship passed on to Spain, Portugal, England, and Holland, the great maritime nations of modern history. The Mediterranean was no longer the focal path of commerce. The argosies and galleons of the new era set their courses into the great Atlantic.

VI

DAWN OF EMPIRE: GOVERNMENT AND CHURCH

Once the conquest was achieved, since the Spaniards were not settlers but adventurers, and since they did not seek lands on which to live but wealth to possess, they only dominated the inhabitants of the land and exploited the mines. These two things complemented each other. The domination gave them Indians to work the mines, and the working of the mines gave them further means of subjugating the Indians.

—ANDRÉS MOLINA ENRÍQUEZ

WHEN Columbus landed in the New World **he thought** that he had found the sea route to India and the other lands of the Orient. Consequently, the Spaniards began referring to America as *las Indias*, or "the Indies." This term in the old histories meant the whole of America; it was not limited, as it is today, to the islands of the Antilles. Later, when Cortés added Mexico to the Spanish Empire he regarded the land as so similar to Spain in topography and climate that he gave it the name of "New Spain," by which this territory was known throughout the colonial epoch. The name "Mexico," probably from *mexintl* the war god of the Aztecs, was originally a more limited term referring to the capital city. It is still widely used in that context by the inhabitants of Mexico, who will generally say *Voy a México*, "I'm going to Mexico," if the meaning is "I'm going to the capital."

Mexico City was the Spanish Empire's greatest metropolis, and New Spain was the empire's most wealthy colony. Hence, the most strenuous efforts were made to govern this territory for the profit and glory of the peninsula. The viceroys, churchmen, and colonists who came here were more closely linked with the homeland by geography and by contact than were those of the other dominions. As a result Mexico received a greater and more constant increment of Hispanic culture than did any other part of the Spanish New World. Mexico

City, despite its large Indian population, always had more Spanish inhabitants than any other colonial city.

This book is not a history of Mexico, so no attempt will be made to list every viceroy, bishop, and colonial decree or law under whose aegis New Spain was formed and governed. These details will be left to others. George Bancroft, W. B. Priestley, and H. B. Parkes are among the historians who have written excellent accounts of the country in these terms in English. What this book does aim to do is to give a picture of the broad currents of Mexican life, the foundations and framework upon which the republic of today has been erected. To describe the political evolution of a country without going into the other aspects of its society, its economy, its art, literature, architecture, and its thinking, without seeing the look of its towns or probing the feelings of its citizens, is to present only one part of the picture. The civilization of a country is made up of the interplay of all these forces, and it is this full ebb and flow of Mexican life that is our main consideration.

New Spain, like all the other Spanish colonial dominions, was originally governed by the conquistadores who had conquered them; in Mexico, this meant Cortés and his lieutenants. These were the men who had shed their blood, sweat, and tears in the conquest, and as a reward they demanded gold, lands, and Indians. Whenever the king or some humanitarian-minded priest like Las Casas attempted to soften this demand, the conquistadores rose and shouted that nobody could "take away from them what belonged to them by their toil and right."

The early years in the government of New Spain, therefore, were a time of jockeying for power between the conquistadores, on the one hand, and the representatives of the crown and the missionary priests, on the other. During the first dynamic century, while the conquistadores, now turned landlords, held tenaciously onto their estates and their Indians, the crown and many of the missionaries did everything possible to aid and to defend the native inhabitants. In Peru a full-scale civil war broke out between king and landowners when the New Laws of 1542 in defense of the Indians were brought into that country. In Mexico there was no war, but when the landholders heard that the king's representative was about to arrive in order to publish these New Laws, they all decided to dress in mourning and go out to meet him. The viceroy then wisely temporized until the crisis was over.

After this there was a long period during which the crown and missionaries slowly limited the power of the aristocracy and protected the Indians. The landed aristocrat certainly did not disappear; indeed, the Church itself became an owner of large estates, the biggest landholder of the colonial period. Nevertheless, anyone who will take the trouble to compare Baron von Humboldt's remarks on the Indian population of Mexico in 1803 with those of almost any writer describing the condition of the Indians under Porfirio Díaz, a hundred years later, will be impressed by how much better off they were at the end of the colonial epoch. This trend was not reversed until after the Mexican Revolution (1910–1920), whose battle-cry of *Tierra y Libertad* (Land and Liberty) turned Mexico back toward its Indian rootstock.

In the Spanish colonial government the viceroy (which means "vice-king") was headman. He had under him a territory for larger than that of any Western European country. He ruled in the king's name and, supposedly, in the king's favor. The king, who was the ruler of all the subjects, Indians as well as Spaniards and mestizos, wanted to keep them all happy, and of course productive. The viceroy, therefore, often had to walk a tightrope in order to avoid inflaming one group of the colonial population against another. He also had to satisfy the king, for he could be retired at any moment. Yet while in power the viceroy did enjoy great prestige and tremendous power. All officers, secular and ecclesiastical, were ordered to obey and to respect him. He was the president or chief justice of the supreme court and commander in chief of the army. "In the exercise of his powers he maintained the state and dignity of royalty. His court was formed upon the model of that of Madrid, with horse and foot guards, a household regularly established, numerous attendants, and ensigns of power, displaying such pomp as hardly retained the appearance of delegated authority." [21]

The first viceroy, and one of the best, Antonio de Mendoza, was sent to Mexico in 1535. He remained in power until 1550. Throughout the colonial period a total of 61 viceroys were appointed in Mexico; their *average* term of office was, therefore, a little less than five years. Historians agree that approximately a dozen of them were outstanding men. By and large the viceroys reflected the character of the monarchs who appointed them. During the reigns of Charles V and Philip II they were generally hard-working and reasonably competent officials. During the seventeenth century, when Spain lost out as a great world power and was ruled by second-rate and frequently moronic kings, the viceroys also showed less talent in government. When the

Bourbons came to the throne of Spain in 1700 there was a great improvement again in the caliber of the ruling caste, but by the turn of the century degeneracy had once more overtaken the reins of government.

The necessities of politics meant that the viceroy at times allied himself with the citizens of the land in which he resided, rather than with the king, who was far away. This eventually led to a most peculiar practice in the Spanish colonies. When the king sent over a royal statute which was considered to be contrary to the colonial interests, the viceroy would read it solemnly before a public assemblage, then holding it over his head in token of submission and humility, he would proclaim in a loud voice: "*Se acata pero no se cumple.* It shall be respected, but not enforced." This act satisfied both the principle of submission to the king and the necessity for realism in colonial government. The common people often referred to such royal statutes as "unconsecrated hosts."

Before we jump to any rash conclusions about the inadequacies of colonial government, it would be enlightening to look back over the list of our own English governors, and of our Presidents. How many of these would qualify as superior statesmen? The Spanish colonial empire endured for three centuries, which in the main were three hundred years of peace and orderly development. The subsequent history of the independent Latin-American republic hardly serves to dim the luster of the Spanish achievement, however much this staggered and sputtered toward the end of the colonial regime. Some writers have come out with the dictum that Mexico was on a toboggan slide for these three centuries. That is nonsense. If it were not for Spain, Mexico would still be a country of barbarians and cannibals whose gods demanded cutting out human hearts by the thousands. Mexican culture at the time of the conquest *was* on a native toboggan slide, already far below its peak, reached centuries before in the Maya jungles. Spain did beat the Indian (though not nearly so severely as the landowners of the republic did), but she also gave him a new look on life. Not all good, of course, but superior to what he was enjoying in Mexico in 1500.

If we compare the Spanish rule in Mexico with that of England in India or Africa, where Britain's own conquest was of the Roman type, that is, English government and culture imposed on great masses of backward natives belonging to another race, the comparison will certainly not redound to the credit of England. Holding themselves racially aloof from the masses of a different color, who were under them, the English did much to improve the material welfare and the jurisprudence of these peoples, but Britain did not create a new race or a new culture. She did not give these people a new language and a new religion, or bring them into the mainstream of her own civilization, but rather intensified their racial and their cultural differences.

Spain of the early colonial period was a church-state, which implies that church and state were inseparable in the colonial government. Ten of the viceroys of Mexico were bishops. This does not mean that the Church pursued a single policy during colonial times, always aligning itself with the landed aristocrats and the governmental clique. The higher clergy naturally favored this group, for they, too, were upper-crust Spaniards. The lower clergy, and especially the early missionaries, aligned themselves with the Indians and against the Spaniards. One *cannot* honestly, therefore, speak of the Church as if it were a totalitarian political party with but a single affiliation. One can say that ecclesiastical and civil government were so closely intertwined that it would be almost impossible to tell where one left off and the other began.

In succeeding years, as the mines poured forth their riches (the Jesuits owned the richest mines in Mexico) and as the Church accumulated more and more land and wealth through bequests, gifts, fees, contributions, etc., an increasingly greater percentage of the clergy identified themselves with the ruling caste, who stood for the *status quo*. Only in this way could they be assured of protecting their own vast economic interests. Gold and serfs corrupt the hardiest of men, and even religion is polluted by an easy life.

The Spanish crown did not hesitate to use the Church as an instrument of state policy. Ferdinand and Isabella were fondly known as *los reyes católicos,* the Catholic sovereigns. Succeeding kings of Spain were invariably referred to as "His Most Catholic Majesty." Whenever a conflict arose between the two groups the crown held the upper hand. Two very specific instruments enabled the Spanish kings to wield this superior power: the Inquisition and the *real patronato*, or royal patronage, the royal privilege of appointing the members of the higher clergy. This patronage was granted in the following devious manner: In 1482 the Pope unwisely appointed his own nephew over the queen's choice for a Spanish bishopric. Ferdinand and Isabella promptly broke off relations with the Holy See, withdrew their subjects from the papal dominions, and threatened to call a general European inquiry into the state of the Church's health, which was none too savory at that time. The papal mission which was sent to Spain to plead the Pope's case was immediately thrown out of the country. Finally, the envoy was forced to come alone, waiving all immunities. The Pope, greatly miffed by the whole affair, reluctantly agreed (1484) that thenceforth the kings of Spain would have the right to appoint all higher church officers. This gave the crown a foothold inside the Church itself, for obviously anyone who failed to show a proper zeal for the king's interests would not be appointed.

The other instrument wielded by the crown in its control of the church-state was the Inquisition. The Dominican, Tomás de Torquemada, confessor to Queen Isabella, was responsible for the establishment of the Inquisition in Spain. He was a religious fanatic and a vigorous anti-Semite. Spain was at the time engaged in an all-out war against the Moors, who were embattled in Granada. The royal treasury was desperately in need of funds. The Jews contributed most generously to this war, but Torquemada was relentless. "Judas sold his Master for thirty pieces of silver," he said. Many Jewish and Moorish citizens were "new converts" whose Christian orthodoxy was suspect, and probably with good cause, for conversion was the only alternative to expulsion.

Putting two and two together, it did not take Torquemada long to convince the sovereigns, Ferdinand and Isabella, that the Inquisition would further their cause. The Inquisition served the Spanish state in a very professional capacity. It simply liquidated all religious minorities. There never arose in Spain a single Protestant church. Spain, therefore, never had to undergo the religious conflicts that divided the other countries of Western Europe. Her unity, perfect and unimpaired, was carried to the New World in what one Spanish author calls a "plenitude of imperium." Unity in religion was an integral part of that imperium.

The Inquisition carefully checked the religious credentials of all who took off for the Spanish colonies. Therefore, few cases of heresy came up before the colonial tribunals, and were mostly those of converted Jews, overzealous eccentrics, or Englishmen or Lutherans who had been shipwrecked or captured. During the three centuries of colonial rule in Mexico the Inquisition executed only forty-three persons. (At Salem our New England ancestors executed twenty-four "witches" at one fell swoop.) The religious policy of colonial Spain was, in this regard at least, not more fanatical than that of the Puritans.

Cotton Mather and various other Pilgrim fathers were religious zealots of the first water.

The Inquisition had another influence on colonial life which was not strictly religious. It attempted to enforce the prohibition against the reading of certain books considered to contain anti-Catholic, controversial, or objectionable material. Such books were listed on the famous *Index*, and included, naturally, the works of Voltaire, Rousseau, Milton, practically all of the French Encyclopedists, books of imagination of many kinds, from both Spain and elsewhere, a total of some hundreds of volumes.

The restriction, however, was not by any means totally effective. Irving Leonard, in his *Books of the Brave*, shows how widely the *Index* was disregarded. Hundreds of banned books were smuggled into the colonies and avidly read. It is a curious fact that when the time was ripe for independence the great leaders of South America—Bolívar, Miranda, and San Martín—were all Freemasons, and Hidalgo of Mexico, despite his priestly robes, was an ardent reader of the liberal French authors. Such is generally the result of any unwise prohibition; too zealously invoked, then opportunely disregarded, it becomes a boomerang in the hands of those who do the prohibiting.

Spain was not always an intolerant country. During early medieval times she was singularly broad-minded in matters of religion. Moslems, Christians, and Jews all worshiped in the same church in Toledo. Intermarriage among them was common. The Moorish-Semitic cast to the Spanish physiognomy was one very obvious result of this mixing. Medieval Spanish literature abounded in unorthodox statements. The war against the Moors, and later the Catholic Counter Reformation, changed all this with a finality that lasted for centuries.

The last decades of the 1400's and the first half of the 1500's gave to the Spanish Church a unique character which still distinguishes it from that of any other European country. Humanism as a philosophy never made much headway in Spain. The Renaissance touched the hard core of the peninsula but lightly, and the Reformation touched her not at all save to intensify her own dark zeal and certainty. Even Don Quixote, who was faith, tilted his lance against the mandarins of reason. During both the Renaissance and the Reformation Spain preserved her medieval soul. She attempted to enclose herself with an impervious xenophobia that fought against the main currents of the times, resisting change like the mollusk.

The church of Mexico differed from the church in Spain in several essential ways. First of all, its primary concern was to convert and civilize the native population rather than administer solely to Spaniards. Second, the Church was brought to the New World when corruption in Rome was at its worst and moral laxity among the priests was general. By the time of the Counter Reformation (around 1550), which resulted in a thorough house cleaning among the clergy of Spain, there were so many hundreds of padres already spread out into the Mexican wilderness that it was impossible to control them. The rigorous peninsular cleanup had no counterpart in the colonies. Distance, geography, and the dissolvent of climate, plus the easy acquisition of Indian mistresses, all argued against it. Third, Mexican Catholicism from the very beginning took on indigenous overtones which became an integral part of the religious life of the natives.

During medieval times the clergy in Spain were notably loose in their sexual morals. The *barragana,* or priest's mistress, was a widespread practice. The Spanish Pope Alexander VI (Alexander Borgia), who headed the church when America was discovered, was not exactly noted for his continence. His illegitimate son, Cesare Borgia, was made a Spanish cardinal at the age of seventeen, and the name of his daughter Lucretia is infamous among the great poisoners of history. When the Inquisition began in Spain it was not at first applied to sexual immorality, but to religious heresy. The Protestant Revolt and consequent Counter Reformation caused it to be extended to a general sweep of all corrupt practices within the church, but Mexico was far away and the flesh was weak.

The archbishop of Mexico in 1575 sent a report to Philip II in which he noted the immoral practices of many of his clergy. Father Angel de Valencia and other Franciscans went so far as to state that "most of the clergy who come to America are guilty of dissoluteness and breaking their vows, which is a great pity." The leading Spanish historian of today, Rafael Altamira, sums up the situation by pointing out that the great distances which separated most priests from their supervising authorities made this looseness possible, and that "trials before the colonial Inquisition, contemporary chronicles, the archives of the courts and of the government, all abound in documents which reveal the exceeding frequency of that immorality."

The regular clergy, members of orders like the Jesuits and Franciscans, were under a more rigorous discipline and were not guilty of these excesses. The isolated parish priests were the ones who continued in Mexico the practice of the medieval Spanish *barragana.* When John Stephens visited the Maya ruins at Palenque, accompanied by four padres, he noted that they packed along bedding, provisions, and many other articles, "besides which, more favored than we, they had four or five women." Many an isolated priest was in a very real sense the paterfamilias of his village.

The Church in Mexico, faced with the problem of converting hundreds of thousands of idolatrous Indians deeply attached to their old gods, made many compromises in order to further its main purpose, which was to make Christians of the natives. Many churches were raised on the ruins of older Indian temples; frequently they were constructed of the same stones. The natives, therefore, easily associated the new religion with the old gods. In many instances the old idols were hidden behind the new altars or inserted in some small niche in the walls, and the Indian who worshiped there went to pay homage to his native gods. Anita Brenner, in her fascinating book *Idols Behind Altars,* gives dozens of instances of the survival of this practice in Mexico even today.

The early priests also noted that the Mexican Indians were a people with a great love for the dance and song. They turned this to their own advantage simply by changing the dress and central theme of these celebrations, substituting battles between Christians and Moors, or devils and saints, for example, for a war dance to the old religion. But they were essentially the same dances, the same music, the same costumes, and at the same place. Even the days were the same. The native gods were generally gods of the *place,* and the new converts participated in the new rites in order to preserve the integrity of their old beliefs. This kept alive the spark of spirit among the natives and more than any other element of the conquest prevented their spiritual annihilation.

The fiesta became an integral part of the religious life of the Mexican village. Integral with it to the finale of pulque drinking, which climaxes the fiesta with temporary forgetfulness of all worldly sorrow. I have witnessed dozens of these fiestas, which are obviously pagan in spirit, being held within the very shadow of the church. A rainbow of Indian color, fireworks, pagan and primitive dances performed to a music which is largely pre-Spanish in its conception. These elements of religious practice still distinguish the Mexican church from that of Spain. Even here, however, there is a groundwork of similarity, for the Semana Santa of Seville (Holy Week) with the weird tremolos and *saetas* of its *cante jondo* is obviously inspired by some ancient pagan feeling in the blood. It was this which doubtless made the imported church of Spain so adaptable to its new environment. The Catholicism of any other European country would not have been so acceptable to the primitive Mexican Indian.

Much of the religion of the Mexican rural population is still *image* worship. The local patron saint occupies a place of preference in the church. It is the material statue of this saint which so often receives the prayers of the ignorant parishioners, not the invisible symbol. The Indian cannot conceive of a purely invisible symbol. His gods stand in the images before him. Remove the image and the Indian becomes bewildered. These images are paraded around the streets, are carried aloft in fiestas, are solemnly borne across the cornfields when there is need of rain.

Even the color of these images takes on an Indian hue in Mexico. The early priests often found that the white saints held no appeal to the Indians, but that when these were colored a darker tone the natives were willing to accept them. Many an Indian Christ adorns the village church in Mexico today. The most venerated of all figures in the Mexican church is the Indian Madonna, the Virgin of Guadalupe. Her image appears in homes all over Mexico, taxicabs carry it frequently on their dashboards, it even rides on many a crowded urban bus.

In 1531, only ten years after the conquest of Mexico, a recently converted Indian, Juan Diego, saw a vision of the Holy Virgin on a rocky hill a few miles north of the capital. She told the Indian to inform the bishop that she wanted a church built on this spot. The bishop, Zumárraga, demurred and demanded some sign of her will. Juan Diego was told to go to the top of the hill and pick roses where only a cactus grew. He plucked them, carried the flowers to the Virgin, and she wrapped them in his cloak. When this was unfolded before the bishop her image was miraculously stamped upon it. A shrine was then constructed, and became the most famous in Mexico. It is now rated as a basilica, the third church rank in Roman Christendom.

An Indian goddess, Tonantzin, Mother of the Aztec gods, was worshiped at this same spot before the Spaniards arrived. Allegiance was transferred from her to Our Lady of Guadalupe. Thousands of Indians who worship her do not even know that she is supposed to represent the Mother of Christ. She has become a goddess in her own right, the brown Madonna of Mexico. Pilgrimages are made from all parts of the country to her shrine, and on the day of her celebration teeming crowds climb on their knees the rocky path leading to the spot where her vision first appeared to Juan Diego. It is a sight long to be remembered, filled with the overwhelming ecstasy of a primitive people. Father Hidalgo carried the banner of the Indian Madonna when he initiated the independence movement in 1810, and a hundred years later Zapata unfurled the same banner to lead his rude legions in the Mexican Revolution for "land and liberty."

Mexican Catholicism is a fusion of Indian and Christian elements, but not on that account is it any less of a real religion. The alloy is often stronger than either of the pure metals taken separately. This seems true of Hispano-Indian alloy in religion. All over Mexico I have seen Indians and Indo-mestizos glide into church, put down their burdens, fall quietly to their knees on the hard pavement, compose their features, and murmur their prayers with a devotion that would move the most callous. If there are images of different saints in niches along the walls, each one will have a group of devotees kneeling before it. The Indian picks his favorite saint for these spontaneous orisons. In the large urban centers most of the worshipers are women, but in the outlying villages everyone goes to church. The people do not enter lightly into the house of God, but solemnly, with the full measure of their emotions. The fiesta is a thing apart, mere trappings of this inner devotion.

As the candles burn and the lips finish their whispered prayers, the worshiper will rise, make the sign of the cross, and disappear silently into the streets. Some moments will pass before he can slip once more into the cold world of reality outside, again altering his countenance for the less solemn attitudes of his fellow man. No one who has observed these primitive congregations can doubt the depth of their fervor. The woman in their black *rebozos*, the men in their loose trousers, for the most part barefooted or in *huaraches*, melt into the cold hollows of the nave, which with the soft curves of their bodies then balances the warm glow of the altar. The Church seems made for these people. No one can doubt that the Indian was miraculously blessed that the Church was brought from Spain along with the soldier. It flowed into the vacuum left by the conquest, grafted itself onto the trunk of Indian culture, preserved the Indian's inner pride and integrity as a human being. Without it the dynamic hybrid that is Mexico today would never have emerged from the chrysalis. The native culture pattern would have survived only as a decapitated body.

Even today, in village after village, the church and the residence of the priest will be the only clean places in town, the only repository of what we call civilization. The priest in these villages is always the most important man in town. He is not only the leader of his flock in a religious sense, but is their political leader, their adviser, their main contact with the outside world, their link with the nation and with the government. Woe be to any federal agency which would operate in these villages without the co-operation of the local padre. Whether it is to build a school or to bring in water or electric lights, the town goes as the priest decides, wholeheartedly, lukewarmly, or not at all. His word is fiat among the ignorant villagers who for centuries have trusted no other leader.

If Spain's economic policy in Mexico had been as Mexican-slanted as the early fervor of her religion, the colony might have prospered. But when gold and silver gleam before the eyes of either man or nation, interest in hard cash quickly overtakes every other consideration. Spain found great mines of gold and silver in her colonies; the English did not. So, while the English colonists tilled their little farms along the Atlantic, Spain became a big-time prospector who struck it rich and immediately threw up every possible barrier to keep others off her claim. The net result of all this was that she established an economy of exploitation, rather than development, and demanded a monopoly on Mexican commerce. By the middle of the first colonial century Mexico was already showing signs of becoming an immensely wealthy colony. In 1553 López de Gómara wrote: "Besides gold and silver, Mexico also produces much sugar and cochineal (both very costly items), feathers and cotton. Few ships from Spain return without a cargo, which cannot be said of Peru, in spite of this land's having the reputation of being richer than Mexico; furthermore, the latter country has preserved a greater number of its original inhabitants. It is a beautiful land, densely populated, and would be lacking in nothing if only the rains were more dependable. New Spain sends to Peru horses, beef and sugar."

This promising start was soon throttled by the monopolistic Spanish trade policy. Mexico was to supply Spain with gold, silver, and raw materials, and Spain was to supply Mexico with finished products. In order to stifle competition before it had begun, the mother country prohibited grape, olive, or silk culture in Mexico, did not allow the manufacture of many needed articles, and held a royal monopoly on tobacco, quicksilver (for mining), gunpowder, salt, even on the sale of snow and ice from Popocatepetl! The supreme irony came in 1557, when a Mexican, Medina, discovered the mercury amalgam process for refining silver, which was a milestone in metallurgical development. Spain, greedy as always, insisted that Mexicans use quicksilver imported from her rather than their own supply. Only Spaniards could trade with Mexico, and Mexico must trade only with Spain. She was not even allowed to trade with her Hispanic neighbors. All goods must be sent in Spanish ships, and finally, for protection, these ships must travel together in a convoy which sailed only at irregular intervals.

The other maritime powers of Europe, Britain, Holland and France, established similar monopolies in their own colonies, but with one fundamental difference. While these countries had a strong and rapidly growing industrial capacity which could supply their colonies at reasonable prices, Spain's industrial system was merely a skeleton. She had a declining navy, a disintegrating merchant marine, a disheartened and impoverished population. The expulsion of the Jews and Moors had subtracted from the national economy two of the most industrious elements of the population, and the entry into the church of countless able workers had taken other thousands from the productive labor force of the nation. Spain's commercial monopoly with Mexico, therefore, was like a mother saying to her famished child, "Take no other milk but mine," when she had no milk to give.

At first, single ships or small groups of vessels were allowed to engage in colonial commerce, but these had to leave Seville or Cadiz and land at Veracruz, the port of entry for all Mexico. In this way supervision could be more efficient. For a time the single-ship system was successful, but later in the sixteenth century, when rich silver mines were discovered in Mexico, and ships began to bring back their treasures of bullion, they were pounced upon by English, French, and Dutch corsairs.

In order to protect her monopoly from these marauders, Spain established the convoy system, which lasted from 1561 to 1748. The effect of this arrangement, however, was the opposite of that intended. By upping the stakes it only made the game more appetizing, and the thieving continued. By 1588, after the defeat of the Spanish Armada, Spain was done for as a great maritime power. Obdurate as ever, she would not loosen the bonds of her monopoly, and her colonies took to smuggling on a grand scale. It was the only way to supply themselves with many of the necessities of life.

Denied the culture of those very items which would be most fruitful in her soil, Mexico was at the same time gutted of her long-stored veins of gold and silver. Humboldt estimates the total production of the silver mines of Mexico from the time of the conquest up to the end of the colonial epoch (1803) at approximately 2 billion pesos, that is, 80 million kilograms or 180 million pounds of silver. The production of gold was only a small fraction of this in value. The dumping of this wealth into European coffers caused a dislocation in Continental economy, because hitherto the amount of these precious metals had remained more or less constant and their value did not vary greatly. Now it was the other way around. There was an abundance of precious metals, and prices began to jump. The value of gold and silver declined, and increasing amounts were needed to pay for commodities. Spain was particularly hard hit by this process; she had neglected both agriculture and industry for this illusory wealth. What remained in Mexico helped to construct the lovely baroque churches of the eighteenth century, for it was in this century that the mines flowed most freely. But what went to Spain was like sand through the fingers; it left only an empty hand behind it.

Humboldt shows that the annual agricultural output of Mexico was only about 30 per cent higher in value than the annual production of gold and silver at the end of the colonial epoch. Yet he has hopeful words for those engaged in farming. "The Indian farmer is poor, but he is free. His state is very much preferable to that of the villagers of a great part of northern Europe. In New Spain there exists neither forced personal services nor slavery; the number of slaves is almost nil. The principal objects of agriculture are not those luxury products to which Europeans have given a variable and arbitrary value, but grains, nutritive roots and maguey, which is the life of the natives. The aspect of the fields reminds the traveler that this soil feeds those who till it, and that the true prosperity of the Mexican people does not depend on the vicissitudes of foreign commerce nor on the uncertain politics of Europe."

VII

SPANISH TOWNS AND INDIAN MISSIONS

The civilization of Spain was an urban thing. From the time when the Greeks and Punic peoples settled in Iberia, Spaniards had lived in cities and shunned the open countryside. If they did not dwell in cities, they grouped themselves in towns and villages for sociability and protection.

—William Lytle Schurz

The Spanish towns and the Indian missions were two very different examples of the colonial policy of the peninsula. The town was, in so far as possible, a replica of its counterpart in Spain, while the mission was an outpost in the wilderness. The town was a sturdy symbol of the Roman type of conquest which Spain imposed on Mexico. The mission was a symbol of the desire of well-meaning members of the clergy to establish in this vast new territory a kind of idealistic, utopian society, a co-operative commonwealth, set apart from the claws of European greed and sin, idyllic and self-sufficient. Although many of the missions accomplished almost miraculous results against the most prodigious odds, in the end they served a purpose which was the exact opposite of that for which they had originally been intended. That is, they softened up the recalcitrant native population for later assimilation into the colonial organism. The missionaries, through absolutely no fault of their own, were the shock troops of the colonization of Mexico.

None of this could be seen in the beginning. The original intent of the early members of the clergy who lived among the Indians was to defend them against the rapacity of the *encomenderos*. Father Las Casas was the first and most famous example of this atttiude. He had come to Santo Domingo in 1502, and settled there on a land grant with his allotment of Indians. Within a few years he became convinced that the *encomienda* system was morally wrong, so he gave up his estate and in 1510 became the first priest ordained in the New World. From this time on, until his death at the ripe old age of ninety-two, Father Las Casas was the "Defender of the Indians" and the famed "Apostle of the Indies."

He labored tirelessly among the natives, he founded the first Spanish mission in America in Venezuela in 1520 (which the Indians promptly destroyed), he appeared personally before the king and pleaded with great eloquence for laws to protect the Indians, and he wrote both a history of the Indies (the New World) and a scathing denunciation of the Spanish conquest. In Spain he told the king that, if the Indians were entrusted to the Spaniards in any way whatsoever, "no matter how many laws, statutes, or penalties are imposed, your Majesty will see that it is the same as if it were decreed that America be made a desert."

Las Casas and his colleagues were always in the minority. He, the Dominicans Pedro de Córdoba and Vasco de Quiroga, and many other missionary priests were regarded as "troublemakers" by the compact majority of the Spanish colonists. Nevertheless, many new laws were passed in favor of the Indians. The most famous were the "New Laws" of 1542, making it illegal to demand personal services of the Indians. These were too few and too late to effect any drastic change in the *encomienda* policy, but they certainly did mitigate it.

When the New Laws reached Mexico the Spanish colonists en masse refused to obey them. Bishop Zumárraga in Mexico City sided with the *encomenderos*, as did most of the clergy. The crown sent over personal representatives to enforce the new regulations, but they were paralyzed by the pressure of public opinion. The crown refused to give up and finally did achieve the liberation of the Indian slaves, about sixty thousand in number, and put the *encomenderos* on notice that their privileges were under scrutiny. In the long run, however, this was a hollow victory, for the enforcement of any law which was against the landed aristocracy was impossible.

Searching for some way to breach the wall of enforced Indian labor, Las Casas urged that Negro slaves and Spanish peasants be imported to do the work instead. Negro slavery had long been taken for granted, and the good father was simply replacing one sin with another. Thousands of Negroes were imported into the Gulf area and promptly took the place of the Indians, who died rather than live as serfs. The Negro became an important element in the population of this region. Later in life, and now a wiser and older man, Las Casas confessed his error "with deep regret and humiliation," for, he said, "the same law applied equally to the Negro as to the Indian." In so far as his suggestion concerning the Spanish peasantry was concerned, there was hardly one among them who wished to come to the New World in order to remain a peasant.

The Catholic Church was the great unifying factor in Western civilization during medieval times. Europe was made up of dozens of petty kingdoms, speaking dozens of different dialects, but despite these political and linguistic divisions, culture and religion were international. Monasteries and universities, where most of the professors were famous priests, were the repositories of learning, the libraries, the centers of art. The language of the church, Latin, was the international language.

When Charles I of Spain was elected emperor of the Holy Roman Empire in 1519 (he became Charles V of the empire), this meant that he had become the sword arm of this medieval Catholic Church. He and his son, Philip II, and to a lesser extent the subsequent kings of Spain, let this be the star that guided their lives. After the Protestant revolt had spread like wildfire over Europe, they engaged in a series of fruitless wars to win these errant peoples back to the fold. This was their sacred mission. But, as some historian has remarked, the Holy Roman Empire was in reality neither holy nor Roman nor an empire. Nor was the power of Spain inexhaustible. Therefore, this part of the Spanish crusade was doomed to failure.

At the same historic moment the conquest of America had gotten under way. Spain was the discoverer and Spaniards were in the vanguard of the conquest and colonization. Spanish priests undertook the work of conversion among millions of natives. Not since the conversion of the barbaric peoples of Northern Europe had the church undertaken so enormous a task. Unsuccessful in Europe, Spain poured the full quotient of her efforts into the conversion and colonization of the New World.

When Pedro de Córdoba spoke against the weakness of the early Laws of Burgos (1512–1515), which were drawn up to protect the Indian, the king asked him to take upon himself the charge of remedying them. From that time forward Pedro de Córdoba became the propagandist in the New World for the plan of the mission. Las Casas, Quiroga, and many other priests were quickly won over to his idea.

When the Council of the Indies was established by Charles V in 1524 to take over the political, judicial, and military administration of the colonial empire, the very first mandate given to this body contained these significant words: "We want nothing more than the publication and spread of the evangelical law, and the conversion of the Indians to our Holy Catholic faith . . . therefore, we order and encharge the members of the Council that, putting all else in second place, they take as their first duty the matters of Conversion and Doctrine, and most particularly that they bend every effort of mind and body to provide sufficient ministers for it so that the Indians of our realms may be converted and keep the knowledge of God, our Lord, in honor and praise of His Holy Name."

The first great wave of missions was implanted in Mexico during the century after the conquest (1521–1600). The ideal of these missions was to restore society to its Christian bases. The missionaries believed that they could achieve among the Indians a social order without social sin. In order to reach this goal "they entrusted direction not to the philosopher, as in Plato, but to the priest, converted particularly into supreme magistrate." [25] Thomas More's picture of an ideal society in *Utopia* (1516) served as a spur to goad them on. They attempted to turn More's dream into a concrete reality. In the mission settlements, all must work for the community, and co-operative effort took the place of competition. Religious law was the basis of the collective as well as the individual life.

Before the first missionaries reached Mexico, missions had been established in Santo Domingo with a fair amount of success, and Las Casas had attempted one and failed in Venezuela in 1520. Three famous missionaries came to Mexico in 1523, among them Pedro de Gante, illegitimate brother of Charles V. They were followed by eleven others who landed in Veracruz in 1524. When Cortés learned that they had reached Mexican soil, he sent word that the roads over which they must pass be swept, that every bell be rung, and that the people of all the villages along the way must come out to receive them. The Indian natives were instructed to carry lighted tapers, and the Spaniards were ordered "to fall on their knees and kiss the hands and habits of the friars, so that the Indians might see this and take the proper example." The good fathers, for their own part, walked the entire distance from the coast to the capital, nearly three hundred miles.

When the contingent reached Mexico City, Cortés himself went out to receive them. He was accompanied by many soldiers, and also by Cuautemoc, the Lord of Mexico, and many other chieftains. When the two groups met, Cortés dismounted from his horse and with great reverence kissed the habit of their leader, Father Martín de Valencia. The Mexican chieftains were deeply impressed to see the great captain, whom they had come to regard as almighty, perform this act of humility before unarmed, emaciated men in coarse and tattered robes. They also noted that Cortés never spoke to one of the fathers without first taking off his hat. All these things, plus the humility and selflessness of the priests themselves, caused the Indians to receive the Franciscans everywhere with the best of will.

These friars and others who soon followed them immediately proceeded to establish their missions and to organize the Indian communities under their direction. Using the native chiefs as their subalterns, they built churches, schools, workshops, and in some cases, dormitories. In Texcoco, Pedro de Gante noticed that the Indians liked to dance and sing before their own idols, so he turned this to his advantage by putting on similar performances before Christ and the Virgin. These highly colored fiestas were and are an integral part of Mexican Catholicism. Pedro de Gante and his helpers quickly learned the native language by mingling with the Indians and playing their games, "becoming children again among those who were children." It was this intimate contact which gave the mission idea its great drive all over Spanish America. Bookish study came later, but in the early years there were no books to go by, no dictionaries, no precedents. The first century or so in the New World was certainly a period of great glory for the Spanish Church.

After three years in Texcoco, Fray Pedro de Gante (1526) moved his school to Mexico City. It became an integral part of the Church of San Francisco, which the group established in the capital in 1524. It was constructed on land donated by Cortés, a site formerly occupied by Montezuma's zoological gardens. Cortés also advanced funds so that the work might begin at once, and the building stones were readily available from the great pile accumulated by the destruction of the Aztec pyramid-temple the year before. In the school headed by Gante the students were taught the Spanish language, painting, music, many of the arts and crafts; some of the most intelligent learned to read and write, and a few of them even studied Latin. Particular attention was paid to music, for the Aztecs were a musically inclined people, and before long many of them had learned something of the more intricate harmonics of European composition. This school had an enrollment of a thousand students, and was the first to undertake on a large scale the work of cultural and spiritual fusion which characterized the later mestizo culture of Mexico. Nearly four centuries before John Dewey it was a true "activity school, a school based on current life."

Gante's school was only one part of the San Francisco establishment, which included a monastery, a hospital, other related churches, a huge refectory, and spacious gardens. The refectory alone seated five hundred friars. The buildings covered an area of more than two square blocks and were connected by magnificent cloisters. This "mother church" was the largest religious center in Mexico for many years. All that remains today of this great institution is a small relic, whose graceful walls of rose-colored *tezontle* are now hemmed in by modern buildings in the midst of the metropolitan center.

The missionary work was primarily under the direction of the regular clergy, that is, those who were members of the religious orders. These were better organized, more disciplined, and in general better educated than the secular clergy. The Franciscans were the first to arrive in Mexico. They occupied the area southeast of Mexico City to Puebla, then west and north to Guadalajara. The Dominicans reached the country only a couple of years later and established themselves south of the capital, around Oaxaca. The Augustinians arrived in 1533 and settled in the state of Guerrero, also near Oaxaca. They also spread out in the area around Mexico City, and are responsible for the two famous early monasteries of Acolman and Actopan, easily accessible from the capital. After the Augustinians came the Jesuits, who remained mostly in the cities. They considered themselves the aristocrats among the regular clergy and frequented the centers of wealth. Last of all were the Carmelites, who erected some wonderful establishments around Mexico City.

Among the more famous missionaries in Mexico were the Franciscan Toribio de Benavente, a member of the group that landed in Veracruz in 1524, who went among the Indians and lived as they did, leading a life of self-abnegation and service to his fellow men. Later he wrote a fascinating history of the Indians of New Spain, containing many details about their rites, customs, beliefs, games, and arts. Among the natives he was known lovingly as *Motolinía*, the "ragged one," because of the manner in which he lived and dressed. In 1529, at Cortés' request, Motolinía established the beautiful Franciscan monastery at Cuernavaca, which in 1891 was elevated to the rank of cathedral. One of the streets in the center of Mexico City today bears the name of this selfless priest.

Then there was the learned Bernardino de Sahagún, who gave sixty years of his life working among the Aztecs, learning their dialects and their history. His dictionary of the Mexican language and his history of the Aztecs are among the finest books to come out of those early years. Juan de Torquemada also wrote of the early Mexicans and left an exceptionally interesting account of their music and dances.

The Dominican Vasco de Quiroga, who arrived in Mexico in 1530, was another of the early missionaries and deeply loved by the Indians. Quiroga was also a great admirer of Thomas More, and got from him the idea of a perfect society after which he attempted to pattern his own. Quiroga's mission was established in Tzintzuntzan near Pátzcuaro in the state of Michoacán, where the natives had been cruelly treated and were deeply hostile to the Spaniards. However, Quiroga's patience and kindness soon won them over, and at its height this mission embraced thirty thousand Indians. Among them Quiroga strove to "restore the lost purity of the primitive church," and to establish a cooperative community in which all would labor for the common weal. He believed that the natives could be raised "to a level of virtue and humanity superior to that of the Europeans."

Quiroga's Indians learned many Spanish arts and crafts, engaged in agriculture, constructed schools, and observed a six-hour workday. His community was a notable success, and Quiroga himself is still venerated by the natives of this area. Dozens of churches were built here during his years of service, perhaps more than in any other part of Mexico. However, after the leader's death the community, lacking focus and inspiration, fell quickly into decay. Dozens of streets and plazas in the state of Michoacán still bear Quiroga's name, and a modern tourist hotel near Lake Pátzcuaro is known as the Posada de Don Vasco.

The last great wave of missions was pushed northward by the Franciscans, with Fray Junípero Serra at their head. They constituted a beautiful chain of Indian settlements which reached up into the present state of California, then Mexican territory. There were also missions in northern Mexico, in Texas, New Mexico, and Arizona, which marked the advance of Spanish culture into the southwestern United States, leaving behind them a colorful heritage and dozens of Spanish names, from San Antonio to Los Angeles. One well-known Mexican historian, recalling these days when the Mexicans came into the land as teachers and leaders, adds wryly that "they would never have believed that there would come a sorrowful time like the present, in which our blood is pariah in the very territories which it then helped to win for civilization."

The mission, the town, the *encomienda:* these were the three most dynamic institutions of the Spanish colonial regime in Mexico. Taken together they were the octopus that engulfed, then digested the country. The town was the trunk and body of this symbolic octopus. The *encomiendas* and the missions were the tentacles it sent forth into the wilderness. But, while the *encomienda* was generally closely connected with the town and with the municipal administration, for most of the *encomenderos* lived in town, the mission was often a completely self-sufficient unit. Even so, it depended on the town for certain initial supplies and for its directive leadership.

The town, therefore, was the concrete symbol of Spanish domination in Mexico. With its central plaza, reminiscent of those of Spain, its municipal buildings and its church, it was a Spain in miniature, despite the brown faces that appeared on its narrow streets. It was the nerve center of the community, for with it everything was possible and without it nothing would have been achieved save the impermanent triumph of a military campaign. The town dominated completely the country around it. It was the seat of the governing power, the military headquarters from which soldiers were dispatched, the bosom of the church from which the missions were established. In a good many instances it was also a strong point of Spanish dominion, a place of protection against the unsubjugated Indians of the hinterland.

Some towns were raised on the ruins of older Indian settlements—Mexico City, for example; others were placed in more or less inaccessible localities in order to be near the mines; but the large majority of Spanish towns were established at the most favorable geographic and climatic points, in fertile valleys, on good harbors, or at strategic locations which would afford a good defense against the Indians. The founders of new towns were enjoined to select their locations with great care, not only from a standpoint of geography but by scrutinizing the color and complexion of the natives of the area in order to make certain that they were choosing a healthful place to live. It is partly due to these considerations that there is not in Mexico, indeed in the whole of Latin America, a town of importance with the abominable extremes of weather found in most of the larger cities of the United States: Chicago, Detroit, New York, Washington, to pick only a few.

Each Spanish town had its village common, used for grazing and for a variety of other purposes. The land around the town was distributed among the colonists, each of whom also received a dwelling plot inside the municipal limits. Soldiers received more than civilians, and mounted soldiers were given four or five times as much. The old Spanish term for foot soldier, incidentally, is *peón,* while the word for mounted soldier is *caballero,* also the Spanish equivalent of "gentleman" or "sire."

In the outskirts of all these colonial towns were more humble Indian dwellings, one-room huts of thatch or abode, which furnished the motive power for the Spanish part of the city. Into these filthy hovels were crowded masses of landless Indians, bereft of pride, without hope or status, whose only requital was to mix their blood with that of the white conqueror.

"Back in the hinterland, far off the beaten track and almost completely separated from civilized centers, were the Indian villages. They were still organized on a communal basis, and pursued their isolated way like small truncated parts of a once-great body. If they had any contact at all with Hispanic civilization it was through the priest and the tribute collector. If Christianized, their religion was permeated with elements of their primitive and idolatrous past." [8]

Closer to the governing centers were other Indian towns, but these were an integral part of colonial life. Here lived the Indians who paid tribute and those who were the workers for the colonial landholder, mineowner, ecclesiastical and government official. Slowly and surely the intrepid zeal of the missionaries and the search for more land, gold, and silver pushed spearheads into the dark interior. Sometimes at the site of a rich mine a large raw Spanish-Indian city would spring up almost overnight, symbolizing and quickening the mestizo destiny toward which all towns were pointed. In the early mining economy such places became the backbone not only of Mexico and Peru, but of Spain herself.

These colonial towns, of course, did not emerge full-blown from the hands of their architects. During the early years after the conquest they offered the appearance of armed camps or impermanent mining centers.

> A large proportion of the population was either just preparing to leave for some other place, or had just arrived. Hodgepodge crowds of every conceivable type milled about the streets. Prospectors were getting ready to go in search of mines; soldiers were receiving their equipment and last minute instructions for the campaign; missionaries were preparing to depart silently into the wilderness, or perhaps some government or church official was about to arrive and the inhabitants had turned out in a mass to meet him. The general feeling was that of living along the borders of a great unknown, that the town was merely a center from which the true promised land was soon to be reached. Moral and legal restraints were thrown to the winds. The streets and central plaza were a bedlam of noise, animals, processions, drunken brawls, murders, prostitutes, Indians, Negroes, priests, showy dressed officials, and general bedlam.[8]

But these encampments, whose necessities were not yet more than those of priests and soldiers, soon took on the more permanent aspects of colonial life. The "gangster interlude" of early government was quickly replaced by the leadership of honorable men. The first viceroy, Antonio de Mendoza, the two Luis de Velascos, father and son, and later still, Revillagigedo—these and many other government officials went hand and hand with honorable church leaders: Bishop Zumárraga of Mexico City, Vasco de Quiroga of Michoacán, Motolinía of the Central Highlands, Bartolomé de Las Casas of Chiapas, and dozens more too numerous to mention.

Cortés himself pointed the way. No sooner had Tenochtitlán fallen to his soldiers, and its demolished masonry been thrown into the city's canals, than a new capital began to emerge. Cortés was a builder as well as a destroyer, the greatest builder among the conquistadores. Even in distant Peru the writer Cieza de León characterized him as "the mirror of governors and captains of the Indies." It was the vision of Cortés that gave rise and form to the Spanish capital of Mexico, the largest, wealthiest, most beautiful diadem in the crown of colonial Spain. Cortés brought in plants, seeds, workers, architects, colonists, and saw to it that they all fitted into a single progressive pattern. He was a stern ruler, but he was neither cruel nor unjust. He gave the land and funds for the construction of the great religious center of San Francisco in Mexico City, he constructed the earliest municipal buildings, he founded and endowed the hospital of La Concepción for the needy sick, he ordered the construction of the cathedral at Cuernavaca, and in the same lovely tropical city erected his mansion. It still stands on the Plaza de la Constitución from which rises the most beautiful Indian laurel tree in Mexico. This tree is not native to the country, but was imported by Maximilian and Carlotta. The house of Cortés has been remodeled and is now further adorned with Diego Rivera's murals on Mexican history, but much of its original charm has been untouched by the passing centuries.

During the colonial epoch there were founded a total of perhaps a hundred Spanish towns in Mexico. They were called *villas,* whereas the name for the Indian settlements was *pueblos.* How many of the latter existed during colonial days there is no way of telling.

The town was of transcendent importance in colonial life. Both power and culture resided there. Invariably built around a central plaza, usually rimmed with stone arcades, these colonial towns, with their lovely churches and monasteries, their narrow winding streets, their dearth of trees and profusion of flowers, their thick-walled mansions and their graceful fountains, were and still are among the most beautiful architectural entities in the wide world. Decorating these old provincial towns, their towers and domes overlooking residential rooftops like irregular sentinals, are a goodly proportion of the ten thousand religious buildings that were constructed in Mexico during the colonial period.

Celaya, Guanajuato, San Miguel de Allende, Morelia, Taxco, Pátzcuaro, Puebla, Cuernavaca, Oaxaca, Guadalajara, Saltillo, Querétaro, and dozens of others bear the indelible stamp of Spain on the architecture which makes them so distinctive. Although there are strong regional variations, some of them due to topography, some to climate and to local custom, there is a mark on all these colonial towns which makes them clearly Hispanic, and, on closer scrutiny, specifically Mexican.

The streets are long treeless lanes paved with cobblestones, bordered by narrow sidewalks, both deliberately made narrow in order to give some refuge from the tropical sun. The houses stand one next to the other in continuous and unbroken lines, and are flush with the sidewalk, as if a yard or garden either between or in front of them were an impossible conception. Ordinarily the houses are of a single story, but in some of the larger centers they will have two stories, with balconies and iron-barred windows on the second floor overlooking the street. First-floor windows also are invariably protected by iron grilles, backed up by solid wood blinds which swing inward to open. Sometimes, too, there is a wrought-iron railing over the entrance. Externally, the colonial houses have a massive, severe appearance. The façades are seldom decorated, except for the enormous wooden doors, which are of beams so huge that it would take a battering ram to knock them down.

These colonial houses are made of adobe brick, or stone, and are nearly always covered with plaster. The walls are solid and very thick, the ceilings high, and the rooms spacious. Very little wood is used in their construction, except for structural beams and vertical supports and the doors and frames of windows. Floors are of clay-colored or white tile, and are scrubbed incessantly. In a country not exactly noted for its cleanliness, the scrubwoman with her pail and mop who makes her daily rounds over the cold glazed floors is frequently an amusing spectacle. It seems such a shame that the hardest work of the Mexican domestic should be this solemn and strenuous expenditure of needless effort when there are so many dozens of other things that cry out for a little cleaning. But try to change them. It is like butting one's head against a stone embankment. *Es la costumbre,* it's the custom. And that is the end of it.

The one invariable distinguishing feature of the city house is the interior garden, or patio. The Spaniard or Mexican could not conceive of a yard open to the public view. He would as soon undress before a window as relax and chat with his intimates in front of the neighbors and passers-by. If the house follows the typical Spanish pattern and is shaped like a square, it encloses and is constructed *around* an open patio. One enters via the massive wooden doors, passes through the *zaguán* and into this interior courtyard, which is lined with open corridors. All the principal rooms of the house are accessible via doors that open onto these corridors and onto the patio.

The patio is the center of family life, a private gathering place shielded from the street and neighbors, where the family unit can meet and talk or sit and nap undisturbed. In the larger houses the patio often contains a fountain and a luxurious garden. If there is space for a tree (orange, fig, lemon, palm), it will be enclosed with a wall of masonry, generally circular or octagonal, called an *arreata*. The patios of the houses of the Central Highlands are smaller than those in other parts of the country, and are usually paved with stone or brick. Decorative flower pots (*macetas*) line the patio with splashes of color, and there is also usually a larger tropical plant such as the morning glory, or the magenta or crimson-lake bougainvillaea which throws its brilliant hues against one of the columns or walls.

The colonial towns were built around the central plaza (*plaza mayor*) in the same way that the houses were built around the patio. The plaza was where the townsmen gathered; it was the focus of community life. Here stood the church, the municipal buildings, and here assembled the Indians and merchants who made up the market. The plaza itself in colonial times was a barren square, "paved with stones and used for military drills and parades." In the nineteenth century Maximilian and Carlotta put trees and flowers where the cobblestones had been. The church was the most imposing building, and lifted its spires above the surrounding town just as the European cathedrals rose loftily above the miserable medieval villages, epitomizing the faith of an epoch.

Every town has one plaza, and many towns have several. But, as has been pointed out by the inimitable Charles Flandrau, "there is always one that more than the others is a kind of pulsating, civic heart, and it is interesting to note how in their dimensions they observe the scale of their environment. Big towns have big plazas, small towns have small plazas, villages have tiny plazas."

Travelers sometimes complain, Flandrau goes on, that "Mexican towns are exactly alike; if you see one you've seen them all." He does not agree with that "bromidically couched observation," and neither do I. But it is easy to understand why the remark is made. "They are not alike," writes Flandrau, "but they are so startlingly different from Northern towns that one is at first more impressed by this fundamental difference, in which they all naturally have a family resemblance, than by the less striking but delightful ways in which they often differ from one another. Without exception, they are, as art critics used to say of certain pictures, 'painted in a high key' . . ." [11]

If we try to get at the heart of this family resemblance we will find that it is the result of a blending of the Hispanic and Indian influences, in the same way that Mexico herself is a blending. The larger, more solid buildings are architecturally Spanish, and although they are frequently decorated with Indian motifs, and invariably adorned with native plants and flowers, it is still conceivable that one might descend into the midst of some very Hispanic part of a Mexican town and believe for a moment that one is in Spain. Taking for granted, of course, that no one is on the streets. But even if the place is deserted, a closer scrutiny will reveal the native quality of the town. Topography, the look of the land, the climate, the plants and flowers, the signs written on the stores, the kind of stones used in the construction, what is in the stores behind the glass windows—these things and many others add up to a quality that is uniquely Mexican. Put people on the streets, and even the most obtuse and casual traveler could not believe himself to be in Spain, or in any country in the world but Mexico. The serapes, the *huaraches*, the *rebozos* of the women and the broad-brimmed hats of the men, not to mention the brown cast of faces that is distinctively Mexican, distinguish the towns of Mexico from those of any other nation.

Yet, similar as they are in these family resemblances, Mexican towns reveal a variety that is delightful. Jalapa, with its riot of tropical flowers, its lush green hills, its houses of white, blue, pink, and yellow, and its incessant rains, is a far cry from Guanajuato, with its crowds of square houses surrounded by denuded hills. And neither place seems to bear more than a distant kinship with the massive earthquake-proof walls of Oaxaca or with the severe façades of Querétaro opening onto patios flooded with charm and flowers. Puebla with its profusion of colorful tiles, which make it the most Andalusian of all Mexican cities, is only a distant cousin; and Pátzcuaro's low tile roofs with wide projecting eaves have a distinctly Oriental flavor as they climb up and down the sloping streets in a continuous stream. Taxco, piled tier after tier on steep mountainsides of rolling green, with the soft pink twin towers of its exquisite baroque Church of Santa Prisca, is different from them all.

There is no doubt about it, the towns of Mexico have a diversification that is enchanting. The traveler who has seen only one part of the country has many a surprise in store for him when he visits the rest. And wherever he is, the streets of Mexico, even when they are deserted, are never monotonous. Put a few Mexicans on the streets or plaza, and they become fascinating, magical.

Mexico City during the colonial epoch was just as distinctive as it is today. It was always *the* city of the Spanish New World, larger and more sumptuous than Lima, a greater city by any measure than the mine-crowded, temporarily more populous Potosí. But in colonial days it was far more Spanish than now and cut more in a single pattern—the pattern of colonial Spain. The Indian, while not by any means apart, was hardly the cultural axis of the place. The city belonged then to its Spanish rulers; just as today it belongs to the mestizo. The colonial capital was the heartbeat of the country, the center of everything. It was so large that it dwarfed every other city in the country. It was one of the great cities of the world. All of Mexico was drawn here, and the best of Spain came here to find a new life. The wealth, the power, and the glory of New Spain all reached their zenith in the capital which was raised on the ruins of Tenochtitlán, at the edge of the water.

The barefoot Carmelite friar Antonio Vázquez de Espinosa, who was in Mexico for several years in the early 1600's, has left his vivid description of the colonial city as it appeared to him in 1612:

> The city is one of the largest and finest in the world; it has an excellent climate, neither cold nor hot, with marvelous skies and healthful air; since it is built on a lake, it is very salubrious. For the reasons given, which also apply to the district, it covers the area of a very large city. It will be over two leagues [about 8 miles] in circuit; all of the buildings are of excellent construction, composed of a very fine reddish stone, unique in the world; there are very rich quarries of it right by the lake; it is very easy to work and so light that a large slab or block of it will float on the water without sinking, as I saw with my own eyes when I was in that city in the year 1612.[34]

The building stone to which Father Vázquez refers is the porous volcanic *tezontle*, which abounds in the Valley of Mexico. It was widely used by the Aztecs in their own construction, particularly as building material for temples and the houses of the chieftains. *Tezontle* comes in many shades of red and pink, and has a warm glow to it "like the soft stone smile of an angel." Many examples of *tezontle* buildings may be seen in Mexico City today, but these have now taken on a grayish hue due to the industrialization of the city. A portion of the National Palace on the Zócalo is made of *tezontle,* as is the Palace of Iturbide, on Calle Madero across the street and toward the Zócalo from Sanborn's, also *tezontle*-walled is the Hotel Cortés, which occupies an old colonial mansion across the Alameda from the modern Hotel del Prado.

Vázquez de Espinosa continues his description of the colonial city as follows:

> The streets are very straight, wide, and unencumbered; taken with the excellent architecture, they make a fine appearance. The city is well supplied with an abundance of cheap and delicious food. Along the streets there are broad deep channels of water from the lake, with bridges to cross over from one side to the other. For the provisioning of the city there come in from all the surrounding country every day over the lake more than 1,000 boats loaded with supplies of bread, fish, game, wood, and grass, which they call *zacate,* and what else is needed; by land every day, come over 3,000 mules loaded with wheat, corn, sugar, and other commodities for the stores. Thus it becomes one of the most abundantly and luxuriously supplied cities of the world.
>
> The city will contain over 15,000 Spanish residents and over 80,000 Indians who reside in the city and in the suburb or city of Santiago de Tlaltelolco and in the other environs or garden tracts (*chinampas*); furthermore there are more than 50,000 Negroes and mulattoes, slaves of the Spaniards or free; so the city's area is widespread and extensive. Business is active, both because the land is rich and the city is the capital of those realms, and also in consequence of the close connections it has with Spain, Peru, the Philippines, and with the provinces of Guatemala and its territory, Yucatán and Tabasco. . . . They usually have four market days there, with great quantities of merchandise, silk, cloth, and everything to be found in the world's best-supplied markets. . . .
>
> There are many large shops of merchandise, and Spanish and Indian artisans of every craft, who practice their professions with skill; accordingly, with this abundance of everything, there is nothing lacking in this famous city. It has a very fine cathedral, built by the most Christian Marqués del Valle Don Fernando Cortés right after he conquered that kingdom and took the city; as bases of the pillars, he used some heathen stone idols. . . . He left his name immortalized by having won that country itself, and its souls for Heaven, whither he went to rest for his reward and recompense for the great services he rendered to both Majesties, divine and human.
>
> Since Mexico City has grown so large and wealthy, they have built

another splendid cathedral; and although it is not yet finished, it can vie in size and richness with the best of all Christendom.

Father Vázquez then describes in detail the many monasteries and nunneries in Mexico City, mentioning the number of friars or nuns in several of them. He gives a detailed and graphic picture of the largest:

There are in Mexico City splendid and famous convents of friars, with sumptuous temples, richly and perfectly appointed, with large incomes and charitable contributions which support them. All of them maintain schools of Arts and Theology; the chief one, Santo Domingo, is one of the best and richest to be found in the Indies, and I doubt whether there be its equal in Spain. It has over 200 friars, many of whom are highly educated and great preachers. In this splendid convent they teach Arts and Theology; the church has become a glowing ember of gold, with great majesty of chapels along its sides. Although the foundations have sunk more than five feet below ground level, the convent is an excellent one, with large cloisters and dormitories, well designed and carried out.

Father Vázquez then lists and describes about three dozen other monasteries, churches, convents, colleges, and hospitals of the City of Mexico. Eleven of the largest monasteries have a total of 1,060 friars, according to his figures, but these make up only a small proportion of the religious establishments in the city. Father Vázquez winds up his description of the colonial capital in these words:

Besides all the above, the city has an abundance of water, coming from Santa Fe 2 leagues off, in a flume on famous arches like the aqueduct of Carmona near Seville; these cost over 300,000 pesos to construct. So all the city's fountains are well supplied with water; it is also well provisioned with bread, corn, meat, fish, and much fruit, both Spanish and native, and such luxuries as sugar, preserves, etc., as will be described in the following chapters. On the lake they have bathhouses with excellent hot-water baths, very healthful and beneficial to the invalids who bathe in them. The city has a brilliant assemblage of titled gentry, knights of the military orders, nobles, and important people.

In the towns and cities that were established Spain reproduced herself in Mexico. Each town was a symbol of her governing power, her culture, her religion. In the *encomienda* Spain reproduced her feudalistic economy of lord and vassal. And in the missions which reached like arrow points into the hinterland she expressed the drive and aspiration of her medieval faith in the world's last great crusade. Spain gave herself completely to the colonies, leaping even over the barriers of race. Yet, what began as a Roman conquest, imposing the Hispanic way of life on masses of native Americans, was bound to conclude as something strikingly new in world history, for the Indians engulfed the invader. They could not overcome him, but passively, like a woman, they could wait for the propitious moment, then thrust forward and overwhelm him. Slowly there was a fusion and a new birth in the wilderness. While Spain herself withered away under the stress of the great enterprise, the colonies, and especially Mexico, grew steadily stronger, more fruitful, more hopeful, more aggressive.

VIII

DAILY LIFE IN NEW SPAIN

The so-called Latins, perhaps because they are not really Latins at all, but a conglomeration of types and races, persist in not taking the ethnic factor into account for their sexual relations. . . . The Spanish colonization created race-mixing: this defines its character, fixes its responsibility and determines its future.

—José Vasconcelos, former Minister of Education in Mexico

From the beginning Mexico presented extremes of poverty and wealth. The Spaniards, by and large, were well off; the Indians were poor. A total of only 300,000 Spanish "heads of families" entered Mexico during the three colonial centuries. Very naturally they occupied a position of privilege among the masses of natives, two or three million of whom were incorporated into the colonial society. At least a couple of million others never became an integral part of the national life. The rapid increase of the mestizo class from the day that Cortés and his soldiers received that gift of twenty Indian maidens from the chief at Tabasco was the bridge that linked the two extremes together. As the bridge took shape and grew it eventually became the mainland of Mexico. The Mexican of today has inherited the culture of both his Spanish and his Indian forebears. A chemical reaction has taken place, and today's compound has replaced the two original elements.

During colonial times the fusion was not nearly so complete. Spaniards were the masters. They lived in towns, in houses, at least with some of the comforts of civilization as they knew it, while the natives lived in one-room huts, called *jacales* or *chozas*, or were gathered into mission settlements. The mestizo, generally born out of wedlock, and with no real family life, was often an outcast, a pariah. Not all Spaniards were rich, but they were relatively rich. They occupied a place in the community much like that of the white minority in some of the heavily Negro-populated communities of the United States

South today. With this difference: they were sexually much more promiscuous, and their consorts were Indians.

We have described the towns and houses in which this upper crust of white overlords resided. They were good solid buildings, picturesque, that formed a harmonious and pictorial pattern. Inside them was the flowering retreat of the patio. The people who inhabited these houses knew all the arts of graceful living. Thomas Gage, who visited Mexico City in 1625, has left a fascinating picture of life in that capital. He overestimates the number of Spanish inhabitants at between thirty and forty thousand, and says that at least two thousand coaches circulated constantly on the broad streets. Then he continues:

> It is a by-word that in Mexico there are four things fair, that is to say, the women, the apparel, the horses and the streets. But to this I may add the beauty of some of the coaches of the gentry, which do exceed in cost the best of the court of Madrid, for they spare no silver, nor gold, nor precious stones, nor cloth of gold, nor the best silks of China to enrich them. And to the gallantry of their horses, the pride of some add the cost of bridles and shoes of silver.
>
> Above all, the goldsmith's shops and works are to be admired. The Indians, and the people of China that have been made Christians, and every year come thither, have now perfected the Spaniards in those trades. . . .
>
> To the by-word touching the beauty of the women, I must add the liberty they enjoy for gaming . . . nay, gaming is so common to them, that they invite gentlemen to their houses for no other end:—to myself it happened that, passing along the streets with a friar . . . a gentlewoman of great birth, knowing us to be *chapetans*, from her window called unto us, asked us if we would come in and play with her a game at primera.
>
> Both men and women are excessive in their apparel, using more silks than stuffs and cloth; precious stones and pearls further much this their vain ostentation; a hatband and rose made of diamonds, in a gentleman's hat is common, and a hatband of pearls is ordinary in a tradesman; nay, a blackmore or tawny young maid and slave will make hard shift but she will be in fashion with her neckchain and bracelets of pearls. . . . The attire of this baser sort of people (which are mixt nature of Spaniards and blackmores) is so light, and their carriage so enticing, that many Spaniards, even of the better sort (who are too prone to venery) disdain their wives for them. . . .[11]

Gage also comments on the fine horsemanship of the mestizos, and speaks of their skill in performing all manner of Spanish dances and in playing Spanish musical instruments. He discusses the afternoon promenade, after which the people returned to the sanctum of their calcimined or rose-colored *tezontle* mansions which lined the better residential streets. The interiors of these were enriched with beautifully carved furniture, massive Spanish chests and cabinets, leatherwork of deep luster, often gilded for added brilliance, with bright tiles from Puebla and silks imported from Manila and other Far Eastern cities. Native pottery of the finest workmanship also filled these mansions, and "throughout the spacious rooms there shone the moonlight gleam of silver mirrors, silver braziers with their glow of hot charcoal, silver dishes on the dining table, reflected in the soft rays of candles held in silver sconces." The age of silver had its comforts too, and its charms and splendor.

Indian servants glided in and out noiselessly, always in a number that seemed excessive to the need. Many native foods appeared on the tables of the Spaniards, and Indian woven goods decorated most of the rooms. The day was begun with foaming hot chocolate flavored with vanilla. A typical Mexican wooden beater called the *molinillo* was twirled in the liquid by holding its handle between the palms of the hands and pushing these to and fro. A little later a more substantial breakfast was served. With the heavy midday meal hot tortillas replaced bread, and meats were often flavored in Indian fashion. *Guacamole* sauce made of mashed avocados also was a favorite. Wine was served after the midday repast, and this was followed by the inevitable siesta, which lasted two or three hours. Every shop in town was closed while the siesta was in progress and the people drowsed away the stupor of their heavy eating. This custom was so ingrained in the Mexican people that it was observed even on military campaigns, as Sam Houston found out much to the elation of all Texans. Houston won his biggest victory at San Jacinto by piling into Santa Anna's much larger army while the Mexicans were sleeping in the middle of a hot Texas afternoon. This resulted in the independence of Texas.

When night came, the main diversion of colonial society was the *tertulia*, or night-at-home, when the neighbors dropped in to chat and enjoy themselves. The *tertulia* lasted from about six until nine, and was followed by dinner. The principal entertainment at these social gatherings was conversation: small talk, heavy talk, always voluble talk, sometimes about the latest bullfight, sometimes the most heated discussions on economics, or on political or intangible subjects. Conversation was, and is, the favorite sport of most Latins; the subject itself is not important. But there were also games of forfeit, dancing, singing, cardplaying, and musical entertainment at these *tertulias*.

All this, of course, in the mansions of the mighty. The great silver mines of Mexico made it possible, and silver was enthroned in the highest chair. Some silver was mined from the very beginning of the colony, but by 1550 several rich finds (Zacatecas, Guanajuato) were pouring forth their wealth, which kept on increasing until the end of the colonial epoch, when it became a veritable torrent of silver. The silver kings of Mexico were among the wealthiest men in the entire world, and many of their stories are fantastic. Rags to riches, riches back to rags again, lavish displays that would have startled many a European monarch, the construction of sumptuous baroque monuments which still adorn the landscape of Mexico from one end to the other.

Despite the surface glow of the larger urban centers, a two-class society of landlords and day laborers, aristocrats and peons, was already one of the marked characteristics of Mexican life. Beggars infested the street, sticking out their filthy and germ-infested paws at maddening intervals. As the moneyed carriage riders promenaded so proudly along the boulevards, hundreds of Indians scurried about in all directions on errands for their masters, their colorful garments a great mural in motion. Atlas-fashion, these barefooted brown masses held on their shoulders the aristocracy of Mexico.

Sanitation and hygiene were never among the strongest points of the Hispanic temperament. Even today prominent signs on the walls of churches and other public buildings carry the warning: *Se prohibe hacer aguas mayores o menores.* (It is prohibited to do either the big or the small wetness here.)

The gutter (which was also the sewer) generally ran down the middle of the cobblestone streets, which sloped toward the center. Hundreds of these old streets are still in evidence. The garbage and muck that sometimes accumulated here emitted a stench that was intolerable. Medieval pictures of saints walking about in high boots in order to protect their feet from this filth had nothing on Mexico. When slop was to be thrown into the street, it was customary to yell out: *Agua va!* (Here she comes!) From then on it was every man for himself. The present-day visitor to the outlying Mexican towns will no doubt remember similar experiences of great pails of dirty water being heaved from upper-story windows onto the cobblestones below. Custom dies hard in Mexico, particularly when it embodies both convenience and an emotional escape valve after oppressive labors.

People took no care with their drinking water, and intestinal diseases were rampant. There were also epidemics of smallpox and other virulent diseases: diphtheria, typhoid, measles, bubonic plague, yellow fever, and rabies. Malaria was widespread in the tropical regions, and syphilis was a menace in every part of the country. According to some authorities, the early visitors to the New World carried syphilis back to Europe; according to others, it was the other way around. In any case, up to the time of the discovery of America, syphilis was not the violent disease that it became soon thereafter. Probably what happened was that the Indians, immune to their own strain of syphilis, were affected violently by the Europeans', and vice versa. In any case, after the conquest syphilis became one of the most general and most horrible of diseases among the colonial population.

In Mexico smallpox killed nearly half the natives during the first century. The terrible epidemic of 1555 was followed by the disastrous run of 1576, which is said to have wiped out nearly two million persons. The white man's diseases were a far greater scourge than his guns or his lash. Polluted drinking water and the continued use of human excrement as a fertilizer were two obvious causes of easily preventable contamination. They still are, today.

Colonial dress was similar to that of the peninsula. Men wore a waistcoat, knee breeches, silk or wool stockings, frilled collars and cuffs, and a broad-brimmed hat. If the man was well-to-do, a large Spanish cape was thrown over the shoulders. Women wore the typical *saya*, a long single-pieced dress gathered in at the waist with colored ribbons. It fitted snugly over the breasts and reached almost to the ground. Hooped skirts, embroidered ruffs, collars, and blouses also were common among the wealthy classes, and some form of the Spanish mantilla was universally worn instead of a hat. Among the poorer classes in Mexico this became the typical *rebozo*. Even today Mexican women rarely wear hats in church, and the *rebozo* probably owes its wide popularity to this need to keep the head covered while in a religious temple.

In rural Mexico the *rebozo* is the *sine qua non* of the woman's wardrobe. It is her coat, her stole, her hat. She wraps her baby tightly inside the *rebozo* and carries it either over her breast or slung on her back. When the child is sleeping at her feet, or beside her, the *rebozo* is its blanket and sheet. When she goes to market, the *rebozo* is often used as a basket, and is filled with fruit and other foods. If she goes to market to sell, she may throw the *rebozo* over her clay pot of tortillas or tamales to keep them warm. When she carries either a water jar or a basket on her head, she first coils the *rebozo* and lays it on her hair as a base. Young ladies and girls wear *rebozos* of many beautiful designs folded or crossed over the shoulders in a half a dozen ways for adornment as well as warmth. In a word, the *rebozo* is to the Mexican woman what the serape is to the man; it serves every possible purpose, both utilitarian and aesthetic.

Rebozos come in many sizes, large ones for adults, smaller ones for children. Grown women usually prefer them about a yard wide and two and a half yards long. Conservative colors are used: grays, blues, browns, with finely wrought designs and deftly fashioned fringes. Some of them are of the finest cloths and take months to make. Occasionally those of the finest threads are pulled through a small ring in order to show their quality. Only recently have tourists begun to buy *rebozos* in large numbers as they long have bought serapes, hence the quality and beauty of this garment have not yet deteriorated so much in an effort to appeal to the particular tastes of the tourist trade.

The sexes were rigorously separated in colonial life, both in education and social intercourse. It was a firm belief (among the men) that women were better off uneducated. It was an equally fundamental belief (among both men and women) that to leave a young man and girl alone for more than five minutes was asking for trouble. Consequently, the whole social code of relationship between the sexes revolved around this one fundamental tenet. Young daughters were zealously guarded within their homes. They were allowed out only to attend church or occasionally to witness some special fiesta. They always went in groups, and were closely chaperoned. The church and the fiesta, quite naturally, became the places where most of the courtship went on. Owing to the pressure of time, it was usually a whirlwind affair, and many a couple got married without having ever shaken hands, and most certainly without having ever kissed.

Outside the matriarchal circle it was common (if not always officially possible) for the gallant to appear before his truelove's barred window at night for a furtive chat, and perhaps a little dark billing and cooing thrown in. This gave rise to the phrase "eating the iron" (*comiendo el hierro*), which is the Spanish idiom for fast and furious lovemaking. On some occasions, if the man was aggressive and the lady willing, it was a good thing that the iron grating stood between swain and lady. Some older aunt (probably very experienced or very frustrated) often fostered these nocturnal meetings and thus brought the two young lovers together, getting a vicarious thrill out of the whole affair.

Women, of course, were expected to be scrupulously virginal, but men followed the usual double standard, and everything that wore a skirt was considered fair game. Rare indeed was the young man who reached his maturity without having had an Indian or a mestiza mistress. The abundant servant supply constantly paraded ripe and willing bodies before the adolescent male; masculine chastity was regarded simply as degrading. Pregnancies, to use an understatement, were rather frequent. These prolific young swains, of course, were performing the very effective function of strengthening the mestizo class. It was a national contribution of the first order.

Although seduction was the outstanding masculine amusement, there were also cockfights, games with dice or cards, cane tilting, running the rings, jousts, bullfights, and riding. Horseback riding and bullfighting were the two great national sports, and both of these were introduced by the Spaniards immediately after the conquest.

In the early years every effort was made to keep the Indians from riding, for the horse was the concrete symbol of the superiority of the Spaniard over the native warrior. In one of his early letters to the emperor, Cortés had written, "After God, our only security was the horses." And in the first years after the conquest, when iron was scarce, he considered the horses so valuable that he had them shod with silver. No Indian was allowed to own a horse. But when the mestizo class became larger than that of the whites this prohibition was no longer possible. By the time of the second century mestizo rancheros (small landowners) had already acquired a national reputation for fine horse breeding and outstanding horsemanship. Vázquez de Espinosa in 1612 praised the large ranches and excellent horses of the southern province of Chiapas, where, he says, they have "the best horses in all New Spain; they can compete with those of Córdoba, and some assert that they can surpass them." Thomas Gage, who was in Mexico only a few years later, also was greatly impressed by the horsemanship of the natives of Chiapas, and makes a point of saying that the governor, Don Felipe de Guzmán, who looked like a pure Indian, "kept commonly in his stables a dozen of as good horses for public shows and ostentation as the best Spaniard in the country."

The best Spanish horses were brought into the peninsula by the Arabs, and when these were taken to the New World they underwent certain physical changes which adapted them to the new environment, and in many cases improved the stock. Those which escaped and ran wild in herds often developed "leaders" of exceptional strength, speed, and intelligence. In Mexico there was a special love of good horses from the time of the conquest, when the animal was thought to be a god, a centaur. Riding skill became the measure of a man.

Those who became wealthy spent lavish sums to adorn their carriages, their riding equipment, and their habits with gold and silver. This showiness reached such extremes of bad taste that a royal decree of 1623 expressly prohibited scandalous overadornment or ostentation, which was believed to have a bad effect on the poorer citizenry. The decree went unheeded, for by this time the Mexican horseman, or *charro*, had become a national institution and nothing could stop him. *Charreadas*, or stunts performed on horseback, were the stock in trade of this new class of mestizo rancheros. The country folk of Salamanca, who wore a similar costume, were called *charros*, hence the origin of the term. In Mexico it has also taken on the meaning of "loud" or "flashy."

The *charro* modified the Spanish saddle to suit his own conditions and aesthetic sense. He often covered it with intricate carvings, embossed work, and invariably with silver adornment. The *charros* may still be seen in Chapultepec Park on a Sunday afternoon; they also participate in parades on national holidays and in all the horse shows and fairs of the republic. They are among the finest horsemen in the world today.

The Mexican herdsman, or *vaquero*, was the *charro* of the rural areas. He was a real working cowboy who rounded up stock, lassoed wild horses, and trained them for the ranch owner. It was from the *vaquero* rather than from the city *charro* that the American cowboy has descended. Indeed, for many years the only cowboys in the southwestern United States (originally a part of Mexico, of course) were Mexicans. When the North American herder began to take over, he learned all the tricks of the trade from his Mexican forebear and also appropriated his vocabulary, some of it unrecognizably Anglicized, to be sure. *Rodeo* is a Spanish word, and so are *lariat* (*la reata*), *lasso* (*lazo*), *bandanna, corral, vamoose* (*vamos*), *hoosegow* (*juzgado*), *calaboose* (*calabozo*), *desperado*, and many other words now in common English use.

Bullfighting was the second great national sport, and it too came in with the conquistadores. In the early days the *toreros* were not professionals, but were distinguished young men about town who took this occasion to display their bravery and their skill. There were no rings, so the fights were held in one of the plazas. In Mexico City the first audiences were composed of Spaniards only, and the archbishop, the viceroy, and all the great officials watched from the balcony of the viceregal palace. The bullfighters entered the square on horseback, wearing habits of the greatest luxury. Town buglers and musicians kept up a constant accompaniment while the fight was in progress. In the provinces native musicians played strange airs on drums, trumpets, and flutes. The early colonial bullfighters were not sufficiently trained, and many of them were killed or wounded. As is the case today, the public cheered a courageous performance and raised pandemonium if cowardice was shown.

The bullfight soon became a part of practically all fiestas, religious as well as profane, "the canonization of a saint, the arrival of a new viceroy, the birthdays of the Spanish monarchs and princes, the queen giving birth to a child, the coronation of a king, a peace treaty signed between Spain and some other country, the news that a shipment of gold and silver sent from Mexico had reached Spain safely, and finally to raise funds for charitable institutions and the royal treasury." [30] In the latter part of the eighteenth century the sport became more highly conventionalized, and professionally trained bullfighters were brought from Spain. Before long Mexicans were rivaling them in skill and daring.

The bullfight had a great effect on the native dances, which were then in process of blending Hispanic and Indian movements. Many of the different kinds of passes with the cape and the motion of the *torero's* body were reflected in the regional folk dances. The Mexican is an extremely mimetic person, and has a great gift for selecting what could be turned to best advantage.

Colonial education was in the hands of the church. The clergy was the "solid rock" upon which all educational institutions rested, even the university. This carried on the medieval pattern of islands of culture in a great sea of illiteracy among the masses. Only the sons of well-to-do families received an education; very few daughters even knew how to read or write. In the mission settlements Indians were taught mainly the arts and crafts; only a talented few learned reading, writing, or music. For the very small minority of Spaniards and mestizos who attended school emphasis was placed on religious doctrine and the three R's, and in higher institutions on Latin and classical authors. Toward the close of the colonial period a few town councils did subsidize and secularize education to some extent, but the efforts were not far-reaching.

The University of Mexico was chartered in 1551 and began to offer courses in 1553. It is the oldest permanent university in the New World, as nearly all writers on Mexico have been at pains to point out. This is supposed to prove that culture in the Hispanic colonies is not only more ancient but more highly regarded than in the United States. Our first university, Harvard, was not founded until 1636, nearly a hundred years later. But how indeed could there very well be a university in the territory of the thirteen colonies if there was not even a permanent settlement here until 1607? The only point of this paragraph is to draw into proper focus the comparison between the two countries. It is certainly *not* to disparage the University of Mexico.

The Carmelite Vázquez de Espinosa, writing in 1612, describes higher education in Mexico City in these words: "It has a splendid university, which can vie with the best in the world, with a large attendance of doctors, masters, and students; courses are given in all the sciences with great brilliancy and with benefit to the students, who are sons of that kingdom, where Heaven seems to promote intellectual keenness and subtlety, but with few rewards, since they are so remote from the eyes of His Majesty, and for that reason may drop out at just the best moment. In this university they confer all degrees in every branch of learning; it possesses all the privileges and exemptions of the University of Salamanca, for it is like it in educational program and in size."

During the three centuries of colonial rule the University of Mexico granted a total of nearly forty thousand degrees. Theology was the highest-paid chair, and the rest of the curriculum consisted of courses in the native languages, in canon law, sacred writings, Latin, classical authors, grammar, and later on, medicine. The more than five thousand books which appeared on the *Index* of the Inquisition were not to be read. During the first two centuries most courses were given in Latin. The liberalizing currents of the Renaissance barely touched Mexico. Professors were not expected to devote their entire time to teaching, and received an annual salary of from 150 to 200 pesos. Most of them were members of the clergy or lawyers. They filled out their income with other jobs, just as they do in Mexico today. In fact, there is no other country in the world where the professor works so hard for so little as in Mexico at the present time.

Because the Inquisition was always on the lookout for ideas that did not "symbolize with revealed truths," professors and students alike were wary of pursuing impartial investigation with too much zeal. The custom of the colonial intellectuals to discuss theoretical issues as if their lives depended on the outcome was indicative of how remote higher education was from the social and economic scene. And the stress on mental gymnastics produced a tradition of verbosity which still plagues many a Mexican intellectual. Scholars of "stupendous rote memory" came from these hallowed halls, but there was hardly a professor of world stature among them. The average North American's lack of interest in "philosophical" matters has caused many well-educated Latins to regard him as an intellectual upstart, interested only in the material things of life.

Universities in the thirteen colonies were under a similar bondage. Prior to the American Revolution the following colleges existed in the territory of the United States: Harvard, Yale, Brown, Dartmouth, King's College (which later became Columbia), Rutgers, Princeton, the University of Pennsylvania, and William and Mary. One American historian, after listing these names, comments tersely: "These institutions devoted themselves chiefly to the training of ministers." There was a difference: the bonds in these places were not as tight, and later they helped to produce the flowering of New England. One of the "ministers" of this period was Ralph Waldo Emerson, whose penetrating mind has influenced the trend of world thought.

Not until the very end of colonial times did the universities in either the English or the Spanish colonies become centers of "revolutionary" ideas. These were the concepts of skepticism and social freedom which had erupted from France and spilled out into the whole of the Western world. The North American Revolution, the French Revolution, and finally the Spanish American Revolutions were all partly attributable to the spread of these ideas.

Although a printing press had existed in Mexico since 1532, only ten years after the conquest, it printed mainly books of a religious nature. Books for use in the lower schools were at a premium, and according to one historian, "Each child read the books that he could bring from home: profane histories, the narratives of which neither they nor their teachers understood; books of chivalry or similar productions; and the most pious fathers gave their sons ascetic works to read which were the products of an ill-digested piety or lives of saints which had been written by authors without judgment and were consequently laden with apocryphal passages and pretended miracles." All the emphasis was placed, therefore, on a subject matter of very dubious value.

The North American colonies were far ahead of the Spanish colonial empire in this field of elementary education. New England took an early lead in public education, and as early as 1647 (only twenty years after the Pilgrims landed) a Massachusetts law "required every town of fifty families to establish an elementary school where children could learn to read and write. The teachers were to be paid by the parents or by public taxation. Every town of one hundred families was further required to set up a grammar school in which students might be prepared for college. This law became a model for similar legislation throughout the United States." [35]

The growth of this public school system from that day to this has been one of the greatest factors in shaping the character of the United States. Popular education became almost a religion, while in Mexico education was for many centuries reserved for the aristocrats. The problems were not at all alike. To teach the reading and writing of English to a few hundred thousands of children whose language was English is hardly comparable to teaching the reading and writing of Spanish to several millions of Indians and mestizos, to a great proportion of whom it was a foreign language representing a foreign culture. In spite of the colossal size of this problem, the burning question of race feeling has never divided Mexico as it still does divide the people of the United States.

IX

COLONIAL CULTURE: THE HIERATIC STREAM

A baroque world, this, of easy wealth and luxury and songs—a world very much in keeping with the baroque period into which Europe was entering after the bloom of the Renaissance. . . . It has been said that, out of the eight masterpieces of the baroque world, four are in Mexico. . . .

—Pedro Henríquez-Ureña

The conquest and colonization of Mexico covered three centuries, and during these years Spain gave her very lifeblood to her colonies, and most of all to New Spain, her favorite child. It was lifeblood flowing away, for while the New World was growing stronger and richer decade by decade, and century by century, Spain was growing progressively weaker. The tremendous wealth that she extracted from the colonies was squandered on useless wars all over Europe. Spain herself became a mere skeleton, a funnel through which this wealth of gold and silver flowed into foreign coffers. The people of Spain were left destitute and in despair. No wonder so many of them were eager to come to the New World, which was the "restless image and the dream caressed" of all the poor devils of the peninsula. Or, as Cervantes put it, "the common deceit of the many and the specific remedy of the few . . . the refuge and shelter of all the despairing waifs of Spain."

The three colonial centuries were far from being a long and drowsy dream. During this period an area greater than any ever before or since conquered and occupied by another race was brought into the orbit of Hispanic civilization. The English, with their thirteen colonies along a narrow coastal strip, were not in the same show with Spain. And this helps to explain the fundamental differences in the societies today in these two regions. Medieval and Renaissance Spain, and most of all *Catholic* Spain, explored and converted, colonized and governed a greater part of the entire territory of Spanish America during those colonial centuries. Therefore, when independence finally came the *old order* was everywhere firmly established. It was difficult to conceive the new, impossible to attain it.

In the United States, on the other hand, when independence was won a vast frontier territory lay to the west, and it was into this new Canaan that the freed colonies, *the United States*, not England, moved with its democratic dream.

The colonial centuries in Mexico have many distinguishing characteristics. The first century was militant, dynamic, expansive; everything was on the march. The army, the church, the explorer, the settler—all impelled by the explosive quotient of their Spanish will, drove spearheads into the unknown, explored mountains, rivers, and jungles, conquered wild Indian tribes, established missions and towns and churches. Nothing was able to stand before them. Mines were discovered, stupendous books were written about the New World, the basis of empire was firmly laid.

The next century was one of retrenchment and consolidation. The newly won lands and peoples were incorporated into the colonial society. Expansion was slower now, the speedy pace had tired the runner out. The mines poured forth their wealth, viceregal society assumed a splendid glow, learning now moved from the battlefield and the explorer's camp into the salon and the intellectual circle, into the university. Firsthand experience and the charm of firsthand records gave way to study, to accumulation, to scholarship and scholasticism. Literature was voluminous, but written now with a desire to impress; it dazzled, shed luster, had little feeling and less light.

The final colonial century began when the French Bourbons came to the throne of Spain in 1700. The pallid Spanish Empire received a sudden injection of French liberalism and took its second breath. The kings improved for a time (they could not possibly have become worse) and the empire again began to move forward. The Inquisition spluttered and faded away. But French culture, then leading the world, was blinding in its brilliance. Voltaire and Rousseau had no counterparts in Spain. French liberalism stunned Spanish thinking into mental inertia. When you mention the eighteenth century in France you think of a summit. When you mention the eighteenth century in Spain you think of a vacuum. Almost, not quite. For Mexico was better than Spain. The New World still had its fruitful soil, its mines, its teeming life. Out of this arose an architecture that was distinctively Mexican, the ultrabaroque, which lifted its splendid flowers everywhere on the branches of the Mexican tree. This architecture is still one of the all-time wonders of Hispanic civilization.

During all these years the church was the mother of art. The Indians gave to it of their labors, the friars dedicated to it their dreams and their strength, the rich men gave to it of their wealth. Religious architecture took root in Mexico and grew and flowered all over the land, as if it were a native plant. Were some holocaust or blight to destroy overnight the entire population of Mexico, and leave it an uninhabited land, there would still remain two things lovely: the churches and the mountains. Ten thousand of these beautiful colonial churches, monasteries and nunneries are scattered all over the countryside.

The church dominates the plaza and the town. It is the nerve center of community life, the one thing above all others which embodies the heritage of colonial Spain. The church rises above many a small and even squalid Mexican plaza in the same way that the ancient pyramid-temples of preconquest days rose above the starkness of the daily life around them. The conquest in Mexico was hard, and the landowner was demanding; the priest was both hard and demanding, but what he exacted in discipline and labor he gave back immediately in something that the Indian could understand, something beautiful that he could call his own, something that dwarfed the mightiest plateresque palace of the richest *encomendero*. These churches were *his*, as the good padre for whom he sweated so patiently told him. Indeed, they were the only place in Mexico where he and the Spaniard, the *gachupín* (wearer of spurs), were at least relatively equal.

With the church as the cradle of culture, it is little wonder that religious architecture was the great art of the colonial period. Where the Indian had been a builder before the conquest (and the Central Highlands of Mexico were clothed with some of his greatest temples), he became very quickly a builder of Christian churches. All he needed was a priest to guide him. When the Indian saw his own temples destroyed it gave him a feeling of panic. He felt that he belonged to a race which no longer had any god. He was desolate. But in this moment of bewilderment and fear the friar stood beside him. Using the same stones, and often building in the same place, even at times on the same foundation, the friar asked him to raise another temple, larger, more beautiful than the one which had been destroyed. The Indian believed that a more powerful god had spoken, and into this structure he deftly fitted his concept of the new religion, viewing it as a graft upon the old. There were always more gods than one. The good padre appropriated the Indian's music, his dances, his many fiestas, and added a few new ones from Spain. The Indian liked that. His robust brown body, however strong, could toil only so many days from sun to sun. Then he needed to rest, and he needed a place to rest, a place where he could feel safe and sure. And, being Indian, he wanted a place that was beautiful. The church gave him all these things.

During the years immediately after the conquest religious architecture was heavy and ponderous, for these were the years of the great *fortress-churches.* The Indian was not yet completely subdued. The church (like the early colonial mansion) had to be a strong point as well as a house of worship. Walls were thick, massive, with few windows and little decoration. And, as with the early colonial mansions, a massive exterior opened onto an interior which was warm and lovely. The artist could be freer inside.

The style of these early days was a mixture of the earlier Spanish styles: the heavy Romanesque, the more graceful ribbed vaultings of the Gothic, with frequent admixtures of the Mudéjar, a Moorish style made popular in Christian Spain in the days of the caliphs. The Romanesque gave these churches thick heavy walls, Gothic fingers lifted and sustained the domes and roofs, and the Mudéjar decorated and carved the wooden ceilings with precious, many-colored designs. A few native influences also came out in the early stonework of the Indian workers. There were occasional native plants and animals, even friars' cords, with serpent heads, oftentimes a group of Indian faces and occasionally an Indian-like design.

Among the early fortress-churches of the Franciscans are the Cathedral of Cuernavaca (the tower was added later), the monastery at Tepeaca, and the old Franciscan church and monastery on the plaza of Xochimilco. There are many others in the vicinity of Puebla, the most famous of them all in the little town of Huejotzingo. The Augustinians constructed two famous buildings in this style at Acolman and Actopan, both in the vicinity of Mexico City. The Dominican church on the plaza at Coyoacán also typifies the early fortress style; its side gateway shows a strong Indian influence. The Dominican church at Tepoztlán, just off the main highway from Mexico to Cuernavaca, is another example of the early fortress-monastery style.

The above first period of colonial architecture might be called medieval. The second period corresponds to the Renaissance, which came later to Spain than to Italy and which reached Mexico later still. Each period of Spanish art (and literature) takes about a generation to work its way over to the New World, so the cultural lag is always at least that great. In Mexico the second stage came only after the soldier was able to lay down his arms and the settler felt secure enough to engage in profitable agriculture and mining. The conquistador and early friars were now turned into colonist-builders. This period extends from about 1550 up to, roughly, 1630, and the style that dominated architecture during these years was the plateresque. The word means "silver-like," and comes from imitating in stone the graceful designs of the early silversmiths, who made delicate lacy patterns against a very simple background. In architecture plateresque designs were usually placed around the entrances, and sometimes over the windows. They were particularly popular on the more sumptuous residences, so much so that Trent Sanford, in his monumental *Story of Architecture in Mexico*, heads one of his chapters "Plateresque Palaces." [28]

The Cathedral of Morelia is the *magnum opus* of plateresque architecture in Mexico; Sanford calls it the most beautiful cathedral in all Mexico. The smaller, but very famous church at Tzintzuntzan, Vasco de Quiroga's original headquarters, is also in the plateresque style. Three huge bronze bells hang from beams in front of the church, placed there so as not to be toppled by earthquakes. These plateresque churches, as well as the mansions in the same style, show the "Medieval reluctantly giving way to the Renaissance."

Examples of plateresque residences are the House of Cortés in Cuernavaca, the mistakenly named House of Alvarado in Coyoacán, the House of Diego de Ordaz, also in Coyoacán, and the House of Francisco de Montejo in Mérida, Yucatán. Many public buildings reflected the same style: the National Palace, on the Zócalo, and the city halls in Tlaxcala and Atotonilco.

The Cathedral of Morelia, perhaps the most beautiful example of plateresque architecture in the world, was not constructed during the period when this style was at its height. It was begun in 1640 and completed in 1744, long after the popularity of the plateresque had given way to the baroque. But, coming late as it did, this magnificent building embodied and recapitulated every element of the graceful plateresque with a unity of form and feeling unbroken by crosscurrents from any other style. This cathedral sits atop the highest point in the city, with spacious gardens on both sides, and faces a wide boulevard. It is not cramped, or cold, or stolid, but rises nobly and unobstructed above the town. From its eminence it dominates Morelia completely, a perfectly proportioned masterpiece of architectural art.

When Philip II came to the throne of Spain in 1556 he was the veritable embodiment of the Catholic Counter Reformation. In every sense of the term Philip was *His Most Catholic Majesty*, a phrase applied to all the kings of Spain during these years, but applicable to him in a very special way. Philip was both the zeal and the sword arm of the Spanish faith which strove so desperately to reconquer the Western world for the Church of Rome. It is fitting that a massive and austere style of architecture should reflect the stern fervor of such a king. Exactly, such a style was the severe Spanish classic, or High Renaissance, which seemed made for Philip. Its most magnificent monument in Spain was the Escorial, tomb of the Spanish kings, which Philip planned and watched go up on the bare hills of northern Castile. In Mexico two great cathedrals embody the classic style: the Cathedral of Mexico and the Cathedral of Puebla. Neither of these structures, however, was carried out in complete faithfulness to a single architectural pattern.

The great Cathedral of Mexico, largest in Latin America, was begun in 1573, and the bulk of the structure was completed by 1667. However, it was 1797 before the last stone of the mighty twin towers had been put in place. The building is 387 feet long, 177 feet wide, and the towers rise to a height of 203 feet. The exterior is of buff limestone, darkened somewhat further by Mexico City's industrial smog. It is an imposing building, a tremendous building, but few will say that it is truly beautiful. It sits on one side of the Zócalo, like some giant frog, squat, massive, and unlovely. Since Mexico City was the great capital, so closely in touch with Spain, this building reflected the changes in architectural fashions during the more than two centuries that it was abuilding. It is classic, with baroque and Gothic overtones, as if the builders could never quite make up their minds which pattern to follow. Indeed, this was precisely what did happen. On two or three occasions the plans were changed to suit the caprices of a king.

Inside it is the same. Sanford calls the interior a museum of styles. But there is a lushness here that is utterly lacking outside. Unfortunately, the beautiful high altar by Balbas has been demolished, and an inferior one has taken its place. The *Capilla de los Reyes* (Chapel of the King and Queen) also by Balbas, does remain intact as a fine example of the later ultrabaroque, also called Churrigueresque. The beauty of many of the chapels along the sides was destroyed by Tolsa in an attempt at renovation in the nineteenth century.

The Sagrario Metropolitano, which stands just alongside the cathedral, is a building in a completely different style. It was begun in 1749 and completed in 1769. The exterior of this building is in effusive Churrigueresque, a lavish brocade in stone standing beside the stolid mass of the gray cathedral.

The Cathedral of Puebla is more of a single piece than the grand pile in Mexico, and also owes its inception to Philip II. The towers of this building, which soar to a needless height of 240 feet, seem too far apart. The exterior of the building, of a gray-blue local stone, is gloomy and almost boxlike in its lack of grace and beauty. But inside is a golden glory, a veritable flood of gold that reminds one of the mythical rain-tree caught in flowering gilt and stone. Even the Mexican Revolution passed this building by, and its splendor is so well kept, so dazzling and new in its appearance, that it might have been finished only yesterday.

In summarizing the styles of the cathedrals of Mexico and Puebla we might say that they are severe Philip II Spanish on the outside and flamboyant Mexican within. As one enters the portals of these imposing but cold cathedrals one enters also into the next and final phase of colonial architecture, the Mexican baroque (1600–1750). The death of Philip released the imagination of the Creoles and *gachupines* in Mexico, who then began to seek their own natural expression. Economics also played its part, and a very important part it was. The silver mines of Mexico began to flow heavily in the 1600's, and by the eighteenth century this flow had turned into a tidal wave as the mines gushed forth their wealth. The baroque was the gem of elaboration into which this richness might easily flow. As this flood of silver entered the great hieratic river which was colonial art, the baroque flowered from one end of the land to the other. It became the style of architecture which Mexico made her own.

The stories of the silver kings of Mexico have often been told, but some of them are so fabulous that they bear recounting here. Joseph de Laborde, a Frenchman, whose name was Hispanized to José de la Borda, was one of the most famous. He arrived in Mexico in 1745, a poor man. After several ups and down he hit it rich in the silver region of Taxco, and wishing to thank the Lord for his good fortune he had constructed the Church of Santa Prisca, whose rose-colored towers still rise proudly above the terraced white houses of Taxco. Borda is reputed to have said: "God gives to Borda, Borda gives to God." After this, he lost his entire fortune, and the archbishop allowed him to take and sell a golden custodia embedded with diamonds which he had presented to the church. With the hundred thousand dollars obtained from its sale, Borda tried his luck again in Zacatecas, and again he struck it rich. Then he built the famous Borda gardens in Cuernavaca, which later became a favorite retreat of Maximilian's.

Another silver king, the Count of Regla, became so wealthy from his mines at Pachuca that he presented King Charles III of Spain with two warships (one of them carried 112 cannons) and further lent the royal treasury a million pesos, still unpaid, according to Humboldt. Another grandee of Zacatecas paved the street between the church and his mansion with bars of silver at the wedding of his daughter. Count Regla did the same thing for his son's christening. He also invited the king to visit Mexico City and promised to pave the entire 260 miles of road between the coast and the capital with silver if he would come. The Count of Valenciana began his career by hacking away at a hill near Guanajuato where the goats were grazing. Before long he hit a rich vein, and a huge boom town of seven thousand people arose almost overnight. His "take" amounted to nearly three million dollars a year over a considerable period, a goodly part of it net. He was one of the wealthiest men in the world.

Mexico doubled the world's supply of silver in 150 years. With this torrent of silver flooding the land it is easy to understand why rich man vied with rich man, and town vied with town, each trying to outdo the next in building the most lavish monument possible to the greater glory of God, and of course to the greater glory also of himself. As Trent Sanford points out:

> The Baroque, even though originally imported from Spain, and added to by the Indians, and further influenced by the Orient, seemed made for Mexico. Like the life and the religion, it was mundane in conception, florid in execution, and intolerant of restraint. The Baroque *gachupines* and creoles gambled with their increasing wealth; and the Baroque churches, boastful in expression and triumphant in scale, seemed to express a desire to gamble with God. There was none of the mystic faith that had produced the Gothic churches of Europe, none of the devout missionary zeal that had built the fortress monasteries of sixteenth-century Mexico; it was a blatant materialism that not only expressed unrestrained joy over the increasing wealth and the greater ease, but seemed to defy God to deny entrance to the Kingdom of Heaven.[28]

During these hieratic years "Architecture was mother to painting as to sculpture and even to music; churches were not only art galleries but academies as well." [16] Statues of saints and virgins in polychrome, oftentimes in garments as well, adorned the interiors. As Manuel Toussaint, the Mexican art critic says, "sculpture is particularly well suited to the baroque spirit." There were graceful reliefs in stucco and stone, carvings in cedar, burnished and gilded; figures with robes of brocade, and faces and hands delicately flesh-tinted. Everything in the baroque followed a curve upward, as, before, the Gothic had lifted itself in pointed ogival windows and archways, which resembled hands in prayer. But the baroque was not a prayer; it exalted the pagan spirit of the later colonial centuries; it invaded the homes also; it even invaded the thinking of the times, which followed a devious curve to its point of no return.

Toussaint writes: "Contemporary furniture for houses and churches show that same unrest and love of movement; legs of tables and chairs turn and twist like the spiral columns of baroque altars. Iron is wrought into lace-like grilles, railings for balconies, lamps that adorn façades; while inside the houses, rugs, screens, writing tables, lattices, rich velvets and embossed leather recall the sumptuous and evocative interiors of Moorish times. All the arts show that same baroque tendency; Mexico has found her own personality in the furnishings of her many magnificent palaces." [31]

It would be ridiculous to attempt any listing of all the noteworthy baroque structures of Mexico, for the land abounds with them as if it had been planted with baroque seed. But here are a few obvious landmarks which are easily accessible to any visitor. In Mexico City the huge four-story Palace of Iturbide, on Madero, opposite Sanborn's and toward the Zócalo, is one of the richest baroque mansions. For many years (until 1928) it also served as a hotel. The National Pawnshop, west of the cathedral, Monte de Piedad, is also a large baroque building. It was the first viceregal residence in Mexico, but was later remodeled in the baroque style. Other fine examples of the baroque style are the National Preparatory School, with a beautiful façade of *tezontle* trimmed with warm gray *chiluca*, the Church of Santo Domingo, on the plaza of the same name, and La Profesa Church, once the Jesuit stronghold in Mexico, on Madero and Isabel la Católica, in the heart of the capital's downtown section. The Church of Santo Domingo in the city of Oaxaca, one of the largest churches in Mexico, has the finest baroque interior of any building in the country. Its massive walls, built doubly thick to withstand earthquakes, have protected the exquisite interior well against war and shock. They even withstood the weight of cannons mounted on the roof. If the interior of the Cathedral at Puebla reminds one of the mythical raintree, here in the Church of Santo Domingo is a raintree in reality, unmistakably stretching itself all over the ceiling in branches budded with figures wearing crowns.

The most famous baroque building in Mexico, of course, is Borda's Church of Santa Prisca, in Taxco, said to have cost over 8 million pesos. Sanford calls it "the most complete example of ecclesiastical art that the period produced anywhere." When I last saw Santa Prisca its twin towers of rose-colored stone were glowing in the sun, while shadows from the Indian laurel trees on the tiny plaza before it made a green embankment for the exquisite façade. One of the huge bells was upside down, apparently stuck, and the hands of the giant clock were stopped at 2:45. Time no longer exists for the Church of Santa Prisca, which has already passed into the realm of the immortals.

As we enter this church and see its interior we walk into another architectural style. Here are a series of twelve altars in carved and gilded wood, which typify the ultrabaroque (Churrigueresque). The mural paintings are all by that colonial master, Miguel Cabrera, and represent his finest work. Even the stonework inside glows with a new and shining light, its pink warmth making a sharp contrast with the huge murals and the Churrigueresque *retablos*.

The definition of ultrabaroque might well be given as follows: it is like the lavish baroque, only more so. In this style columns often disappear completely under a mass of decorative details, and interiors in the ultrabaroque often form decorative incrustations which actually jut out from walls and ceiling like heaps of multicolored shells and leaves in which are embedded small cherubic figures. This style was also called Churrigueresque because in Spain the architect Churriguera is reputed to have been its initiator. But on reaching Mexico the Churrigueresque simply burst from the already flowering baroque with a naturalness that marked it for the country's own. "It was a religious art in its anxiety to make the House of God not only as splendid as possible, but also a sort of celestial vision. . . . This exaggeration of the baroque is the incarnation of an epoch and of a people." [31]

One fine example of the ultrabaroque, the Sagrario next to Mexico City's cathedral, has already been mentioned. Many altars of the cathedral itself are strongly Churrigueresque. By the time many of the great church buildings were completed this new style was at its height, and it is natural that the interiors, which were the last parts of the building to be done, should follow the latest fashion.

Among the churches which have ultrabaroque exteriors is the one at Tepotzotlán (Aztec for "On Hunchback Hill"), a few miles north of Mexico City. (This town is not to be confused with Tepoztlán near Cuernavaca, studied in such detail by Redfield and Stuart Chase.) The Church of San Cayetano at Valenciana, near Guanajuato, also has a façade in pure Churrigueresque style. The story goes that in making the mortar for this church silver dust was mixed with some of the finest Spanish wines. The Count of Valenciana, who defrayed the cost of its construction, was reputed to have made a fortune of some 800 million pesos.

In the area around Puebla the ultrabaroque took on a strong regional flavor. Puebla was (and still is) the great tilemaking center of Mexico. It was started from scratch as a purely Spanish city, and became a popular place of residence for emigrants from Andalusia, who had learned their tilemaking from the Moors. This art was quickly taught the natives and, as the Puebla clay was ideal for the purpose, the industry soon began to flourish. Before long, tile was used in decorating almost anything in Puebla: the façades of residences and churches, the sides of stairways, the wainscoting, the bases around fountains, on park gates and benches, in patios and in kitchens. The Puebla tilemakers applied a heavy glaze of color to the white tile, giving it a thick wavy appearance which stood out beautifully in the open air. Blue, yellow, green, and red were the favorite colors and were reproduced in many shades.

The tile-covered façades of Puebla's "Sugar-Cake House" (Casa del Alfeñique) and the "Doll's House" (Casa de los Muñecos) are both justly famous. The Church of San Francisco has a notable tile façade, as does the Church of San José. The monastery of El Carmen, and the churches of Nuestra Señora de la Luz, Nuestra Señora de Guadalupe, Santa Catalina, and Santo Domingo all reflect the lavish use of tiles. Outside Puebla the Santuario de Ocotlán (Aztec for "Place of Pines"), near Tlaxcala, has a gorgeous tile-embedded ultrabaroque façade, and the Church of San Francisco Acatepec (Aztec for "Windy Hill") is a bejeweled maze of tile-dazzling splendor. There are many, many others. Although Puebla is still the great tile center of Mexico, many of the glaze formulas were lost in the early nineteenth century during the War for Independence and the chaotic years that followed, and the tiles of today cannot always hold their own with those of yesterday, despite the wear of centuries.

The Church of La Compañía (Company of Jesuits) in Puebla, constructed before tile façades had become popular, is a baroque building which enjoys another kind of fame. It holds a plaque which is the epitaph of the mythical Chinese princess who, according to the legend, was stolen by pirates, brought to Acapulco, and sold there to a kind merchant of Puebla. She became a Christian and put away her Oriental finery for a red skirt and embroidered white cotton blouse. Her disposition and devotion quickly won the hearts of the townfolk. The costume of this *china poblana* ("Chinese girl of Puebla"), with a few added embellishments, has become the national costume of the "typical" Mexican girl today. Wherever the *jarabe tapatío* is performed, the female dancer will invariably wear the dress of the *china poblana*.

The most famous tile-bedecked building in all Mexico is not in Puebla, but in Mexico City, where it is visited daily by hundreds of North Americans. This is the well-known House of Tiles, on Avenida Madero, which houses the original Sanborn's restaurant. (There are now several branches, including one in Monterrey.) The building was put up in the sixteenth century, and was sold in 1596 to Don Diego Suárez de Pereda for 6,500 pesos. When Don Diego's wife died, he became a Franciscan, and left the place to his daughter. She married into the family of the Counts of Orizaba, in whose hands the house remained for many generations. A century and a half later this family spawned a ne'er-do-well spendthrift son who was the black sheep of the Orizabas. The old man, irked at his son's extravagance, one day snorted at him: "Son, you'll never own a house of tiles!" The phrase implied simply a noble mansion and well-ordered family, but the son took it to heart most literally, gave up his improvident life, found himself a well-to-do wife, and set about turning the ancestral mansion into the most elaborate house of tiles in the country. During the regime of Porfirio Díaz, many years later, the place passed into other hands, and eventually wound up as the famed and high-toned Jockey Club, a landmark often referred to by the poet Gutiérrez Nájera and many other Mexican writers.

The back part of this House of Tiles is a more recent addition, but the rest remains much as it was in 1750. The interior has changed little since the first construction, a couple of centuries earlier. It is one of the finest seignorial mansions in Mexico, and is an excellent example of Mudéjar (Spanish-Moorish) architecture.

The tall slender columns of the patio, somewhat grayed with age, and the ancient stone fountain in the center are exquisitely carved. Blue and white tiles almost completely cover the exterior, and the roof is surmounted by ancient battlements.

The price that this mansion sold for in 1596 (6,500 pesos) gives us some idea of the purchasing power of the peso at that time in terms of real estate and construction. The building would now probably bring (not counting the addition) a price of something like 650,000 pesos, or a hundred times as much. In early colonial days, then, a man did not have to possess an enormous fortune in order to be most comfortably wealthy.

The movement for independence, which began in Mexico in 1810, brought to an end the epoch of great religious architecture, which expressed so perfectly the hieratic culture of the colonial period. Sacheverell Sitwell has said that "the last good church ever built" was that of the Carmen, Our Lady of the Garden, in Celaya. The Mexican architect Tresguerras put up this church in classic academic style in 1802–1807. It is a fitting conclusion to three centuries of magnificent church building in Mexico.

There are four things about these wonderful churches which always amaze the visitor: first, their number, perhaps a total of ten thousand; second, the locations of many of them in remote corners of the country; third, their size, for hundreds of the old colonial structures are truly imposing; and fourth, their beauty, which seems to spring from the land as if they had all been planned in the mind of Providence since the beginning of time. Take a small town like Cuernavaca (small, certainly, in colonial days), and stand next to the tremendous tower of its cathedral. Or take the small and isolated (isolated in colonial days) town of Oaxaca, and stand next to the colossal walls of its Church of Santo Domingo. Confronting this grandeur, and in this position, one cannot help feeling somewhat inconsequential about the structural achievements of our own more technical civilization. Everything in these great piles was done by hand. The soft pink tower of Cuernavaca, the warm green walls of Oaxaca, the gray borders of *chiluca*, the vibrant many-colored tiles of Puebla, the flamboyant interiors of white, silver, and gold—all these were made by hand, by Indian hands mostly, under the guidance of padres who were no technical geniuses (they made many mistakes in building), but who kept the great river flowing until the colony came finally to its end. Up-to-date stores, homes, and hotels are now going up beside these relics of a bygone era, too often destroying the harmony of the older picture. Many a street widening, done in the name of progress, has caused the demolition of irreplaceable loveliness. A few towns (Taxco, San Miguel de Allende, for example) have been declared national monuments, and as such are untouchable, while others, just as beautiful, are feeling the inroads of our highway civilization. There is a planned way to avoid much of this destruction, but the towns themselves must take the initiative, and pride in the past is hardly a strong point of Mexican character. Newer additions should be kept separated from the "old city"; they should be given a place and a perspective of their own. Contemporary Mexican architecture certainly deserves this. Meanwhile, the old buildings must not be destroyed. We North Americans who do not have such a heritage in our own country, and never will, can view this problem as unbiased observers, and the above, I am certain, will be the dictum of us all. "Mexico, keep your wonderful treasures. It is so easy to destroy, so impossible to replace."

In literature as in architecture the baroque spirit characterized the last two colonial centuries in Mexico. In Spain the Counter Reformation had put an end to the free expression of ideas which might expose their holder to inquisitorial scrutiny. Denied this outlet of skeptical inquiry, the Hispanic mind turned toward the overadornment of form. Images poured forth in a golden stream from the great pens of the peninsula. A powerful and beautiful literature arose, and in Spain's Golden Age equaled the world's finest. Cervantes, Calderón, Lope de Vega, Góngora, Gracián, and dozens of others wielded their magic scepters and entered the mainstream of universal letters. The baroque now became a style as well as an escape. Since the rational quest for ideas was not basic to this literature, the great gift of these authors was in the linking of their images. The eternity of a poem depended on the quality and union of its metaphors.

Mexico did not produce a great literature comparable to that of Spain's Golden Age, which had been reached only after many centuries of literary production. A garden will often burst into its greatest flowering on the very eve of the day that its plants are fated to die. The literature of Spain was something like this; it was a zenith, after which there was a descent into a valley. Mexico had not yet had the time to reach a similar summit.

But if the colony as a whole did not produce a great literature, it did at least produce one outstanding writer, the greatest of all writers of the colonial period in Spanish America—Sister Juana Inés de la Cruz. Sister Juana (*Sor Juana* in Spanish) lived between 1651 and 1695; she is often called the Tenth Muse. She was the illegitimate child of a poor country couple and very early showed signs of being a prodigy. According to her own story, she could read at the age of three, and in her early teens was so consumed by the desire to learn that she begged her mother to cut off her hair and dress her in the clothes of a boy so that she might attend the university, which was only for men.

About this time in her life she was sent to Mexico City to live in the home of her grandfather. By the time she was fourteen her fame had spread all over the capital, and the wife of the viceroy asked the young girl to come and live in the viceregal mansion. When she was seventeen she was given a public examination by forty outstanding professors and Mexican intellectuals, in which she defends herself "like a royal galleon beating off the attacks of a bunch of rowboats."

Shortly thereafter she entered the convent, where she spent the rest of her life writing, surrounded by her library and musical instruments, and tending to her religious duties. She died in a plague, taking care of the ill, at the age of forty-four. While in the convent she was criticized for her worldly writing and for not immersing herself sufficiently in religious things. She answered the criticism with a brilliant defense of her God-given right to study all things. Her words were also a defense of womankind in general, for in those benighted days it was not thought fitting that a woman should develop her intellect. Sor Juana found herself out of step with her times. She was a feminine prodigy living in a man's world, subject to man's law and man's customs, and she rebelled violently against it. However, the criticisms she received (the bishop of Puebla was one of her strongest critics) finally had their effect on her, and toward the end of her life Sor Juana disposed of all her books and material possessions, gave the proceeds to charity, and wrote two protestations of faith in her own blood. The intolerant atmosphere of her epoch had swallowed up the finest, most sensitive spirit of colonial Mexico.

Why did Sor Juana decide to enter the convent? She herself writes: "There were so many things in the mundane world that were repugnant to me . . . marriage seemed to be a total negation . . . my one wish was to live alone that I might have absolute liberty to continue my studies." In other words, she was clearly not a born nun. Another obvious reason for her leaving the outside world lies in the illegitimacy of her birth. She must have felt uneasy socially on account of it, and realized that most men regarded her as a phenomenon rather than as a person. The security of the cloister was her only chance for self-expression.

Sor Juana wrote many different kinds of things. Her religious poetry is intense and moving, her gongoristic writings are obscure but filled with golden images, her occasional verse is in keeping with the high-sounding tone of the times. But it is in her more simple pieces, her lyrics of love and loss, that Sor Juana achieves her finest writing. No amount of formalism was able to destroy the spontaneous flame of this sensitive soul crying out the tragedy of her life and of womankind.

Mexico now was overwhelmed with form. The colony was a cumbersome vehicle which barely moved along the path of progress. There was only a slight cohesion of the heterogeneous elements of society in Mexico, and the dictatorial, complacent hauteur of the ruling Spanish minority did little to bring these elements together. Once the symbol of the Spanish crown was removed, the frail chain of union would be destroyed forever. Mexico then must seek out her destiny, alone.

1.
Temple of
Kukulkan,
Chichén-Itzá

2.
Church of
Santo Domingo,
Oaxaca

3. Ultrabaroque façade of Church of Tepotzotlan

6.
Cathedral
and (right)
Sagrario,
Mexico City

7. Colonial street, Jalapa

8. Old hacienda dining room in Fortín de las Flores

9. Chapultepec: under these *ahuehetes* Montezuma walked

10. Old colonial street in Guanajuato

11. Airport, Mexico City

12. Ministry of Communications Building

13.
Paseo
de la Reforma,
Mexico City

14.
Monument of the Revolution, Latino-americana apartment house, and building of Recursos Hidraulicos

15. Interior of home in "Pedregal," Mexico City

16. Home with pool, "Pedregal," Mexico City

17. Biology Building, Science Tower, and Medicine Building, University City

18. Administration Building and Library, University City

19. Highway from Mexico City to Cuernavaca

20. Housing project, Mexico City

21. Mexican students at University City

22. Interior of Library, University City

23.
Library,
University City

X

INDEPENDENCE AND CHAOS

After the Mexicans won their independence, the terror inspired by the Spanish authorities, which had been passed down from fathers to sons, disappeared. In its place were substituted the broadest and loudest declarations about liberty and equality. However, since ignorance could not and did not disappear, it has given rise to a political charlatanism which has taken possession of all public affairs and has led the state to confusion and to chaos.

—LORENZO DE ZAVALA

AT THE close of the colonial regime all things conspired to make Mexican independence a reality: the growing appeal of liberal French thought, the example of the United States, the French Revolution, which universalized this example before the Western world, the invasion of Spain by Napoleon and the flight of the Spanish king, the rise of liberalism in southern Spain both during and after the Napoleonic invasion, the harsh stratification of the classes in New Spain, the bitter rivalry between Creoles and Spaniards, the century-long frustration of the mestizo, the oppression and blind hatred of the Indian masses—all these things went hand in hand to bring about the end of the colonial regime and the independence of Mexico.

An enlightened king in Spain might have spared the country the horrible bloodletting of the War for Independence, but Ferdinand VII of Spain was anything but an enlightened prince. A progressive monarchy in Mexico also might have turned the trick, but the attempt to establish such a monarchy came too late and fell through on account of the chaotic conditions both in Mexico and in Spain. However, Mexico did twice try the institution of monarchy, once in 1821, under that grand Creole opportunist Iturbide, and again in 1864, under the foreigner interloper, Maximilian. Neither of these princes had the ghost of a chance of succeeding on the Mexican throne. The first had stacked everything against himself, the second had everything stacked against him. Both of them wound up before the firing squad.

On the eve of the struggle for independence, the population of Mexico was between six and seven million. Humboldt estimated the national income from agriculture at that time at approximately 30 million pesos a year, from industry about 7 million, from all other sources (mines, etc.) perhaps 50 million, making a total of approximately 100 million pesos yearly. On a per capita basis this would be an absurd 14 pesos yearly, but we must remember that many Mexicans never saw a peso. Even so, since the wealthy minority received far more than that, the average wages of those who did receive them, could not have been more than a very few pesos a year per family in 1810.

The classes in New Spain at the close of the colonial epoch were:

1. At the top the Spaniards, or *gachupines,* who held the highest government and church positions. They numbered around 15,000.

2. The Creoles, or persons of pure or almost pure Spanish blood, who were Mexican by birth. They occupied the administrative positions of lesser importance, and were the merchants and in many cases the miners of New Spain. They numbered about 500,000.

3. The mestizos, of Spanish father and Indian mother, who were the outcasts of the colonial regime. An immense number, perhaps the majority, were born out of wedlock, at least in the early years of the colonial era. They numbered approximately 2,600,000.

4. The Indians, who made up the majority of the Mexican people. They numbered between three and four millions.

There were a few thousand Negroes and mulattoes, but these were not of sufficient number to exert any great influence on the national life.

In this rigorous stratification of the classes each group felt itself in conflict with every other group. However, it was the conflict between the top two which was to decide the independence and the hegemony of Mexico. During the early years after the conquest the Creoles had naturally felt that they were Spaniards and rightfully belonged in the same social and political group as the Spaniards. But as the decades passed, and as the sons, grandsons, and great-grandsons of these old families were born, they were more and more confronted by two things: first, they felt progressively less Spanish and more Mexican; second, they saw that the choicest political and ecclesiastical offices were invariably reserved for new arrivals from Spain, who were in reality strangers to Mexico. The realization of these two facts caused a burning resentment among the members of the Creole class, and when the possibility for revolt arose, the spark was applied by Creole leadership. It might even be called a revolt of the classes, rather than a revolt of the masses. But in Mexico (as did not happen in the Indianist areas of South America) the Indians and mestizos did take a very considerable part in the fighting for independence. They also hated the *gachupines*.

On the night of September 15, 1810, the church bell began to toll in the small village of Dolores. Father Miguel Hidalgo, the white-haired parish priest, was calling his humble parishioners together. Captain Ignacio Allende had just arrived on the run to tell Hidalgo that their conspiracy had been denounced. Action must be taken at once. When the gentle priest took the pulpit and began to speak, there was an impassioned tone in his voice. The poor Indians and Indianist mestizos who made up his flock leaned forward intently.

> I have been your priest and your protector for seven long years. Together we have made a community of which we all have a right to be proud. Together we planted mulberry trees and grapevines, raised silkworms, and made wine, in spite of the Spaniards' opposition. Together we put up our factory where pottery and leather goods are produced. Always, as you well know, I have been your friend. Always I have zealously defended the poor and the oppressed. When the Spaniards came and uprooted our trees, because of the competition, I protested with all my might, but it was in vain. Finally the time has come for us to unite and rise up against our oppressors, both yours and mine. So now in the name of our beautiful land, and in the name of our beloved Virgin of Guadalupe, let us take back the lands that were stolen from Mexico three centuries ago.
>
> *¡Viva la Virgen de Guadalupe! ¡Viva México!* Long live the Virgin of Guadalupe! Long Live Mexico!"

These last two sentences are known in Mexican history as the famous *grito de Dolores*, or "cry from Dolores." They mark the opening salvo in the struggle for freedom, and are repeated each year by the President of Mexico, who comes out on the balcony of the government palace on the Zócalo and shouts them to the multitude assembled below. The President adds the phrase, "*¡Viva la independencia!*" The crowd then cries out an answering "*¡Viva!*" and Mexico's greatest celebration is begun.

It is reported that Father Hidalgo, after giving the famous cry, added a spontaneous peroration: "*¡Y ahora a coger gachupines!* And now let's get on with the killing of Spaniards!"

Whether or not Father Hidalgo actually said that final sentence, we do not know. But the rabble that erupted over the countryside and followed him certainly made these words a historic fact. Possibly this is the reason for the story.

In any case, it is well to point out the great difference between this speech of Father Hidalgo's and the restrained and poetic Declaration of Independence of the United States. The one called forth the dark hatreds of racial feelings and cried out for the killing of Spaniards. The other announced in some of history's noblest words the declaration of the rights of man, and of a people to be free.

Father Hidalgo put himself at the head of his parishioners and their neighbors, and the War for Independence was under way. Had Captain Allende headed the rebellion as planned, there would have been discipline and the revolt would have followed a different course. But, as a Mexican writer has pointed out, "Leaders are not named. They spring forth from the necessity of the moment." The motley contingent moved slowly across the land, taking on numbers as it advanced. With the banner of the Virgin of Guadelupe unfurled before it, this lowly multitude grew by leaps and bounds as it advanced toward the wealthy city of Guanajuato. The *gachupines* entrenched there refused to surrender, and the battle was joined. Like locusts the mass army swarmed into the city and captured it by sheer weight of numbers. The streets ran scarlet, the carnage was revolting, and the aftermath of the battle was more revolting still. The undisciplined horde killed, looted, raped, and destroyed like a pack of wild beasts. The Mexican historian Alamán, who witnessed the scene as a boy, remembered it graphically in later years when he described it as "a monstrous union of religion with assassination and plunder."

In Mexico City both the government and the Inquisition were now after Hidalgo. It was pointed out that he had in his library certain prohibited French books, that he had two illegitimate daughters, that he had read the Scriptures critically, had spoken insultingly of the popes, and that he had even expressed some doubt regarding the virginity of the Mother of Christ. He was excommunicated from the church. It was too late; the swarm of locusts behind Father Hidalgo did not desert him now. They regarded the accusation as lies, and the excommunication merely as a weapon of the *gachupines*.

But the multitude that Hidalgo headed, however numerous—and some estimates place it as high as 100,000—was by no means an army. The general himself made serious strategic mistakes, and when his horde was met by a well-organized fighting force it collapsed and dispersed. Father Hidalgo was taken prisoner and shot. His head was displayed on a pole in Guanajuato. Thus ended the first chapter in the Mexican War of Independence.

Hidalgo and his hundred thousand insurgents had failed, and failed miserably, because they had no program, no organization, no discipline, no army. Hidalgo himself never renounced his allegiance to the Spanish king. On the contrary, during his campaign he frequently cried out, "*¡Viva el Rey Fernando VII! Long Live the King!*" He was naïve enough to believe that the king, once he returned from France to the Spanish throne, would give royal support to his struggle against the Spaniards. Therefore, Father Hidalgo died without having called for the independence of Mexico. He had striven for a nebulous freedom within the disintegrating existent political order. He and those who followed him constituted only an idea instead of a program, a mob instead of an army.

His former pupil and follower, José María Morelos, a mestizo, had a greater success in the field than did Hidalgo. Morelos also was a priest. He had studied under Hidalgo at the seminary of Valladolid, now named Morelia. Learning from the failure of the leader, Morelos organized his followers on a more disciplined basis, and also organized a congress which announced a liberal social program for the country. This congress proclaimed the independence of Mexico. If the mestizo class had been in a position to unite behind Morelos, mestizo government might immediately have taken control of the country, and more than half a century of chaos might have been avoided. But Morelos was a generation ahead of his class and ahead of his time.

Morelos won many skirmishes, but he could never decisively defeat the Spanish army. Moreover, as a general he was responsible for many prisoners being executed in cold blood. This set a precedent which was repeated in every revolutionary campaign in Mexico's future history. In the end Morelos himself was captured and shot.

Hidalgo and Morelos are both glorified in Mexican history as great national heroes. Hidalgo was the initiator of the movement for independence (although he renounced it all when he lay in prison awaiting execution), and Morelos was the patriot martyr who announced the country's independence and called out loudly for fundamental social reforms.

Neither man was a model of achievement. Both were martyrs, and there are too many martyrs in the history of Mexico. A well-known

Mexican writer, referring to Morelos alone, adds: "To elevate to the highest peak of patriotic fame a person who suffers such blemishes, subtracts authority for us to demand of the officials and leaders of our own day that they display the elemental virtues of honorable men. For, how can we ask of the ordinary governing official that which is not demanded of the national hero?" [33]

The writer of these lines, José Vasconcelos, then adds bitterly: "Morelos accomplished more than Hidalgo, but Hidalgo had not done anything. The only object of any war is to win it." These words may be too harsh and somewhat misleading. But certainly neither Hidalgo nor Morelos ranks in caliber or character with Bolívar, Washington, or San Martín. Bolívar, for example, never had one-fourth the number of soldiers of Hidalgo, yet he liberated half a dozen countries. Washington and San Martín had even fewer men.

As a result of the glorification of Hidalgo and Morelos, several things have happened. First, the great stress placed in Mexican history on "dying for the country," a phrase that is familiar in song and story is repeated today even by school children who hardly know the meaning of the word. While the fact, of course, is that one should not die for one's country, but should live for it in order to make it grow in strength and liberty. Second, the way in which the insurgent patriots executed prisoners and let their followers get out of hand and loot whole cities opened the way for the wholesale shootings and lootings which characterized the history of Mexico for the next hundred years, right into the twentieth century. Third, while the arousing of racial antagonisms (to spark the revolt) might have been a historic inevitability, the blind direction of these hatreds stirred up the worst aspects in the character of the Mexican masses. These worse aspects soon came to dominate the nation. The Indians and Indianist mestizos, now that they had a taste of being soldiers, were reluctant to return to a subservient life. Soldiering became the national profession. After Hidalgo and Morelos died, they were soon replaced by Iturbide and Santa Anna, scoundrels of the first water. Not long thereafter came Porfirio Díaz, and after him the bloodiest revolution of them all. Mexico had embarked on a course of savagery and chaos which made anything of Spanish colonial times seem pale by comparison.

Mexican independence was achieved by Agustín de Iturbide, political opportunist par excellence. He was a well-born Creole who had left school because of idle and vicious habits. Then he became a soldier, and when Hidalgo's revolt broke out he was a young lieutenant of twenty-seven. There had been some talk of his "parlor liberalism," so Hidalgo offered him the rank of lieutenant general in the revolutionary forces. Iturbide must have sensed how the wind would blow, and refused the offer. In fact, he took arms against the insurgents and won several small victories. Soon he became "Colonel" and eventually "General" Iturbide and was placed in command of the districts of Guanajuato and Michoacán. He was thoroughly disliked by the citizenry of the areas under his command. In Guanajuato he speculated in articles of prime necessity and ordered sold at ridiculous prices the grain supplies of several haciendas. In his personal life he was arbitrary, cruel, dictatorial, and untrustworthy. Complaints against him now came so fast and furiously that he was removed from his command and transferred to Mexico City, where he was put on trial. But the trial lagged and Iturbide was neither condemned nor reinstated.

In 1820, the king of Spain, who had returned to the peninsula after the defeat of Napoleon (1814), was forced to recognize a liberal constitution. Immediately, the conservatives in Mexico placed the government of the country in the hands of the conservative viceroy, who was enjoined to rule according to the old colonial laws. However, freedom of the press was declared and the Inquisition was abolished. It was manifestly impossible to block completely the path of progress.

There was still in field one noteworthy insurgent general, Vicente Guerrero, in the area of Acapulco. The viceroy looked about for an apt leader to demolish Guerrero, and his eyes fell on Iturbide, who was selected for the job. With a sizable force at his heels the new commander, now exonerated from all his crimes, went after Guerrero. But, instead of meeting Guerrero in battle, he negotiated with him, and together they issued a proclamation declaring Mexico to be a free and sovereign nation. It was agreed that she was to be governed by a monarch, of the House of Bourbon, which ruled in Spain. The new Mexican government would embody three guarantees: the Roman Catholic religion, independence, and a *rapprochement* between Mexicans and Spaniards. "Liberty, Union, and Religion" made an appealing battle cry.

Iturbide had played his cards with consummate skill. He appeased the clergy, appealed to the Spaniards, and deceived the Mexicans. The majority backed him with enthusiasm. Without fighting a real battle he had achieved (*a*) the independence of Mexico and (*b*) the undisputed leadership of the new state. Negotiations for a Spanish prince were dropped, and Iturbide rose rapidly from generalissimo to His Highness to Emperor Agustín I of Mexico.

Opposition now began to show itself: Iturbide had overstepped the mark, and substituted himself for Spanish royalty. Among the members of the opposition was an aged and liberal friar, Fray Servando de Teresa y Mier of Monterrey, who had just returned to Mexico after three decades of exile. He was promptly elected to the Mexican Congress. Fray Servando was a man of unflinching intellectual convictions. He had been deported from Mexico for having openly expressed his doubt of the miracle of the Virgin of Guadalupe. In Congress he began immediately to hack away at the regal affectations of Iturbide with the edge of his mordant wit. People at first smiled cautiously, then laughed, and finally applauded. The stalwart friar was clapped into jail, but the seeds of discontent were already widely sown.

A few months later, when one of Iturbide's own leading military supporters, General Santa Anna, joined the opposition, the emperor was forced to flee the country. He had remained in power for a couple of years (1821–1823). The following year he returned to Mexico, hoping to recoup his fortunes, but on this occasion he was caught, given a summary trial, and shot. He was the third revolutionary leader whose life had come to an end before the firing squad.

The Emperor Iturbide had brought forth another reprehensible element which was to mar the progress of Mexico until our own times: large-scale embezzlement of public goods. Add this to the emotional savagery of the hordes that backed Hidalgo and Morelos and you have the two outstanding characteristics of the Mexican political scene for the next hundred years. With this beginning, therefore, Mexico was launched on her way as a sovereign state. Independence was the only boon that she had gained at the cost of nearly all the rest.

During the next fifty-five years—between Iturbide (1821) and Porfirio Díaz (1876)—Mexico had two emperors, forty presidents, and half a dozen provisional governments. It was the arena of every violent passion of every political party and suasion. However, among the dozens who rose briefly to the top, only to disappear in smoke, three men were of outstanding significance in the national government during the nineteenth century:

Antonio López de Santa Anna, *The Scoundrel* (1832–1855)
Benito Juárez, *The Reformer* (1855–1872)
Porfirio Díaz, *The Despot* (1876–1911)

The careers of these three men characterized Mexican history for a century after the wars for independence.

López de Santa Anna, The Scoundrel

Santa Anna, the Creole, was perhaps the most miserable political clown ever to govern Mexico. He strutted across the national stage for nearly half a century, coming and going like the flashbacks of a repeated nightmare. Once he had himself dubbed "His Most Supreme Highness." Under Santa Anna the country merely continued its old colonial pattern, except that now Creoles instead of Spaniards held the positions of highest power. The masses who had fought and died for independence had achieved only a change of masters. Mestizo government was delayed for more than a generation. And if this were not enough, Santa Anna lost half the territory of Mexico to the United States: first Texas, and then New Mexico, Arizona, and California were cut off from the Mexican tree.

During the government of Santa Anna, Mexico went through her formless years. She was a republic in theory, but a reality of chaos. A corrupt militarism dominated the country. Four times the Mexican people wearied of the grandiloquent gamecock antics of this "Napoleon of the West," and four times they deposed and exiled him from the country. But, finding no substitute, four times they restored him to power. He lived through the Reform War, the empire of Maximilian, the presidency of Benito Juárez. He was almost indestructible. The last time he returned to Mexico uninvited, and wandered down the streets of the capital, wooden leg and all, no one recognized him. In 1876, the very year that Porfirio Díaz became president, he died in obscurity and poverty in the city where he had ruled so shabbily for thirty of the sorriest years in the history of the Mexican people.

One episode in the life of Santa Anna is noteworthy for the effect which it still has on our lives today. In 1855 the general left Mexico with 100 trunks and 12 servants and spent several months of exile in the United States. While in this country he hired an American secretary, James Adams, a resident of New York. Adams noticed that the general was constantly chewing on something which he never swallowed. He was told that it was chicle, sap from a tree that grew in the jungles of Yucatán. A sudden idea hit Adams like a bombshell. He got together all the money he could beg or borrow, imported several bales of chicle, added a few popular flavors, and started the chewing gum business in the United States. It developed, as we all know, into a billion-dollar industry. Santa Anna had given chewing gum to the United States. It was perhaps the only worthy bequest of one of the greatest scoundrels of Latin-American History.

Returning to a more serious tone, during the governments of Santa Anna several national problems began to come to a head:

1. The mestizos had fought and won the revolution, but the Creoles had taken over the government of independent Mexico. The society of the grand old aristocrats was replaced by the society of the upstart generals. Santa Anna commissioned over 10,000 army officers.

2. The church tried to shake off its back the royal control which had given the kings of Spain the right to appoint the higher church officers. The Creole government latched onto this control, and refused to relinquish it. Thus began the church-state conflict in independent Mexico.

3. The Central Highlands of Mexico, the country's heartland and corn basket, were under the control of the federal government, but the rest of the country was floundering about in various stages of local bossism, with precious little linking to the federal government. Mexico, in a word, was not yet a nation.

4. The economic situation of the people was extremely miserable. As Madame Calderón de la Barca recorded, "there was hardly a connecting link between the blankets and the satins." Independence brought with it no change of social status; it was purely political.

5. In the sphere of government, demagogy had taken the place of statesmanship, verbiage the place of reason.

Point number three bears further comment. The government of sovereign Mexico resided in the Central Highlands; from this center it must slowly spread itself toward the periphery. It must repeat the process of the Spanish conquest of Mexico. But in early colonial days every Spaniard in the country was the epitome of his nation; and the Spaniards all together constituted a united hard-hitting force which recognized no obstacles. Now things were different. The Creoles were in the governing chair, but there were also Spaniards, and mestizos, and Indians. All these were *Mexicans*. Yet only in name were they united; it was a far cry from the close union of the early Spaniards. Consequently, the central government could not control the periphery, great parts of which inevitably were sloughed off the national territory before the Mexicans began to think of themselves as a nation.

In the United States exactly the reverse had happened. The new nation here occupied the periphery, a very thin strip of land along the Atlantic seaboard. This territory was firmly consolidated and united. From the periphery the Union's course was to move slowly toward the west into then unsettled land. As the frontier edged westward, the American dream was planted in the wilderness, and the new nation emerged rooted firmly in the traditions of its first independent government.

Mexico's first government was not a thing to give inspiration to any people. And Mexico's periphery was already firmly colonial and Indian-Spanish. When the new state tried to establish itself upon the old way of life it met with deeply rooted obstacles on all sides. Tradition everywhere obstructed the path of progress. Hence, the United States and Mexico began their lives under entirely different conditions, which may help to explain their very different histories in the nineteenth century. The United States, democratic, stable, expanding, became the land of promise to Europe's downtrodden masses, and 40 million immigrants poured into the open door during the next 150 years. Chaotic Mexico received a bare 200,000.

The two wars in which Santa Anna's administration engaged, first against Texas, then against the United States, were hardly of world-shaking consequence. But their importance for our two peoples is profound and shocking. There is scarcely a Mexican today who respects Santa Anna, and there were many Mexicans in his own day who thoroughly despised him. One of these men was Lorenzo de Zavala, a distinguished writer and liberal, who had served as governor of the state of Mexico. When Santa Anna became dictator of the country, Zavala fled to the outlying Mexican province of Texas. Here he corroborated what the people had already heard about the rank corruption of the central Mexican government. It was futile, he said, ever to expect reasonable treatment at the hands of that group of scoundrels. Zavala's eloquent oratory was an important influence in fanning the flames of discontent and separatism in Texas. Later, when that state did declare its independence of Mexico (1836), Zavala, the mestizo Mexican, was elected its first vice-president. There was no racial antagonism between the Anglo-Saxon and Mexican settlers in Texas at that time.

Santa Anna changed all this overnight. His capture of the Alamo and slaughter of its defenders may be excused according to the rules of war, for this was a fight to the death. But at Goliad, when 347 soldiers surrendered, and the terms of their surrender were duly signed by the commanders on both sides, Santa Anna had the lot of them butchered in cold blood. The Alamo and Goliad were the fuses that inflamed the fanatical fires of prejudice and racial venom, which ignorant Anglo-

Saxons soon turned against all Mexicans regardless of their station.

A decade later Mexico engaged in a war with the United States. This was beyond a doubt the most unjust war in which the United States ever took part. Our own history books at last have the decency and honor to describe this conflict as it actually took place. Ulysses S. Grant, by no means noted as a great humanitarian, participated in the Mexican campaign as a young lieutenant. In his memoirs, written many years later, he referred to the war as "one of the most unjust ever waged by a stronger against a weaker nation. . . . Even if the annexation itself [of Texas only] could be justified, the manner in which the subsequent war was forced on Mexico cannot. . . . We were sent to provoke a fight, but it was essential that Mexico should commence it."

Many distinguished North Americans opposed the war vigorously. Thoreau was slapped into jail because he spoke out too loudly against it. Abraham Lincoln, who was then a member of Congress, voted for a resolution thanking the officers of the armed services for their gallant conduct "in a war unnecessarily and unconstitutionally begun by the President of the United States."

However, not all of the American soldiers were honorable and gallant. What Santa Anna's men had done in Texas, they repeated in Mexico. Captain Kirby Smith, later a distinguished Confederate general, who took part in the War with Mexico, wrote in words of burning shame and disgust of the raping of women and shooting of Mexican civilians. And U. S. Grant, after dwelling on the duties of a good soldier, added these words: "I know the struggle with my conscience during the Mexican War. I have never altogether forgiven myself for going into that. I had very strong opinions on the subject. I do not think there was ever a more wicked war than that waged by the United States on Mexico. I thought so at the time, when I was a youngster, only I had not the moral courage to resign. . . ."

Benito Juárez, The Reformer

Santa Anna abdicated and fled from Mexico in 1855; symbolically, he traveled in a ship named *Iturbide*. The leader of the liberal opposition which had deposed his Most Serene Highness was Benito Juárez. From that day until the year of his death (1872) Benito Juárez was the outstanding leader of his country. Juárez was a full-blooded Zapotec Indian. As a boy he had come down from the hills into the city of Oaxaca. He worked as a houseboy. There was a burning light in his deep brown eyes. His diligence, honesty, and intelligence appealed to his master, and he was given an education. At first he studied for the priesthood, but later gave it up for a career in law. As a lawyer he was soon known far and wide as a man of scrupulous honesty; before long he had become the governor of his state. He kept open house, and received complaints from the poor Indians and mestizos in person. He was deeply loved by the masses. One of his greatest admirers in those days was a young mestizo named Porfirio Díaz, who later became dictator of Mexico.

Benito Juárez represented a new psychological element in the national life. He was an Indian, but he had not been educated as an Indian. He was a Hispanized Indian, that is, an Indian with the mestizo outlook and the mestizo psychology. The Indians looked up to him because of his race, the mestizos respected him because his leadership vindicated their Indian blood. Both Indians and mestizos admired him because of his political liberalism and his personal integrity. Benito Juárez was the ideal man to bring mestizo rule to Mexico, a country in which the mestizo class represented the most progressive element of the population. It was poetically fitting that this mestizo rule should be embodied in the form of a humble Indian, for thus it became doubly effective.

Up to the time of Juárez the Catholic Church had enjoyed enormous economic and political power in Mexico, both in the colony and in the independent state. During the administrations of Santa Anna there had been some jockeying for control of the Church's temporal power, but little had been done about it. The Creole class was divided on this point, and this cleavage finally assured the triumph of Benito Juárez. The historian Pallares summarizes the wealth of the Church as follows: the clergy had a capital of more than 150 million pesos, and an annual income from it of 8 million pesos; the bishop of Mexico received a yearly income of 130,000 pesos, the bishop of Puebla 110,000 pesos, the the bishop of Michoacán 90,000 pesos, the bishop of Jalisco 35,000 pesos, etc. The total federal budget was only 24 million pesos a year, and the president and other ranking officers of the state never received more than 36,000 pesos a year. These figures refer to the early years of Benito Juárez.

A few years later the Abbé Testory, chaplain general of the French army which had entered Mexico in order to support the Emperor Maximilian, wrote as follows:

"When in 1856 the law for the sale of the clergy's property was proclaimed, the amount of that property was already enormous. The fortune owned by religious orders reached the sum of 200,000,000 pesos; the income from that property plus tithes, voluntary contributions, fees, the proceeds from dispensations, altar offerings, etcetera, gave the clergy every year a revenue greater by far than that of the state itself. It is not, then, to be wondered at, that the state looked upon this vast wealth as an obstacle in the path of public prosperity. . . . Consequently, we may assert without hesitation that the state was strictly within its rights when it expropriated the property of the clergy on the ground of public welfare. . . ."

Maximilian and his empress were both good Catholics, but when the papal nuncio arrived in Mexico in order to size up the situation he was very firmly told that the conflict was essentially an economic one, that it had nothing to do with church dogma, and that they strongly supported the government of Mexico in its attempt to break up the tremendous vested interests of the Mexican clergy.

In order to put an end to this temporal power of the church and in order to give lands to the dispossessed masses, Juárez initiated the Reform Movement (*La Reforma*). In 1856 a law expropriating church and other corporate lands was passed. The liberal constitution of 1857 embodied and recapitulated this reform legislation. Church lands were to be confiscated and sold, education was to be directed by the state, cemeteries were secularized and placed under the newly created Department of Public Health, religious liberty was proclaimed, civil marriage was approved, special courts for church and army officers were abolished. The constitution made one colossal error: it expressly expropriated *all lands* owned by corporations or groups. The intent was to expropriate church-owned lands without making specific mention of the church. But, as stated, the law also included the communal lands of the Indians.

The church reacted violently, and all who supported the "iniquitous" constitution of 1857 were threatened with excommunication. Churches were closed to liberals and their supporters. The Pope himself came out and condemned the constitution in the strongest terms. Mexico now split into two clear-cut camps: those favoring the new constitution and those against it. That is, the liberals and the conservatives, the anticlericals and the proclericals.

The church-state conflict in Mexico now began in earnest. The two parties were soon joined in mortal combat, which was known as the War of the Reform. It lasted until 1860, when Juárez and the liberals were victorious. One noteworthy weapon in that conflict was the Reform Laws of 1859, proclaimed by Juárez, whose forces then were in Veracruz while the conservatives still held Mexico City. These laws were an even stronger blow against the church. They specifically nationalized church properties without compensation, separated church and state, suppressed all monasteries and nunneries, prohibited priests and nuns from appearing in their traditional habits.

These Reform Laws had three immediate effects:

1. They showed that the liberals did not mean to yield ground, but that, on the contrary, they would push the struggle against the temporal power of the clergy to its conclusion.

2. The Reform Laws showed that the new class of mestizo intellectuals could strike out at vested interests of the church without being smitten from heaven.

3. The Reform Laws specified the nationalization of church properties and annulled the unpalatable expropriation of communal village lands. Up to this time many Indians had supported the clergy; now they threw their undivided support behind Juárez, and a liberal victory was assured.

In theory, the liberal constitution of 1857 and the Reform Laws of two years later had decreed the end of the feudalistic structure of Mexican society. The lines of the struggle to achieve this social revolution were now clearly drawn, but it would be nearly a century before the theoretical dream became an economic and social reality.

XI

NATIONHOOD: DREAM AND RESPONSIBILITY

The Mexicans united behind Juárez because of his personal integrity and the vigor of his convictions. Benito Juárez was worthy of the role which history offered him. He was a man who deserved his Plutarch, a man of whom any nation might well be proud.

—EMILIO OLLIVIER, Minister of Napoleon III

AT THE time when Mexico gained its independence there existed no such thing as the Mexican people. Much less was Mexico a nation. The country was a formless mass, split into many classes and economic groups, mutually distrustful each of all others. In the United States federation had meant integration; in Mexico it meant disintegration. Our motto *e pluribus unum*, "one out of many," became in Mexico "many made out of one." [10]

Under Juárez a new psychological spirit and a real sense of nationhood began to arise. The invasion of Mexico by the French under Maximilian quickened the process. Many exiled Mexican conservatives had appealed to Napoleon III of France to place a European prince on the Mexican throne. The United States was engaged in civil war and could not interfere. Maximilian of Austria, a Hapsburg, was selected for the job. He entered Mexico naïvely believing that the majority of the Mexican people wanted him to be their ruler. His advisers never let him believe otherwise. With their well-trained army the French captured Mexico City (despite a resounding defeat at Puebla on the famous Fifth of May) and then drove Juárez clear to the Texas border. Maximilian was almost the master of Mexico. The brief reign of this cultivated, well-meaning European prince (1864–1867) was merely an interlude in Mexican history, yet has left its mark on the physical beautification of the capital and on the psyche of the Mexican people.

Among the Mexicans only the most conservative supported Maximilian. The moment the French army withdrew from Mexico his downfall was inevitable. To all classes in Mexico Maximilian was a foreigner, an invader, a symbol of that very European domination which they had already fought one bloody war to end. Opposition to Maximilian slowly united Mexico; the war forged Mexican nationality. The more Juárez was defeated on the field of battle the higher rose the Mexican people's admiration and respect for him. He became the hope of all Mexicans fighting the foreign invader. He became a symbol of Mexico herself, an ennoblement of her Indian blood, no longer inert and silent but now standing with dignity and honor before the world.

The sequence of events was fast and furious: in 1865 the Civil War in the United States came to an end, in 1866 the French army began to withdraw from Mexico, in 1867 Juárez surrounded the remnants of Maximilian's force at the city of Querétaro and took the emperor prisoner. A short time thereafter Maximilian was given a summary trial, found guilty of usurping the government, and executed. He died like a man. He went to each member of the firing squad and gave them a few gold coins that he had with him. He begged them to shoot at his heart. Then he made a little speech saying he had really come to love Mexico and had always tried to do his best to govern her wisely and with justice. He concluded with the words: "*¡Viva México!*" The shots rang out, but the riflemen were nervous. Maximilian was not dead. He writhed in pain. They came closer and killed him. The invasion was over, the empire had ended.

Juárez presided over a nation in ruins. In his black carriage he returned to the capital and took up the reins of power. In that same year (1867) he was elected to his third term as president. Less than twenty thousand votes were cast in the entire country. Juárez labored unceasingly for the betterment of his people. He built schools, distributed lands, re-established justice. Austere and implacable as a pagan god, he distributed no political favors. There were flurries of revolution, but Juárez suppressed them quickly. His face had become saddened, inscrutable. He was not what the Mexicans refer to as a *persona simpática.*

The constitution of 1857 was much too idealistic for Mexico. Besides its advanced social legislation, this document imposed on all males over twenty-one years of age the "obligation to vote." It established universal male suffrage in a country that was 90 per cent illiterate. Therefore, we have the grotesque situation that in order to carry out the constitution and hold an election it was *necessary to violate the constitution.*[25] This simply turned the polls into a mockery. Since the illiterate masses supposedly had to vote in order for there to be an election, a handful of political bosses (representing the government slate, of course) merely voted in the names of all of them. In 1872, when Juárez presented himself for a fourth term, the usual electoral fraud was repeated. This time the President had two opponents: Porfirio Díaz and Lerdo de Tejada. Juárez was re-elected, but there was a widespread belief that he had not indeed received the majority of the votes of those who had in truth cast their ballots. Díaz rebelled, and Juárez whipped him in the field. One night shortly thereafter Juárez slumped over his desk with what looked like a heart attack; a few hours later he was dead.

With Benito Juárez was solidified the sentiment of Mexican nationality. With him the mestizo class was elevated to rule the nation. With him the Indian blood of the Mexican people was vindicated. With him the church-state conflict in Mexico was fiercely joined. With him was born a strong program of social reform. And with him also there emerged a new tradition in Mexican politics: the government candidate was bound to win in any election. This tradition still plagues the more enlightened Mexico of today.

Porfirio Díaz, The Despot

Porfirio Díaz was the most efficient dictator in Latin American history. Mexicans of the old regime, dissatisfied with everything that has taken place in Mexico during the past fifty years, still sadly wag their heads and say, "Ah, the good old days of Don Porfirio! Now, there was a man for you!" And part of what they remember is true. What they do not remember is truer still.

In the days of Porfirio Díaz business hummed in Mexico, harbors were dredged, thousands of miles of rails were laid, trains ran on time, bandits were suppressed, capital was secure, the Indian was kept in his place, and the hacienda owner lived off the fat of the land. Mexico was about as safe for the foreign (or native) investor as things ever get on this unreliable planet. Therefore, we have the legend of Díaz the builder. Tolstoi referred to Don Porfirio as "the solitary silhouette of a modern Cromwell" and said he "possessed the reconstructive force of the English Puritan without his fanaticism." Andrew Carnegie and Cecil Rhodes called him one of the world's great builders; and Theodore Roosevelt, who admired the big stick, also lifted his voice in praise, as did the German Kaiser.

Elihu Root, Secretary of State under the first Roosevelt, visited

Mexico not many months before the fall of Díaz, and stated that of all men living Don Porfirio was the one most worth seeing. Then fulsomely he added: "If I were a poet I would write eulogies. If I were a musician I would compose triumphal marches. If I were a Mexican I should feel that the steadfast loyalty of a lifetime could not be too much in return for the blessings that he had brought to my country. As I am neither a poet, musician nor Mexican, but only an American who loves justice and liberty and hopes to see their reign among mankind progress and strengthen and become perpetual, I look to Porfirio Díaz, the President of Mexico, as one of the great men to be held up for the hero-worship of mankind."

As these men spoke, and as the superstructure of Mexico became so attractive before the world, the people who raised it, the dispossessed masses of Mexico who had given their very souls to make it so, were withering away. The country was building on sand. Back of the façade the structure was weak—gorgeous stage decorations covering the hull behind it.

A Mexican author comes closer to seeing the true picture: "Díaz made Mexico presentable before the world. He gave her a good bath, for she stunk to high heaven with all the filth of her revolutions, and then he dressed her in clean clothes in order to present her to the other civilized nations. On the other hand, if Don Porfirio was an admirable tamer of wild beasts, he completely lacked the spirit to give a soul to his work." [27]

Yet Díaz was the greatest of all the Latin-American *caudillos*. He was also one of the most astute politicians that Latin America has produced. He was the symbol of the mestizo class now elevated to the presidential chair. From this position of eminence he was able to make Mexico presentable before the world. He did not rush things too fast nor did he too openly oppose political reforms. He played parties, factions, and individuals against one another with consummate skill, never placed his own trust in anyone, and achieved his own ends like the octopus, literally encircling and suffocating his opponents.

In 1871 when Juárez defeated him in the field Díaz' stock sank to rock bottom: there is no political popularity that can resist defeat. But the man who replaced Juárez, Lerdo de Tejada, was of a haughty mien, superior, disdainful. He very quickly alienated his supporters. Díaz bided his time, waited patiently, and built up his reputation. In 1876, when Lerdo decided to succeed himself, Díaz led the revolt against him, and this time he was successful. Díaz was still a liberal, but many conservatives supported his rebellion against the unpopular government. As leader of a victorious revolution he was the inevitable candidate for president, and was overwhelmingly elected.

Juárez had given Mexico nationality, autonomy, agrarian reform, and had left her with a tradition of electoral fraud. Díaz made full use of the last of these and got himself elected not once but seven times. Up to 1900 he would undoubtedly have won any election, but none of the elections was legitimate, because the constitution of 1857 made honest elections impossible. Díaz entrenched this illegitimacy by perpetuating himself in power as long as he was able, for a period of nearly thirty-five years.

Díaz was a man who knew how to use the catchwords of the day to achieve his own purposes. It was an epoch of positivism in Mexican thought, and the positivists (called the *científicos* in Mexico) believed (*a*) in Darwin's idea of the survival of the fittest, (*b*) that in Mexico they were the most fit, and (*c*) that the fittest were given by nature the right and the duty to rule the not-so-fit, who, of course, were the Mexican masses. The positivists also believed ardently in order and progress, the "scientific" way to hasten the evolution of human society. Díaz capitalized on this current of thought and began to preach *Nada de política y mucha administración* (*No politics and plenty of administration*). He also made a fetish of the two positivist catchwords: *Order and Progress,* with a capital "O" and a capital "P." And as more than one Latin American has pointed out, this has been the panacea of many a Latin-American dictatorship, its *raison d'être,* its justification, its perpetuation.

Why are Latin Americans so taken in by abstract ideas? Why do they so often fail to see the natural end results of these ideas or ideals? It is because among peoples who are not truly equipped for democratic government theory and ideals are bound to have a tremendous value in drawing up *programs.* And it is on the basis of programs that many a government has risen or fallen. Among the Latin Americans, impassioned as they are for ideals, these have frequently been the very soul of the most intense conflicts and the deepest revolutions.

Porfirio Díaz went the idea-mongers one better: his program became a reality. He not only promised Mexico "Order and Progress" but delivered them in full measure. Little wonder that his reputation soared to the zenith.

Díaz put an end to the long period of revolutions, he crushed Mexican militarism, suppressed banditry, brought Mexico a long period of peace such as she had not known since the end of the colonial epoch. During these years of peace he went zealously about the task of material progress. Mexico entered a period of growth such as she had never experienced before in her entire history. Some of the achievements of the Díaz regime in this order are truly amazing. The table below comparing the Mexico of 1876, when Díaz took over, with the Mexico of 1910, when his government began to crumble, is self-explanatory:

1876	1910
691 kilometers of rail lines	24,717 kilometers of rail lines
51,760,000 pesos of foreign trade	499,588,000 pesos (ten times as much
one bank, capital and assets of 2,500,000 pesos	32 banks, capital and assets of 764,000,000 pesos
Mexico bankrupt, in abysmal debt	136,000,000 pesos surplus in national treasury
7,500 schools	12,500 schools
federal income of 19,776,638 pesos	federal income of 111,000,000 pesos
5,000,000 pieces of mail carried	200,000,000 pieces of mail carried
$50,000,000 in U.S. investments	$1,000,000,000 in U.S. investments

The above table is indicative of the percentage of growth of Mexico in nearly every sphere of material progress. Cities were cleaned up, streets were paved, lands were drained, mines produced abundantly, sugar refineries sprang up all over the country, there were between seven and eight thousand factories, oil resources were developed, and Mexican credit was firmly established before the world.

When the naturalized Frenchman Limantour, who was Díaz' astute treasurer, floated a loan for $40 million in Europe, he was able to stand before the Mexican Congress and proudly state: "The present loan will have no special guarantee, will carry no collateral; the Government of the Republic backs it only with the name and credit of the nation."

Nor did Díaz neglect the small towns of Mexico. In every plaza a bandstand arose; property was secure and on Sundays there was music. Operatic melodies played by Indian brass bands mingled with native airs and drifted from the cast-iron rotundas across the low-flung plazas. A man could put a bag of gold on a donkey and travel from one end of Mexico to the other without being molested. The foreigner was again safe in Mexico, and for the first time in years the Mexican abroad did not have to feel ashamed of his country. A Mexican author of those days has written: "For the first time since the independence of Mexico, the Mexican traveler in Europe, in the United States, in any foreign land, heard only words of praise for his country and words of admiration for its government, and the traveler felt proud of his nationality." [25]

This certainly was no mean achievement for a single man. But in the meantime the political life of Mexico began to wither and fade. When Díaz said "No politics" he meant the words to be taken literally; he meant "No meddling." There was a more pointed phrase for it: "Bread or the club." He gave bread to those whose influence made such a gift advisable and he clubbed down those whose lack of influence made this course of action possible. In both cases he resolved the matter quickly. Díaz had his filthy prisons; he had his efficient police. No dictator has survived for long without these less savory appendages of the governing power.

At the beginning of his presidency Díaz was a liberal. He had supported the Reform Movement, had taken an active part in the war against the conservatives who opposed it, had fought bravely against Maximilian, and had for a time been the right-hand man of Benito Juárez, the Indian President. But Díaz was also a man of ambition. To wait patiently for his cue so that he might take his place in the apostolic succession of the presidency went somewhat against his grain. Nevertheless, this very enforced waiting taught him the means of effective control. When he led the revolt against the liberal Lerdo de Tejada, Díaz himself was a liberal using the support of the disgruntled conservatives to overthrow an unpopular government. But once in power he began to change his political views.

It was the old story of the liberal who attains power and then becomes a conservative in order to conserve the power that he has won. This is not only a psychological truism but a political fact, which history has proved over and over again. During his early years in office Díaz did give some lands back to the Indians, and his government was clearly aligned with the liberal party. But as the years passed and he surrounded himself with the better-heeled elements in Mexican life, it was hardly possible that the President would alienate these elements which he himself had created by continuing to support the impoverished masses. Certain portions of the Reform Laws and constitution which were objectionable to the persons who counted were allowed to remain dead letters. Anticlericalism was soft-pedaled. The country was made safe for foreign investors. Thousands of acres of oil lands were sold to American interests at $2 or $3 an acre. Wall Street looked at the Mexican dictator with a big smile. Financial indexes jumped 500 and 600 per cent. Never before or since has Mexico been such a bonanza for the American investor.

What, then, was the price? It is a fundamental law of economics that a society cannot get something without paying for it. What did Mexico pay for her progress under Díaz? The answer is not difficult to find, but it is a two-pronged answer. First, the best lands of Mexico were concentrated in the hands of a chosen few; second, in order that these lands might become productive, the Indianist masses, who made up 75 per cent of the population, were sold into debt peonage and made to till the soil for a pittance. Despite the amazing material progress of Mexico under Díaz, the kernel of *Diazpotism* lay in the buildup of the big hacienda. Under Díaz the hacienda became a way of life, and the vast majority of the Mexican rural population became landless peons.

When Juárez came to power the lands of Mexico were mainly in the hands of the Creole landowners, the clergy, and the communal Indian villages. These properties did not circulate, and the rising, ambitious mestizo class owned almost no lands at all. But under Juárez they did what the Creoles had long wanted to do: they began to take over the properties of the clergy. Resistance was immediate and violent, but in the end the mestizos won. Things were at this stage when Porfirio Díaz became President.

Diaz had been in power barely seven years when he began the systematic alienation of the Mexican lands. At first, the distribution was largely of public lands in order to encourage colonization (which failed), but when these public lands were exhausted the dictator passed on to the rape of the Indian villages. In other words, he exactly reversed the policy of the previous pro-Indian government of Mexico. He winked at the ownership of lands by the clergy and clamped down on all lands owned in common by the villages. In two circulars of 1889 and 1890 he declared categorically that all *ejido* lands must be broken up and distributed as private property. Thousands of *ejidatarios,* rural farmers who formerly had worked these lands in common, suddenly found themselves without the means of earning a living. The small plots of land which they received as individuals were not only insufficient for their needs, but they had no equipment to cultivate these parcels, and having pursued a co-operative economy for centuries they did not know how to farm as individuals. Nor did they have any conception of the meaning of private property. In this state of bewilderment most of the *ejido* lands slipped out of the hands of the Indians and quickly found their way into the hands of the large landowners or unscrupulous speculators.

According to the study of George McBride, over 14 million acres of Mexican land was given to seven *concessionaires* in the state of Chihuahua; another company received 12 million acres scattered over four states; in Lower California four individuals received 25 million acres; in Durango 5 million acres were divided by two recipients; and in Oaxaca four grantees received more than 8 million acres. By the end of the Díaz regime a total of 134.5 million acres, or almost 27 per cent of the total area of the republic, had been concentrated in the hands of a few individuals. These lands alone were more than the total *combined* areas of Great Britain and Western Germany. For this immense amount of land the government had received about $12 million, mostly in depreciated bonds, or about 9 cents per acre. When Díaz fell there were no public lands left in twelve of the states of Mexico, and very little in the entire country. The Mexican Luis Cabrera estimates that 90 per cent of the villages of the Central Highlands, Mexico's corn basket area, had no communal lands whatever. Probably 85 per cent of the rural population of Mexico was landless in 1910. The transition from a semi-*ejido* economy to an hacienda economy was an accomplished fact. Díaz, the mestizo, had oppressed the Indian more violently than the white Spaniards had ever done in three hundred years of colonial rule, and the new mestizo *hacendado* was a far more ruthless taskmaster than the worst *gachupines* had been. Mexico emerged from the Díaz regime with practically no public domain, no village commons, and with an impoverished and hopeless rural population. It was as if the country's very heart had been eaten out by a pernicious worm.

In the colonial period the hacienda had developed from the old Spanish land grants and the *encomiendas* of Indian labor. But the big-time hacienda that covered Mexico from one end to the other, the hacienda as a way of life, the hacienda that deprived the Indianist masses of their very sustenance, was the creation of Porfirio Díaz. Land was a far better gift than money, for while funds could easily be wasted, and the recipient come back for more, land produced its own income and gave the owner a definite social status. Since the days of Rome land had been the mark of the aristocrat. In the days of Díaz the mestizo landlord clung to his hacienda with a very special tenacity, for it was the outward and visible sign of his newly acquired status. It gave him security, income, prestige, servants, and power, a principality where he was a little king. It gave him fine horses, on which to display his equestrian skill, and a hardy outdoor way of life (when he was not in Mexico City or Paris) which appealed to his strong masculine instincts inherited from the conquistadores.

A hacienda in Mexico is a parcel of land of more than 1,000 hectares (about 2,250 acres). At the end of the Díaz regime there were 8,245 haciendas in Mexico. Three hundred of these contained more than 10,-000 hectares, 116 of them were of 25,000 hectares each, 51 haciendas contained approximately 30,000 hectares, and 11 haciendas contained more than 100,000 hectares each. The vast Terrazas estate in Chihuahua contained 13½ *million* hectares. It was approximately the size of the countries of Belgium, Holland, Switzerland, and Denmark *combined*. Thus, the agricultural wealth of Mexico was concentrated in the heads of approximately 10,000 families. In fact, a mere 834 haciendas occupied about 90 per cent of this land. Less than a thousand families owned most of Mexico. This Mexican *latifundismo* was a social plague without precedent in history. Not even in the days of Rome, Persia, or in feudal times did a single person own such vast estates. And Mexico, despite her phenomenal material development under Díaz, was still fundamentally an agricultural country. Not until the 1950's did she truly begin to enter the industrial epoch.

Díaz himself created a goodly number of these ten thousand haciendas. He not only helped to build them up but gave them protection before the law, security from revolution, and allowed them almost complete autonomy. Naturally, the *hacendado* class vigorously supported Díaz. The hacienda was an almost completely self-sustaining economic unit. It rarely had a resident population of less than a hundred persons, and frequently entire villages were included within its borders. While the arable land area was the heart of the hacienda, generally there were also woodlands, pastures, an orchard, many kinds of livestock, and of course a supply of water in the form of streams or lakes.

The hacienda also included a church, a store, a post office, a jail, a cemetery, and occasionally a school. The big house was an elaborate and picturesque building of massive stone or adobe walls, built around a huge patio. It had a red-tile roof and thick iron bars over the windows. It was comfortably and beautifully furnished, had a large retinue of servants, and was surrounded by a parklike garden. Off to one side were the huts of the peons, the granaries, stables, and shops. Invariably there were fine-quality horses, for horsemanship was one of the most attractive elements of hacienda life to the proprietors. While the *hacendado* grew rich, the peons ate beans and corn.

The hacienda produced all of its own needs except for a few luxuries imported by the owning family. Agriculture was carried on intensively, but not according to modern, scientific methods. Manual labor was used almost exclusively; the tools and methods were similar to those employed in Egypt four thousand years ago. Production was so inefficient that Mexico never produced enough corn for her own consumption. Many millions of dollars' worth of grains had to be imported every year in order to feed the people of Mexico. The great initial outlay of capital necessary for a more efficient production on these vast estates was unthinkable to the *hacendado*. Why go to such expense when the present primitive means of production more than sufficed to keep him and his family in velvet? In this way the hacienda agriculture slowly drained away the effective lifeblood of the nation. Díaz spoke much of "Order and Progress," but the economy of Diazpotism was in fact an economy of exploitation, not real development. The *hacendado* lived in luxury while the earth itself and the landless peons yielded up their last reserves of spirit and energy.

But the hacienda was no market, and herein lay another of its fundamental weaknesses. The mass of its workers were unable to buy anything except a few primitive necessities of daily life, which they had to purchase on credit at the *tienda de raya*, or hacienda store. A market of a mere ten thousand families in a country of several millions is but a drop in the bucket. Foreign investors had to be encouraged to enter Mexico on a large scale. Under the hacienda system it was manifestly impossible for the Mexicans themselves to develop their own country. With foreign investments and a top-heavy hacienda economy Díaz built up the surface progress of Mexico, but he stifled the possibility of a more widespread, more contented, and more economically productive labor force which in time would also have constituted a vigorous market. By forcing the growth of the country in the way that he did Díaz set back the natural development of Mexico for more than half a century.

The *tienda de raya* was an integral part of the hacienda economy. At this central store the peon bought his necessities, the cost of which was deducted from his pay on Sunday. Often, he received no pay at all at the end of the week. The few pesos in cash that he did receive (for fiestas, marriages, etc.) swelled still further the sum that he owed the *hacendado*. The peon made around 120 pesos a year and was lucky if he could get through the year without going into debt. Oftentimes his debts would reach four or five hundred pesos, a truly astronomical figure for the impoverished peon. He was reduced to virtual serfdom. It was all strictly against the law, but the peon had no standing before the courts. He did not even know that such rights were his in theory. His master could flog or kill him at will; he could seduce his daughters, enslave his sons. But before the courts the *hacendado* and the foreign investor always won the case. A psychological factor made this system of debt peonage even more effective. The illiterate Indian looked at the incomprehensible figures on the account books and was fascinated by them, as some people are fascinated by a snake. Accustomed as he was to being dominated for over three centuries by forces he did not understand, these strange characters exerted over him the potent influence of a malignant idol. He did not dare attempt escape; it would be defying destiny.

What was the actual economic situation of these peons and their families? They lived in one- or two-room huts without water, ventilation, or sewerage. The floors were of earth, the beds of straw mats, the kitchen usually in a lean-to outside, the diet was of corn and beans. Medical and educational facilities were almost completely lacking. There was a church, under the aegis of the *hacendado*. Since the 1790's the peon's daily wage had remained more or less stationary, between 25 and 35 centavos a day, but prices of the necessities of life had gone up by many hundred per cent: corn about 250 per cent; flour over 700 per cent, beans 600 per cent, etc.

In plain language it cost the peon and his family about four times as much to live in 1908 as it had in 1792, at the end of the colonial epoch, yet his income was essentially unchanged. The purchasing power of the average North American farm laborer at the turn of the century was about fourteen times as great as that of his Mexican counterpart. For each hour of work that he put in, the North American could buy 12 times as much corn, 15 times as much wheat, 19 times as much cotton cloth. It is hardly necessary to elaborate further on the wretched economic condition of the Mexican peon in the latter days of the Díaz regime. In reality there were two civilizations living side by side in Mexico under Porfirio Díaz: the twentieth century of the wealthy and cultivated minority and the twelfth century of early medieval serfs.

In spite of all this, Díaz slowly built up the myth of Mexico's modernity. Things looked impressive on the surface, but it was merely a façade, a false front, behind which lay a stinking shambles. Yet with peace, order, and wealth among the ruling few, upper-class culture also took a new lease on life. Writers of the previous generation had used their pens for a political purpose in order to bring about social reform. Now the outstanding Mexican authors turned their backs on social problems and made literature into an art form. In the movement known as *Modernismo* some of the greatest literary figures Mexico has produced wielded their ivory pens: Gutiérrez Nájera, the poet and marvelous writer of prose sketches and chronicles, Amado Nervo, editor of one of the country's most famous journals, and also a poet of finest quality, Díaz Mirón, Díaz Dufoo, Othón, and many, many others. In the long-winded novels of these days the Indian entered only as an element of local color. It was an upper-class literature, pure and simple.

This new generation of writers went hand in hand with the astonishing material progress of Mexico. In their poetry and prose they reflected the language of luxury. They produced an aristocratic literature of rare quality and exquisite grace. It was art for art's sake, divorced from the society around it. These writers wrote from their ivory towers which stood in the clouds high above the sordid social reality of Diazpotism. In an epoch of stability and upper-crust well-being they were the cream that rose to the top. Díaz was too astute a politician to pass up the opportunity to use these men in order to bolster his cause. He doled out government subsidies, made Amado Nervo the Mexican ambassador to several countries, kept the gifted pen either on his side or strictly neutral. He thus helped to build up the cultural façade, as he had already built the material surfaces of his nation.

The *modernista* writers of Mexico, however, did perform one essential function. They fused French and Spanish influences onto the Mexican rootstock and produced a literature which was the equal in beauty and power to that of any European nation. In achieving this they defined Mexico's new literary sensibilities and asserted their country's cultural independence from Europe. What the generation of liberators had achieved in a political sense, they achieved culturally. They took Mexican literature abroad and made it a thing to be admired. With them Mexican literature entered the mainstream of world letters. They gave dignity to the word *Mexican* in universal culture. By the very same token these writers, who might have been the intellectual leaders of their generation, were separated from the Mexican masses by an abyss. They expressed in refined language the agony of the individual but did not reveal the agony of the race. They did erect a beautiful façade fronting the stage of a Greek tragedy.

In the final years of his dictatorship Porfirio Díaz lost some of the political astuteness which had formerly been his greatest asset. The mass of the thinking people of Mexico, including the intellectuals and many members of the upper classes, had at last grown weary of his continual re-elections. Díaz was approaching eighty, and so far no successor was in sight. The words of Louis XVI of France must have been in the minds of many intelligent people: "After me, the deluge!" However, these same persons opposed the violent removal of Díaz from the presidency with the same vigor that they opposed (this not too openly) his continuance in power. The dictatorship, therefore, rested in very delicate balance.

As the historian H. B. Parkes has pointed out so pungently, the Díaz regime, apparently so invincible, was rotten with age. The President's policy of playing his followers and opponents off against each other had destroyed all internal cohesion in the government. Díaz himself was a respected administrator, but many of the less-important officials, especially the political bosses, were not. Two of the state governors were over eighty, six others were over seventy, sixteen more were over sixty. The generals were equally ancient, and the army was almost impotent. Díaz had boasted that he had killed militarism, and it was indeed true. The dictatorship needed new blood to survive, but the new blood was not found. In spite of all these things, Díaz as a person still enjoyed a very great popularity. The urban masses cheered the aged dictator when he appeared on the streets or on the balcony of the presidential palace. It was an almost unconscious reflex with them, for they saw in the proud old man the symbol of their newfound nation. The voiceless rural masses, who never saw Díaz at all, must have identified him in a bewildered sort of way with the long-continued misery of their state of life. It was these voiceless masses who held the balance of power, but it was first necessary that some individual awaken them to action.

Strangely, the first spark was thrown by an American journalist, James Creelman, but the real fire was started by a wealthy landowner of the North, Francisco I. Madero. Creelman had been sent to Mexico by *Pearson's Magazine* to interview Díaz. The interview was written up in the issue of March, 1908. Creelman referred to Porfirio Díaz as "the greatest man on the continent," he presented an impressive array of figures, and then quoted the President verbatim. Díaz said that he was not only willing but eager to find an intelligent successor. He had tried frequently in the past to leave the presidential chair, but the people would not let him.

"I can abandon the presidency of Mexico without the slightest pang; but I shall continue to serve my country as long as I live. . . . It is true that when a man has occupied a position of power for an extended period, he must begin to look upon it as his property, and it is good that a free people protect itself against the tendencies of personal ambition. . . . I can state sincerely that the position has not corrupted my political ideas, and that I still believe that democracy is the true and just principle of government; although it is possible only for the most advanced nations. . . ."

He concluded by stating that Mexico, he felt, was now ready for democratic government. The country had developed a middle class, and this class was numerous and intelligent enough to rule Mexico. He, Díaz, would welcome an opposition party, if it really meant to govern and not to exploit the people, and he would gladly aid such an opposition with his advice and even his support.

When this interview was translated and published in Mexico it had the effect of a bombshell. The Mexicans had gotten from an article published in English in New York the statement for which many of them had been waiting for many years. Francisco Madero, who was noted as a parlor liberal, took Díaz at his word, announced his candidacy, and headed the opposition. He wrote a book called *The Presidential Succession of 1910*, in which he praised Díaz to the skies, pointed out his complete personal honesty and admirable family life, then went on to call for honest elections and a one-term limit to the presidency. Madero waged a vigorous campaign, but when the election took place Díaz not only won hands down but failed to lose a single deputy. Madero received a grand total of 196 votes. He knew perfectly well that the election was dishonest. He did not hesitate to say so, and his campaign cry of "Effective suffrage and no re-election" still echoed on the streets. Díaz clapped him in jail, but a few days later turned him loose on bail. Madero jumped bond and fled to the United States. In San Antonio he drew up his proclamation calling on the people of Mexico to overthrow the dictatorship of Porfirio Díaz. In view of the obviously dishonest elections, he felt duty bound to take this action in order to keep faith with the people who had placed their trust in him.

Madero announced the exact day and hour that the revolution would begin. "On the 20th of the month of November, *at six o'clock in the afternoon*, all citizens of the Republic will take up their arms in order to throw out of power the authorities who are now governing us."

Madero crossed the border, but the revolution failed to materialize. In despair he returned to the United States and just as he was about to leave for Europe news reached him that a band of revolutionaries had defeated the federal troops in the state of Chihuahua. Pancho Villa was one of the rebel leaders. Madero returned to Mexico and the Revolution was under way. It is called in Mexico the Revolution with the capital "R" in order to distinguish it from the other armed uprisings which have so frequently marked the course of Mexican history. This Revolution was a veritable holocaust which swept over the land in blood and destruction, upsetting completely the social and economic fabric of the nation's life.

On the day when Madero, the softhearted idealist, met Pancho Villa, the blind force who killed with his bare hands, the two opposing poles of the Revolution began to stand forth. One Mexican writer has called them the Eagle and the Serpent: the Eagle, which represented the early ideals of those who rose in rebellion; the Serpent, that blind savagery which defeated their dearest dreams. The idealist intellectuals by their very nature made up the element which was least adapted to the struggle. For more than a decade Mexico was to be given a bath in blood until finally, exhausted, the fighting would stop and the country would again gropingly seek to find a peaceful way of life.

An outstanding Mexican economist of today, Jesús Silva Herzog, has written that the Revolution was caused by a hunger for land, a hunger for liberty, a hunger for justice, a hunger for bread. Madero's idealism, however, led him to view the struggle primarily in political terms: "The people are not asking for bread, they are asking for liberty." This misjudgment (and his soft heart) incapacitated Madero for effective government. With Villa's backing he soon entered the capital in a blaze of glory, but he survived as president only a few brief months (Nov. 6, 1911, to Feb. 19, 1913). The whole country was soon in an uproar. The nephew of President Díaz headed one rebellion, and in the state of Morelos Emiliano Zapata and his men refused to lay down their arms until they received both "land and liberty." Madero temporized, and failed. He did not execute the young Díaz, and he was unable to suppress Zapata. His supporters deserted him, the United States minister turned against him, he was captured by General Huerta and shot to death, a hapless martyr. The Revolution now entered its bloodiest phase. The "lyric" interlude of the idealist was over.

Carranza rose up and led the fight against the usurper Huerta, one of the vilest political leaders Mexico has ever produced. Zapata continued to fight in the south, Villa and Obregón in the north. First one, then another general dominated the national scene. Before the Revolution was over, three of them—Zapata, Carranza, and Villa—were assassinated. Obregón finally came out on top. But this was not until 1920, ten years after the first revolt against Don Porfirio. In the interim Mexico had lost nearly one million dead, many killed on the field of battle, many from disease and hunger, thousands of them from the world-wide epidemic of influenza. During this decade the population of the country actually decreased as the pillaging bands made any semblance of orderly life impossible.

The Revolution was born without a program. Madero had protested against electoral fraud and perpetual re-election, and Zapata added the cry of "Land and Liberty." But this hardly constituted a program. The generals and the Indianist soldiers who made up the revolutionary armies simply struck out against all authority; they sacked, burned, robbed, raped, and destroyed on a gigantic scale. In their blind and fumbling way they were perhaps groping toward some better social reality, but in the beginning they felt only a compulsion to uproot and to destroy. The old order must be peeled away, clean down to the core. The haciendas must be captured and gutted with purifying fire. The factories must be demolished, the churches pillaged, the women violated, the opposition (anyone who resisted) obliterated. It was a war with no quarter asked or given. Prisoners were shot by the hundreds.

One novel, *The Eagle and the Serpent*, by a writer who took part in the Revolution, Martín Luis Guzmán, contains a chapter called "The Fiesta of the Bullets," in which a Villa general enjoys telling a large group of prisoners to run for it, then shoots them down one by one as they attempt to scale a wall. After the fiesta has ended, his trigger finger is so swollen that he can hardly get it out of the pistol.

Another novel, *The Underdogs*, by Mariano Azuela, who also took part in the Revolution, describes the revolutionary leaders as bloodthirsty opportunists, caught up in the whirlwind. Each scene of this graphic novel is an etching of some bloody episode, punctuated only by the blind gropings of an occasional man who thinks, and so wishes to find some meaning to it all, or by the serene and everlasting beauty of the Mexican landscape, which is untouched by man's inhumanity to man. Azuela portrays the soldiers of the Revolution as Darwinian ants, engaged in a fierce struggle to determine the survival of the fittest. The positivism of the days of Díaz has now come to grips with the human reality; it is no salutary sight. Man walks hand in hand with death; he seems unworthy of the nature about him. Individual after individual dies, but the Revolution goes on. Mexico herself has reaped the whirlwind.

There were literally dozens of novels of the Mexican Revolution. A new kind of Mexican literature was born on the battlefields out of the emerging social reality. It was a literature full of blood and life and death. These novels broke with the European literary traditions. They were inspired completely by the contemporary scene. The author submerged himself and went about like a camera, catching the disjointed episodes which thrown together made up the Revolution. The writing was direct, impassioned; action was constant. In these novels the pistol was elevated to the position of a symbol; it was as important as Fate in Greek tragedy, as character in modern drama. The pistol decided everything; the pistol knew no appeal. The Indian masses, who had entered into the novels of the Díaz regime as mere elements of local color, were the heart and guts of these novels of the Revolution.

One of the characters in Azuela's novel, *The Underdogs*, looks down on a burning village, sees the smoke spiral upward into the clear sky, and watches a mob of ragged women dressed in black descend on the town to strip the bodies of the dead of their belongings. For a moment he feels that he is suspended at the core of death and life. The picture before him is the embodiment of natural law.

> "How beautiful is the revolution! Even in its most barbarous aspect it is beautiful," Solís said with deep feeling. Then a vague melancholy seized him, and speaking low he added: . . . "Robbery! Murder! What a colossal failure we would make of it, friend, if we, who offer our enthusiasm and our lives to crush a wretched tyrant, became builders of a monstrous edifice holding one hundred or two hundred thousand monsters of exactly the same sort. People without ideals! A tyrant folk! Vain bloodshed!"

This soldier knew the four horsemen of death. Perhaps he saw the vast outlines of a class struggle, the blind fighting of the masses against all power and wealth and privilege. Against the landlord, against the church, against the political bosses, against the government. But the Revolution was more than death. It was the birth of a new nation, it represented the pangs of birth on a gigantic scale. Mexico was torn bleeding from the umbilical cord. Only after this could the seeds which had been sown find a place to grow. The Revolution which had begun as a hunger came to an end as a regeneration. It revitalized the Indian past of

Mexico; it left the masses with a heritage of hope. It incorporated the Indian into the social, cultural, and economic fabric of the national life, no longer as a minor partner but as an equal. Juárez had elevated the mestizo; the Revolution placed the Indian beside him, and gave him land, the very bread of life, and liberty, which all men cherish.

The Revolution with the capital "R" was the first real social revolution in Latin-American history. With it Mexico became the leader of all the Indianist countries. Although the Revolution itself was long and savage, the gains achieved as a result of it were merely those which every advanced nation has long taken for granted: political justice, a fair distribution of lands, destruction of the feudal order.

Spanish colonialism, the chaotic beginning of Mexico's independence, and Porfirio Díaz—all these contributed their share toward making these problems so acute that only a revolution could resolve them. As the colonial period advanced, Spain herself began to fall out of step with the other nations representing Western civilization. While others went forward, she stood and watched, still cherishing the days of her glory. A set of values was developing in Western civilization which Spain with her poverty, her ignorance, her fanaticism, and her backwardness would not accept. Industrialization, economic progress, the growth of democratic ideas, improved working conditions, religious tolerance—these were the things that carried Western civilization forward as Spain lagged behind, nurturing her medieval dreams. Spanish literature is full of this feeling. The caustic pen of Mariano José de Larra blasts at Spain's intransigence and backwardness with a pen dipped in gall. This was in the 1830's. Sarmiento does the same in Argentina. In Mexico, Fernández de Lizardi, Francisco Zarco, Ignacio Ramírez, Benito Juárez, and dozens of others also blast at the old entrenched traditions which so urgently need a reform.

Mexico was only one country among many of this Hispanic civilization which had fallen to the rear. But in Mexico the problems were more acute because of the tremendous Indian population. Consider the reality: out of 15 million people, nearly 12 million Indians or Indianist inhabitants. And of these a bare 20 per cent could read or write. The amazing thing is not that Mexico took a century (1810–1910) to overthrow the old order, but that she was able to accomplish it at all. The nations of Europe had taken many centuries to achieve a sense of unity and nationality. Even with their homogeneous racial stock, they had split up into dozens of petty states which lasted from medieval times until the nineteenth century. Mexico, with a heterogeneous racial make-up and a huge Indian population at a completely different cultural level from that of the ruling class, was able to demolish the old order and achieve nationhood in approximately a century. She is now achieving a modern social and economic fabric at a more rapid rate than has been recorded by any other nation in the pages of history.

What about the many uprisings and revolutions which she has suffered? Is it fair to criticize Mexico for them? These revolutions have been the mark of distinction of the Mexican people, who had no other way to protest against the sterility of permanent despotism. The revolutions continued only until the people had won, and then they stopped. Mexico, democratic and progressive Mexico, has now enjoyed peace and order for several decades, and it is not a *pax romana,* a *pax porfiriana*—it is a *pax populi,* truly of the people.

XII

LAND AND LIBERTY

The right to be free is not sufficient; we must deserve to be free.

—Adolfo Ruiz Cortines, President of Mexico

Under the administration of President Carranza, on February 5, 1917, emerged the constitution under which Mexico lives today. It was promulgated on exactly the same date as the constitution of 1857, hence February 5 is one of Mexico's great holidays. This liberal constitution was an attempt to take the country in one great hurdle over the obstacles which had held her back for four centuries. While not immediately successful, its long-range power and influence have helped to guide the modern nation into the period of real peace and progress which she enjoys today.

Some of the most important parts of the constitution of 1917 are:

Villages which have been deprived of their *ejido* lands will have them restored. The word *ejido* is defined as "the waters, woods and lands which the village may need." The large haciendas will be broken up, their lands distributed to the peasants, and their owners compensated with government bonds.

The church will not be permitted to own real estate, or to engage in primary education. All primary schools are to be secular. All priests must register with the civil authorities. The state legislatures are empowered to limit the number of priests within their jurisdiction. Public education is the exclusive function of the government. Foreign priests are prohibited in Mexico.

The nation owns its subsoil and all mineral and oil rights therein. Only Mexican citizens may own lands or develop mines or wells. The nation will grant such rights to foreign nationals only on condition that they agree to become Mexicans before the law, who cannot ask for the protection of a foreign government.

Workers may form unions, bargain collectively, and strike. There is to be an eight-hour day, with double pay for overtime. The larger industries must provide schools for their workers' children. There is accident and sickness compensation. Certain minimum wages are established.

President Carranza began the redistribution of Mexican lands but was assassinated before he had carried the program very far. Obregón, who became President in 1920, the year generally given as marking the end of the Revolution, distributed approximately 3 million acres. President Calles, who followed him, distributed nearly 8 million acres; after 1929 there was a brief lag in the program, and it was not until Lázaro Cárdenas became President in 1934 that the problem was attacked on a grand scale. Cárdenas, on his retirement from office in 1940, announced that his administration had distributed 45,330,119 acres of lands. With some interruptions the program has continued up to the present, and a total of approximately 200 million acres have been given back to the communal villages and to small property owners. In some parts of Mexico 90 per cent of all cultivated lands are now organized as *ejidos*.

At first, these *ejidos* were extremely inefficient, for the natives had neither the tools, the capital, nor the experience to run them properly. The old traditions had been slowly strangled by the conquest, the colony, and most of all by Porfirio Díaz. It is not easy to turn a slave population into efficient farmers. During the past decade *ejido* agriculture has improved greatly, more scientific methods of tilling the soil have been introduced, and production had grown rapidly. Even so, in many areas there is a strong desire to create more small property owners, individuals with a personal pride in their own farms. This movement is particularly strong in the state of Jalisco.

Approximately 90 per cent of all *ejidos* operate on the "individual" basis, that is, the crop lands are distributed to families, and each family works its *parcela* as it wishes. The average size of these plots was for many years about ten acres. Actual ownership of the land resides in the community, and if the soil is not properly worked it may revert to the community. On most of these small plots only subsistence crops are raised, principally corn and beans. The "collective" *ejidos*, which are the really big ones, are worked on a co-operative basis. One of the largest, La Laguna, has a population of about 120,000 people; this *ejido* grows and markets cotton on a large scale. Collective farming, in theory, cuts down costs, provides better marketing, more social services, and easier credit. It can, and often does, produce a very unwieldy organization. The individually cultivated *ejidos* also have their group organizations, which appoint a leader or leaders who help the group get credit, obtain tools and seeds, market their crops, build up their schools and medical facilities, and so on. There is an Ejido Bank which lends funds to both the large and small groups; individuals have no *ejido* credit. Despite all this, La Laguna was a notable failure.

Some *ejidos* are show places, with every modern facility: up-to-date dormitories or apartments for the members, a hospital, dentist, school, motion-picture theater, public recreation hall, even a common dining room. Others are very poor communities, which seem on the border of starvation, as indeed many of them are. There are several reasons for this: erosion, which is a tremendous problem, unproductive soil, small plots, inefficient farming, bad organization. Mexico's forest lands, which should be holding the water, are being destroyed at a rapid rate. So are vast areas of so-called crop land. Thousands of acres yearly are being gnawed away. Furthermore, in many cases lands have not been distributed in such a way that they can be efficiently farmed. Ten acres, just because it is ten acres, will not give a family even a subsistence living in many parts of Mexico today. Thousands of *ejido* workers have already deserted their lands and are now working as farm or urban laborers, in which jobs they are able to earn an easier and a better living. Over a fourth of the *ejido* workers are at present engaged in either part- or full-time work off the *ejido*.

The larger "collective" *ejidos* also had a hard time getting started. Their workers were inexperienced, they had no tools, they were unused to working together. There was a great lack of trained agricultural specialists. The old *hacendados* paid their administrators $10,000 a year, and got the best. Naturally, the early *ejidos* balked at laying out any such sums as this for management, so for years they just floundered along.

However, the government has done everything in its power to help. It has established the Ejido Bank, made available many kinds of agricultural services, developed irrigation projects, built roads and highways, and helped in a dozen other ways. Perhaps the most important thing of all was to change Article 27 of the constitution so that the size of the plots distributed might be increased and their actual extension depend on the kind of soil involved in each individual instance. At present the National Constitution states that the individual unit or plot of the *ejido* grants *must not be less than* 25 acres of irrigated, or "wet," land or less than 50 acres of lands depending on seasonal rains, or less than 100 acres of dry land of good quality, or less than 200 acres of dry land classified as arid soil. This new manner of classification has done away with the major complaint of the *ejido* workers in regard to land distribution. The administration of President Díaz Ordaz has distributed approximately 57 million acres of land during the past six years. This has been parceled out in both small farms and *ejidos*, the average plot containing more than 100 acres, a far cry from the 10-

acre plots that characterized the early years of the Agrarian Reform program.

This has all paid off magnificently, for during the past two decades agricultural production has soared! The statistics are impressive; the last survey (1970) indicated that:

Per capita production of corn, beans and wheat, Mexico's essential foods, was twice that of 1950.

Corn and beans are in oversupply and large quantities of each are being exported.

Approximately 3 million rural families, consisting of some 15 million persons, have directly benefited from the government agrarian reform program.

Mexico's annual agricultural output in 1970 was worth 34 *billion* pesos, double that of 1960. Poultry production, 123 million birds a year, was up 50 per cent since 1964.

Mexican production in 1970 supplied 95 per cent of all farm products consumed in the national market.

Mexico has come a long, long way since the last days of Porfirio Díaz. But the land of Mexico is poor, and most Mexicans are still farmers. Eight million acres of newly irrigated lands have helped, but they have not solved the problem. The *ejido* was once looked upon as Mexico's way out. It was believed that a redistribution of land would turn a nation of serfs into productive individual farmers. It is now clear that much more than this is needed. Irrigation must be carried to every possible acre. Soil erosion must be controlled. Farming must be made more scientific, crops rotated, better seeds planted, more fertilizers used, better marketing facilities made available.

Little by little, all these things are being accomplished. Let us not forget that the United States has its dust bowl and its deserts on the march. Mexico has already made the most impressive progress in the face of the greatest possible obstacles. The many thousands of Mexican *braceros* (farm laborers) who have come to this country to work for a season or two, and have then been able to carry both money and experience back to Mexico, have also been a factor in pushing Mexican agriculture forward. This program, which came to an end in 1965, should be reinstituted and carried out under strict United States government supervision.

In conclusion it can be said with certainty that, while agrarian reform has not solved Mexico's agricultural problems, it has brought an immeasurable improvement over the old hacienda serfdom. No farm worker or his family would trade today's freedom for yesterday's vassalage and misery. Even under the worst circumstances (sadly, too many farms fall into this category) a man can now call his soul his own. Nothing in the world could ever make him surrender this priceless feeling that he has won for himself and his children.

The Revolution of 1910 marked the turning point in the social and cultural history of Mexico. The great Indian past of the country was awakened from a spiritual slumber of centuries. The progress of Mexico's indigenous culture, interrupted by the conquest, now resumed its march. By giving the Indian land and liberty, the Revolution gave him dignity as a human being and revitalized his long-dormant cultural creativity. Thus one of the most vital forces of contemporary Mexican life was rescued from the very doors of the tomb.

During the nineteenth century art was nearly dead in Mexico. The country was exhausted by the War for Independence, the chaotic years of Santa Anna, and the heroic struggles of Juárez. There was a small group of academic painters and a small group of folk artists. They produced a few interesting items here and there, but there was no real Mexican art. When Díaz re-established the landed aristocracy, academism flowered as never before. The wealthy *hacendados* not only collected European art but decided to send the most promising young Mexican artists to Europe to study. Francisco Goitia, Dr. Atl, Alfredo Ramos Martínez, and Diego Rivera were among those who went abroad. In 1889 when Mexico contributed a pavilion to the Paris Exposition she built it in Moorish style. The native arts were considered unworthy of attention. And the great artistic monument of the Díaz regime was the 7 million peso Opera House (now the Teatro de Bellas Artes), built of white Italian marble in a style reminiscent of nineteenth-century Paris and with a seating capacity for only a handful of the elite. Another and perhaps even more symbolic monument of Don Porfirio was the steel shell of an enormous "Legislative Palace," left in its skeletal state when the despot fled from Mexico. The giant hull of this building rusted away for many years before its wings were finally demolished and its central dome was transformed into today's Monument to the Mexican Revolution, an architectural atrocity now straddling the Avenida del Ejido.

In 1909, on the eve of the fall of Díaz, Diego Rivera and Dr. Atl returned from Europe, and a new breath entered Mexican painting. The young artists, inspired by these dynamic personalities and sensing the tormented state of their own countrymen about to be caught up in the whirlwind, broke out into a fever of productivity. Even the Revolution did not stop it, for these artists became the pictorial aspect of that mass upheaval, catching its writhings in permanent form and color. The great mural art of Mexico today was born of the Revolution.

During colonial days architecture was the supreme artistic expression. Society and culture moved in a broad hieratic stream, which suggested the European period of cathedral building when the spirit of an epoch was poured into the towering Gothic spires that rose above the mire of medieval villages. The lovely architecture of colonial Mexico captured the serene faith of those benighted times, and today's great art of fresco painting reflects the tortured struggle of the Mexican masses for a better way of life.

As a distinguished Mexican, Antonio Castro Leal, has put it: "On the Mexican walls were written the life of the people and the history of the nation, the silent tragedy of the humble and the sordid ambition of the wicked. Shining above all was the hope of a better world." [17]

The great mural painting of Mexico today did not spring full grown from a vacuum, nor from any mind of Zeus. During the latter years of the Díaz regime its main features were already beginning to emerge timidly from the academic chains that enthralled it. The fine landscape painter Joaquín Clausell, that master of poignant oils Francisco Goitia, and the superlative engraver José Guadalupe Posada, all contributed their fair share to the renaissance in Mexican art which the Revolution set free with its explosion.

The powerful political caricatures and grotesque skeletons of Posada captured in black-and-white woodcuts the stark reality of Mexican life. His macabre skeletons, which dominated so many of his cuts, were a prophecy of the bloodletting to come. Posada died in 1913, just as the most savage phase of the Revolution broke out. Francisco Goitia, one of Mexico's finest painters in oil, caught the social tragedy of his people in some of the most impressive canvases ever to come out of Mexico. At first, unable to pin down the feeling he sought in the parade of wretched faces that characterized his models, Goitia's attention one day fell on a woman wringing her hands. Then he knew he had found it. From this moment he concentrated on the hands and feet, in which the Indian's torment became a spontaneous, almost animallike convulsion, and the effect was one of overwhelming tragedy. Goitia's "*Tata*

Jesucristo" ("Father Jesus Christ") is one of the most magnificent pictures ever produced in Mexico, and bears comparison with the best canvases of modern Western art.[22]

With this beginning, twentieth-century Mexican painting was off to a solid start. In 1909, when Rivera and Atl returned from Europe, the necessary push was given. Rivera had studied in France, Atl had seen the marvelous frescoes of Italy, and José Clemente Orozco, who was to develop into perhaps the finest painter of his country, had spent many hours standing beside the engraver Posada. Rivera exhibited his best pictures, and Dr. Atl spoke enthusiastically of the magnificent murals of da Vinci and other Italian Renaissance artists, whose technique, he said, had been lost for four centuries. Atl's eyes flashed fire and he began to preach nationalism in art. He experimented with colors, invented new and more durable tones suitable for painting on paper, canvas, or plaster. Orozco and the other young painters at the Academy caught Atl's enthusiasm and began to paint with strong, brisk, rapid strokes. Sometimes they even sketched models in motion. Before very long each one had found his own personal style. Gone forever was the photographic immobility of academic art. In his autobiography Orozco writes of this period in his life:

> In those gatherings of young apprentice painters there appeared the first revolutionary bud in the arts of Mexico. During past epochs the Mexican had been a poor colonial servant, incapable of creating anything or thinking on his own. Everything had to come full born from Europe, for we were an inferior and degenerate race. We were allowed to paint, but it had to be as they painted in Paris, and the critics of Paris must be the final arbiters of our work.
>
> In those nocturnal gatherings where we heard the inspiring voice of Dr. Atl, we began to suspect that all this colonial vassalage was just a deception of the international merchants; that we did have a personality of our own which was worth as much as any other. We could and should learn from the foreign masters, but we also possessed creative abilities as great or greater than theirs. We began to feel not pride, but confidence in ourselves, and an awareness of our own being and of our destiny.

Dr. Atl himself went to live on the volcano Popocatepetl, and made the painting of volcanoes his unique contribution to contemporary Mexican art. Since that time Dr. Atl has painted nearly a thousand pictures of volcanoes, and has become Mexico's leading vulcanologist. When Parícutin erupted in 1943 Dr. Atl hurried to the spot and promptly bought up the volcano, which had exploded in a corn field.

He set up a hut there and studied the life of a volcano in progress. The old man also injured a leg, which had to be amputated in order to save his life. Orozco began to explore the slums and brothels of Mexico City, and gradually there emerged "like a new dawn," Orozco says, "the land of Mexico itself and the forms and colors that we knew so well. This was the first timid step toward our liberation from the tyranny of foreign art."

In 1910 the Mexican government set up a huge exhibit of Spanish art in order to commemorate the 100th anniversary of Hidalgo's famous "Cry from Dolores." Many thousands of dollars were appropriated to bring from Spain some of the largest canvases of Sorolla, Zuloaga, and many other peninsular artists. The young Mexican painters, with Dr. Atl as their spokesman, protested their exclusion from the exhibit. Finally, the ridiculous sum of 3,000 pesos was given to defray the expenses of an exhibit of Mexican art.

Never before or since has there been such an exhibit in Mexico. Paintings and pieces of sculpture flooded every available hall and gallery, and in spite of the fact that most of these young artists were exhibiting for the first time, the Mexican pieces were more varied, more dynamic, and more inspired than those from Spain. They were acclaimed with enthusiasm. The young artists organized themselves into a Centro Artístico with the central purpose of painting the walls of the public buildings. Dr. Atl got permission for them to start on the newly constructed Preparatory School, but the Revolution broke out and the project was abandoned in panic. A dozen years passed before fresco painting actually made its start.

The young artists went on strike, the Academy folded up, Dr. Atl went to Europe, and Alfredo Ramos Martínez returned to Mexico from France. There was a hiatus in the development of Mexican art. Ramos Martínez was a devotee of the impressionist school, and when he was appointed director of the new School of Fine Arts he set up an outdoor school of painting at Santa Anita, which he called "Barbizon," after the name of the artistic village made so famous by Corot, Rousseau, Millet, and other French painters.

"This," wrote Orozco, "was like establishing on the banks of the Seine, near Paris, a Santa Anita with wooden carts, *pulque*, *charro* horsemen, *enchiladas*, *huaraches*, and the flash of Mexican knives." Orozco went on to state that so much open air was not to his liking and he separated from the group and set up his own studio in Illescas Street. His criticism is not entirely valid, for the new school did break away from the academic tradition and brought to Mexican painting a luminous quality which captured the sunlit clarity of the high plateau air.

The Revolution was now in full swing, and the whole country smelled of blood and the smoke of battle. Orozco himself took no part in the Revolution and was never in any danger. The whole sorry spectacle passed before his eyes like a savage carnival scene. At last, sickened by the chaos and the killing, he left Mexico and came to the United States. He was always the "lone wolf" among the Mexican painters of our times.

Other artists were not so separated from the political upheaval around them. In 1913, when General Huerta assassinated Madero and Carranza rose against the usurper, many artists joined the revolutionary forces: Dr. Atl, Goitia, Guillemin, Alfaro-Siqueiros, Escobedo, Bolaños, Cabildo, and many others. There was little time for painting while Mexico was receiving her bath in blood, but in 1915, before he left Mexico, Orozco exhibited a collection of his slum and brothel scenes in a bookstore. The exhibit passed almost unnoticed; only a few artists admired the stark and somber pictures. In 1919 the Revolution was almost over. In the state of Jalisco a government of revolutionary artists was set up. Alfaro-Siqueiros was sent abroad and met Rivera in Paris. They fired each other with new ideas. In 1921 Siqueiros issued a manifesto in Barcelona in which he called for a return to the indigenous base of Mexican art and the abandoning of outworn European patterns. This new revolutionary art would, he said, express the hopes and sufferings of the masses. Both Siqueiros and Rivera became Communists and added frequent Marxist slogans to their violent outpourings of what art should and should not be. Orozco kept himself apart from politics. In fact, he states in his autobiography that, "Artists do not have and never have had political convictions of any kind, and those who believe they do, are not artists." This was putting it a little too strongly, but it was his way of denouncing the loud certainties of Rivera and Alfaro-Siqueiros. Orozco, of course, could not possibly keep himself cut off from the social realities of Mexican life and never attempted to do so. But what he did try to do was to portray that reality as a spiritual rather than a political quality, and by so doing he made himself into a more universal artist.

Diego Rivera now returned to Mexico from Europe by way of Italy, where he was deeply impressed by the frescoes of the Italian Renaissance and the Byzantine mural mosaics. In the early 1920's José Vasconcelos, the new Minister of Education, turned the walls of many public buildings over to the young artists, and Mexican mural painting was born. Rivera, Orozco, and Alfaro-Siqueiros are the three best-known fresco artists, but there are many others. At first both Rivera and Orozco followed the Renaissance tradition, using limited, transparent colors, and fine, close brush strokes. Later on, the strokes became bolder, the colors more varied.

Miguel Covarrubias, himself one of the finest Mexican artists, explains that "the true fresco is painted with earth colors and water on a surface of wet plaster. Only an area that can be completed in a day's work is plastered, the next being prepared the following day and the two joined as inconspicuously as possible. The palette of the fresco painter is limited; Rivera uses only ten colors: six natural earths (oxides of iron), emerald green, two blues, and black. Orozco uses even fewer, resorting freely to an opaque white. Fresco painting requires great technical knowledge, speed and complete sureness of hand and intent, since no alteration is possible once the plaster dries." [6]

Another Mexican painter, Jesús Guerrero Galván, has interpreted the mural art of Orozco in these words:

"The horrible is its chief strength, and, though it may seem paradoxical, its chief beauty also. By means of the eye it produces a trembling, a shudder. Instead of producing a pleasure for the eye, as the scholastics understood esthetic enjoyment, it gives a sensation of anguish, or horror, of desperation." [13]

Rivera and Orozco are very different kinds of men, and very different artists. Rivera is the out-and-out propagandist, politically sure of himself, and rather insistent on defiantly shouting out his opinions. His pictures are always strongly pro-Indian, pro-masses, and even more strongly anticapitalistic. It is a strange commentary on his proletarian canvases that they were nearly all snapped up by people of wealth, who liked their colors or thought they were funny. (A withered John D. Rockefeller eating a meal of gold coins is an example.) The proletariat hardly knew what the artist was about. The people of wealth knew, but didn't care, just so long as he didn't put Joe Stalin in a public building. This political propagandism has given to many of Rivera's best-known murals a cluttered effect which is certainly not the best art. The artist is so intent on getting in every bit of evidence which supports his preconceived point of view that the perspective of the work of art is often destroyed. Great crowds often flood Rivera's pictures and resemble a May Day parade rather than a distilled essence of artistic feeling. However, Rivera has at times painted the human face and form with profound emotion and a marvelous mastery of artistic technique. Often, too, his colors have a shining quality which is like that of the Mexican landscape itself, suggesting the colors of tropical birds and flowers.

Orozco is a man of torment who sees human suffering as inevitable in life and strives to capture that tortured feeling in his forms and colors. He is obsessed with fire, and flames of orange, red, and blood contort many of his most magnificent figures. Fire is man's conscience, fire purifies and cleanses while man struggles to move forward and to be free. Rivera is always sure that a new social state (Rivera's own particular brand of Marxism) will solve the difficulties of mankind. Orozco is not certain of anything, except that man is a biological organism that lives, learns, desires, hurts, screams, aspires, and dies. Orozco admires dignity and justice. He detests pretense, debasement, corruption, and deceit. He believes that man is here for a purpose, and that purpose is to improve himself.

Alfaro-Siqueiros, who uses duco and other new paints, sometimes applied with a spray gun, has tried to create "a monumental and heroic art, a human art, a public art, with the direct and living example of our great pre-hispanic cultures in America." He believes that the mural art of Mexico today "is moving toward the accumulation and fusion of every plastic value of worth that history has left us. And it is the only movement in the whole world which is realizing such a purpose." The frescoes of this artist, with their monstrous figures and vivid forms and colors, are unique in modern art. They have a cumulative grotesque effect that is overwhelming. Alfaro-Siqueiros makes a point of stating that mural painting is such a gigantic undertaking that the individual painter can no longer handle it alone. He becomes, in effect, an architect and director technician who inspires, guides, correlates, and trains those who paint with him. The art thus produced is a public, not a private art.

Mural painting, now welded to modern architecture, is the great art of Mexico today. The Mexican frescoes are not paintings on a wall; they are paintings which are a wall. Together with the magnificent buildings which house them they have caught the surge of history, the suffering, growth, and aspiration which make up the spirit of Mexico in our time. Better than any other expression they link the present with the indigenous past, and in this fusion reach toward an even more powerful future.

XIII

TRANSITION TOWN

When Mexico shall have become a nation of good workers, from the top to the bottom of society, she will have been saved forever. She will belong to herself.

—ANTONIO CASO

AS IN colonial times, the town plaza is still the heartbeat of community life in Mexico. You can sit on the plaza and see a cross section of the town's life go by. Wait for a while and you are likely to see a midwife scurrying across the plaza on her way to deliver a baby. Wait a little longer and you are certain to see a funeral. If you remain on the plaza you are bound to witness a fiesta, more certain still of seeing a market in full progress. You will hear most of the town's problems and most of the town's gossip thrashed out, then thrashed out all over again. You will see and hear the children play, and you will watch the old folks sit or snooze and nod. You will observe the young blades and belles stroll around the square, courting. The plaza is the pulse that catches them all.

Take, for example, the plaza of the little city of Tepic, in the state of Nayarit. Tepic is not one of the most-visited towns in Mexico. It has nothing very noteworthy or very beautiful to show. It is not in any stupendous geographic setting, for Tepic is neither on the seacoast nor in the highlands. It has no brilliant Indian market. True, it was the birthplace of Amado Nervo, one of Mexico's greatest poets, whose home carries a plaque to commemorate the event. But for all that Tepic is not a particularly literary town. On the contrary, it is a town of very ordinary Mexican people, bent on the multiple tasks of making a living.

When I began to work on this book on Mexico I held the tenuous thought that Tepic might be an ideal town to study in detail, as Robert Redfield and Stuart Chase have studied in detail the life of the community of Tepoztlán, an isolated Aztec community of about four thousand souls not far from Cuernavaca. Once, many years before, I had visited Tepic on the train, before the highway was opened. I remembered it as a sleepy, picturesque little village, cleaner than most

Mexican towns, with one foot in the past, the other moving toward today. It was a typical mestizo town, and most of Mexico is made up of such mestizo towns and villages. The old Indian way of life, the economy of machineless men, the economy of almost complete self-sufficiency is becoming less and less typical of Mexico today. In the twenty-five years that have elapsed since Redfield and Chase made their fascinating studies, Mexico has moved forward with great strides into the age of the automobile and the tractor. One of the things that was bound to go is the economy of machineless men.

Tepic is still a typical Mexican community that one might profitably write a book on, for the town is a cross section of mestizo Mexico. But such a study would be far too voluminous to have any interest for the general reader; it would probably take at least a thousand pages. As an example of the larger in-between towns of Mexico, the transition town that is in process of going modern, Tepic calls for a different kind of treatment, and fills the bill perfectly.

When I first saw Tepic fifteen years ago, it had a population of perhaps 4,000 or 5,000. The census figures today say 13,000. To be exact, they give Tepic a population of 13,239 souls. The Mexicans like to count inhabitants as *almas* (souls). It is part of the Hispanic heritage. But census figures are no sooner taken than they are out of date in Mexico today, particularly in an expanding region. Tepic must have a population of close to 30,000 now. It is no sleepy village; it is a bustling little city, an interesting combination of the old and the new, but definitely bustling with automobiles, Coca-Cola signs, hot-dog stands, and all the other accouterments of civilization. This despite the decoration of an occasional Huichol or Cora Indian who comes in from the hills to buy or to sell his wares. When the Huicholes put on their real finery they outdo any other native group in Mexico, but in Tepic they now merely represent an element that is exotic to the town's daily life.

Perhaps it was Tepic's reputation as a clean town that really took me there. Many travelers and natives have referred to it as being the cleanest town in Mexico. This I wanted to see for myself.

Tepic is the capital of the state of Nayarit, not long ago one of the more isolated regions of the country. The town lies at the base of an extinct volcano, Sanganguey, and goes back to an old Indian village of the seventh century. Cortés occupied the place in the year 1524, only three years after the fall of Mexico City. So Tepic was one of the very first Spanish colonial towns. It still preserves many picturesque aspects of the colonial past, combining this with an enterprising modern air of large athletic stadiums, pleasant parks, tennis courts, and a wide, well lighted main street. In fact, Tepic takes great pride in the paving of all its major streets.

The largest buildings in town are a modern cigarette factory,* the new Pepsi-Cola plant, and the fine eighteenth-century cathedral. An even more ancient structure, the Church of the Cross, was once part of a Franciscan monastery from which Fathers Serra and Kino departed for their spiritual conquest of the northern Mexican states and, finally, for California. In both of these regions Serra, Kino, and those who followed them constructed a long chain of missions which brought Spanish culture into the southwestern United States. They gave California its famed Mission Trail, adorned with some of the finest Mexican religious architecture of the final colonial century. These missions represent the last flowering of the missionary ideal; they were outposts of Spanish Christianity in a primitive wilderness. They were the last flare of the tremendous apostolic fire which had consumed the early Spanish church fathers. It is fitting that Fathers Serra, Kino, and their brothers, like those other earliest missionaries, were also Franciscans. Their labors were long and strenuous; the buildings they made were massive, simple, imposing, white as the rocks from which they arose. They were like the fortress-monasteries of the first years of the conquest in Mexico itself.

Like every town, village, or city in Mexico, Tepic has its central plaza, as a relic of colonial days. Here the old meets the new, blends with it, clashes with it, sometimes takes it on and then rejects it. In any case, the central plaza gives a pretty fair picture of the racial make-up of the community, the activities, the rate of progress, the milieu, and the economic and social levels of community life.

The plaza in Tepic is spacious. It is not as large as the central Zócalo in Mexico City, but for a town this size it is certainly not a cramped plaza. On one corner stands the cathedral, its two slender spires reaching upward with Gothic fingers. They are gray and tall and tower above every other building on the square.

The other buildings around the plaza line up something like this: on the side next to the cathedral are a clock and watch shop, an old hotel with tables out on the sidewalk, a corner café. Down the next side are a drugstore, which has a sign stating that it is selling "without the degree of pharmacy," which means that it cannot fill prescriptions. Then there are six clothing stores, two of them called *almacenes*, sup-

* This factory employs approximately 400 people and turns out 10 million cigarettes per working day. The wages for a semiskilled factory worker are about $3.00 per day.

posedly department stores, but they are only a little larger than the others. Across the sidewalk in front of these stores are half a dozen little wooden stands in which are sold cold drinks, candy, popcorn, stationery, dime-store knickknacks, and *lonches*, the Mexican word for "lunches." One of the favorite luncheon items was a ham sandwich, but more popular still were the *exquisitos hot-dogs*, as the red sign called them. A bottle of Coca-Cola sold for 50 centavos, or 4 U.S. cents. A bar of chocolate cost a nickel. A hot dog cost a few pennies more. Twenty cents would buy one of these "lonches" with candy, drink, and all the fixings.

On the next side of the plaza were a hat shop, a candy store, loaded with every conceivable kind of sweets, and not far from the *dulcería* was the big market building, which does not open directly onto the plaza. Mexicans love candy and sweetmeats of all sorts. There is candy wrapped in paper, homemade candy in the open, fudges, nut-flavored nougats, preserved and sugared fruits of half a dozen kinds, delicious Mexican chocolates, peanuts, popcorn, chewing gum, and every kind of cold drink under the sun, all well sugared. Mexicans eat heartily of them all. The *dulcería* is always one of the best-patronized places in town. Children, particularly, consume huge quantities of candies. Little wonder, then, that their teeth and skins show the results of this overindulgence. The dentist is rapidly coming up in the new Mexico, the Mexico that has money enough to buy beans *and* candy. The dermatologist has not found his place but, if this candy consumption continues and incomes keep on growing, he will soon surely have a firm spot in the new society, for no one likes to have a greasy or a lumpy skin.

The last side of the square was occupied by another *almacén*, a bookstore, two cafés, a paint and enamel shop, a large garage with its sign reading *Productos Pemex*. (*Pemex* is the Mexican Oil and Gasoline Co., meaning *Petróleos Mexicanos*. The word *Pemex* is formed by taking the *Pe* of the first word and adding the *Mex* of the second.) Then came a pharmacy, a shoe store, and another pharmacy. This brings us back to the cathedral, in front of which runs the main street of Tepic, the Avenida México, which extends across the little river and into the hills, the buildings getting smaller and poorer the farther out it runs.

In the center of the plaza is a new bandstand, a kind of Roman rotunda, built in a semicircle with tall Doric columns of sand-colored stone. It has replaced the old cast-iron bandstand of an earlier date. Every Mexican town of more than five hundred inhabitants once had one of these cast-iron stands. Hundreds of them were put up during the regime of Porfirio Díaz, when the bands began to play on regular days their very irregular versions of the melodious music of Rossini, Verdi, and other operatic composers along with the native tunes. The Roman rotunda of Tepic hardly fits beside the Gothic cathedral, but it is new and the cathedral is old; thus there was no argument among the town councilmen of Tepic. Always the new must replace the old. Rarely is there a rebuilding in the same style or fashion. Not far from the plaza's center, and near to the stone bandstand, rises a single lordly evergreen, almost but not quite as high as the towers of the gray cathedral. It resembles greatly the splendid cedar of Lebanon which rises so nobly from the grave of Luther Burbank, who lies buried in his own yard in Santa Rosa, California. The evergreen of Tepic rises from no grave; it merely adorns the plaza, another anomaly in this town once noted principally for its quaint colonial streets.

I take a seat on a bench in the plaza. A boy of ten, wearing tan pants and a once-white shirt, comes to shine my shoes. He asks a peso (8 cents). It is too much; the regular price is 75 or 80 centavos, 2 cents less. While he is at work on the shine another little boy (he seems about eight) passes by calling out *panes calencitos*, "hot corn muffins." He carries them in a small open basket. An old gentleman about seventy, with a kindly face, heavily stubbled, draws near and holds out the inevitable box of Chiclets. Every street and plaza in Mexico is filled with these sellers of Chiclets, two white tablets in each little box. Generally they are carried in a small pasteboard carton. Boys of six sell them, and men of seventy. You get three boxes (six pieces of gum) for 20 centavos, less than 2 cents. I open a box of Chiclets and begin to chew. The shine boy and the old man are still standing beside me. The corn-muffin boy is just behind them. School is just letting out, and a stream of children start across the plaza. One of these, a bright-faced, very bronze-skinned boy of ten, pauses a moment, and stares at me intensely. He knows that I am a gringo, a foreigner, and he is eager to cross the strangeness between us. Finally, he spurts the question: "*¿Usted es gringo, verdad?*"

He says the words without the slightest malice. To him gringo *

* The Spanish word *gringo* comes from *griego*, meaning "Greek." It means only a foreigner, but usually refers to the foreign element which happens to be dominant in a given locality. In Mexico the gringo is a North American; in Argentina he is an Italian. The old wives' tale about the word being derived from the words of a song which had a refrain "Green grow the rushes" is completely untrue. The word was in Spanish use years before there ever was such a song. Just as we say "It's all Greek to me," the person of Spanish speech refers to the foreigner as a gringo.

means very simply a North American. I answer very simply that he is right. I am an American. Then I note that he is carrying his schoolbooks in a little homemade wooden case, one side of which has a small door swung on tiny hinges. I ask if I might see some of his books. His bright little Indian face is wreathed in smiles as he opens the case and takes out his books. His notebook catches my attention, and I open it. On each page is a brief essay, written in a very clear childish scrawl. I examine the notes. The first essay, very fittingly, is on Christopher Columbus. Then there is one, a little longer, on Benito Juárez, the great Indian President of Mexico who died suddenly on the job in 1872. The next essay is on "The Indians." It interests me particularly because the boy himself, and most of his classmates, are largely Indian in their own racial make-up. The child before me could easily be taken for a pure Indian, but the essay ran something like this:

"Our country, Mexico, was once inhabited by a people very different from us, the Indians. They fought with arrows and hunted animals. They also killed each other. They had many human sacrifices. They used signs called hieroglyphics instead of real writing. The 'sun' was just a bunch of crossed lines, all bursting. [Beside this sentence there was a childish picture of a sunburst, in yellow.] A very thick green line represented a plain. If this line was straight up, it was a tree. [A green rectangle, upright.]"

There were several other Indian signs, all of which the boy had studiously illustrated in various colors. Other essays followed: one on "The Senses," another on "The Human Body," one on "Our School," a brief paragraph on "The Cardinal Points," and an essay on "Corn," which was pointed up as the most important plant in Mexico because it gives food to so many people. There was one page which I turned rather quickly. It had an essay on "Los Niños Héroes," the "Boy Heroes" of Chapultepec, lads in their early teens whe defended Chapultepec Heights when the North Americans took it by storm. When their ammunition gave out and defeat was certain, the remnants of this gallant band, who were only students in a military school, wrapped Mexican flags around their bodies, and plunged to their deaths over the cliffs on which Chapultepec Castle stands. One of these "Boy Heroes" was born in Tepic, and his house is still regarded as a local shrine. The child whose notebook I was handling seemed not to notice that I had rapidly turned this particular page and had gone on to the essays on "Geography" and "Hygiene." In this latter essay it was carefully stated that "children must be very careful not to put things either in their noses or in their mouths, for things that we handle have a lot of microbes on them, and they can make us very sick."

I thank the boy for his courtesy and let him go on his way. He wishes me well. The other bystanders also depart, slowly as if afraid of missing something. I sink back on the seat and survey the people who are on the plaza at this moment. It is now about five-thirty, and the afternoon sun is almost down. A breath of chilled air floats over the plaza. On the bench next to me an old gentleman sits slumped into his black poncho, an old-style poncho with a hole in the middle for the head to go through. Only his forehead is sticking out. He wears a white sombrero, and is obviously taking his siesta. An old lady dressed in solid black walks by. She even wears a black *rebozo*. Black is the favorite color of the older Mexican woman in all the small towns. It gives these the aspect of being places where the women are always in mourning. But the woman in black is quickly followed by a young lady wearing a white *rebozo* and a light-gray dress. After her come two young men, with white scarves across their shoulders. They have on blue shirts and trousers. Their eyes are fixed on the hips of the girl in front. Farther down the sidewalk are two women in blue dresses; one wears a brown *rebozo*, the other a blue. There are about thirty-five men and boys on the plaza at this moment. Half a dozen are shine boys or sellers of Chiclets. Another half dozen are school children. The men are of all ages and kinds and descriptions, but their clothes have a certain uniformity, a colorless uniformity which is the mark of civilized men everywhere. The Mexican uniformity is on a somewhat lower economic scale than ours, that is all. The coats and trousers are mostly khaki, blue denims, grays, or faded browns.

Suddenly the jukebox in the café across the plaza begins to blare. Mexicans like their music loud. It is Elvis Presley, singing "Love Me Tender." The people sitting at the sidewalk tables are listening intently. This is followed by a piece of typical Mexican music, and then comes an old-time favorite "Lady of Spain, I Adore You." It is so old I had almost forgotten that it existed. Then comes another piece of Mexican music, and this is quickly followed by "In a Little Spanish Town, 'twas on a night like this."

As the music blares on, one piece after the other, in its odd medley of American jazz, old and new, and popular Mexican airs, the traffic cop on the corner gets down from his little wooden stand (with "Coca-Cola" written all over it) and walks over to one of the sidewalk stands to get a cold drink. He lets the traffic light take care of the cars while he is gone. And there is plenty of traffic in Tepic. The business of this town, despite an occasional burro, certainly moves on wheels. Trucks of all descriptions pass down the street. Scattered among them are the little two-wheeled carts, drawn by horses, which are still typical of the town. They all have rubber-tired wheels now, replacing the steel-rimmed wood of an older day. But they all still have, very carefully placed just beneath the horse's tail, a little catcher of some kind, a basket, a piece of burlap, or a piece of rubber, which is so stretched that it will catch whatever the horse may feel like dropping as he trots along. The streets of Tepic must be kept clean; the town is proud of its reputation for cleanliness, and these two-wheeled carts are a proof of it.

I get up and begin to walk around the plaza, carefully examining the buildings. The stone arcades along the sides of the square have been touched up with fresh plaster. Tepic is having its face lifted. New lampposts line both sides of Mexico Street, their fluorescent lamps leaning out over the road in a sinuous curve that reminds one of serpents. They are mounted on slender cement columns, colored red. Many buildings along the same street are being remodeled. The whole town is in a fury of rebuilding. Colonial façades are being demolished, and replaced by modern fronts in new stucco, colored dark yellow, blue, or gray. The tones are all subdued; Tepic does not like garish colors. New iron railings are being placed outside the second-story balcony windows. The whole main street is taking on a modern tone, which contrasts strangely with the older colonial parts of town.

Along these older streets the buildings have faded plaster walls of clay-ocher, gray, blue, or green. Most of them are of a light clay-ocher, and are chipped away in several places despite the accumulations of paintings. The walls are very thick; the windows are covered with iron bars. The great wooden doors are wide open, and every store and shop is a part of the street. (I had noticed the same thing in other Mexican towns, especially Mazatlán and Veracruz.) Barbershops, print shops, doctors' offices, ticket agencies, stores of all kinds, even banks and offices where typists and bookkeepers are bent over their tasks—all these are wide open to the public view. The streets are filled with people, and the people stroll in and out with complete nonchalance. Business, pleasure, and social life are all thoroughly mixed. No one stays cooped up at home; half of Tepic must be on the streets.

In this the old Indian way of life persists, and the Spaniards, having something of the same quality to their own social fabric, have not only not destroyed it; rather, they have widened the base with the addition of new kinds of work, industries, stores. The colonial walls of Tepic are massive and thick, but they are not impersonal. They let you out, they let you in. No alienation of productivity here.

I walk down the streets and past the movie houses. One of the largest is called the Cine Amado Nervo, honoring Tepic's famous poet son. (*Cine* means "movie.") "The Vagabond King" is playing here. At a second theater is "The Monster from Mars," and at a third there is an American western. Not a Mexican film among them. There are Mexican films, plenty of them, but Hollywood far outbalances the entire Mexican productivity. The names of our stars are on every Mexican's lips, somewhat garbled in pronunciation but instantly familiar.

A man in a rust-colored suit suddenly stops in front of me and asks the time. He is wearing a white shirt, open at the collar, and no tie. He has a notebook in his hand.

"You speak English, do you not?" he then asks, very correctly. On receiving an affirmative reply he proceeds:

"How do you say in English 'Usa muchos ademanes'?" he asked. "Is it '*He uses many gestures*'?"

I tell him that you may say it this way, or you may say "He makes a lot of gestures," or even "He gesticulates a lot," or "He gesticulates a great deal."

"Ah," the man said, and he repeated the words after me. "Will you write that down on this book?"

After I had written the words down, he turned the page and came to another English sentence which read "This law is void of effect."

"Is this correct?" he asked me.

"No, you do not need to say 'void of effect,' you simply say 'This law is void.' "

"Ah," responded my friend, "I thought the English was shorter."

"And how do you say in English," he went on, " '*México es un país católico, por excelencia*'? How do you translate those last two words into English?"

" 'Mexico is a Catholic country, par excellence,' " I said, "would be the easiest way. We sometimes use the French phrase. But you might also say more colloquially 'Mexico is a real Catholic country' or 'Mexico is an outstandingly Catholic country.' "

My friend repeated the words very slowly after me. His pronunciation was labored, but clear.

"This interests me intensely," he went on. "I must learn English fluently. I must learn it."

"Do you study it at school?"

"No, I do not. I study it at home, and I go to the American movies when I can. But mostly I study it from books at home, from books, and newspapers and magazines. I go to the movies to correct my pronunciation, and to understand."

"Won't you sit down?" I said. We had both been standing during the entire conversation.

"No, I am in a hurry," he said. "I should be home by now. Well, good-by, and thank you very much. Perhaps I shall see you tomorrow." He extended his hand and, after shaking mine, went on his way.

It was a typical Latin leave-taking. Never leave a person in Mexico without shaking his hand, even if you meet him casually. It is an expected courtesy which must come after almost any conversation. Indeed, it is more expected that one shake hands on parting than on meeting. And certainly the custom makes sense. By then you know each other better. This is exactly the way the Mexican looks at it too, and he would be greatly chagrined and would feel definitely rejected if there was no shaking of the hands on leaving *after* a conversation.

As my man went away I noticed that he had two small white stains on his very poor rust-colored suit. He wore a mustache, his face was clean shaven, and his eyes were brown and bright. Rarely have I seen a Mexican with sluggish eyes, unless he is a Mexican who is physically ill. In the young people, most of all, the eyes are quick and bright as though they are searching eagerly for something. They *are* looking for something, and that something is knowledge. It is not always a properly organized knowledge, but the Mexican learns quickly and his judgment is often very penetrating. Unconsciously, in his short conversation, this man had deftly characterized his people: a great use of the hands in gestures, a very Catholic country, a people with a tremendous urge to learn, a fascination for things American, and many laws that are void of effect.

The bells of the cathedral now begin to peal, and the jukebox suddenly blares out again as if deliberately to drown out the sound of the bells. I do not see many people going into the church. I do see the hot-dog man doing a rush business, and the seller of *paletas* (Mexican popsicles), who has his little cart parked near the popular hot dogs, is also taking in good money. People are drinking Coca-Cola and Pepsi-Cola all over the place. There is a brand-new, spanking-clean Pepsi-Cola bottling works in Tepic, and Pepsi is giving Coca a good run for the money. Soft drinks of all kinds are a big business in Mexico. When the colas outsell the pulque you will know that the Revolution has finally been achieved.

It is almost time for supper now and I retire to my hotel. Located only a stone's throw from the plaza the Sierra de Álica is a good but old hotel. It has a profusion of blue tiles which line the walls and climb the wide stairs. It is a very clean and pleasant hotel, and my room there cost exactly 42 pesos, or $3.36. The shower bath was separated from the toilet in typical Mexican fashion only by a plastic curtain, but it was spacious. Nearly all Mexican hotels now have baths in all their rooms. And nearly all Mexicans eat a hearty breakfast. In these two ways they take after the Americans, and differ from the Europeans.

Back in my room I lie on the bed for a few moments' rest before going down to supper. It is dark and the great hum of Tepic at dusk comes floating on the air. Suddenly I am aware that the noises of Mexico are very different from the noises one is accustomed to at home. Here I am within four walls, lying on a bed from which it is impossible to see any part of Tepic, but it is very obvious that this is a foreign country. The shrill voice of a boy is yelling out his papers, an organ grinder on the plaza is playing "*La Golondrina*." There is a clatter of dishes far away, the murmur of an electric engine, the rumble of a car, the frost-far sound of voices in the kitchen, and from the street comes the high whir of grinding steel as the scissors sharpener puts a new edge on shears or knife. From the plaza comes the crackling symphony of many singing birds. Over all there is a kind of reverberating echo which seems to flow on soft air waves down marble halls. The door of my room has a kind of lattice on the bottom, which lets the air (as well as the sound) in and out. Silence is unbearable to these people. Mexicans do not like to be isolated. They want to be a part of something, even if it is just a part of the hotel assemblage. They do not like to be shut off.

Now I hear a dull pounding of some kind, the strains of a distant accordion, a clump-clump of heels and voices in the corridor. The voices are musical but penetrating. Spanish is a sharply melodious language. It is not a lazy-sweet melodious language. It is quick and clear and crystal-bright. All these sounds blend into one great wave of sound which is Tepic, which is Mexico. It could never in a thousand years make a person believe that he was in the United States, surrounded by the endless cacophony of the traffic in our streets by day or the muffled silence of our residential neighborhoods by night. It is at such times as these that one can feel very alone, and I began to wonder what it is in history that really divides men into linguistic and national groups, so that even our noises are different. If we could fathom this wall we might know understanding, cross the barrier of fear, and even come to love our brothers.

The following afternoon I have a late lunch in a boardinghouse which has a charming patio, open to the air and sky. An American I know enters the patio and takes his seat in the corner. He has put away his street smile and is now merely alone and bewildered. He has been in Mexico for five months working for a U.S. tractor concern. He does not like Mexico, he says. At least he does not like Mexico today. It is a dark pitiful thing that springs from the abysmal depths of racial feeling. The American has a gaunt, thin face, and his stomach aches.

There is no aloneness, he says, like that of being alone among a people who speak a strange language and belong to a foreign culture. The Mexicans speak a strange language. It is not at all the language our high school teacher pronounced for us in a totally different manner. You cannot get a word. You are furious at the inefficiency of our expensive educational system. You are more furious still at the natives who insist on speaking at breakneck speed, obviously to annoy you.

But language is not the only barrier here. From a quarter of a mile away these people can tell at once that you do not belong to them. No need to open the mouth. You do not look like them. You do not walk as they do, much less talk as they do. You are a curious intruder, a visitor, businessman, enemy or friend, but you do not belong to them. After years you may think that you belong to them, but you never will. You may live in one spot and become rooted there, and the people there who saw your roots go down will take you for their own. But step into another province, another town, and see what they will say. No matter if you speak like a native, see how strangely they regard you. Even your fluent Spanish is an anomaly. They like you for it, but they are suspicious. Why should a gringo, whose idiom is money, learn Spanish so well? Some trick up his sleeve, no doubt.

Nothing is said or done. Politeness is a byword here. But the eye can quickly tell there is a strangeness in the air. I have often wondered if a blind man could feel it. Would the voice give it away? In any case, the eye can clearly see how the picture is colored. It is the jolt of the unexpected. One moment the *abrazo* (a welcoming embrace); the next, "too busy to see you, my friend." Great duties to perform. The duties of strangeness.

Then you are alone, truly, unaccountably alone. You hate Mexico, and your hatred is a dark river in which you are drowning. You hate the woman who comes swishing the grass broom that throws eddies of unpalatable dust in your face. She laughs at your discomfiture. You hate the chatter that comes from the market place, a medley of cries in the distance. You hate even the little urchin who splashes water on the red geraniums from an old perforated gasoline tin. And you are very much alone with yourself. You consider every Mexican a scoundrel, and wonder why you ever came to Mexico in the first place.

You look at the sky and it is unalloyed. The sun is the sun of Mexico, blistering and bright. The red flowers seem redder than before, and the mountains that are everywhere are floating across it, a woolen sterility against the blue. Your darkness makes the colors breathe with light. The flowers catch a glory from the sun; they are as alive as you. An artist might see in this moment a painting. Mexico is a color pattern that does not fade. Mexico is made up of such unguarded fragments of time, fixed in the memory, and of a pictorial intensity that is abiding. But to you, in your aloneness, it is a pattern of strangeness. There is no time here, no distance. There are no goals that you can feel or understand. It is another dimension.

But your aloneness has caught the flow of your thoughts and has stopped them. A dam of strangeness has pushed you into yourself. You are no longer wallowing in the great foreign sea. You feel only the present moment, the kernel of self. This is your core, your axis, your life. In a moment you will expand again, and the strange brown faces will all be smiling. You will again find peace among strangers. But for a fragment of time you feel that all of humanity is hurting, alone, in your heart, and the world is a great luminous wheel whose slow passage is fixed forever in your sight.

The dining room of the Hotel Sierra de Álica is a spacious place which opens onto the side street. The tables are placed away from the door, and are served by two Mexican girls, one plump, one tall and slender, both wearing black flat-heeled shoes. I have never seen a Mexican woman (unless she was ill or old) walk in an unqueenly manner. Even the fattest of them have in their stride an air of regality which is striking. Their steps are quick, light, and airy. The men too walk briskly, using smaller steps than the North Americans. To the Mexican eye the North American, man or woman, is an awkward, ungainly creature. The Mexican man will admire the figures of American girls, and their white skins, but he will never admire the way they walk. To him it is athletic, but ugly, mannish, and utterly preposterous.

The slender waitress takes my order, and I am served with a regal air. She is a peasant, but her manner is queenly, and aloof. Her regular features, part Indian, part Spanish, are perfectly blended into a harmonious whole. She is not beautiful by any stretch of the imagination, but she has great charm. I look at the menu and order a *filet mignon* steak, which is 20 pesos, or $1.60, a piece of *papaya* melon (10 cents), a cup of coffee and a dessert (8 cents each). Mexican coffee is not cheap, and it is not good. It is either strong and black or it is weak and watery. It has a burnt flavor which comes from overroasting. Many Americans carry jars of Nescafé around with them in order to have the taste of home. One kind of Nescafé is made especially for sale in Mexico, and only rarely is any other instant coffee seen.

My steak is served practically raw. I send it back, and it returns well done. No matter how it is cooked, though, the steak you will find in Mexico is grainy and tough. Mexico is only in the process of becoming a meat-eating country. The cattle are allowed to wander up and down the hills, chewing on weeds and grass, until they are slaughtered. Their fibers and muscles are admirable, but their meat is abominable. Rarely are they penned in and fattened for the dinner table. Moreover, Mexicans do not know how to cut meat. The butcher simply takes a huge knife and goes at it. What comes out is often in lumps, cut wrongly on the grain, full of gristle and strings, and it is almost never aged. Meat comes straight from the slaughterhouse to the table and seldom has more than a passing acquaintance, if that, with the refrigerator. But the fruits of Mexico are delicious. Papaya, with lime juice on it, fresh pineapples, strawberries, mangoes, mameyes—all these are delicious if properly ripe.

There is no real lobby in the hotel, merely a few chairs alongside the entrance hall and a few more off in one corner. Most of the lodgers sit at the entrance. After supper I take a padded seat and look out at the Club Tepic across the street, a saloon filled with men drinking Mexican beer: Bohemia, Carta Blanca, Dos Equis, all first-rate beers. Mexican music comes from this *cantina*. The lights of the city are on now, a maze of neon signs blinking like those of any American city. I see across the way a hardware shop, a store selling electric machinery, a Casa Goldman (Goldman's House), which is a haberdashery, a *lonchería* (a place to get lunch). and a barbershop. A haircut in Mexico costs 8 pesos, exactly 64 cents. No tip is expected. In a de luxe shop the price might go up to 10 pesos, or 80 cents. To pay more than this would be stupidity. Mexican barbers are excellent.

An American couple from the state of Idaho take a seat beside me.

There are Americans in every part of Mexico at every time of the year. If they were suddenly to stop traveling, practically every hotel south of the border would promptly go bankrupt. This old couple drove a trailer down, but they decided to leave it three hundred miles up the road, as trailer facilities are limited in this part of Mexico. Electricity is lacking in so many parks, and other services are few and far between; the farther one gets off the main highways the more quickly all these disappear. But there is always some kind of garage where one can store the car safely for the night, at rates that are extremely low.

The couple from Idaho were not talking to me, but it was impossible not to overhear them. They were discussing two topics which always interest Americans everywhere: business and sex. Business in Tepic was good. The new tobacco factory, in which the man had an interest, was expanding and large increased sales were expected. It already occupied a spacious and beautiful new building. Then the man went on to tell about a friend of his, an American of nearly seventy, who had lived in Tepic for some years. This man was retired, and lived from his Social Security income. He was not a permanent immigrant, so he had to return to the States every six months to get another tourist's visa. He had found a house and had a Mexican girl of about twenty as housekeeper. He paid her nothing, but gave her food and kept her in clothes. He called her his "long-haired dictionary." She was getting too fat, he had said, and her teeth were troubling her. He was feeding her too well. The man was not sure that I had taken in this story, so a moment later he repeated it to me, with a good chuckle. His wife did not blink an eye. The only thing that amazed the storyteller was his friend's age, nearly seventy. I looked out of the corner of my eye, hoping that no Mexican hotel guest had overheard. Mexicans, of course, are also interested in sex. But they do not discuss it publicly, most particularly if it happens to cross the lines of nationality and age, as in this instance.

One morning I walked slowly through the market in Tepic, notebook in hand. The market occupies a large building on the other side of the plaza from the hotel. It is cluttered with stalls selling nearly every kind of merchandise, from clothes to food, but the vast part of it is of local origin. I entered, passing between two stalls selling ready-made clothes, ducked under a great heap of *huaraches* (leather sandals) and shoes hanging from the ceiling on strings, and finally reached the food emporium. On one table was an enormous sea tortoise, lying on its back. It must have weighed a good eighty pounds. Beside the dead tortoise was a large fish, in process of being cut into pieces, and alongside that were piles of shrimp. Only the shrimp were lying in ice.

There were literally dozens of vegetable and fruit stalls, selling such items as chile peppers, cabbages, tomatoes (pear shaped) by the bushel, frijoles, corn, potatoes, onions, bananas, papayas, pineapples, lemons, oranges, squash, and lettuce. The little stalls of groceries (*abarrotes*) sold mostly canned goods and things in pasteboard cartons; they did not sell fruits and vegetables. Canned milk was much in evidence, for fresh milk is always suspect in any smaller Mexican town. There were also cans of fish, fruits, vegetable oils, olive oil, vegetables, sauces and ketchups, tubes of Crest and Colgate, boxes of Fab, Tide, oatmeal, syrup, corn flakes, and Jello. Many Mexicans now take oatmeal with their breakfasts. Nearly all of them like hot cakes; and eggs, of course, are a *sine qua non*. They are also beginning to serve American bread, which is a great pity. Old-style Mexican bread is crunchy and flavorful. The new style American loaves, made in brand-new factories by the thousands, are doughy and tasteless as our own. But toast will be expected for breakfast by the visitors from the North, and it is not easy to make toast out of a Mexican loaf, which is much the same as the long French loaf, only not quite so long.

The Tepic market also had its stalls of chickens, both alive in crates and freshly butchered. There was no refrigeration. The chickens were simply slaughtered, plucked, quickly quartered and then slapped down on the counters or strung up on strings until they were sold. At the dining table they are invariably as well muscled, stringy and tough as the Mexican beef. A few stalls in the market sold dime-store items of various kinds: combs, mirrors, cheap jewelry, toys, knickknacks. I was told that the main butchershops were outside, along the street. At the door I met a man carrying half a roasted pig, head attached, on a wide board. Head and all, it was probably for somebody's feast.

There were seven butchershops on the street, only one with refrigeration. Meats of all cuts were hanging from the rafters or ceilings. One of the butchers specialized in pork products. There were flies, of course. The meat markets were clean, except for the flies and the blood. The floor of the main market building, although regularly swept, was anything but clean. One could not truly say that it was filthy, but it certainly had on it a coat of dirt which no amount of sweeping was likely to pick up. Remembering Tepic's reputation for cleanliness, I simply shrugged and muttered that all things were relative. Mexicans can be the cleanest people in the world in some things, but there is usually one item or possibly more than one that they nearly always overlook. For example, the floors of the hotels and houses are given a vigorous daily scrubbing. It is the custom to scour these tiled floors incessantly. But rarely does one see even a good hotel room with a clean bedside rug. These small throw rugs, which could easily be kept spotless, are allowed to turn a dark gray from use, with hardly ever a washing.

I step again out onto the plaza. The same old gentleman in the large black serape is dozing on a bench. He probably sleeps there day and night. The plaza this time of day is filled with women going to market. Dozens of men are chatting idly in front of their stands and stores. Two things strike me at once: the number of pregnant women and the number of people (male and female, but mostly male) who are spitting on the sidewalks. Pregnant women are everywhere, and are all ages, ranging from fifteen to nearly fifty. The expression "making a baby" is so common in Mexico that it might almost be said that it is the national pastime as well as the national occupation. Certainly, it is the Mexican woman's *raison d'être*, her prime mission in life. Seldom does one encounter a family of less than half a dozen children, and many families have ten or a dozen.

I stroll down Mexico Street toward the park. In spite of its being during school hours there are several children playing. I count six of them in a single block, five boys, one girl, all less than twelve. Beyond the park is the creek, with a thick stream flowing. Half a dozen women are kneeling on the banks soaping their clothes on big rocks, scrubbing them to and fro, dipping them into the stream, then again scrubbing and rinsing. When the wash is clean enough, it is placed on other rocks or branches to dry in the sun. Two of the washerwomen, more enterprising than the rest, had strung up rude shelters of stakes and thatch in order to do their work in the shade. I walk on down the street to where a man has parked his little cart and is selling *paletas* (popsicles) and also little cones of sherbet. He is not doing much business. A bus comes along and I hail it. It will be pleasant to drive aimlessly a few miles into the countryside.

It was a small red second-class bus, like so many hundreds that ply the roads of Mexico ferrying their loads of ordinary families and workers. Their rates are ridiculouly cheap. For fifty cents they will take you to almost any town in the state. For a dollar you could travel halfway across Mexico. They bang, rattle, and jolt and they stop at every hole in the road. They even drive a mile off the road to stop in a village of three houses, but somehow they keep fairly close to their schedules and they usually arrive safely. These second-class buses are nearly always full, and they are constantly filling up and emptying as they run. One can get on or off practically anywhere. One can also carry a load of chickens, a pig, three babies, a hundred pounds of pots. Everything goes, and only the passenger has to pay. My bus that morning was crammed with people, and several chickens. When the wheels hit a deep chughole, our feathered passengers would let out a muttered squawk, but they were certainly not obstreperous. It was almost as if these chickens were by nature used to second-class Mexican road travel.

We passed the last clump of outlying adobe houses and entered the open country. The sun was out and the morning was warm and clear. We drove through fields of sugar cane and corn into the brown hills. The hills contrasted strongly with the waving green of the fields. As we climbed I could see Tepic below us, in its small valley. Nearly every town in Mexico is in some hollow or valley. The elevation of Tepic is something over three thousand feet, which gives it an admirable climate, winter and summer. The earth is rich in the state of Nayarit and the farms are flourishing. They need almost no irrigation. The earth holds enough moisture to mature the crops. From an eminence above the town the domes and towers of the churches of Tepic stood out, as they do in every town in the Mexican Republic, gaunt and lovely reminders of another epoch. Smoke spiraled upward from two big smokestacks at the edge of the valley. The towers of the cathedral dominated the urban landscape completely; the green and waving sugar cane dominated the country.

XIV

RURAL SCHOOL

Our task is to demonstrate that mestizos and Indians are capable of assimilating and of equaling, at least of equaling, the culture of white men.

—José Vasconcelos, former
Mexican Minister of Education

Thirty, forty, fifty miles or so we drove into rolling hills. We passed few houses, but people got on and off constantly. At one stop I noticed a little adobe building bearing the crude whitewashed sign: *Escuela Federal Rural* (Rural Federal School). Around it were grouped half a dozen houses, a tiny store, a cold drink stand, a mule, three pigs, two burros, and a few dozen chickens. This was where I would get off. So much has been written about Mexico's "little white schoolhouse" that I was determined to enter one, unannounced, and see for myself exactly what was going on. No classwork would be interrupted because the yard was now filled with children playing.

The first impression was hardly favorable. There was nothing "white" about this schoolhouse except the scrawled letters in irregular whitewash which designated it as a rural federal school. The walls were of adobe, and once upon a time they were probably neatly calcimined all over, but that was long ago. Now their adobe bricks were gnawed away, exposing the natural adobe. It was as if some strong corrosive had been poured upon them, dissolving entirely their edges and their white. They were, therefore, a dusty gray, the precise color of the earth from which they had been made. Small strands of straw stuck out of the walls here and there. This was the straw which had been put into the adobe to hold it more firmly together.

The front door was wide open, as were two of the windows. The other two were boarded shut. I noted that none of the windows held panes of glass. They were roughly boarded, and only two of them swung open on hinges. The other two did not. The door also was of weather-worn and unpainted boards. In front of the school, hanging from a rope, was the old steel rim of an automobile wheel. This was obviously the bell.

The school building was on a little mound, four or five feet above the level of the surrounding terrain. It consisted of two very meager rooms. You had to climb up six steps cut out of the earth in order to reach it. I began to climb. By this time every eye in the place was fixed on me. The children in the yard all stopped playing and stared in sudden fascination. The children inside who were gathered around the teacher asking questions suddenly lost all interest in the answers, and looked quizzically in my direction. A young girl of seventeen, who was the teacher's helper, came out to escort me in. The whole schoolyard was at our heels, and the young lady was obviously bewildered.

The two rooms which made up the school had no lights of any kind, and the interior was brightened only by the open windows and door. On a cloudy day it would have been dim gray inside.

The *maestra* (teacher) was talking with half a dozen girls as we entered. She was a plumpish Indian-looking woman of about fifty. She wore a gray dress flecked with white. It was badly frayed at the waist and it could have been cleaner. The teacher's face was pleasant, and she had a rotund little stomach. Her hair was dark and stringy. She was definitely more Indian than Spanish in her racial make-up. Her figure was low and ample; she waddled slightly as she walked. She dismissed the girls and came to greet me, obviously somewhat on guard. The girls withdrew a few steps and then stopped. They had no intention of missing anything. Their little brown faces were all eyes. When I told the *maestra* that I also was a teacher, her face relaxed. At least here was no gringo businessman, after a fast penny. By this time so many children had gathered around us that she turned toward them and shouted:

"*Niños, váyanse a jugar!* go on out and play! We have a visitor from the United States. You must not be rude to him. I will call you in later."

Reluctantly the children withdrew. Soon they were playing their games outside. As the teacher and I exchanged a few amenities I heard one group of them go through the Spanish version of our familiar "Eeny meeny miny mo. . . ." It ran like this: "*Tin marín dedó pingüé, cúcara mácara títere fue.*" The words are meaningless, as in English, but unlike the English they have no offensive second line. They include all the full Spanish vowel sounds, and rhyme pleasantly.

"It is now recess time," the teacher explained unnecessarily, "but I will soon call the children in." She was still feeling her way and was quite plainly embarrassed at the appearance of her school.

"Our *mobiliario* [furnishings] are very poor," she said. "This is an overflow school, you see. There is another school down the road, but it is full. It is more than full. And we had either to place the children in this older building or leave them ignorant on the roads and in the fields. I believe it is better that they learn something." She looked toward me for confirmation, and I heartily gave it.

"We are about to whitewash the inside walls," she went on, "but so far the men have been too busy to do it. I think I will do it myself soon."

The interior walls, I saw, were very much like the exterior walls, except that they were not quite as much gnawed away. They were gray and pockmarked and, judging from the window sill, were almost a foot thick. Two old well-beaten blackboards were nailed to the inside adobe. They were pasty looking from long use and had an almost pinkish cast. There was no desk. When she was not standing the teacher occupied an old chair with a side arm. It was the only one in the school. She insisted that I occupy it now, while she remained on her feet. Above our heads were eight or nine old beams of wood, completely exposed, which held up the corrugated roof. I thought this was cast-iron but was told later that it was a special kind of corrugated paper, made especially for roofing. The children had no desks, but sat on board benches at long tables, both very roughly made.

There were about a hundred children in the school, nearly all of them in the first three grades. The rate of dropout is rapid in rural Mexico, and only a small percentage of children ever really finish school. In the year 1965 an estimated 35 per cent never got beyond the first grade. Today this has probably been reduced to about 25 per cent. Some rural areas, of course, are far worse than others. In the community of Tlaxcala, the valley from which came those Indian allies who helped Hernán Cortés capture Mexico City from the Aztecs, out of a total of 23,435 children who entered the first grade only 187 finished high school. In 1970 in Mexico as a whole only one out of ten completed the sixth grade.

It was now time for class to begin again. The teacher went outside to the automobile rim hanging from the rope and rapped it sharply with an old piece of pipe which was kept nearby. At the sound the whole school rushed pell-mell back into their rooms. Five or six occupied each board bench, so every table held ten to twelve children. The teacher explained that they had a guest and must be on their best behavior. This was really not necessary, for they were all mannerly and serious. There was not a joker in the whole room. The teacher asked them to open their books so that I might pass down the aisle and look at their work. Their only school possessions were a five-cent notebook, and a pencil. They used no texts. Yet even at this level (most of them had been in school only five months) they were all able to write, and many of them wrote surprisingly well. Their letters were clear and straight, and the sentences they wrote indicated quite a high level of achievement. Offhand, I would make a quick guess and estimate that at least half of this particular class, which contained fifty-five, was at the writing level achieved by the end of our second grade in the United States. And not more than half a dozen of these students were in the second grade; the rest were all beginners. The quality and clarity of their handwriting very frankly amazed me. Here in this isolated rural school, without a single modern educational tool to help them, and with a teacher whose preparation was certainly anything but exceptional, these children of six and seven had all learned how to write, and write well, simply by concentrating on doing just that. There was no folderol, no social play, no dramatic acting out about it. They simply read and wrote.

I had picked up as many of the little dog-eared notebooks as possible in order to examine them individually, but had left out a good many of the students in the far corners of the room. It was too hard to reach them across the tables. Now suddenly, all at once these children began to rise up in the seats and crawl out over their neighbors in order to show me their handiwork. They simply could not be overlooked.

"*Sentaditos!*" the teacher said, and then repeated the word again "*Sentaditos!* In your seats!"

The children obeyed reluctantly, and passed their books down to me in a great jumble.

"Here's mine! Please look at mine, señor!" they all seemed to say at once. Again the teacher admonished them.

"*Calladitos,*" she said, and repeated it "*Calladitos!* Quietly now!"

They were certainly as well behaved and quiet as could be expected of any group of eager little children who have just learned how to read and write and want to show this to a visitor. When I told them that they were the equal of our second-graders in the United States, their little Indian faces beamed with smiles. The teacher was not convinced. She took it for a courtesy, but it was the truth.

After looking at every notebook in the entire class, for now I could do no less, the children were willing to sit back quietly on their benches and wait. The majority were boys, which rather surprised me.

"The boys drop out faster," the teacher explained. "So we left most of the girls at the other school, which is much better than this."

"It may be larger and newer, but I doubt if it is better," I said. And then I added a sentence which made me feel easier, and which I believe made them all feel easier as well. It is a sentence which I repeated in nearly every Mexican school that I visited.

"A fine building does not make a good school," I said. "Not even books make a good school. The only two things that are really necessary are good teachers and students who want to learn. You have both of these elements right here in this classroom, so you are very fortunate indeed."

The children in this particular classroom were among the poorest in the state of Nayarit. Many of them were wearing the only clothes they had, clothes which had been passed down to them from some older brother or sister. A few of the shirts were in tatters. Not all of the faces were clean. Some of the little bodies looked as if they had not been given a good bath in weeks. Dresses were cleaner than pants, but then I suppose girls are just naturally less liable to get filthy than boys. But every face, without exception, was eager and bright. There was some spark behind all that poverty and dirt. And there was pride, pride in accomplishment, pride in being a Mexican and in being able to show a gringo what a Mexican child could learn. It was good to see this spark and to feel this light.

Naturally, I wanted to find out exactly how these children had been taught so quickly to write. The teacher had referred two or three times to certain "exercises" which had helped them to learn how to form letters easily. The children apparently enjoyed these exercises, and their result was certainly excellent.

"Could you show me exactly what exercises they do?" I asked the teacher. "Are they muscular exercises?"

"Oh, no," she laughed, "not exactly that. But they do involve the muscles too. Look, I will show you."

Then turning to the class she said:

"*Niños,* our visitor would like to see how we learn to write. Let us all remain in our seats and show him just what we do. Do not make any noise. I want all of you to take part."

The class became quiet as a mouse. The teacher went to the blackboard and picked up a piece of chalk.

"First, we will do *The Little Drum,*" she said.

Then drawing little circles on the board she began to sing. The class knew every word and joined in the song. They also joined in the drawing, each one using his own notebook. As they sang, the teacher kept on drawing: circles above, circles below, then straight lines joining them, and finally crisscrossed lines between these straight lines, which were the lacing on the little drum. In a few moments the drum had emerged complete, and song was ended.

Without realizing consciously what they were about, the children had been given practice in making small lines of several shapes preparatory to forming letters. They had also learned co-ordination, so that when the time came to write the letters of the alphabet, neither the small size of these nor the necessary co-ordination would make them nervous. The alacrity with which all of the children participated in the singing and drawing was refreshing. Not one of them held back. Every little mouth was wide open, and every little voice was giving its all.

There were half a dozen other exercises which interwove the singing of simple folk tunes with apt words and easy drawings in order to condition small hands for writing. The teacher explained that at the beginning of each day's lesson the class would sing and draw, and the accuracy and co-ordination of the lines they drew steadily improved as they went along. After a few days they advanced to writing down the simple letters, forming a few familiar words. Then they took up the more difficult letters. After three months they knew the entire alphabet, and after one semester they were writing quite well. There is no doubt that they acquire this skill more quickly than our own students, that their handwriting itself was superior, and that even though their full energies and attention were directed toward writing, this never made them nervous or tense and they never found it a chore.

In examining the children's notebooks I noticed that they all had written down sentences about an imaginary girl named Lila. I asked the teacher who this Lila was, and how they had been introduced to her. The teacher then went to the wall and lifted up a piece of rough drawing paper which measured about two feet on each side. This was the only physical "tool," if we wish to use that term, in the entire school.

On the paper, drawn in crayons of different colors, was the picture of a little blonde girl of about ten who was asleep in her bed. The colors were mainly gold and blue. There was a romantic crescent moon and there were golden stars in a deep-blue sky. Lila was under her blanket below them. beside an open window, sleeping. There were two words written below the picture: *Lila sueña. Lila is dreaming.* The children were to imagine what she was dreaming about: the moon and the stars, her mother, her family, her little kitten, a soldier. . . ? They asked for the right words, the teacher wrote them on the board, and then the children copied them down. At first they all wrote the same sentences, then after they had learned the words they made up sentences of their own.

When the teacher had finished explaining how the picture was used, she called her assistant and asked the time. She herself had no watch. It was ten minutes after twelve.

"We are ten minutes late in letting them out," the teacher said. "Perhaps you had better ring the bell."

The gong was sounded and the children prepared to go out. The teacher asked them to say "*Hasta la tarde*, professor," as they left. And without a single exception, as they filed out before me, slowly, every one of them said pleasantly, distinctly, and individually:

"*Hasta la tarde*, professor."

In the state of Nayarit most of the schools have a recess period of a couple of hours in the afternoon. This is the siesta period. If the school is located so the children can go home for lunch, they do so. Then at two or three they return to school and stay there until five o'clock. This not only observes the customary siesta break but keeps them off the streets most of the day. After the last child had left, I turned to the teacher and said:

"I like very much the way you teach. The children are learning rapidly, and you have every reason to feel proud of them."

"*Gracias*, señor. I follow mostly my own methods. The state Department of Education has asked us to follow 'el método natural'; I think this comes from the United States, and that is where I got the sketch of little Lila dreaming. They almost insist that we use this method now. But we use it in the way we like. Frankly, I like the phonetic, or rather the onomatopoetic method better. When children learn the sounds of letters they really know them, and they do not forget. If we use the natural method too much, they do forget. They imagine too much, they take in too much, they do not concentrate on what they should be learning, which are the ABC's."

I asked the teacher what she meant by the "onomatopoetic method," and she explained that this was a method "invented" by the Mexican professor Gregorio Torres Quintero. It consists of using primarily the sounds that animals make. For example, "bow-wow, meow, baa-baa, moo," and so on. Students are taught to write out these sounds, which are much more phonetic in Spanish than they are in English. Slowly other sounds are added, familiar Mexican sounds that we do not know, like *glu-glu,* the sound that a liquid makes as it comes out of a bottle, or *cataplúm,* the sound that an object makes as it falls (similar to our "boom"). After they have mastered these phonetic onomatopoetic sounds, the children can go on to more difficult words.

"But many administrators today," the teacher went on, "don't seem to like this method. Apparently they believe that it is better to go from the firmament to the cloud and to the star, from the whole picture to the smaller parts, rather than from the star to the sky. I like the last way best myself, and I believe the children like it best also. There is nothing so stimulating in the process of learning as learning itself. Here, we start with something perfectly familiar, and we begin to write immediately. The children are enthusiastic and learn quickly. Language, of course, is the basic skill on which all other skills depend. Without it we live encaged. And language is made up of sounds, so why not teach sounds to begin with? Writing and reading should begin with sounds, I think."

This teacher, I am sure, had no acquaintance with the squabbles which are at present going on in our own educational system, but she had summarized one viewpoint very well. The words that she chose interested me especially. No person whose native language is Spanish can speak truly without metaphors. The poetic image is basic to the Hispanic pattern of thinking, and this teacher, I felt, had taken an especial pride in justifying her methods with such imagery.

"You have a large group," I said.

"All our schools are crowded," she said. "The classes average between fifty and sixty pupils, and many of them have sixty-five. We do not think this is too large. We do need more teachers and more school buildings in order to keep the children off the streets and highways."

"Yes, this morning I saw a great many children who were not in school."

"There is absolutely no way to make them come," she said. "In the first place, we do not really have room for them. In the second place, many of the boys have to work in order to help support their families, even at the age of ten or twelve, and many of the girls have to remain at home in order to take care of the younger children so that their mothers can work. The government has almost no monitors to check up on the children and find out if they are telling the truth about their absences. It is a vicious process, and we are only just now beginning to break it. But at least those of us who teach love to teach, and we are doing our part to *formar patria,* to form the nationhood." She pronounced these final words with great verve, as if this were the real reason for her being in the teaching profession. And to a great extent what she said is completely true. The Mexico that is emerging today, and the Mexico of tomorrow, is now being molded by what is going on in these thousands of little Mexican schools.

"How many years does a prospective teacher have to study before getting a job?" I asked.

"It varies in different places, but the minimum is to have finished elementary school, that is, six grades. The girl assistant who is here is now studying in secondary school. She receives only fifty pesos [about $4] a month for her work here, but that helps considerably."

"Are there many church schools in Mexico?"

"We do not refer to them as religious schools," she answered. "They are always called 'private schools.' Yes, there are a great many, especially in the towns and cities."

"Do they teach religion?"

"They learn to pray. Yes, I am sure they learn to pray."

She spoke from hearsay, I am sure. It was very clear that she had never actually visited one of these Catholic schools.

"Nobody bothers them any more," the teacher went on. "It's not like in the days of President Calles when the churches were all shut down. That was real persecution. There's none of that today. We are all Catholics here, you know, but we are not all fanatics. If parents want to send their children to Catholic schools, why not let them? If people like to carry their little saints up and down the streets from one church to another, let them do that too. These fiestas and pilgrimages don't hurt anyone, and everybody is happy."

The teacher spoke sincerely but not intensely. It was clear that so far as she was concerned the religious problem had disappeared from Mexican education. As she talked, I noticed that around her neck she wore a little necklace at the end of which was a small gold-colored medallion that bore the image of the Virgin of Guadalupe. She unconsciously fingered this as she talked. It was her only piece of jewelry.

"If you would not mind having a simple *caldo* [beef broth] and some eggs and tortillas, I would like to invite you for lunch," the teacher then said.

After the proper protestations, I went.

I recalled, vividly, the difficult beginnings of Mexico's present-day program of rural education. In 1920 there were almost no rural schools. But in 1923 José Vasconcelos, who was then Minister of Education, managed to get 15 per cent of the federal budget set aside for schools, and there was a broadside assault on rural illiteracy. However, the rural folk, particularly in the Indian areas of the country, were mostly belligerent, or at best apathetic. The teachers who were sent into these regions had not the faintest idea as to how to cope with the situation, and it soon became apparent that a new slant had to be found if any headway was to be made. The new slant was the idea of the "cultural missions," small carefully trained groups of specialists in rural education who were sent to several strategic spots throughout the country to train the local teachers, and the local population as well.

The teachers of the area came in to take a rigorous eight-week course with these cultural missionaries, whose goal it was to bring the rudiments of sanitation, agriculture, hygiene, as well as the ABC's, to the rural population. Eventually, thousands of schools were aided by the program. These cultural missions threw away the inadaptable textbooks. The anthropologist Manuel Gamio made it clear to them that no good would come of teaching the rural Indian the city man's culture, which he would resent and which would only make him forget his own. Besides, this would serve no purpose. The central problem, Gamio said, was to acculturate the Indian, to incorporate him into the national life. In order to bring this about the teacher had to go out among the rural people as the colonial friars had done. He must learn the Indian's ways, his language, he must understand his culture, before he could begin to teach successfully. He must, in a word, be a modern "missionary," hence the origin of the term "cultural missions."

By 1955 there were 73 cultural missions in Mexico, 41 of them in rural areas. (Some are now highly specialized, and work in the urban centers.) Each cultural mission is made up of about a dozen members: a well-trained chief, who is a specialist in rural education, a nurse, a social worker, teachers of agriculture, carpentry, masonry, and instructors in the plastic arts and music. The mission remains in the area as long as is necessary to get the local program well under way, and then moves on to another region. Many missions are now at work in the most remote mountain sections of Indian Mexico.

The program was so extraordinarily successful that UNESCO's regional school known as CREFAL (Central Regional de Educación Fundamental en América Latina) was set up in the former home of

President Cárdenas (who gave it to CREFAL) on Lake Pátzcuaro, in the state of Michoacán. Students from all over the world come here to learn how to deal with difficult rural situations in their own countries.

The *maestra* had studied with one of these cultural missions, and had the highest respect for them.

"Without them we would have been completely lost in Mexico," she admitted frankly. "With them we have taken the lead in rural education among the Indianist countries of Latin America."

We were walking slowly along the highway as we talked. Not a car had passed us on the way. The teacher's house was a good quarter of a mile down the road, and then up and behind a hill. It was of the usual gray adobe. On one side was a yard enclosed by a rude stake fence and a few odd stretches of wire. However, it seemed not to be in use, for the chickens and pigs were wandering about on the hill outside. I commented on this.

"We put them in the corral for the night," she explained. "That way they learn where they are supposed to live. Besides, then nobody can steal them."

The house consisted of three rooms and had an old red-tile roof. The teacher lived there with her mother, two sisters, the husband of one of these, and three children. The sisters were not there for lunch. They were in town sewing. It was at a *taller*, a shop run by an aunt, which had six Singer sewing machines. The shop was doing a very good business of late; everybody was ordering a dress at the same time.

The inside of the house was clean and the walls had been given a good coat of lime not too long ago. There was a little tin shrine hanging on one wall, a picture of some saint I did not recognize, a picture of the Virgin of Guadalupe, and a calendar advertising automobile tires. It had a large yellow tractor on it. The furniture was of the cheapest wood, and was covered with a yellow varnish. There were four chairs with laced-palm seats, a table, and an ancient brown sofa.

We were served *caldo* in glazed bowls of clay. It contained large chunks of pork, small pieces of chicken, and gobs of liquid soup heavily greased, and piquantly flavored. The tortillas had just come off the charcoal fire, and were crisp and tasty. The eggs were fried in heavy grease. The coffee was thick and slightly bitter. I reminded myself to be sure to buy a box of *bicarbonato de sodio* at one of the pharmacies before returning to the hotel.

After lunch was over we all sat back to relax. There were two or three magazines lying on the saggy sofa, and I picked up one of them.

It was a copy of *Life,* in Spanish. The other two were Mexican periodicals, dog-eared from use. One of them contained a long article on how to raise healthy chickens. Two or three elementary textbooks stood on a rude shelf nearby.

"I don't have much of a library," the teacher said.

It was an understatement.

An hour later we went back to the school. It was difficult to shake off the combination of a heavy meal and the sultry drowsiness of that tranquil afternoon. It seemed a very long quarter of a mile that we walked. When we arrived the children were playing outside. At the sound of the gong they came in quickly and quietly. They stood at the benches, waiting. The teacher asked them to bid me "Good afternoon." With a single voice they all said: "*Buenas tardes,* professor."

That afternoon they read and practiced their numbers, doing most of the work in unison; there was not time for much individual attention. After an hour or so I took my leave, because the last bus for Tepic would soon pass by. They all stood again and bade me a warm good-by.

Then I descended the six earthen steps and picked my way through the dusty loam to the highway to wait for the little red bus. Even Tepic seemed far away, but the warm blue sky of Mexico was soft and friendly. The brown hills bayed out on either side of the road, and the green sugar cane in the valley below swayed gently in the breeze. The few houses that I could see, gray and white, appeared to have been there since the beginning of time. A splotch of poinsettia against the walls gave them their only distinctive color. The pictorial intensity of the whole scene melted against the earth with a harmony that was almost perfect. When the red bus came, crowded to the roof, it was like life-blood coursing through the old arteries of a great organism which is now beginning to wake up and move after a long, long sleep.

XV

DAILY LIFE IN TEPIC

Respect for the rights of others is the way to peace.
—Benito Juárez

I reached the central plaza of Tepic and got off the bus just as the sun went down. The jukebox blared forth a piece of American jazz as I headed for the hotel. The policeman atop his Coca-Cola stand under the red light waved me across the street. Inside the portals of the Hotel Sierra de Álica the lights were just going on. No sooner had they lighted up than there was a sudden brilliance and they were off again.

"*El fusible*," somebody yelled. "It's the *fusible* again, the fuse."

One of the bellboys came out with a new one.

"The damn thing is always blowing out," said the American from Idaho. "These Mexican lines just won't take a heavy load. Turn on more than two lights, and ping, out goes the fuse."

Tepic is not confined to its central plaza or to Mexico Street. It is rapidly spreading out across the valley floor. On one hillock, near the edge of town, is a large new hospital. Half a dozen blocks away is another, not so new and not so large. There are tennis courts and ball fields with large stadiums around them. There are four parks. There is also a church in which they show you a cross which suddenly appeared in the grass many years ago and is still visible. They call it the green cross of Tepic. The cross can be seen from inside the church; it grows just beyond one of the walls. It is clearly a cross formed of grass which is taller than the other grass around it. The miraculous cross bore obvious marks of having been trimmed, not to say cut out, in order to maintain its shape. The whole thing reminded me of the carnival days of my youth when the pictures outside invited one in to see some mighty wonder, and when you got inside the wonder turned out to be figment. But people do not say this about the green cross of Tepic; they cross themselves humbly before it.

One afternoon I went into one of the parks of Tepic to watch the children play. It was about five-thirty. There were sixty-two children playing, most of them under twelve. The majority were girls.

Most of the children were playing in groups gathered around one or the other of the seven balls which were in evidence. One group of boys, the oldest, was playing soccer. Occasionally there would even be a good strong American block or tackle. All the rest were simply batting their balls to and fro. A point was made when your adversary let the ball hit the ground. Three out of the sixty-two children were obviously maimed. One girl had a badly twisted knee and was forced to walk like a spider. One of the boys had a hand missing. Another girl of eight had a badly withered arm.

I looked down Mexico Street toward the brown hills and saw that the houses gradually diminished in size until they disappeared completely in the distance. The hull of an old ruined chapel could be seen on one side of the road. Washing was strung out to dry on the half-fallen brick walls. On top of the highest hill far away was a large cross, placed there to overlook the town. The bells of the cathedral began to toll. On my way back to the plaza I stepped inside the door. At the far end of the cathedral the altar was a glow of gold and polychrome, and candles burned brightly here and there along the walls. But hardly more than a corporal's guard were in the church. The candles certainly outnumbered the people. The great vault of the cathedral soared above a great emptiness. But Mexicans do not take their religion as a daily chore. When the big fiestas come, they will be there. They will walk for miles and they will carry torches and pray until their mouths are numb. They will walk on their knees until their joints are sore in order to participate in the saintly fiesta. But this is not every day.

If there was a great emptiness inside the gray cathedral of Tepic, there was also peace. The doors were open, but the walls were thick and they shut off the sound of the world outside, which could be heard as only a faint hum in the dusk. The worshipers were all in deep concentration. They sat motionless in their pews or remained on their knees, like statues in immobile stone. The cathedral was their refuge and their rock. When disaster struck, or death, it would always be there, waiting. As I arose to leave, the sound of a man's voice came flowing inward on the air:

"*Paletas! Pale-e-etas!*"

It was the popsicle man with his white cart, crying out his wares. The plaza was filled with people on their way home from work. A dozen neon signs were blinking on the square. There was a line of cars and trucks two blocks long. The traffic was almost like that of an American town on Saturday night.

Although Tepic is a town of no more than 50,000, or at the outside 60,000, inhabitants, it boasts four newssheets. Compared with the five newspapers which appear in Los Angeles, California (a city of nearly three million), the record is not a bad one. It goes without saying that the Tepic papers are not exactly voluminous. They range in size from four to twelve pages, and in the main limit themselves to subjects of local interest. In Tepic the struggles of the local Pepsi-Cola Company to employ workers who do not belong to the *sindicato* (union) and stories about a local bandit referred to as "El Yoyo" replace dramatic tales about the Suez Canal, the Viet Cong, and the international situation generally. Tepic, at least that portion of Tepic which tries to keep up with the world, is perfectly aware of these larger problems, which come to them through *Time* magazine, or the Mexican *Tiempo* (no kin to *Time*), or in capsule form in the Spanish version of the *Reader's Digest*. But literate Tepic has long ago made up its mind that the Tepikians cannot do very much about international problems, and so these are left for the larger arenas. It is a wise decision, which gives the Tepic dailies the flavor of a news sandwich composed of local industrial problems, melodramatic human interest stories, and assassinations, with plenty of oversize Pepsi-Colas to carry it down.

Nine-tenths of the news is of a local nature. Most of it is small talk. The papers appear to have picked out the seamiest episodes of Tepic's daily life; yellow journalism is on the march. The ads in the four papers (besides what the doctors, the dentists, the funeral parlors, and the colas have to say) tend mostly to automobile accessories, office furniture, copper tubing, machines of all kinds, farm implements, tractors and bulldozers for hire, cigarettes, and ads of a few of Tepic's stores. I noticed particularly that whenever people appeared in these ads (drinking a cola, sitting in a store, even standing beside an automobile tire), the commercial artist invariably drew them as well-dressed persons who might have stepped out of the pages of the *Los Angeles Times*, or even *The New Yorker*. There was not even an Indian tinge to their appearance. In general, I found this same thing to be true of magazine and newspaper advertising all over Mexico. Racial equality is supposed to exist in Mexico (and Mexico is certainly much closer to this than are we in the United States), yet there is a strong, often subconscious undercurrent, which gives Mexicans the urge to move as far as they can out of the Indianist category.

The only other item of Tepic's daily newssheets which merits special comment tells about the Catholic priests who are going to the States to minister to the Mexican itinerant workers. After reporting the above fact the paper goes on to make the editorial comment that the priests will try to "make less burdensome the lives of these workers in those foreign lands where they are often looked down on, molested (*vejados*), and frequently robbed." The priests have promised to bring both comfort and faith to the contract fields "where our racial brothers weep the absence of their families and the distance of their native land."

For many years the United States and Mexico had an arrangement whereby, during the height of the harvest season in the United States, Mexican workers might cross the border as *braceros* and work as long as the season lasted. They were not permanent immigrants; after the labor period was over, they had to return to Mexico. The *bracero* program ended in 1965, but in 1970 approximately two and a half million Mexicans still held "border-crossing cards" and 100,000 others were "green card" immigrants who live on the other side of the border but cross over to work and often to follow the seasonal harvests as far north as Michigan. The lower wages paid to these workers frequently causes resentment among the farm hands of the United States. On the other hand, the Mexican workers themselves have often been exploited to the limit. These workers perform a valuable service for the farmers of the United States, and the money they are able to earn in this country has enabled many of them to send large savings in dollars back to their families in Mexico. This has helped to raise the Mexican standard of living and to increase the Mexican consumer market. Once people get a taste of some of the good things of life they work harder than ever to hold on to them. This obviously stimulates the Mexican economy, extends the buying market for both Mexican and U.S. products, and can become an effective instrument in bringing the two nations closer together.

There had been a slight shower the day before, most unusual for the dry season, and the sky was pure gold and blue as I strolled up and down the narrow streets of Tepic's old colonial quarters looking into patios to see what was going on. The patios were all small; Tepic's houses do not run to a very large size. But they were all neat and green. Pots of every size and description held plants: ferns of many kinds, philodendrons, banana trees, tropical flowers. Poinsettias of a dozen varieties were in bloom. Bougainvillaeas of purple and red climbed up the inside adobe walls, on the patio arcades. The red tile of the floors made a strong contrast with the brilliant green. I walked by the house of Amado Nervo, Tepic's famous poet of the Modernist Movement, whose verses range from tortured love to mystic serenity.

I passed several schools. Not one of them had a real playground. They all did have enclosed patios, with a small space for volleyball and basketball, where the children were supposed to play. Some of the patios were paved; others were still muddy from yesterday's shower. None of them was larger than a small lot, perhaps a hundred feet on each side. In this restricted area as many of five hundred school children had to find room for their games. And they did play here, without fighting, without undue noise, all enjoying themselves greatly, in spite of their belonging to at least six different age groups in six different grades.

Tepic does not believe in co-education. The little rural school that I had visited in the hills was an exception. The schools in town were nearly all restricted to one sex or the other. When I asked about this arrangement, very general answers were given: "It's the custom here. Parents like it that way better. The children learn more. There aren't so many problems in discipline."

The particular school that I wanted to visit was the Escuela Amado Nervo. Even in passing this school one could see that it was a model plant. Studious faces were bent over books and papers; the quiet rhythm of concentrated work prevailed. Both students and teachers were neatly dressed, and represented the most progressive elements of Tepic's daily life. An enormous oil painting of the poet Nervo looked down on everything from one side of the patio; his dark-brown eyes, mystic face of aquiline features, and thinning hair held before the teachers and children of this school the example of one of Mexico's greatest intellects and greatest hearts.

The patio itself was paved and was one of the largest in town. The arcades were covered with cream-colored plaster, not recently applied. The building was not one of the newer ones in town. I walked in unannounced and, as was the case all over Mexico when I stepped into a school, the welcome was warm and friendly. It almost made me feel a little ashamed, for I felt that no Mexican visitor suddenly appearing in an American school would receive such generous attention.

The Amado Nervo School was for girls in the elementary grades, first to sixth. One of the pupils happened to be in the arcades as I entered, and took me to the principal's office. The principal was an intelligent, motherly lady of middle years whose life was obviously dedicated to these children.

The office was small and bare. Although the school had over eight hundred girls and seventeen teachers, there was no secretary, not even a typewriter. In addition to all her other work the principal had to write every letter and draw up every report by hand. If a teacher was absent, the principal invariably took her class. She had no vice-principal to help her. In spite of this overload of work, when I entered the office she dropped everything and insisted on taking me personally around the school so that I might visit every class. The average size of the classes was fifty-five students. One class in homemaking was sewing and embroidering. Twice a week they gave a few minutes to this task. Another class was doing decimals and fractions in the metric system. Grade one was learning to read and write. Lila appeared again on the walls of this room, but her horizon was somewhat extended. She was no longer confined to a single picture of "Lila Dreaming," but appeared in three others: (*b*) Lila is a little girl, (*c*) Lila's home, and (*d*) Lila and her mother. In each of these pictures there was a profusion of flowers.

"The state gives us the central idea, but I drew the pictures," the teacher of the first grade said. She was a young girl of not more than eighteen. "Would you like to hear the class read?"

And so they read, first all together, then singly. After one semester they were all reading exceptionally well. They were cleaner, healthier than the poor children in the rural school, but I do not think they were any brighter. It was obvious, of course, that they would be able to stay in school longer, make a greater use of the knowledge that education can give.

"I have almost no dropouts in my school," the principal said. "We have one of the best records in the state of Nayarit."

We walked on down to the sixth-grade room. Here the girls were making up a bulletin board display. It was almost finished. There was a large photograph of George Washington and below that another of the signing of the United States Declaration of Independence. This was referred to as the beginning of freedom in the Americas. Above Washington were pictures of a group of Japanese Virgins, who greatly resembled Mexico's own Virgin of the Guadalupe. The bulletin display was taken into the arcades and hung up beside another which had been prepared by the fifth grade. This latter showed the Aztec Virgin Xochi offering flowers to one of the Aztec gods, as the great chief of the tribe sat immobile on his throne in the background. A few feet from the chieftain was another Indian wearing an immense headdress of feathers in many colors which stood erect on his head in the shape of a great circle. The picture called to mind the ancient Aztec celebration at which a very beautiful dance was performed for the war god, Huitzilopochtli. In this ceremony the dancers all decorated themselves with roses and covered the walls of the temple with garlands of roses. In the temple sat a woman representing Xochi-quetzalli, the goddess of love, beauty, and flowers. As the dance progressed, little boys dressed as birds and butterflies, in costumes of brilliant feathers, climbed the artificial trees placed in the temple, and moved from branch to branch, sipping the nectar of its garlands of flowers. The principal said she thought the students enjoyed making up these bulletin boards immensely, for it made history come alive for them.

"The girls like to celebrate different holidays and events in this way," she said. "And we let them choose the pictures they want to display. The ideas are all their own. You see how much they think of the United States?"

At this moment the bell rang and the girls all came out into the patio for their recess. Half a dozen of them set up little stands under the arcades and began to sell tortillas, popsicles, Pepsi-Cola, and cake. A long line quickly formed before each stand. There was no teacher direction, but there was no shoving or horseplay of any kind. The girls themselves took care of the selling and the making of change. Within a few moments they had several peso bills in their care.

"That is the way we teach them to calculate and use their figures," the principal said. "They make a mistake occasionally, but they never make the same mistake twice. They know what it costs us. And they love to do this work. Besides that, it keeps them from buying contaminated food on the streets."

"How much do you take in during one day?"

"I really don't know. Let's count it."

The girls put their money together and counted seventy-six pesos. It was not all profit, but earnings were sizable. There would be more coming in before the day was over.

We returned to the principal's office and had a cola ourselves. The principal spoke frankly of her main problems.

"We are overcrowded, of course, but we can't help that. Parents are all eager to send their children to school now, at least more of them than we have room for. When the year began we had pupils standing and sitting all over the floor, even out in the corridors. There were not even enough seats to go around. So we canvassed the homes and began to take up a collection. One family sent us six chairs, another family contributed fifty pesos, and so on, until we at least had enough seats. I think we have added about a hundred chairs."

"What time are you able to leave school for home?"

"School lets out at five, but many of the girls do not want to go straight home. They stay on here until six or seven. We never rush them off if they want to stay. Sometimes they just play, at other times they have studies that they want to do."

"Do the teachers receive any extra pay for these additional hours?"

The principal laughed at this.

"No, indeed," she said. "Being a teacher in Mexico is a full-time job. I always stay on myself, and the others take turns. Most of them enjoy being here with the girls."

"Why do you have your schools separated here, some being limited exclusively to girls, others to boys?"

She hesitated a moment, then said:

"We don't have as much culture in these matters as you do in the United States. Mexicans are not accustomed to having the two sexes thrown together freely in the way you are. It almost always causes more trouble than it avoids. Someday, I am sure, we will change; but if we were to throw the boys and girls together right now, the parents of half the girls would promptly jerk their daughters out of school."

I found out later that the principal had been in California, where she had visited our schools, and was impressed most of all by the way boys and girls got along together in the same classes.

"What would be the average income of a teacher in a Mexican school in a town this size?"

"Teachers are placed in two categories, A and B, depending on preparation and length of service. Their salaries range from 840 to 1,002 pesos, plus a slight priority increment. Many rural teachers get more than this."

Roughly, this would be between $72 and $84 a month.

"I don't see how anyone can live on that," I said.

"No one can live on it, and certainly not if there is a family to support. That is why nearly all the teachers here are daughters in a family which has other sources of income, or are wives or widows whose husbands or children also work. I myself am the case of a woman who makes her living from teaching alone. But as my income from this position is not enough to live on—and remember I am the principal of the school—I have to hold an additional job. So I teach at a secondary school between six and eight every morning before coming to work here at nine. With this increment I am able to get along."

We were just winding up this discussion when one of the Tepic co-ordinators walked in. This lady went from school to school trying to keep things running smoothly and more or less at the same pace. She also had the onerous task of having to apportion her small budget in such a manner that each school received its just share for minor expenses, equipment, etc.

"We are all going to get a raise soon," this lady said. "They will give us ten per cent without much of a fight. But we are asking for a forty per cent increase, and for that we will have to fight."

The principal agreed with her on this point.

"But how will you fight?" I asked. "Go to the parents?"

"No, we will go to the government. Then we will strike. All the teachers in Mexico belong to the teachers' union, and although we hate to strike, because of what it does to the children, sometimes we are forced to, because we have to live, too, you know. And who can live now in Mexico on 840 pesos a month, when even a couple of rooms cost 300 pesos a month?"

"Do you think you will get the raise?"

The co-ordinator said:

"We will get it, but there will be some difficult times."

"Who pays the teachers—the city, the county, or the state?"

"We are paid mostly by the state. Nayarit is a rich state and is certainly able to pay us more than we are now getting. Business has been good here for several years, workers' salaries are up, profits of industry are up, incomes have improved all along the line, but teachers' salaries have remained much the same. It is time for a change."

It was the same old story of education everywhere. Those who are willing to devote their lives to a profession of human service are invariably underpaid, and primarily because they are people who are willing to make sacrifice after sacrifice in order that their work may continue.

"Do any of your schools have libraries?" I asked.

"Just what you see here," the principal said. I saw possibly fifty books on a shelf.

"That new encyclopedia there," she said, "the *Enciclopedia Salvat*, I was able to buy that this year so that the teachers here might check their materials with documentation. They have made much use of it."

"What about textbooks?"

"We use as few as possible. The parents buy them and they are very expensive. Everyone is always kicking."

At this juncture the co-ordinator arose to leave, and I followed suit. The principal had a pile of papers on her desk which needed attending. My eyes wandered from the desk to the pockmarked walls where the plaster was wearing away, then to the little "library" on the shelf, and finally to the principal herself, in her inexpensive black dress. Down the corridors came a wave of small voices, happy voices, saying their lessons aloud. Behind the principal's desk were half a dozen trophies which the school had won for volleyball championships, and above them were two pictures of recent champion teams, smiling healthy girls dressed in neatest white.

The principal escorted us to the door. The co-ordinator left, and the principal turned to me and said, by way of farewell:

"You can see that I love my children and my work. Every teacher must. Please come back whenever you can, and know that here in Tepic, even though we are isolated from the world, you will always be warmly welcomed. *Adiós*, señor. *Que le vaya bien.* May all go well with you. *Adiós.*"

A rapid look at the history of education in Mexico will show us how gigantic a problem illiteracy has been in the story of the Mexican people. At the end of the colonial regime (1810), after nearly three centuries of Spanish rule, only 30,000 persons were able to read and write. Perhaps another 20,000 could sign their names. That is, out of a total population of 6.5 million, 99.5 per cent were illiterate. In the year 1874, during the administration of Lerdo de Tejada, the index of illiteracy stood at 93 per cent, out of a population of 9,343,470. (Russia's percentage of illiteracy in that year was 91 per cent; India's was 98 per cent.)

When Porfirio Díaz took over the reins of government in 1877, illiteracy was approximately 90 per cent, and when he was overthrown in 1910 it had been reduced only to 78.4 per cent, despite the superstructure of railways, industrial expansion, foreign investments and trade, all of which were humming. During the years of the Mexican Revolution, and the decades immediately following (1910–1940), illiteracy was decreased to 63.04 per cent. In 1944 there were still between 10 and 12 million people unable to read or write. The real struggle against illiteracy in Mexico has been waged since that year, beginning under the presidency of Avila Camacho, when the Law of Emergency (to decrease illiteracy) was promulgated. According to this law, every Mexican between the ages of 18 and 60 who knew how to read and write was obligated, as a national duty, to teach the ABC's to at least one other person between 6 and 40 years of age. Although it was manifestly not possible to enforce this law rigidly, such was the enthusiasm and pride generated that 69,881 teaching centers were organized during this crusade, and here instruction was given on a collective basis. The illiterates gathered in these centers where their more fortunate brothers and sisters served as teachers, and the problem was attacked with all the vigor and enthusiasm of an awakened people. In 1970 only 30 per cent of the population was classified as illiterate. The Mexican schools today are doing an admirable job of teaching under economic conditions which are often lamentable.

There are at present approximately 9,500,000 children in the primary grades in Mexico, 700,000 in the secondary schools (junior high schools and high schools), and approximately 350,000 studying at the college level. The second largest appropriation of the government is now going toward the improvement of the school system. (The largest is for public works.) This is an economic as well as a cultural necessity, for, while machineless men may be perfectly well able to work and produce their arts and crafts without knowing how to read or write, skilled workers are at a serious disadvantage without this knowledge.

Before becoming overenthusiastic at the inroads which have been made on illiteracy in Mexico during the past twelve or so years, we should in all justice point out that a very large percentage of those now classified as "literate" possess such a low level of education that if they lived in the United States we would classify them as "illiterate." To be specific, in 1965 approximately 35 per cent of those who could read and write had not reached the second grade. The extremely high percentage of dropouts is at the heart of this problem. Out of every 100 children who enter the first grade, only 65 now reach the second grade, 41 reach the third grade, 29 reach the fourth grade, 17 get into the fifth, and only 10 reach the sixth grade. This represents a loss of 90 per cent by the end of elementary school. In the United States, England, Germany, and Japan, a person is not classified as literate unless he has reached at least the fourth-grade level. Consequently, the present figures for illiteracy in Mexico are somewhat deceptive, for the actual or "functional" percentage of illiterates, those who stand merely at the first-grade level of education, would take in 50 per cent of all those at present (1970) classified as literate.

Formerly, what these people read, if they read anything at all, were infantile stories, comic strips, and occasional news items which would certainly depress rather than elevate them. There is nothing creative in such readings. In order to combat this, the National Campaign for Literacy is publishing what it calls the Popular Library Encyclopedia, composed of cheap and easy editions of works which present different phases of Mexican and universal culture. Several hundred titles are already available, and an additional one appears every week. The books sell for the ridiculously low price of 16 cents, and their popularity has become widespread. It is a matter of great pride when a reader can tell his friends he is enjoying one of these books.

Schools in Mexico are supported by both the federal and state governments, with poor rural areas getting most of the federal aid. In the state of Nuevo León, for example, in 1969 there were 597 state, 731 federal, and 101 private elementary schools. A "crash" program of school building was carried out in the 1960's. Government architects designed a cheap but sturdy pre-fabricated frame adaptable to nearly any building material: adobe, stone, wood, brick. The easy to assemble frames are made available at less than cost. The community does the assembling and pays only $1,760 (in time payments), while the government's share is $2,720. These pre-fabricated schools come fully equipped with furniture, phonographs, projectors, and an adjoining teacher's apartment. During the years that Pedro Ramírez Vázquez, Mexico's great architect, occupied various posts in the Ministry of Education, a grand total of 35,000 pre-fabricated schools were constructed.

Teachers' salaries have doubled since 1960. In the larger cities the average monthly salary is now $160. Many government agencies—Social Security, Petróleos Mexicanos, the National Railways—have schools for their own employees. In the area of higher education Mexico has 103 institutions, but there is still a critical shortage of doctors, nurses, engineers, technicians. In oversupply are economists, architects, and accountants.

Alfonso Reyes, the famous Mexican writer, in his essay "Mexico in a Nutshell," proudly affirms that the great achievement of the Mexican Revolution was education. "A grand crusade for learning electrified the spirit of the people. Nothing to equal it has ever been seen in the Americas. It will be Mexico's highest honor in history."

XVI

GUADALAJARA, JALISCO

May slavery and class distinctions be abolished for all time, and one American be distinguished from another solely by his vices and his virtues.

—José María Morelos

Every city in Mexico has a distinctive personality of its own, and this gives a flavor to travel in the country which even the rapid growth of industry and the mechanization of life cannot erase. Guadalajara, in its great valley, is the colonial past come to a new life in the industrial present. Monterrey is the United States spirit of organization, enterprise, and efficiency transported to a Mexican locale. Mexico City is a little of everything: Indian, mestizo, white man, colonial past, dynamic present, overcontemporary architecture and art, glorification of industry, noise and bustle unlimited. It is a colossus now emerging from the colonial cocoon; many observers would say that it has already emerged. In any case it is Mexico on a gigantic scale, a loud bawling cosmopolitan metropolis which would be the envy of any urban lover anywhere in the world. It is one of the great cities of the Americas today.

The tremendous growth of urban life in Mexico during the past three decades has created many new problems. The country folk have poured into the cities in an ever-increasing stream. They are in search of a better income, better living conditions, better schools, and all the other accouterments of urban civilization. At first, they did not seem to "belong" in their new environment. They had not learned the necessary techniques of city life. They were not accustomed to the impersonality of urban society. They felt uprooted, alienated, lost, and the cities in which they lived gave the same impression. They were cities composed of wandering and apparently rootless men in a restless search for their destiny.

A Mexican novelist, López y Fuentes, has a novel on this theme called *Entresuelo*, which means "mezzanine." It is a symbolic title. The Doblado family (also a symbolic name, for it means "bent double") came to the city from the country, and lived in a nondescript apartment on the middle floor. They lacked the class feelings and strength of the poor family on the first floor and did not have the money or position of the well-to-do family on the third floor. They were caught between the two and had no real place in the great city. The novel tells the story of a country boy lost in the city, overwhelmed by the impersonal tragedy of urban life, unable to make convincing headway against the stormy urban sea. The Doblado family is symbolic of the emerging middle class in Mexican urban life. Caught and pressed between those below and those above, it loses lifeblood and withers away.

The novel came out in 1948; it reflects the tragedy of the past three decades. The tragedy was widespread, but it was really more the tragedy of individuals than of the middle class. For the Mexican middle class, which is the educated white-collar urban class, certainly never withered away. It staggered, faltered, felt restless and lost, rootless and without a soul, but it never ceased to push forward with a kind of instinctive will to survive and to progress. Also with a will not to surrender the best of its Indian past nor to forgo the best of the mechanical civilization which was moving down upon it from the United States. The story of the large Mexican cities is the story of this emerging middle class.

Industrialization and the great growth of the urban centers in Mexico have gone hand in hand during the past few years. Since 1940 the percentage of the rural population in towns and villages of less than 2,500 inhabitants has declined from 66 per cent of the total to approximately 40 per cent, and the total number of settlements in Mexico (rural and urban) decreased from 122,434 in 1940 to 73,134 in 1970. The number of settlements classified as cities (over 10,000) increased from 97 in 1940 to 251 in 1970, and the increase in urban population was tremendous and has affected all levels of Mexican life. (Even so, 30 per cent of all Mexicans still live in settlements of less than 1,000 persons.)

In 1940 the total urban population stood at 4,308,240 inhabitants, or 22 per cent of the total; in 1950 it stood at 7,464,854 inhabitants, or 29 per cent of the total, and at present (1970) it will approach 30 million, or 60 per cent of the total population of Mexico. Although about twenty million Mexicans still live in small rural settlements and still engage in agriculture, the output per man (and output per man-hour) of the urban worker is many times that of his rural counterpart. For example, the 1970 census shows over 8 million agricultural workers in Mexico (those under age twelve are automatically excluded), while there were only 3,850,000 workers in industries, 4,630,000 in services and communications, and a mere 93,000 in mining. However, the productivity per man of each of the 8 million farmers comes to only $467 a year, while the per capita productivity of the industrial worker is $2,669, productivity per miner is $2,577, and productivity per worker in the communications and services is $3,734. The higher standard of living which these figures indicate for the urban and industrial worker explains the attraction of the city for the enterprising Mexican country boy.

It is less than two hundred miles from Tepic to Guadalajara, but the landscape that lies between is some of the most forbidding in North America. The earth is scored with sharp, deep ravines and canyons which pierce the valleys and rising mountains with a series of long and imposing cuts. The highway is not as spectacular as those of the Central Highlands, which reach upward beyond the timber line one moment and the next sweep downward to a riot of tropical jungle. It is from the air that the stark serrated gorges of Nayarit and Jalisco (called *barrancas* in Spanish) are seen to best advantage.

The airplane takes less than an hour to make the trip. It is a small DC-3, of the Aeronaves Line. The airport is deserted that afternoon. An ancient porter, who looks the spit and image of Sitting Bull, grabs my bag and shuffles to the counter with it. Then he begins to help with the freight. There are many packages of cigarettes and a few odd accessories of agricultural machinery.

The plane comes in and I get aboard. The purser is a man, as is the case in most Mexican planes, especially inside Mexico. About five minutes before take-off time a taxi screeches up, tires burning, and out jumps a last-minute traveler. He and I are the only passengers aboard. He is a clean-cut, well-dressed young man of about thirty, obviously a businessman of some means. He takes off his coat, loosens his tie, and settles back in his seat. We strike up a conversation. I find out that he is selling automatic temperature controls for a concern in Mexico City. He says that business has been extremely favorable, even in Tepic. He had also made a quick trip to the west coast, only a few miles below Tepic, and had done well there too. The west coast beach towns Puerto Vallarta and San Blas, once completely isolated, are now booming. Every tourist tells the next one that these places are the real Mexico, off the beaten track, tranquil, and despite a certain squalidity, also delightful. And tourists are already beginning to go there by the hundreds. Within four or five years we will probably have half a dozen rivals for Acapulco, which, with the present great influx of North Americans, has practically ceased to be a Mexican town.

I tell my passenger friend about having visited the Nayarit schools and comment warmly on the achievements of the Mexican school children. When I say frankly that I believe they are further advanced than children of a similar age in our schools in the States, he looks dubious, hesitates a moment, then comments:

"Latin children are all extremely bright, especially at an early age. They learn quickly, imitate readily, and give the impression of being unusually talented.

"But this slows up as they get older. By the time they have reached their teens they are already getting indolent and lose interest in study. They prefer to substitute a good flow of words for concentrated effort; they can speak fluently on almost any subject, but cannot talk profoundly on even one. They drop out of school in droves, and want to work."

"Many of them *have* to work," I interpolated.

"Yes, I know, but there are thousands of dropouts among those who do not have to. They simply grow weary of study, hard study. Now, in the United States," my friend went on, "I have noticed that, while the children may not appear so bright in the early grades, their intellectual development is steadier, more sustained. They mature more slowly, but they never seem to stop learning, growing."

I suggest that nutrition may be just as important as temperament. Mexican children suffer a nutritional deficiency and their body reserves are quickly burned up as they advance in years. These reserves are never replenished. Temperament sets the spark, and nutritional deficiency does the rest.

My friend agrees, but points up Mexico's great surge forward of the past few years.

"Ten years ago Mexico was a *pueblo enfermo,* a sick nation," he said. "Now we are beginning to cure some of our worst ills. I have just come back from a long trip through Guatemala, Colombia, and Venezuela, and compared with those countries Mexico is well off indeed. Our people are *free.* They can say whatever they want to say without fear of reprisal. We have a free government. Even if there are elements which are still corrupt, and still rob the country, we are getting them under control. We are getting rid of them. And they have no power at all to obstruct the free flow of ideas. This is Mexico's great advantage over those nations which live under a dictatorial government. We have been through dictatorship and revolution, and are sick of it. We are through with it for good. Therefore, a great stimulus to progress exists in Mexico in all levels of the population, as it does not exist in the totalitarian countries of Latin America.

"The concept of the family is gaining in Mexico too, the concept of the family unit as something basic, and sacred, and indispensable. Men are getting drunk less, there is less running around and hell-raising generally, the pistols have been replaced by the ball-point pen. The streets are no longer full of swaggering drunks and soldiers; they are crowded with honest and hard-working husbands and fathers."

My friend paused a moment, then added, very seriously:

"I've traveled a great deal in the United States, too—our company has two branches there. And I know that whatever we have been able to achieve in the matter of organization here in Mexico we owe to you. There are some Mexicans who are not willing to admit this, but it is very true."

"Yes," I said, "and there are some North Americans who still believe that a Mexican simply cannot run a tractor or bulldozer, or drive an automobile, or handle an electric machine. There still exists the myth that the Indian cannot learn anything about mechanical gadgets, yet some of the best mechanics in the United States are Mexicans. The border states are full of them. It is one of those old legends that die hard."

"This is very true," agrees my friend of the automatic temperature controls, himself a cultured Mexican businessman who makes an excellent living out of just such mechanical gadgets.

Mexico is full of such men. Industry has come to Mexico to stay. Forty years ago Stuart Chase wrote that the country could never support a population of more than 30 million, unless it became industrial like Great Britain and sold its manufactured articles in order to import certain goods and foods. Mexico is not yet ready to be compared with Britain industrially, but in the years that have passed since Chase wrote his book real miracles of industry have been accomplished in the southern republic. The country stands today on the threshold of a new era of expansion which only some catastrophe could bring to an untimely close. As these thoughts run through my mind the plane swoops in over the Valley of Guadalajara, and I see the sharp twin towers of the cathedral as we curve in for the landing.

It was January but I remember the roses. There were roses, roses everywhere. Their blossoms were full and firm, their leaves were strong and green. At the airport, in the city parks, in the plazas, in the patios of the homes, everywhere there were roses. Guadalajara is a city of roses and other flowers of every imaginable kind. In March the violet-blue jacaranda trees burst into bloom; in April the royal poinciana adds its fire-red blooms to the scene. There are pinks, carnations, gardenias, and flowering raintrees covered with racemes of gold. Guadalajara is Tepic on a gigantic scale. It is the second city of Mexico, with a population of well over a million. It is the most charming *city* in Mexico. Monterrey is too close to the United States, Veracruz is too near the sultry hurricane coast, Mexico City is a colossus of such dimensions that one simply cannot take it all in. It lacks cohesion and beauty of form; it is still an inchoate monster emerging from the green and denuded hills. Guadalajara is the most charming of them all. It was founded in 1542 and was named for the old Moorish city in Spain.

Downtown Guadalajara is plaza after plaza of colonial splendor still surviving. On the main plaza the ornate sharp-towered tile-embroidered cathedral (begun in 1571) lifts its great bulk above the town. It is a vast conglomeration of colonial styles, Byzantine and Gothic predominating. It is a cathedral unworthy of the town. Fronting an adjacent plaza, the beautiful baroque Palacio del Gobierno (Government Palace), constructed in the 1600's, contains an enormous fresco by Orozco which covers the entire walls and ceiling above one of the stairways, and shows a gigantic figure of Father Hidalgo freeing the slaves. It is perhaps the grandest mural painting in all Mexico, and one of the finest in the entire world. It is certainly fitting that Bernard S. Myers in his recent book, *Mexican Painting in Our Time,* should reproduce this fresco on his jacket as representative of the best in Mexican art.

At night stone fountains send their sounding spray into the balmy air, for Guadalajara, at an elevation of 5,000 feet, enjoys a mild climate throughout the year, broken only by the occasional violence of a tropical thundershower. The tempo of life moves unhurriedly here, and the business of living has been raised to the status of a fine art. Because of the wonderful climate the people spend much of their time out of doors, thronging the streets, strolling through the parks, visiting with their friends in the cafés. The band plays regularly in the Plaza de Armas. The bandstand is a romantic piece of cast bronze composed of eight beautiful female figures, nude from the waist up, which support the roof with one of their arms, while the other holds a musical instrument over the middle region instead of the usual fig leaf. Each of these seductive beauties has rounded breasts fully exposed.

On a third adjacent plaza stands a huge figure of Father Hidalgo, who on December 6, 1810, made in Guadalajara his famous emancipation proclamation, as famous in Mexico as is Lincoln's in the United States. Beneath the enormous bronze figure of Hidalgo are written the principal articles of this proclamation:

1. All slaves in New Spain will henceforth be considered as free men.
2. Tributes of all kinds are abolished, particularly the tributes exacted from the Indian population.
3. The government no longer holds a monopoly on the manufacture of gunpowder. Henceforth, anyone may make powder with the single proviso that he will give the government the first option to buy his product.
4. Special stamped government paper need no longer be used in legal transactions. Regular paper of any kind will suffice.

The figure of Father Hidalgo stands over the plaza in its great flowing cape, surmounted by an enormous head and brow (also notable in Orozco's mural). An occasional passer-by stops to read the inscription printed below. Behind the statue, on Hidalgo Street, the buses pass in a constant stream on their way to the outlying areas. The plazas of Guadalajara are less crowded than those of the smaller towns. Now that colonial Guadalajara has become a great city, the axis of life, as in the United States, has moved into the suburbs, where "California" homes are replacing the colonial mansions of an earlier day. One of the most imposing of these suburbs is called Country Club Estates; one of the best motels is California Courts.

This is no guidebook on Mexico, but it would be unforgivable to mention Guadalajara without referring to its famed pottery and to the suburb of Tlaquepaque, whose very name suggest the clap-clap of man or burro heavily laden with the brittle ware.

Another landmark is the Museo Orozco, the former home of the greatest of Mexican painters, left just as it was when Orozco died. The artist designed the four-story house and left many of his paintings in it, also his brushes, his thick-lensed spectacles, and many of his preliminary sketches. In one room of the house is a marvelous picture of the archbishop of Mexico and in the next is a collection of grotesque bawds in various stages of undress.

The University of Guadalajara, founded in 1792, now occupies a new physical plant. The university has over fifteen thousand students and there is a large summer school, held under the joint auspices of the University of Guadalajara and Stanford University, which attracts many North Americans. The summer climate is delightful.

Guadalajara also has its bullfights and is particularly noted for its *peleas de gallos* (cockfights), which are held almost daily in nearby Tlaquepaque. But the city is especially famous for its music. Little bands of strolling musicians wander about the streets ready to play for you at the drop of a hat. They are called *mariachis.* (It is said that the name is derived from the French word *mariage,* for during the reign of Maximilian and Carlotta these bands appeared so frequently at marriages among the French that Mexicans began to refer to them by the French word, *mariage,* badly pronounced of course.) If a band stops and plays a request for you, the rate of pay is seven to nine pesos per song, for six or less musicians. Guadalajara is the real home of the *mariachis,* and several of these bands can be found at the various markets of the city, where they entertain the customers and where they may also be hired to play at a fiesta party, a birthday, a wedding, or to serenade one's best girl. These serenades, called *gallos,* usually played just after midnight, are a traditional part of courtship in Guadalajara. A wealthy young man of the town once created a sensation by hiring the entire Russian Cossack Chorus to serenade his lady love.

Guadalajara also has its Boys Town *(Ciudad de niños),* and its famous Cabañas Orphanage *(Hospicio Cabañas)* which houses other impressive murals by Orozco. These frescoes are in the great dome of the building and contain the famous "men in fire" figure, one of the artist's finest. The Cabañas murals were attacked by a very destructive fungus a few years ago, and doctors were called in. They made a culture and then proceeded to inject a ton of medicinal plaster into the dome. This destroyed the fungus, and the murals were then expertly restored.

In nearby Zapopan is the famous basilica of the famous *Virgen de Zapopan,* a dark Madonna who antedates the *Virgen de Guadalupe.* She is probably the oldest saint in Mexico and is given credit for having performed several "miracles": stopping a flood, putting an end to a smallpox plague, winning a battle against the Indians, etc. This Virgin is deeply revered by the religious people of the region. She is an image only ten inches high, in beautifully adorned clothes; her skin is dark. While her "home" is in the baroque Basilica of Zapopan, a little town just outside Guadalajara, such is her fame that she spends four months of the year visiting all the churches of Guadalajara and its environs. There are so many of these that she is able to spend only three or four days at each. When she appears, the church visited is decked out with streamers and flowers, and its congregation have a big fiesta.

The Virgin returns to her own sanctuary on October 12, on which day the biggest fiesta of all is held. An estimated *three to five hundred thousand* people from the city and countryside turn out to participate in the impressive *marcha* of return. Lovely and haunting songs are sung in her honor, and the natives put on colorful Indian dances. The pageant is noted for its rainbow of color, its fervor, and its intensity.

Twenty years ago Guadalajara, colonial "pearl of the west," began to go modern. It was decided to widen some of the main thoroughfares, particularly the Avenida Juárez (nearly every main street in the republic is called Avenida Juárez). Buildings had to be condemned, demolished, pushed back off the street, jacked up and moved out of the line of traffic. Citizens who for years had been enjoying immense tax savings by reporting buildings they owned along the right of way at ridiculously low figures, now saw these figures turned against them and were stuck hard. They let out a howl that could be heard to the Texas border, but the work of modernization went on. One large new building, that of the telephone company, was too expensive to demolish, so it was put on stilts and moved off the road. Now Guadalajara has several wide, well-paved arteries which help keep traffic flowing smoothly. One of these leads all the way out to the village of Zapopan and to the Country Club Estates. Sears, Roebuck has come to town with a large new store in the center of the city, and the better hotels have done a complete job of modernization. The city no longer rests on its laurels as the "most Spanish city" of Mexico.

Before dismissing the hotels of Guadalajara I should like to mention one of them, the Hotel Francés, which is a true architectural gem. This hotel was once a monastery. Its lovely patio, surrounded by corridors that rise four stories high and enclosed with flowing stone arcades, decorated with great leafy plants and brilliant tile and surrounding an old fountain, is one of the finest in the city. Here, many years ago the Mexican revolutionary generals gathered to discuss their strategy before the campaign. For years the Hotel Francés was the social center of the colonial town. Then, as other hotels arose, it began to descend the scale, and fell into a second-rate category. Recently its management decided on a program of complete modernization: now every room has a bath and old floors and walls have been repaired. The hotel still caters to visitors at rates which are most reasonable. Rooms go at 50 to 100 pesos per day, from $4.00 to a little over $8.00. The Hotel Francés is one of the most charming hostelries in the country. It is located at 35 Maestranza Street, in the heart of the downtown area, just off the Plaza Mayor, and offers a visual retreat into the colonial past that is almost like a dream. There are, of course, several newer, de luxe hotels.

Mention Mexican music to any foreigner, to any Mexican, and probably the first song that will come to mind is the *Jarabe Tapatío,* which had its birth in the vicinity of Guadalajara. *Jarabe* is a common type of folk song and dance evolved in Spanish America from the *Jota* of the province of Aragon in Spain. *Tapatío* simply means "from Jalisco," the state of which Guadalajara is the capital. After the Mexican Revolution, around the year 1920, the *Jarabe Tapatío* became set in a pattern which was rapidly adopted by the country at large. When danced by a couple, the man wears the costume of the Mexican *charro* and the girl is dressed as the mythical *China poblana.* The *Jarabe* consists of nine gay melodies and dance figures, the dancers meeting and moving around each other with strong and rapid movements of body, heel, and toe. The dance ends with two figures known as *La Paloma* and *La Diana* (The Dove and The Diana). In "The Dove" the man follows the girl as she dances around the brim of his hat which he has thrown to the floor; as she picks it up he passes his right leg over her, and the two partners finish the dance facing the audience, the man's arm around the girl, as they move back and forth to the rapid rhythm of "The Diana." Everyone joins in with loud handclapping at the "Diana" finale. It is a picturesque and "cute" dance, but has been performed so frequently, especially by North Americans who have studied at summer schools in Mexico, that it has lost some of its early freshness and charm. In years gone by such famous dancers as Pavlova and La Argentina learned the *Jarabe* and danced it on their tours through Mexico. Since the 1920's, with the widespread popularity of radio in Mexico, many other beautiful folk songs and dances, formerly known only in their native regions, have become popular all over the country. Others are dying out as urbanization pushes them aside. Among these are the lovely Christmas carols of the *Posadas* which recall the wanderings of Joseph and Mary from inn to inn as they seek shelter for the night. These were once sung on the streets of nearly every village in Mexico during the Christmas season.

Guadalajara is about four hundred miles northwest of Mexico City, edged in by mountains in one of the larger pockets which make up the Central Highlands. In order to reach the capital by train or automobile, it is necessary to go up over the mountain barrier which separates the Jalisco pocket from that of the capital and then to go down again. This brings to mind the matter of communications. As Mexico's second city, Guadalajara is the center of a fine network of roads and airlines, and lies also on the main line of the railway from southern California to Mexico City.

Guadalajara's airport is one of the finest in Mexico, and is clean as a pin. Why they have built it so far out of town, halfway across the state, I cannot fathom, but this is the way airports are planned. Guadalajara also boasts the largest and finest bus terminal in Mexico. It is a huge modern building whose great bulk stands out above the low-lying structures which surround it almost as much as the high-towered cathedral. On the left there is a waiting room for first-class passengers, and on the right-hand side of the building is the second-class waiting room. Both rooms are commodious and so clean that they would shame most of the bus stations in the United States. This goes for the second-class portion of the building as well as for the first-class. The buses all have their numbered tracks back of the building, and there is an immaculate restaurant inside the terminal. One could not possibly expect anything finer in bus communications.

A person who has traveled over considerable parts of Mexico in second- and third-class buses may well wonder why so much money has been put into this one terminal and so little into the other hundreds of smaller depots (often little holes in the wall) at which the second- and third-class buses stop. However, the Guadalajara depot has a perfectly valid reason for being. It was put up by the state as an investment in public welfare, and it yields a neat 200,000 pesos' yearly profit, which goes to hospitals, orphanages, and other public institutions which otherwise would require support by taxation. (The tourist who reads somewhere that he can travel all over Mexico enjoying buses of Greyhound quality and terminals of Guadalajara quality will be doomed to bitter disappointment. On many runs only second-class buses are available. They will get you there, but you will certainly not find clean rest rooms, depots, or appetizing restaurants on the way.)

Guadalajara's rail depot is something very different from the shining bus terminal. It occupies a dilapidated tin shed, which is not only dirty but looks on the verge of falling to pieces. It is even risky to set your suitcase on the grimy, oil-soaked floors of this miserable structure, for this may mark your luggage for life. The depot, in a word, is a disgrace to Mexico, to Guadalajara, and to the rail lines which use it. The overnight train which pulls out of Guadalajara at about suppertime for Mexico City, which should be the best run in the country, starts off in this run-down barn. Only one thing is good about the trip: the price. A round-trip first-class rail ticket between Guadalajara and Mexico City, covering a distance of over 800 miles, comes to only 92 pesos, plus 47 pesos for a lower berth, a total of about $15, including a berth both ways.

What goes on in a city the size of Guadalajara that might lure the interested outsider? Take, for example, a couple of weeks during the midwinter season:

On January 24 there is a fashion show in the Hotel Fenix at 9:00 P.M. On January 25, at the Degollado Theater, the Guadalajara Symphony plays Beethoven's Seventh Symphony, Handel's Concerto Number 1, and the Classic Symphony of Prokofieff. On January 27 there is a bullfight, a *novillada,* in which Emilio Rodríguez, one of the top *novilleros* (new fighters) of the season will perform. Also on January 27 the Argentine football team plays the Mexican champions from Guadalajara.

On January 30 (lasting into February) there is a big fiesta at San Juan de los Lagos, a town not far distant from Guadalajara, where hand-embroidered work is sold on the streets. On February 2 comes the culmination of the nation-wide pilgrimage to the venerated Virgin of Rosario de Talpa, where thousands of pilgrims murmur their prayers and carry torches honoring this sacred Lady, as her image is carried from a cave deep in the ravine, up the cliff, and into the village of Experiencia. The little village of Arenal also holds a fiesta for this Virgin, with serenades, dancing, and unique fireworks. February 8 through 17 there is a carnival at Tecototlán, 115 kilometers down the highway. Twice weekly there are concerts by the State Band of Jalisco in the Guadalajara Plaza de Armas. These concerts are held Thursdays and Sundays at dusk. Other things to see would be: cockfights, markets, pottery factories, nearby native villages, the play at the Degollado Theater in which the leading actor of Mexico, Fernando Soler, has the principal role, the architectural exhibit at the Mexican-North American Cultural Institute, the promenades in Revolution Park, the Benjamin Franklin Library (maintained by the U.S. Information Agency), the State Museum, the new Ceramic Museum, the nearby canyons and huge falls, the marvelous frescoes of Orozco in the Government Palace, the Cabañas Orphanage and the university, and of course the groups of strolling *mariachis,* and the many, many fine examples of colonial architecture (Zapopan, the San Francisco Church, Santa Monica, the Church of San Felipe Neri, and the Santuario de Nuestra Señora de Guadalupe). There is always plenty going on, and plenty to see in Guadalajara.

One night I went to see Fernando Soler in the play *La muralla (The Wall),* which had attracted considerable attention in town. My orchestra center seat cost 30 pesos ($2.40). The people who came to the play were all well-dressed, well-groomed members of the well-to-do upper middle class. One could almost point out the prosperous businessmen, the bankers, the surviving scions of the old aristocracy. There was one general, spotless in his uniform, and perhaps half a dozen students. The women were fashionably garbed. It was a notable fact that there was hardly an Indianist face in the entire audience.

The theater was a truly imposing one. Its dome was covered with paintings from Dante's *Divine Comedy*, its boxes were strung out in tier above tier along the sides. Everything was in good romantic nineteenth-century style. The play began at nine o'clock, and the cast, I must in all frankness hereby state, left much to be desired, Fernando Soler included. The play was not well directed, well written, or well acted. It was by a Spanish writer. Mexico's own dramatists are not as popular as those of Europe or the United States. Many dramatic pieces expressly written in order to teach the people something are useful and interesting, many Mexican motion pictures are well directed, and a few Mexican dramas present current social problems reasonably well, but as a whole the theater in Mexico is unequal to its prose fiction. Plays by Tennessee Williams, Edward Albee and Arthur Miller have been the big hits of the Mexican theater in the past decade. In the field of native entertainment the lowly *carpas*, or tent shows, where the inimitable Cantinflas got his start, are perhaps the most vigorous force. This fine pantomimist and actor has become a national institution in Mexico, as Charles Chaplin was in the days of the silent motion pictures in the United States. His peasant naïveté plus a very un-Chaplin-like string of high-sounding but meaningless words are always good for a laugh, and the ways in which he pokes fun at the mighty, his own dignity always shining through, have made him a worthy symbol of the Mexican masses.

One notable exception among Mexico's generally unimpressive dramatists is Rodolfo Usigli. His play, *Corona de Sombra* (Crown of Shadow), about Maximilian and Carlotta, was praised by Bernard Shaw. His *El gesticulador* is a bitter version of "the perfect revolutionary general." Usigli sees the central fact of the past fifty years in Mexico not as the Revolution, but as the Revolution betrayed. He sees his countrymen as great in putting on the *gesto* or mask. "The Mexican's capacity for gesticulation is infinite . . . always opposed to reality; it is his manner, quite primitive, of fleeing reality and avoiding the truth." The students who strike instead of studying, who destroy instead of working hard politically are examples of similar *gestos* in the United States.[51]

XVII

NAHUALTEPEC: MEXICAN VILLAGE TODAY

The greatest resource of a nation is not its lands, nor its mines, nor its industries. The greatest resource of a nation is its people.

MEXICO'S population is mostly rural. Despite the tremendous growth of the great urban centers, approximately 50 per cent of all Mexicans live in the rural areas in settlements of less than 2,500 inhabitants, and 60 per cent in settlements of less than 5,000 inhabitants. Only a portion of 1 per cent live on isolated farms, the rest in small clusters of houses in rural hamlets and villages. Each morning these country folk rise early and go off in different directions to their fields and pastures. At night they all drift back along the well-worn paths into the village. The preconquest Indian population lived in villages; so did the Spaniards who conquered and settled Mexico. It was the only safe way of life in either country, where warfare was a constant threat. In Spain it was war against the Moors. In preconquest Mexico it was war among the Indian tribes. In independent Mexico, centuries later, it was the threat of revolutionary bands.

The village was a protection for a man and his family. And in a literal sense a man's home became his castle, at least his fortress, if castle seems too dignified a term. Today village living is mostly custom, the result of many centuries of deeply ingrained group feeling. A rural Mexican still just *feels* better if his home is one of a cluster of houses. He does not face his destiny alone. His frame of mind is more steady. He feels better, works better. If he owns livestock, these accompany him as he goes out into the fields in the morning. They accompany him when he comes back into the village at night. He closes them into his corral, sometimes in his very house, to prevent their being stolen. This way there are problems of sanitation, but the animals are more secure. Over 50 per cent of the cattle in Mexico live in this fashion.

It is obviously onerous to have to bring the animal fodder into the hamlet, only to have the manure pile up in the corrals or on the streets far from the fields where it might have been of immediate value in enriching the soil. The village way of life, therefore, is inefficient, unsanitary, wasteful of time and energies, but it is also more secure, and it continues the age-old pattern of community living in which the race and the group have always overshadowed the individual. It is natural that in such a society the group, rather than the individual, would become the great creative force. Hence, folk culture, folk songs, ballads, songs, dances, legends, and all the folk arts and crafts expressed, and still express, the finest creative instincts of the Mexican people.

Aside from the daily labors in fields and pastures, and the daily journeys to and from the home cluster of primitive dwellings, there was, and still is, another and larger aspect of rural living: the market. In the Mexican Highlands the larger villages all have their market days and their markets, always on or adjoining the main plaza. Every village of more than a thousand has a set market day, designated as such since colonial or even preconquest times. People from the smaller population clusters come to these markets to dispose of their produce and to obtain those goods which they cannot produce themselves. If the village is fairly small, there is a market on one day a week. If it is larger, there might be a market on two days of the week. In the cities markets are held every day. The villages in a given area alternate their market days so that the surrounding population may be able to attend each market held in the region, one after the other. If a given village has its market day on Monday, for example, the next village will hold a market on Tuesday, and the third on Wednesday, and so on down the line. Itinerant traders may attend all the markets in a given area, bringing in goods from the world outside.

Another aspect of the market economy is that each village is generally noted for a particular product. While one village may enjoy a reputation for pottery making, another may produce wool serapes, another embroidered work, another *huaraches,* and so on. In addition to this home "specialty," a cross section of other regional products also will always be offered for sale or exchange. These products are usually limited to the necessities.

In preconquest days geography and the lack of an efficient transportation system made the local market an economic necessity, as well as a social boon. Goods could not be carried great distances, for there were no pack animals, and everybody had to walk. Many still walk to market in rural Mexico, but many also now ride their burros, their mules, their horses. A few even go in trucks. Goods, too, may be carried on human backs, on burros, in oxcarts, or occasionally in trucks. If the market village is on or near a highway, large numbers of participants may go and come on the local second- or third-class bus.

From a modern industrial standpoint the efficiency of the market economy might be called into question. But there is at least no "cost plus" way of arriving at the price in this kind of economy. The middleman is almost entirely eliminated. Transportation costs are not added, for they do not exist. Overhead, rent? They hardly exist. And as for the *actual* cost of the materials used, how can even this be accurately calculated? A handful of clay to make some kind of jar or jug, some wool off one's own sheep to weave a blanket, some straw out of which to make a *petate*. . . . These items, plus the time that a man or woman puts in working, what do they come to in terms of dollars and cents? The time spent in making or raising the things displayed for sale in the market is leisure time. It is, also, very often time spent in work which was inseparable from recreation. How, then, to calculate the cost? This kind of productivity need not be costly. On occasion it can undersell our own large-scale industry and its outlet, the five-and-ten. What industry could manufacture, transport, market, pay the overhead on, then sell a beautiful clay jug for a nickel? A tiny straw toy doll for a penny?

When market day arrives, the country folk leave their homes at the crack of dawn and return late at night. If the distance is very great, they sometimes arrive on the night before the market and on reaching town simply wrap themselves in their serapes, and sleep on the plaza or in the streets until the market opens. Each product has a particular space in the market, and so does each seller. A small tax is paid to the municipality in order to use this space. In the earlier days the direct exchange of products frequently took the place of money. Among the Aztecs cacao beans were often used instead of currency, as were little quills of gold dust. Today direct exchange is a rarity except in the most isolated primitive communities.

In the outlying villages of central and southern Mexico everyone goes to market. It is the only real social life many of them enjoy. The women who have been cooped up in their drab and dingy *jacales* all week cooking, washing, and sewing, and the men who have been laboring all week in the shops or fields can on market day toss their labors aside and enjoy the catharsis of human contact.

On market day, as the morning begins, the paths are filled with wives, husbands, families on their way to the market place. Like drops of water they suddenly appear on the immobile countryside, increasing in number as the sun goes up, flowing and growing as they move ever closer to the town. Market day is so deeply ingrained in their daily lives that almost without conscious thought, and with clocklike regularity, they head for the village plaza. As soon as the majority of them have arrived the drowsy village will be transformed into a lively and authentic pageant.

As they near the market place the chatter increases. After they have arrived it becomes a great buzz of human delight. Buying and selling come second. Profits mean nothing. Bargaining for its own sake is accorded a high position, but to dispose of one's product is never a necessity. To see, to speak, and to commingle. The spark of human contact is the magnet that draws them. The need to stand on bedrock, not alone, and join the folk in feeling, rhythm, color, voice, and motion. Without this no folk culture could last for a moment.

Market day is still a vital force in the daily life of the Mexican Highlands and the surrounding regions. It survives where the greatest concentration of preconquest Indian population lived and begins to die away along the northern fringe of that area. North of a line which might be drawn through the city of Aguascalientes market day disappears. Ask a villager in one of the states bordering the United States about market day, and he does not understand what you are talking about. He may direct you to the nearest grocery store. But market day is still very much alive for the tremendous population of central and southern Mexico.

Even today the number of villages in the Mexican republic reaches an almost astronomical figure. The 1970 census lists 43,050 settlements with a population of from 1 to 99 inhabitants, and 19,863 settlements with populations ranging from 100 to 500 inhabitants. Despite the increasing migration of country folk toward the urban centers, the rural population of the country has continued to increase *numerically*. And with a more mechanized farm life its productivity also has become greater. Total agricultural output has practically doubled in the past fifteen years, and approximately 46 per cent of all Mexicans who are gainfully employed today are engaged in agriculture.

Only eight-tenths of 1 per cent of the Mexican rural population lives on isolated farms. Rural life, therefore, is village life, community life: in big villages, small villages, middle-sized villages, and in smaller clusters which should hardly be dignified by being called villages at all. Here the old preconquest culture of Mexico goes on, making such adjustments with the mechanical civilization which has enveloped it as must be made but clinging as tenaciously to its traditions as the picturesque little hamlets and clusters of *jacales* cling to the cliffs and banks of the ravines on which they appear so precariously perched. There is nothing precarious about them; they are the true tendrils which for centuries have fed the great trunk of the Mexican tree. If now they are reaching out and flowering again in the urban centers, in an entirely new kind of florescence, this is but an additional proof of their indestructible essence.

R. S. and H. M. Lynd are the authors of a book analyzing the economy of a typical community of the United States to which they gave the name of Middletown, U.S.A. Based largely on a study made of a specific community in the state of Ohio, the analysis would apply to the great majority of towns in the United States. Middletown might be in almost any part of the country, and might be in any state. Its daily economic life is a microcosm of the national economy.

It is not so easy to find a typical Mexican community. As my friend Leslie Simpson has written, there are indeed "many Mexicos." This is one of the basic truisms of Mexican life. Not many years ago the city was as different from the rural village in Mexico as the night differs from the day. Northern Mexico also differed radically from the lands of the Central Highlands. But in the past ten years great changes have taken place. Mexico has been catapulted into the air age almost overnight. No longer are her remote mountain-rimmed valleys isolated and inacessible. Twenty-five years of peaceful living, a growing population, an expanding economy, and a progressive government have all done their part. A fine network of highways and airlines now link the far corners of the republic. The Mexican people, with the help of the automobile and the airplane, have done the rest. The result: Mexico is in the process of becoming a modern nation.

This *process* of blending the old culture with the new is the most notable single characteristic of Mexico today. Therefore, it is now time to describe the economy and daily life of Mexico's Middletown. But to make the picture more complete, to give it better balance, and to avoid the stresses of regional specialization, let us make this Middletown of Mexico a composite, and a symbolic, village.

I have given it the name of Nahualtepec. You will find no such name on the map, though you may locate several settlements which bear some portion of this name in their own. Nahualtepec is, in fact, a composite of three different Mexican villages which I studied in some detail. These villages are all in central Mexico and are not widely separated from each other. However, they are separated sufficiently so that when they are combined in one symbolic settlement the regional does not overbalance the general. Nahualtepec, in a word, is my Mexican Middletown.

Not one word that I shall write about Nahualtepec is invention. Every sentence states a fact, and the sum total of these facts will make up the daily life of Nahualtepec. But no fact must be taken to apply to a specific community. In addition to the reasons given above, I have also done this in order to lend anonymity to the people whose lives I speak of so frankly in the following pages. It would not be in good taste to identify them as individuals or to point out their places of residence as specific communities.

Not far from a small attractive lake, about 95 miles east of the state capital, is the village of Nahualtepec, which is Nahuatl for "Land of the Werewolf." It was one of the first Indian villages established by the Spaniards in the early sixteenth century; the founders of the new village received their title to the land from Hernán Cortés. The town now has a population of something like 4,000, but it gives the impression of being much smaller. Nahualtepec was more or less isolated until quite recently; it was not accessible by road until President Cárdenas, who is from the town of Jiquilpan, in a neighboring state, had the highway from Guadalajara to Mexico City pass through his native village. A branch of this road was also supposed to link the town of Morelia with Nahualtepec, but somehow the funds never materialized for this particular segment, and so today Nahualtepec can be reached only over a rough unpaved road. Yet the village is too near the main lines of communication to fall into the category of isolated Indo-mestizo settlements. It is rather a semi-isolated, semimechanized village which typifies that great segment of the Mexican village population now in rapid process of transformation from a primitive to a mechanized society, from the old folk culture to the new hybrid culture called civilization. As applied here the word *civilization* is taken simply to mean a non-isolated national way of life in which a system of rapid communications has molded all the minor units into a closely knit cohesive whole. This molding includes ideas as well as materials. When the process of "thinking and feeling" becomes national, we have the kind of civilization to which I am referring.

At the state capital I take the second-class bus for Nahualtepec. First-class buses do not make this run. The bus is already half full, although it is not scheduled to leave for twenty minutes. I climb in and sit down. The driver is a young man of twenty, very precise in his movements. Exactly at departure time he presses the starter and takes off, not a second early, not a second late. He has an assistant, a boy of about fifteen, who helps him with the tickets and helps the passengers load and unload their bundles and boxes.

The bus finally leaves the last straggling houses of the city, enters the open country and heads for the hills. It does not travel directly to Nahualtepec, for at intervals of from five to ten miles it swerves off the main highway, takes out across what looks more like a cowpath than a road, and eventually finds its way into a tiny hamlet, where half a dozen passengers invariably get off and a dozen additional ones invariably get on. These off-the-road stops almost double the distance one has to travel to reach one's destination.

As we arrived at one of the villages a funeral procession was just coming out of town. The driver stopped, and turned off his motor until it had passed. As the casket went by, carried aloft on the shoulders of six pallbearers, the passengers all took off their hats and observed a moment of complete silence. Everyone in the cortege was walking. There were possibly 150 persons in all, about twice as many women as men. The women were all dressed in heavy black, and the entire procession kept up a constant muttering of the rosary as the mourners advanced down the cobbled street toward the treeless cemetery which lay on a rocky hill.

It was a wretched-looking town, dry and dusty as an old oven, its plaza dilapidated beyond repair. Several stones were missing from the lofty tower of the church, which raised its single Gothic spire above the powdery streets. While the bus waited I heard about the deceased. He had been killed in an automobile accident at the crossroads, where three cars had collided head on, one of them a heavy truck. Bricks from the truck had been tossed all over the road, blocking traffic for over an hour.

It was a relief to get out of this funereal village and be surrounded again by the open fields. We passed the ruins of several old haciendas, great empty shells, unoccupied since the Revolution, ghostly reminders of a way of life that had passed away with the Díaz regime. The rebelling *peones*, overwhelmed by a blind hatred of the landowner and not having the faintest idea as to how to use his tremendous house, simply set fire to the buildings and let them burn. The central states of Mexico are filled with such ruins, which in the days of Porfirio Díaz were self-sufficient economic units packed with produce, animals, people, and flowers that drew their sustenance from the famishing land. Today, in some of the old patios and gardens a few farm families reside in the adobe huts that once served as the servants' quarters. Once in a great while a new hacienda dwelling, always on a far less pretentious scale, will have been raised beside the old.

The fields along the road are filled with *parcelas* of corn and row on row of the maguey, which reach up onto the bordering hills. There has not been a real rain, a *lluvia formal,* in more than two months, and the land is parched and sere. Along the sides of the road the ditches expose the red-clay soil.

Every time we approach a cluster of houses or a village there are warning streams of smoke spiraling into the air. These do not come from the dwellings, but from the little gray piles in the fields nearby where the men are making adobe bricks. First, the soil is gathered and mixed with water and straw, then the bricks are formed in little wooden rectangles and laid out in the sun. Finally they are piled up in small truncated pyramids about eight or ten feet high, and are then fired. Branches are piled on the ground alongside the pyramids and burned in such a way that the heat and smoke penetrate the bricks, hardening them almost completely. For the pure fun of it I began to count the number of pyramids, and within a few miles had gone beyond a hundred.

The earth here was perfect for the making of adobe bricks. And so the principal structural material of Mexico lies right in one's own back yard. It does not have to be sought for, or mined, or lumbered; it does not even have to be transported. It can be readily utilized, and it costs absolutely nothing. The structure that has adobe walls is insulated by nature, and is solid and strong. It is cool in summer, warm in winter, withstands both rain and storm. In many ways adobe is the ideal structural material, and I have no idea why it is not more widely used in the United States. Many Mexican adobe buildings are well over a hundred years old, and are still in first-rate condition. Of the approximately five million dwellings in Mexico today, more than two million are made of adobe.

A heavy-set Mexican man of about forty shared my seat. He had a boy on his lap. Across from him were his wife and three more children. We spoke about automobiles, and I marvelled at the number of cars on the road, all of which had cost twice as much as the same make and model would bring in the United States. The import tax is close to 100 per cent.

"It does seem hard," my companion said. "But if there were no import tax on cars Mexico would buy a million automobiles tomorrow. You can see what that would do to the country. Money that ought to be invested in other more necessary products would be drained off in order to support a national luxury, for here in Mexico a passenger car is a luxury. Yet even as things now stand Mexico has more Cadillacs than any other country in the world except the United States. We are as crazy to own a car as you are. This is one of the things we have gotten from you, and the government must protect us against it. The policy is a wise one, I assure you. Of course, there is no such tax on farm machinery. Tractors, plows, and things like that pay only a very small tax. Agriculture must progress, but people don't have to ride on soft private seats. These little red buses will get you anywhere, cheap."

By this time we had crossed over the final barrier of hills and were entering the valley of Nahualtepec. Its low-flung houses seemed to cling to the ground. Its streets were narrow and very rough. Over the plaza rose the usual spire, but not so tall as that of many a larger and more important town. The bus creaked to a halt and we all piled out. We had traveled 95 miles; it was the end of the line. My body ached in every joint, but somehow I managed to unscramble my valise from the jumble of cartons and bundles and stagger for the door. I soon found a boy who would carry the grip and lead me to the boardinghouse, which was two blocks from the plaza where we had stopped.

Nahualtepec lies at the foot of a high range of mountains, only a few miles from a lake which has been called the most beautiful in Mexico. It is surrounded by magueys and cornfields, and its inhabitants are still noted for their hand-woven products. Black serapes are one of the specialties of Nahualtepec, and most of the houses contain hand looms and spindles. The villagers take great pride in their weaving. It is not refined stuff by any means; but it is typical, useful, durable.

The plaza of Nahualtepec is smaller than that of Tepic. It is almost squalid in appearance. The buildings are all of a single story and not well kept. Such efforts as have been made to freshen up the plaza are pathetic and touching—for example, the plantings, which show more care than the surrounding buildings. One large bed of low-lying red-leafed flowers spell out the words "V-I-V-A M-E-X-I-C-O." Then, in order not to overlook the source, in smaller letters credit is given for these flowers to the Honorable Ayuntamiento de Nahualtepec, that is, to the Hon. Aldermen, who obviously supplied the pesos.

Another note of the gardener's hand lies in the bushes that adorn a portion of the plaza. These are carefully trimmed to resemble animals and birds. One bush has been trimmed to look like a moose, another resembles a goat, others are cut in the shape of a burro, a large duck, a turkey, and three or four other kinds of birds or fowls. The plaza also contains half a dozen poinsettias (called in Spanish *Nochebuenas*, or Christmas Eve flowers), whose scarlet blossoms contrast vividly with the golden mass of the yellow trees of spring. The plantings are not large or lush, but they do show a certain care. The town loves flowers, and this is reflected in the care given the central plaza.

However, the tree of spring is beginning to fade and drop its yellow flowers; the poinsettias are drooping too. Even the plants seem to reflect the dilapidated appearance of the buildings which line the plaza. The largest of these is, of course, the church, which lies off to one side, separated from the plaza proper by a small courtyard. The next largest building, which occupies almost an entire side of the square, is the Ayuntamiento, or Municipal Building. The jail, police headquarters, and courtroom are in this structure.

As I sit on the plaza, notebook in hand, the town's police force passes by. It consists of two men. One of them is wearing a blue denim uniform, which needs ironing, and an old floppy green cap. He is carrying a long rifle and a huge billy club. He is evidently the police captain, for as he passes he doffs his cap in token of good morning. It is the official welcome to an outsider. His bailiff is wearing gray pants and a light-gray shirt. He has an enormous pistol in an oversized holster and belt. Following the chief's lead, he turns and grants me a perfunctory nod. Then both men disappear into the Ayuntamiento.

Across from where I am sitting is the village saloon and liquor store. The bartender carries a small but potent supply of alcoholic beverages. The favorite drink of the citizens is a shot of tequila flavored with a kind of red juice jocularly referred to as "the widow's blood." It is a kind of concentrated pomegranate juice, but the drink tastes as if it had been flavored with chile ketchup, for the tequila itself has a bite that would knock over an elephant, not to mention the weak stomach of an American in Mexico.

As I am gazing into the bar, the heavy-set Mexican who had shared my seat on the bus sits down beside me. He turns out to be the owner of one of the two tiny motion-picture theaters of Nahualtepec. We chat a while then he asks if I would not like to accompany him to the theater. It had recently been modernized and cleaned up inside. My friend pointed out the improvements: new paint, new seats, even a better screen.

"But I'm almost sorry I did it," he said. "Because now the whole town is talking about it and the tax collector will soon be on my tail, I'm sure. Try to get anything cleaned up here, and it costs you more in taxes than it's worth."

I leave my friend at the box office, where a sign says that the price for a ticket is eight cents, then turn around the corner and enter the churchyard, where men are stringing up firecrackers for the fiesta on Sunday. There are six long rows of them, all tied to wires strung from one end of the yard to the other. Each row must contain at least two hundred high-powered firecrackers. At fiesta time Mexicans go in for noise on a grand scale.

The priest of the Church sees me taking in the decorations, and stops to explain that "these humble people like things like this, and the Church tries to please them."

As we spoke, the sound of children's voices repeating their catechism came from the vestry nearby. There must have been at least a hundred of them, all girls studying for their confirmation. The priest smiled.

"They are doing well," he said. "Soon they will be ready."

"Do you have to teach them religious subjects in the church or can you do that in the Catholic schools?" I asked.

"We have freedom to teach as we like," he said. Then he continued:

"The same laws are on the books now as in the days of Calles, when the Church was persecuted. But now we do enjoy freedom *in fact*, if not legally. We do not teach religion openly in the schools, but we do teach it. We also conform to the federal and state programs of education. Our schools are all incorporated in the government educational system."

Federal opposition to the Church has decreased steadily since the days of President Calles. When I was in Mexico in 1926 religious services were at a standstill, priests and nuns were forbidden to wear their habits on the streets. Soldiers stood on the streets guarding every religious structure. The government appeared to be trying to suspend religion. Tension was explosive. Yet in those days the churches were full of people, at all hours of the day and night. They came as if driven by some inner compulsion to pray, to express their opposition to the official policy, to defend their churches. It was an act of faith.

On that visit I went to the Church of the Virgin of Guadalupe. It was a mass of lighted candles and kneeling figures, all huddled in the strange brightness murmuring their prayers. I shall never forget the wild look in those eyes. At the slightest spark the volcano would erupt. It was so disturbing that I was afraid to remain inside for more than a few moments. It seemed that every eye was fixed on me personally, as if in some incomprehensible way all these people held me personally accountable for what had happened.

Not all of my fear was due to an overzealous imagination. At Cuernavaca the crowd pelted several of us with stones, creasing my head with a deep cut, merely because we had entered the cathedral. Any stranger who dared to enter a church in those days was taken for a federal spy, and was so treated. For several years thereafter the situation remained tense. The faithful answered the government's anticlerical policy with an antigovernment crusade, which, under the *Cristeros* (the Christ-ers) became a violent and bloody eruption of fanatical bands. Hundreds of innocent people, most of them good Catholics, were robbed, beaten, and murdered by these religious fanatics: many simply because they had spoken for moderation, others because they resisted having their fowls and livestock stolen by the pillaging *Cristeros*. The Church never gave its official support to the *Cristeros*, but it was certainly guilty of criminal negligence in not speaking out more constantly and more forcefully against them.

The Mexican educational system was in these days called *la escuela socialista* (socialist education). Emphasis was strongly anticlerical. Not only was it forbidden to teach religion in the public schools, but teachers were instructed to give the curriculum an antireligious tone. All Catholic schools were closed. Enmity was at a high pitch. Finally, when Lázaro Cárdenas became President (1934) and was successful in booting Calles from the country, the tide slowly began to turn. (The same Cárdenas booted the American oil interests out of Mexico when he expropriated their properties in 1938, after they had refused to raise the wage scale and to provide their workers with the safeguards and compensations which the government had sanctioned.) Ávila Camacho who was elected in 1940, gave official recognition to the easing of the official antichurch campaign when he announced in one of his first presidential statements, "I am a believer too." Feelings now relaxed on both sides. The Church became more tolerant of the government point of view, which was to keep priests out of politics, and the government became more tolerant of the Church point of view, which was to enjoy freedom of religion.

The priest in Nahualtepec was mistaken when he stated that the anticlerical laws which Calles attempted to enforce were still on the books unchanged. Article 3 of the constitution of 1917 (Calles had tried to enforce it) stated that education in Mexico must be free, compulsory, and public (that is, nonreligious). The Church was expressly forbidden to run primary schools. In 1934 this restriction was partially lifted in an amendment to the constitution which stated that public education would be "socialistic," would exclude all religious dogma, would combat fanaticism and prejudice "for which the schools will organize their teaching and other activities so that these will create in our youth a rational and accurate concept of the universe and of society." But the amendment then went on to say that, while the state would impart primary, secondary, and normal school education, "private groups might be given authorization to establish schools in these three categories, but only if they rigorously observe the statement of aims specified above. The teachers of such schools must prove to the state their willingness and competence to teach according to these ideas, hence religious corporations and those connected with them are expressly prohibited from running schools or supporting them financially. All teaching plans and programs must conform to those of the state, and no private school shall function without having first obtained its authorization from the government."

The amendment sounded almost as anticlerical as the original article of the 1917 constitution, but at least it left the door open for the establishment of "private" schools, and with the passage of time this actually came largely to mean "Catholic" schools. Proceeding very warily in the early stages, and hiding behind all kinds of "private" names and groups, the Church gradually enjoyed more and more freedom as president after president allowed the anticlerical portion of the law to become a dead letter. At present the only actual consequence of Article 3 is that "Catholic" schools are still called "private" schools in Mexico today.

At the present writing the greatest harmony exists between church and state in Mexico. Leaders of each group respect the members of the opposition, and they can now sit down and speak to each other as friends who simply hold to a different point of view. The members of the Catholic group are now so restrained that they may aptly be referred to as "her Majesty's loyal opposition." Thirty years ago one would have thought that such cordiality could not possibly have been achieved in less than a century. This is a further proof of how quickly Mexico is coming of age.

XVIII

NAHUALTEPEC DRILLS A WELL

Water always takes the form of the vessel that holds it. Sister Water, let us praise the Lord.

—Amado Nervo

Nahualtepec had no municipal water supply until 1955. Approximately half the houses had shallow wells, but these were neither hygienic nor abundant. Finally, the town council decided to drill an artesian well. They appropriated as many pesos as they could spare, and began drilling. After a while the pesos gave out, and they had not yet hit water. There was further canvassing for funds, and when these had been obtained the drill again began to bore. This time they got down pretty deep, but when the money ran out they had still not hit water. The priest was called upon to deliver his opinion. He told the townsfolk that probably God had not intended them to have water. The people took their way home, brokenhearted.

In the middle of that night a great bursting sound was heard, and the following morning a tremendous gusher of pure artesian water was spurting eight feet into the air. It has now been captured in a large pipe, which spouts it out at a more convenient level, but the water is still flowing in great abundance. The well lies at the edge of the churchyard, just off the plaza. It has not been siphoned into any fountain or waterworks. It has not been piped into the houses. The people of Nahualtepec, and also the neighboring farmers, come to the well with their huge jugs and cans, their burros and their backs, and carry the precious liquid to their homes in town or in the surrounding hills.

Water, especially drinking water, has long been one of the fundamental problems of Mexico. Polluted water is still the main cause of diseases of the digestive tract, and the abnormally high death rate due to enteritis and kindred ailments is directly attributable to unclean drinking water. Diarrhea, enteritis, and typhoid cause 30.6 deaths per 10,000 population in Mexico, whereas in the United States they cause only 1 death per 20,000 people. Mexico's death rate due to these diseases is over 60 times as high. Put another way, 75,000 Mexicans die needlessly each year because of polluted drinking water. This is the reason why Coca-Cola, Pepsi-Cola, and other bottled drinks have gained such a vast market for themselves in Mexico. Thousands of wealthy and middle class families buy whole cases at a time, and drink nothing but these carbonated beverages. On every country road you will find little shacks where carbonated drinks are sold. The colas are rapidly supplanting pulque as the national drink of Mexico today.

In 1960 there was no running water in over 60 per cent of the homes (this includes apartments) in Mexico. The actual figures were: running water within the house or apartment, 1,505,003 units; running water outside the dwelling, perhaps in a central patio or corridor, 564,978. Houses and apartments without running water, 4,339,115. The residents of these homes had to go to the town fountain, or to a nearby stream, pond, or well, or had to have water brought to them in tin drums. Much of the water obtained from streams or ponds is, of course, contaminated. During the six-year term (1964–70) of President Díaz Ordaz pure drinking water was brought to 899 towns and to 3,119 rural communities totalling 6,740,000 inhabitants, but still about 60 per cent of the homes in Mexico are without running water inside their own walls. My own estimate of the number of homes without running water in Nahualtepec would be much higher than this.

Country areas suffer most from lack of available drinking water, but conditions in the slums of the big cities are equally intolerable, as Oscar Lewis points out in *The Children of Sánchez*. The building in which the Sánchez family lives in Mexico City contains 157 one-room windowless apartments, occupied by 700 people, an average of more than four to each room. Water has to be drawn for all 700 people from a common tap. Filthy toilet facilities and baths are also used in common, and are always desperately overcrowded.

The Mexican rural inhabitant has learned to be frugal in all things. Water is not wasted, neither are containers of any kind which may carry water, or almost any other thing. The principal container in Nahualtepec is the big square cast-iron can, sometimes a gasoline can, sometimes a large vegetable oil tin, which has been transformed to serve a dozen new purposes. The tinsmith in town gives most of his time to redoing these cast-iron cans. With his shears and soldering irons he can turn them into a garbage can, slop jar, dustpan, a small stove, a milk or cold-drink can, a container for foods or fuel or for almost any other goods. He can put a handle on a can for easier carrying on either human or burro back. Filled with topsoil these cans also serve as flower pots in the colorful patios of the village, and of course practically all water is carried and stored in them. The cast-iron can has made tremendous inroads on the pottery industry all over rural Mexico. Sometimes I marvel that any pottery is still being made. But a trip to any pottery town will quickly convince one that this is most certainly not the case. The tin can serves a *utilitarian* purpose; the handmade jug, jar, or vase is not only useful but is beautiful as well. And of course in Mexico, as in the United States and all over the world, almost anyone would prefer a jewel to a piece of glass.

All day and all night long the water flows from the artesian well alongside the plaza of Nahualtepec. It is a shame to see all that water wasted, particularly in the long hours of the night. During the day it is at least put to constant use, even if the waste is tremendous. As the water spurts out of the great pipe onto the street it rolls downhill in the dirty cobblestone gutter, forming a little rivulet about two feet wide and six inches deep. At the end of the first block it turns the corner to the right and veers off down another street, following the course of the gutter, with a little help from some enterprising damming at the turn. Halfway down this second block another small dam forces it to cross the street and to run down the other side, under the shade trees, which are utterly lacking on the opposite side of the street.

Here half the wives and daughters of Nahualtepec come to wash their laundry. The other half wash away heedlessly in the sun. All of them use the water as it passes in the gutter. They soak their clothes generously, give them a good soaping, pound them on the rocks, rinse them out in the gutter, then soap them up and rinse them out again. The process seems long, but this is one kind of work which the Mexican woman has reduced to a fine art. There is not a wasted motion, at least of the hands. But while the hands are working with such efficiency, the lips are flapping constantly. All the gossip of Nahualtepec and environs is told and retold across that flowing gutter. Never was a phrase more applicable to a neighborhood than "it all comes out in the wash" is to the gossip of Nahualtepec.

Today I see that the little red flags are out again, half a dozen of them hanging on their sticks above the entrances of the butchershops. On days when there is meat, out comes the little red flag. When the meat has all been sold, down comes the flag and the shop is closed. The schedule of butchering is most exasperating, for every butcher in town slaughters on the same days, and all the shops have meat on the same days. But on alternate days you can't find a red flag in the entire town. Why don't they split up the market, each taking a certain day or portion of the week? No one can give a sensible answer to that question. In any case, the whole thing is very Mexican. While the men butcher they can chat and swap stories and, besides, in that way they can all be sure that their competitors are not getting the jump on them. A man would rather lose a whole day's sale of meat than let a competitor have that day scot free. It is a kind of vicious circle in which everyone is partially cheated, for on alternate days the town simply does without meat, and buyers go begging. Of necessity, these have become the turkey and chicken days on the village menu.

The slaughterhouse in Nahualtepec (the name is a euphemism) is merely a spot back of a couple of run-down adobe walls, not far from the central plaza. Here the seven town butchers assemble and slay their animals. Often, curious childish eyes are watching. The town's dogs receive the entrails and the town's buzzards clean up the residue. After an hour or two you can hardly tell there has been a butchering.

The meat is then carried to the markets in washtubs or burlaps, or the animal is quartered and thrown into a truck. As soon as it is unloaded the little red flags go up outside the shops. Inside, the butchers whack the meat into long lumpy and unappetizing strips, and hang it up on strings in front of their counters. Refrigeration is unknown. The consumer carries in some kind of pot, basket, or can and the meat is dropped directly into this. There may be a cloth lining the can, or there may not. Maids can be seen walking down the streets on every meat day with cans full of this freshly slaughtered meat. It is all about as tasty and tender as the thews of a mountain goat, and the local cooking does little to enhance the flavor. Mexicans like chile peppers with everything, and they are used to swallowing their meat in lumps.

It was getting near to fiesta time now, and the village was making its initial preparations. The first salvo, and it was really just that, caused me to leap out of bed into the cold dark about 5:00 A.M. with the terrifying thought that the town must have been pelted accidentally by an atomic bomb. It was only a salvo of rockets and firecrackers, promptly accompanied by a fanfare from the village band (nearly all brass) which has lined up just outside my open window. The synchronization of these two horrendous sounds was enough to raise Lazarus from the dead. The same procedure was repeated on the following five mornings.

"Just warming up for the fiesta," the maid told me. "They don't always play in key," she added, referring to the band.

An American town can open a fair with a pair of shears which cut a ribbon at precisely 11:00 A.M., or at any other hour which has been selected, and everybody will be happy. A line will be formed and ready to pile in. There are always a number of people in the United States who like to be first, even in getting into the fairgrounds.

In Mexico this would be fantastic, impossible. The people here have to warm up for the fiesta, else they feel that they have been cheated out of half the fun. If the spirit does not move them very warmly the first day they make a stab at it, things just sort of fold up and everyone goes home, silently. On the morrow they will try again. Finally, the spark has caught, and the fiesta gets under way and then goes on and on. It is somewhat like going on a beer drunk or a pulque binge. The first glass may not have much effect on you. In fact you may think you do not feel it at all. But just keep on downing the stuff, and soon the results will be highly effervescent.

While the noisy preamble for the fiesta was going on, one of the Mexican gentlemen at my boardinghouse became violently ill. It was the usual thing: a fever and a terrific bellyache, the most awful stomach cramps, vomiting, then a dozen trips to the bathroom in the night.

At the crack of dawn the town doctor was called in. The whole place was anxious to see what would happen. In fact, the maids all stopped work and slicked themselves up in readiness for the doctor's arrival, a bit of needless presumption, I felt at the time.

When the doctor arrived this was all easy to understand. He was a fine-looking young man, well dressed, and was accompanied by a plump Indian-looking nurse. The doctor was the envy of every unattached female in town. I wondered why the doctor and I had never met each other on the plaza, for the young man seemed hardly to belong in Nahualtepec and could have been spotted half a mile off.

When he came in he was all business. Pulse, temperature, tongue, hands on stomach, a light in the eye, et cetera.

"A shot of penicillin," he said, taking out the bottle.

This he gave to the nurse and then turned to chat with the boarders, grouped around the door. His work was done. The nurse, so I was told later, took great relish in ramming the needle about a foot deep in the poor man's buttocks, and said she would be back the next day for another stab. The doctor also left a prescription. One of the flunkies around the place, a ten-year-old boy, was sent to the pharmacy for this. The druggist, who had his shop in a little hole in the wall next to the funeral parlor, filled it without batting his eyes. It was Terramycin.

Cost of treatment: the doctor received $1.60 for the house call. The nurse got 40 cents. Three shots of penicillin came to a total of $3 more. The boy got a peso (8 cents) for going after the prescription. It almost pays to get sick in Mexico.

I rapidly made friends with all the children in the neighborhood. The little girls were especially friendly, and when they heard some of the songs the teacher had used in that rural school outside Tepic they were greatly impressed, and begged to have them repeated again and again. A day or so later while walking down the street I ran into a group of five or six singing out one of these little tunes at the top of their lungs. They had memorized both words and music. They all pointed to me and shouted: "There's the señor who taught us this song." A couple of women standing in one of the doorways, arms akimbo, gave me a critical stare, and I was not sure that they appreciated what had been done for the culture of the town.

The girls always came out in the morning in neat little dresses, but unless they went straight to school they were filthy in no time at all. They sat down anywhere, played in the street, fingered every filthy dog. One of the girls, about eight years old, was named María Mercedes. She was a bright little trick, with gray eyes and a charming smile. She was also a little devil. She told me that she had twelve dresses, and it was not difficult to believe, for she had worn most of them in the last three days. She took a fancy to a pencil I was using, so I made her a present of it. The next day her mother formally invited me in for a cup of coffee.

María Mercedes immediately showed me her twelve dresses, all hanging on a little string. They were as cute as they could be, and must have taken hours to make. There were eight other children in the family, and I met them all. The oldest, a son, was nineteen. There was only one bed in the place. There were several *petates*, the primitive Indian straw sleeping mats. How many slept on the bed, and how many on the mats, I did not find out. The house had two rooms, and a spacious patio. One room was a kind of entrance and parlor. The other was the bedroom. There was a Singer sewing machine in the parlor, a wooden table, and four wooden chairs with straw seats. There was a calendar on the wall, a little tin shrine, a picture of Christ Crucified, and another of the Virgin of Guadalupe. The coffee was served in pale-green cups of local make. It was hot and black. I downed it with three well-spaced gulps; it was too bitter to be left trickling on the tongue.

"How do you keep so many dresses clean?" I asked the mother, estimating her wash at several dozen.

The mother laughed, and pointed her thumb at María Mercedes.

"She washes her own," she said. "But I do help with the ironing," she went on. "I like to iron, but I do not like to wash. I only go to the stream to talk."

Over in one corner of the room was a cast-iron pail with one side cut out of it. This was so the charcoal could be put in. The embers inside the pail were now very red, and on top of the pail was a grill on which the iron was resting. The coffee stood beside the iron. The same kind of portable stove was used when the family wanted to iron clothes or cook tortillas, which was at least twice every day.

The patio was considerably larger than the house itself and contained several small trees and flowers. A turkey wandered around grubbing in the earth, and there were four brown hens taking a dust bath in the sun.

"We also have a pig, a cow, and three burros," María Mercedes said.

"And my son has just bought a truck," the mother proudly put in. "It is only three years old. He has been working in the United States as a *bracero*, and he put all of his money into a truck. He says it will make money for him. I hope it does."

The Mexican family is a close-knit unit and functions as a single organism. Marriage itself, however, is not always the basis of family life, and herein lies the difficulty for so many Mexican children. One of María Mercedes' friends, Bertita, who lived across the street, belonged to this unfortunate category of families without fathers. One day when I asked a perfectly innocent question about what Bertita's father did, María Mercedes sniggered and replied that Bertita didn't know who her father was.

"Well, who is Mrs. Gómez's husband?" I asked, still unconvinced.

"*Tiene mil esposos*," María Mercedes said. ("She has a thousand husbands.")

I found out later that this was quite true. Men came and went from that house with a considerable regularity, each leaving a child or two in his wake. Mrs. Gómez (Spanish for Mrs. Jones, for it was probably not her real name) was responsible for the care of them all. Strangely enough, she did a fairly decent job of it, but in thousands of similar cases the children are not so fortunate, and are left to wander about the fields or streets like little waifs, without shelter, care, or food.

In the year 1895 Mexican families were composed of an "average" of six persons. This of course included all families, even those who had just married and had no children at all. By 1940 the average size of the Mexican family had gone down to 4.5 members. In 1970 it was up to 5.2 members. (In the United States the average family has only 3 members.) Urban life invariably causes a decrease in the size of families. In Mexico today the "average" rural family is made up of 6 members, whereas the urban family is composed of only 4. That is, the most enterprising and best-educated element of the national life is reproducing itself at the lowest ratio.

A recent study of several hundreds of juvenile delinquents in Mexico reveals that 10 per cent of these delinquents were out-and-out vagrants, with no fixed homes; 57 per cent were illegitimate; 32 per cent had no fathers, and 11 per cent had no mothers. These latter two groups were referred to as "orphans," but the word is probably not accurate. "Deserted by father or mother" would be the more accurate descriptive phrase.

The proportion of "free unions" in Mexico, without marriage rites, embraced 1,360,000 persons in the year 1930; in 1970, it was 1,472,000 persons. (In 1930 there were 1,660,000 people married by a priest; in 1970 only 1,358,600.) The number married by civil law alone, a weak bond in a country which is so predominantly Catholic, reached 2,423,000 persons in 1970. Many Mexicans do not regard as valid any marriage which is not performed before a priest, and this includes a goodly number of those who are married in civil ceremonies, some of them for that very reason. Not long since, I saw eighty couples married at one time in Mexico City's National Auditorium, as a result of the Social Welfare Department's campaign to legalize common-law marriages. These couples had been living together already and many of them had children.

Legalized divorces in Mexico increased from 23,293 in the period 1926–1935 to a total of 95,682 in the decade from 1960 to 1970, that is, an increase of 300 per cent. The increase in population during these years was only 200 per cent. And these legal divorces do not, of course, include by any means all the unions which were broken without sanction of the courts. The three most common causes given for divorce in the Mexican courts are: unjustified desertion of the home, incompatibility, and mutual consent.

The domestic servant class in Mexico contains a considerable proportion of what the Mexicans call *madres solteras,* or bachelor mothers. These poor women represent the extreme example of the dissolution of family life. Approximately 35 per cent of them have had children by more than one father. Many of these women later enter the ranks of the prostitutes. Little wonder, then, that domestic service holds so little dignity in the eyes of the average Mexican woman. The first modern census of Mexico (1895) showed 12,632,427 people and 276,456 women servants; in 1970, with total population four times that large, women servants had increased by only 24 per cent to 342,896. (These figures include only those servants who receive wages. Many families take in country girls and give them food, clothes, and shelter, but no pay, in return for domestic services. In nearly all cases the boys of the family look upon these maids as fair game.)

The mother of María Mercedes told me heart-rending tales about the many unwed mothers of Nahualtepec, for whom she felt the deepest pity. Her own family was honorable and respected in the community, she was at pains to point out. It was also a cut above the average family in economic position, and I was anxious to find out how this had come about.

The mother explained that her husband had twice been to the States as a *bracero,* and on the last occasion had taken his son along with him. When I had been in Nahualtepec six years previously this family was one of the poorest in town. The children (there were six of them then) were ill-nourished, ill-clad and perpetually filthy. As soon as the father began to send his savings back, things began to improve. The mother bought a Singer and yards and yards of cotton cloth. She turned out dresses and pants by the gross. The children began to dress better and look cleaner. Now they were among the upper level of the middle class in Nahualtepec. The son's truck had done the final trick. Anyone with a truck in a Mexican village is like anyone with a Cadillac in Pea Ridge, Arkansas, except that the truck is a real capital investment, yielding a good profit, and the Cadillac is not.

As I was saying good-by to María Mercedes, her brothers, sisters, and mother, there was a sudden burst of rockets and firecrackers from the plaza.

"It's a strange time of day to be shooting them off," the mother said, twisting her face wryly. Then she lifted her shoulders in a simulated shrug, and shook my hand. I started down the street, but had not gone half a block when it was obvious that something unusual had happened. Several people were running toward the plaza. As I rounded the corner a goodly crowd of spectators loomed up about a block farther down the street. They were staring at something on the plaza, and obviously had no desire to get much nearer. I joined the crowd and soon made out two men lying on the edge of the sidewalk, as if they had been walking together when something had suddenly mowed them down. Blood was flowing across the walk and into the flowers and grass.

When I finally got the story straight it went something like this. The two men's families had been at odds for many years, and every once in a while the feud would break out into open battle. On two previous occasions there had been knife fights in which critical wounds had been inflicted. This time, under the influence of tequila, Pablo had told the whole town he was going to shoot Pedro deader than a doornail. When Pedro heard this he got his own gun and headed for the plaza, where Pablo was still drinking. Pablo came out and went after him. Pedro was not drunk and let him have it right in the middle. Pablo doubled up and fell to the ground, and then Pedro made his fatal mistake. Thinking that he had done his man in for good, he walked up to him and rudely kicked him over on his back. Pablo was not dead, and at this precise moment he let Pedro have three shots in the chest. Then they both fell dead.

"Where were the police when all this was going on?" I asked. After all, the mayor's office and police headquarters and the whole municipal government was not more than half a block away. It seemed strange that they had not intervened. At first I got only evasive answers. Then somebody said with a malicious smile:

"They were chasing a mad dog at the other end of town."

There were several sniggers. My friend of the funeral parlor, who was on the prowl, heard my question and also the rejoinder. He took my arm and sagely explained:

"It would not have been good judgment to interfere. After all, nobody was hurt except the two who had been causing all the trouble, and they were both killed. Now we are rid of them for good. We'll have a little peace in town."

It did not seem such a bad way to settle things when you see them from that angle. Two days later there was a big funeral for which the town turned out en masse. Twelve men carried the two black-draped caskets down the cobbled streets to the rocky pantheon just outside the town, as the mourners murmured their rosary. The funeral put a crimp in the preparations for the fiesta, but it did not cause any change in the final date. It merely toned down the warming-up period.

On the following morning I spied María Mercedes washing her dresses in the gutter. Her brother, Eduardo, aged three, and her sister, María, five, were playing close by. A few feet above her, two boys were soaping down a dog. Across the street five women were on their knees under the stringy shade trees pounding their wash. I walked slowly toward the plaza over the cracked and hunchy cobblestones. The sun was out in a cloudless sky, although a storm had threatened the night before. The light was almost blinding. Suddenly a door of one of the adobe houses opened and a woman came out to empty a can of urine onto the sidewalk. It was a vivid reminder of that faint musty order which seems to pervade so many Mexican villages. A little farther along the sidewalk I stepped over an enormous cow turd, a reminder of the night before. Sometimes there were similar calling cards that people had left, on the sidewalk or beside the curb.

María Mercedes, her ears straining, edged toward the five gossiping washerwomen. Eduardo toddled after her like a shadow. He was her duty, and she never let him out of her sight. Eduardo had a runny nose and, as is too much the custom in Mexico, it had been allowed to run all over his face, which was now black and wet. One of the very few things about the children in Mexico which has often disgusted me is the number of two- and three-year-old snot-nosed little tots. Even the older children are not immune, but those just beyond the baby years are the worst. Nobody ever seems to carry a handkerchief. Sometimes a shirt sleeve or the hem of a dress is used, rather ineffectively. But almost never a handkerchief.

María Mercedes that morning had on a neat little red dress, although she was on her knees washing clothes and although she constantly cuddled Eddie, wiping his nose on her skirt. I felt the strongest sort of compulsion to ram Eddie's little face into the water and scour off all that filth, for it would have taken but a minute. It never passed through María Mercedes' mind.

The way María Mercedes watched over Eddie and María was a wonder to behold, yet it was typical. Mexican families, among the poorer village classes, run to a large size, and from the beginning the older children learn to take care of the younger. Under any other setup family life would be impossible. The younger ones always have a kind of second mother in these little keepers, who are with them night and day.

The Mexican family at home observes the old-style patriarchal (and matriarchal) standards. Whatever father and mother say must be right and whatever father and mother want done must be done, and without quibbling. Obedience is almost automatic. Discipline is no problem at all where there is really a family life. On this basis of respect for parents Mexican family life runs smoothly at all times, perhaps not always as progressively as one might like, but always smoothly, which is sometimes preferable. There is none of that yelling at parents that is so often heard now in the United States, and which is somehow supposed to indicate a wholesome lack of frustration. Mexican children know frustration of many different kinds, but this particular kind of emotional frustration that is supposed to ensue if you insist on obedience and no back talk is completely unknown to them. And it is only fair to point out that one seldom runs into a maladjusted Mexican child. Out of their respect for parents has grown a warm integrated feeling, an emotional security, and a naturalness of manner which is completely charming.

Just behind María Mercedes and her two little charges were playing two other little tykes, sans diapers and sans pants. Each of them was wearing a nice little blouse or shirt, but no bottom. Until the age of four or five this is quite a common custom, for it saves an incalculable amount of wash.

"Why only the tops, señora?" an American lady of my acquaintance once had the effrontery to inquire. The retort came quick as a bell:

"It is the bottom end that causes all the trouble, señora."

Little wonder that the streets of Mexico are not always clean.

One day, about four o'clock in the afternoon, I went into the church. Eight people were there, seven of them women on their knees. The lone man, dressed in a not-too-clean whitish pair of pants and coat, and with a black serape across his shoulders, was sitting immobile in one of the rear pews. In a moment he arose and walked to a statue resting in a niche along the left side. Reverently, he kissed the feet of this image, then drew his right hand slowly and vertically down his own brow and face. He repeated this three or four times, murmuring a prayer as he did so. Finally, he kissed the image's feet again, and after this, crossed himself devoutly and departed.

In the front part of the church, above the altar, was an image of Christ Crucified. The figure was colored a brownish pink, but the blood was very red. Nearly all of the images in the churches were colored, many of them wearing clothes of brilliant hues. Their eyes and hair also seemed very real. In colonial days they used to put human hair and fingernails (even eyelashes) on these statues in order to make them more lifelike. Now color generally has to suffice. Sometimes this is old and faded; at other times it is rich and new. Frequently real clothes, exquisitely made and embroidered, drape the most venerated images. Occasionally these garments are adorned with rare jewels.

The crucified Christ above the altar was mostly without garments of any kind, in order that the wounds of the crucifixion and the scarlet blood flowing from them might be seen more clearly. On each side of the figure of Christ was an angel, its wings tilted out over the head of the Son of God. The trio of images made a very imposing tableau above the main altar.

One of the kneeling women now lifted both her hands to heaven as if offering her very soul to God. Her green *rebozo* fell behind her shoulders as she raised head and face and repeated the gesture. It was obvious that she was in a very tense emotional state. As she held her hands aloft, two more women entered the church and fell to their knees at the beginning of the main aisle. On their knees they then moved forward toward the altar, praying as they advanced. They were dressed in black; one wore a blue *rebozo* on her head, the other a brown one. On reaching the front of the church they briefly rose, crossed themselves, entered one of the pews, and again fell to their knees for further prayer.

The whole town was now hived with energy in preparation for the fiesta. The funeral of the two feuders had been pushed out of people's minds, and everyone was intent on taking a part in putting up decorations over the streets. In a way, this was a pitiful thing, for the decorations, though most abundant, consisted merely of several dozen rolls of very cheap tissue streamers in pink and white. These were strung up across the streets down which the images, the band, and the procession of pilgrims was to pass, and telephone and light poles along the sides of the streets were similarly decorated. The first few tissues were certainly a sad sight to behold, but as the nimbler young men of town began to climb poles and tie down strings full of streamers, the street look on an air of carnival gaiety. I wondered at the choice of colors, for in view of the Mexicans' love of brilliant hues, it seemed strange that the streamers should be only pink and white. I was anxious to learn the reason. The boys who were putting up the decorations said that this was the custom; they did not know why. But one of the older ladies, dressed in rigid black, gave what I am sure was the correct answer:

"Those are the colors of the little angels, señor, that live in heaven. This is a religious fiesta, señor."

It was good that she had reminded me, for there seemed nothing at all religious about the way the decorations were being put up. But to the Mexican Indian (and the near-Indian mestizo) religion is fun. The early priests made this concession, and it still stands today, rockets, firecrackers, streamers, bands, and all. The first rockets and firecrackers of colonial times were in all likelihood used merely to impress the Indians with the white man's power. Gunpowder, of course, was one of the decisive weapons of the conquest. When used in fiestas by the Church the Indians were so impressed that the good fathers undoubtedly thought next of the idea of scaring away the bad spirits with loud explosions. Perhaps some intelligent Indian suggested the possibility. Soon the fusion of firecrackers and fiesta was permanent. It was built on the deeply ingrained fact that the Mexicans dearly love *noise*, and most particularly the noise that they themselves are making. If the God is big he must deserve a big voice. In the fiesta noise becomes a kind of common tongue which unites individuals in the broader soul of the community bedlam.

On the following day a truck came into town bearing nine heavily powdered and highly painted girls, another strange element of the fiesta. It very soon became apparent that they were to be "the girls" while the town's celebration was getting into swing. They set up shop in the vacant lot against the walls of which the butchers slaughtered their meat. Soon whorehouse and slaughterhouse were going concerns, side by side. A small *excusado* (privy) was rigged up of cornstalks and fibers in one corner of the lot. The "girls" then strolled around smiling and chatting with every potential customer. They did not actually do business there on the lot; this was carried on in a little hovel farther down the street. But the vacant lot alongside the streamer-flowing street was their central rendezvous. It was just far enough off the plaza to afford a modicum of privacy and just far enough away from the church to afford a modicum of decorum. I soon noticed that the older ladies, the mothers, wives, and indeed all the respectable folk in town, gave the place a wide berth. But the young blades of the community swarmed there like bees after honey.

Soliciting, of course, was done mostly after dark. During the bright daylight hours all one could see on the lot was the little cornstalk privy. But when dusk began to fall the bees began to hive. Soon the place was thick with the scent of heavy rice powder, cheap perfume, overrouged faces, thickly painted lips, lush sensual voices, and sinuous bodies. Virile hands followed the exploratory instinct, so much a part

24. Ixtaccíhuatl Volcano, Mexico City

25. Oil refinery, Guanajuato

26.
Sleeping dog vase, Colima culture, circa A.D. 600. In many Indian cultures of Mexico it was believed that the dog escorted his dead master across the River of the Dead to his final resting place. (Author's collection)

27.
Entrance to the Museum of Anthropology, Mexico City

28. The architecturally famous circular waterfall that pours down from the 4,000-square-foot floating canopy onto the pavement of volcanic stone in the central patio of the National Museum of Anthropology in Mexico City

29. Cobblestone street, Taxco

30.
Colonial aqueduct,
Querétaro

31.
Olympic Stadium, Mexico City, during the Olympic Games, 1968

32.
Camino Real Hotel,
Puerto Vallarta

of the old conquistador temperament, but the "girls" never allowed things to get out of hand. If a hand strayed too wildly, they simply snatched it away or grabbed the boy by the arm and pulled him off down the street toward the little hovel, where they apparently took turns using the bed.

I asked one of the more respectable lads in town why the whole thing was permitted to go on so flagrantly, and he, not at all abashed, answered:

"Well, they only come to town when there's a fiesta. That's not very often, señor."

"What do you think of it, personally?" I asked.

"Who, me?" he said. At first, I thought he would not give me a sensible reply, but then he added:

"Their customers are mostly men who come in from the hills, you know. They come into town from *way* up in the hills."

"You mean the town boys don't patronize these girls."

"I didn't say that, señor."

It was easy to see that he was beginning to feel embarrassed, so we let the subject drop.

John Steinbeck has some notable pages in one of his novels on the church and the whorehouse as two of the fundamental institutions that fashioned the society of the American frontier. That thought came back to me in Nahualtepec as I watched the girls go about enticing their men. There was a great difference, however. The "house" of Nahualtepec and the houses of most of the smaller Mexican villages are constantly on the move. They are not exactly stationary in the United States, but in the early days the saloon-dance hall and its "girls" were a definite fixture of the frontier settlement.

The Spaniards did not introduce prostitution into Mexico. Long before the conquest the Aztecs had it, and on a rather widespread scale. In colonial days, it is true, prostitution became vastly more popular, because so many thousands of Spanish men came to Mexico without their wives. There was a time when ten cacao beans was the "price." In Nahualtepec it was 40 cents. Just how many cases of syphilis and gonorrhea this particular group of girls left behind them in Nahualtepec, it would be impossible to calculate. But based on the premise that all the girls were infected with something (a fairly safe premise, I believe) and based further on the rapid eye-scanning estimate of at least five men a night for each girl, we would have a minimum estimated total of 45 to 50 cases per day. The girls stayed in town five days. Roughly, then, 250 cases. These, in their turn, must have passed their infection on to at least five or six hundred more. It is no surprise, then, that the incidence of venereal disease is so high in Mexico, and there is really no accurate way of getting at the total number of cases. Most of them are never examined by a doctor.

The streets of Nahualtepec are narrow and rough. Cracked and uneven cobblestones lead between dust-gray adobe walls to the low-flung plaza atop the rolling hill. A few cars, some trucks, and many bicycles pick their devious paths along these knobby streets, but by far the most important means of transportation is on human or burro back. It is six in the afternoon as I walk down one of the streets. Just ahead of me is a twelve-year-old boy with four burros, three of them loaded with dry branches broken to even lengths, which are the firewood of Nahualtepec. Each little burro is piled high with these splintery gray sticks which are so placed that they form a high semicircle on the small loam-colored back and sides. The wood is tan and resinous at its ends where the branches have been broken off. I inquire about the business, and the boy tells me that he has been ten kilometers up into the canyons to get his loads.

"The trees used to be closer to town," he said. "But now that's all gone, señor."

He also told me that each burro load brought 6 pesos (50 cents U.S.) and that if he and his father were lucky they might gather three loads in a long day's work. His father always helped him do the gathering, but he alone brought the wood into town. This boy was an exception, for most of the firewood boys do their work alone, and if they take in 6 pesos in two days they are lucky. Practically every house and store in Nahualtepec uses this fuel, as they have done for centuries. It is no wonder that the town is surrounded by hills that are gaunt and bare.

It is now beginning to get dark or, as the Mexicans say, it is beginning "to night," and the livestock is coming in from the pastures. Half a dozen cows follow the herd of goats, and not long afterwards five burros and a tiny horse pass by. They all walk with dignified slowness, turn at the proper corners, and enter the home corrals. I notice that when the cows arrive the doors are not open, and one of the animals begins to pick at the wood with her horns. A boy opens up from inside and lets them in.

The livestock of Nahualtepec is always brought in for the night.

Each house has an adjoining patio or yard where the animals are kept, but as the animals disappear behind each entrance they give the impression of going straight into the house. Both dwelling and corral are back of the solid adobe wall that fronts the street.

By day or by night Nahualtepec is hardly a beautiful sight. At night the lights are dim and far apart. Only a pale gleam comes from the barred and wood-covered windows or from the cracks around the massive doors. In the sunlight the streets are equally unlovely. They are but narrow cuts in the little one-story squares of adobe which make up the town. Only the rarest house looks appealing or neat from the outside. Walls facing the street were once painted in different tones of rust, cream, or white, but now nearly all have worn to a dusty and feral hue.

The boardinghouse in which I am living has walls that are at least a foot and a half thick. The structure is a hundred fifty years old. Outside, it resembles every other place in town. Inside, it is one of the more pretentious. Its large patio is planted with big-leaved and flowering vines, over which the tall graceful stalks of a doubly red-tipped poinsettia hang their clusters of scarlet. Arched corridors lead around three sides of the courtyard. At the end of one of these is the common privy, one of the very few water closets in town. But half the time there is not enough pressure to make it flush. Probably because of this fact of life many Mexicans have acquired the filthy habit of dropping their used toilet paper into a basket beside the bowl instead of into the bowl itself. The slightest lump of paper will stop the latter's functioning completely.

Most of the houses in Nahualtepec have no sewerage facilities. Their *excusados* are similar to our old-style outhouses, only worse. Sometimes there are four walls, sometimes there are three, stuck up next to the adobe fence, and sometimes only one behind which to crouch. Frequently, there is no shelter of any kind, and a corner of the yard has to suffice.

While the dwellings of Nahualtepec appear gaunt and poor from the street side, once a person has gone inside this aspect undergoes a remarkable change. Many of the patios are neat and attractive, with well-kept plants and gardens. If the family is relatively well off, the corridors of the patio will be arched, the floors will be of tile, and the plants will be in large clay pots of oval form, like the ancient water jugs. Furniture, at least tables and chairs, will be placed along the corridors for comfortable outdoor living, for the climate is mild throughout most of the year. The family dines, sits, naps, meets, and chats in the patio. Friends gather here when they come to visit. As in colonial days, the patio is the center of family life just as the plaza is the center of the life of the community. Even before the Spaniards arrived the Aztecs had built their better homes around courtyards, so the patio has a double ancestry in Mexico.

This is the principal reason why the North American's first impression of most Mexican towns is a distinctly unfavorable one. The cared-for "outside" yard or garden of Mexican houses is really "inside," behind the adobe walls that front the street. These walls are in part merely a fence, shutting the family away from the public view, affording them a private open-air retreat from the city streets. Of course, not by any means all these patios are attractive. Everything depends on the income and enterprise of the family concerned. If the family group has initiative and some money, the patio and also the dwelling will be clean and appealing inside, but if the family is extremely poor and apathetic it will be a miserable-looking affair. Well over half the patios of Nahualtepec are just enclosed patches of lumpy earth from which an ocasional cactus or other native weed raises its spindly spines. A well-worn hammock will be hanging in one corner of the yard. There may be a pig and a few chickens grubbing in the dust, and the smell of the open-air privy will spoil any possible enjoyment of outdoor living.

Through many of the open doorways of Nahualtepec one can see a sagging mattress on a yellow wooden bed. Yet less than 50 per cent of the population of Mexico sleep on beds, as we use the term. The *petate* is the most common mattress of all. It is a handwoven straw mat measuring about five feet long by three and a half feet wide, and is perhaps one-fourth of an inch thick. This mat is placed directly on the floor. One person out of every six in Mexico sleeps on the ground, or floor. Another kind of "bed" commonly used in the Central Highlands is the "pole bed," which consists of poles or ropes strung across a quadrangle of cross sticks attached to poles which serve as the legs. A blanket, or *petate*, is then placed on the strung poles, and the sleeper occupies a bed above the ground level.

I am sure that less than half the inhabitants of Nahualtepec occupy real American-type beds, and even when these are used they sag in such a radical curve toward the middle that it is difficult to see how a sleeper could long occupy such a couch without suffering a permanently twisted spine. The beds are almost invariably of a sallow, maple-yellow color, of the cheapest wood, and the mattresses are so ancient and lumpy that they evoke a picture of the cobbled streets.

Many of the dwellings of Nahualtepec are of one or two narrow rooms. The children in these homes can hardly grow up without observing the intimacies of their parents, and while this may have the effect of making sex appear as a normal adjunct of daily family life, it also destroys the charm and mystery of this fundamental phase of human contact. By the time a Mexican child reaches the age of twelve or fourteen there is little left in life that he may still look forward to. The rapid maturity of the Mexican body and mind quickens the pace of adulthood, improper sanitation and diet hasten the process, so that by their middle years thousands of Mexicans are already old.

How do people keep themselves clean in houses where there is no running water? The answer is, many don't. Not one house in twenty in Nahualtepec has a bathtub. In Nahualtepec there are two common ways to take a bath: One can get out the family pail or scrub tub and pour the water over body and head, then, if the person bathing really wants to be clean, he can empty that water and rinse himself in another tubful. When there are seven or eight children in the family, as is often the case, it is easy to see why the personal bath is hardly a daily occurrence. Or, one can go down to the public bathhouse, which is on the street adjoining the main plaza, and there pay for the privilege of using the facilities. The cost is 1 peso (8 cents) for soap, water, and towels. The facilities are shower booths which resemble those in many of our second-rate trailer parks or swimming pools.

There is one other way of bathing that is not exactly common, but is now becoming more popular because it is the cheapest, and in many ways the most convenient, way of all. It might just possibly also be the cleanest. This is to wait till the night is good and dark, then head for the plaza where the well spurts out, shed all the clothes and get under the water. On several occasions in the early morning or late evening hours I have seen men and boys here, stripped down to a brief-cut pair of pants or shorts, dousing themselves vigorously. The women, I was informed on excellent authority, make a considerable use of the place during the later and darker hours of the night.

On one of my first visits to Mexico, many years ago, our train was ambling down the west coast route not too many days after a heavy rain. The ditches alongside the tracks were still filled with water. Yet practically all the children and grown folks that we passed, most of them belonging to railway gang families, were extremely dirty. One passenger commented on this and another passenger (both Mexicans) countered with the remark that the people were terribly poor and that their filth was therefore excusable. An old lady, also Mexican and immaculately clean, then remarked somewhat caustically:

"They may be poor, but there's plenty of water right there. No reason why they shouldn't be clean, if they wanted to."

Perhaps the old lady was right in this particular instance, but in Nahualtepec there is definitely not plenty of water easily available and the lack of a daily bath is somewhat more understandable. But habit, the result of centuries of near-waterless living, does go a long long way.

XIX

FIESTA AND MARKET DAY

It is a dry town. But for the great fiestas the flowers break from their cloistered patios and come out to the streets, toward the church, delicate and humble flowers: magnolias, lilies, geraniums, tuberoses, marguerites, carnations and violets, laboriously given water from the town's deep wells.

—AGUSTÍN YÁÑEZ, from *Al filo del agua*

SUNDAY is market day in Nahualtepec. People come in an ever-flowing stream from the hills and canyons that surround the town. From the air it must resemble a procession of slowly moving brown ants all heading toward a common hill, or like drops of water trickling toward the sea, which finally envelops them completely in a greater but less separated motion. Every road and pathway is filled. It is difficult to tell whether there are more people or burros; the burros practically disappear under their loads, and many a human back is piled high with goods to be put up for sale in the market. When Sunday is a fiesta day as well as market day, the number of incoming burros and humans is more than doubled. On a very important fiesta day four or five times the average number of people will come to town.

On this particular Sunday in January there was to be a big fiesta for *Nuestro Señor del Valle* (Our Lord of the Valley). The big church in town was the sanctuary of this image, and its parishioners were responsible for the fiesta. The smaller church across the street would hold its fiesta a few days later. The pink-and-white tissued streamers were now up, forming a canopy of waving color above the main streets leading to the church and to the plaza. On Friday people began to arrive from the hills, three days before the fiesta. A few of them put up with friends in town, but the vast majority simply picked places along the plaza or curbs, and there put down their packs. By Friday noon the choicest spots had been occupied; by Friday night the streets and plaza were fairly crawling with people. The absolute limit seemed to have been reached.

During Friday afternoon I walked up to the plaza to see what was going on. In one corner of the square half a dozen men were busy putting together a tall tower of reeds. First, the framework was tied together with strands of palm and strips of wire. Then they attached crosspieces, which stuck out in front and on two sides like protruding axles. On these were fastened the hubs of a couple of dozen reed wheels, representing dogs, rabbits, foxes. Each object was handmade of bamboo. Then around the exterior were carefully tied long strands of fireworks and rockets so placed that when lighted their propulsion would send the objects into a flurry of motion. The fireworks were all made in the local plant which occupied an adobe shack just outside of town, deliberately placed there in case the barrels of powder should someday accidentally get out of hand.

The workers took the greatest pains in fastening their objects to the axles, testing them again and again in order to make doubly sure that they would move freely when the powder went off. They referred to their handiwork as "The Hunt," and no sooner had they finished it than they began to set up a smaller tower which was called *El Castillo* (The Castle). This had the shape of a slender steel tower like those used on the electric power lines. On the three sides which would be visible from the plaza were a mass of reed wheels. The Castle is an integral part of nearly every display of fireworks in this part of Mexico.

That evening after dark the countryfolk who had parked along the streets opened up their *petates*, serapes, and blankets and went to bed, some of them using the curb as a pillow. As if it were an everyday occurrence, they stretched out on the cobblestones and were soon asleep. The whole place resembled a refugee center of some disaster area where the homeless must live and sleep temporarily in whatever quarters they may find in order to save their lives. But these Mexicans had all come to enjoy themselves, the thought of disaster (or of discomfort) had never entered their heads. Indeed, this very discomfort, slight though it was to them, would heighten the fun on the day of the fiesta. By ten o'clock at least five hundred men, women, and children were lying asleep under the cold starry skies of Nahualtepec, the smaller children wrapped snugly in *rebozos* beside their mothers. I picked my way home among the hunched and curled figures overwhelmed by the eerie feeling of being in a world so strange that it seemed almost to belong to a different planet. The strange faces of bearded men, half hidden under wide sombreros and serapes, the rounded bundles of children completely covered with *rebozos* of every hue, the softer forms of the mothers as they lay asleep beside their husbands and children, all suggested a dream or a painting rather than a raw reality.

Half a block ahead of me a little girl of twelve or thirteen was standing beside a figure wrapped in a blanket. She was the only person on the street besides me who was not in a horizontal position. The figure in the blanket raised its head, looked at the girl a moment, then gave a negative nod. The girl made a slight motion as if to wring her hands. Then she saw me and ran in my direction. A beggar, no doubt, I thought. But when she reached my side the girl burst out:

"Señor, do you know where is the house of the doctor? My mother is very very ill. He must come at once, señor."

"Yes, I'll show you," I said. "It is just off the plaza."

I turned around and hurriedly we walked toward the plaza. The girl was breathing hard, as if she had walked a long way. Her hair was stringy and her dress was torn. She had been crying.

"What is wrong with your mother?" I asked.

"She is spitting blood, señor."

The words were a sudden dagger that punctured all the unreality around us. We were now two human beings bent on a common mission, she for her mother, I with a child and for a woman I had never seen, and would never know. We arrived just as the doctor was about to retire. He slipped on his coat, grabbed his bag, and came out into the night. At the corner I left them disappearing into the darkness that led toward the hills. I never saw the child again and never knew what happened to her mother, but for a moment tragedy had linked us all together, the little girl, her mother, the handsome doctor of Nahualtepec, and me, a gringo from California. A soft warm wave seemed now to stretch itself slowly over me and the strange figures asleep on the cobbled street. We were in one world now, no wall between us, no separation.

Again on Saturday, long before the dawn, firecrackers crackled like shrapnel on the plaza, and outside my window the brass band began its noisy roundelay. It was impossible to sleep beyond this moment, but the bed, despite its notable sag, was warmer than the cold air, and I drowsed until the sky was bright. Then I threw the window wide and sniffed at the morning. A pungent odor entered the room. It was not difficult to guess its cause, but rather than investigate on an empty stomach I waited until after breakfast. It was the proper decision. The sleeping figures were now all out of their blankets, and half a dozen little fires were crackling along the curbs. Tortillas and coffee were cooking on rusty grids over the flames or atop braziers of live coals. But the one thing which distinguished the street from the night before was the odor, that very sharp and definite odor of a latrine, sans lime. Unmindful of the scent, the people went about their breakfast, eating with gusto. One mother paused temporarily in her cooking in order to bed her baby on the street. Deftly she wound another rag around the child's bottom, and then quickly went back to her tortillas on the grid. Several persons were on the other side of the street on their knees, washing their faces in the gutter. One old gentleman squatted on a rock, mirror in hand, scraping the stubble from his face.

All that day the countryfolk continued to pour into town. Up at the plaza some of the fiesta operations were already in full swing. Two shooting galleries were going at full blast, and a large hand-powered merry-go-round was revolving gaily with its full complement of passengers. Another smaller one was quickly being assembled just beside it. The power for each of them was applied from a steel cross bar fastened to the vertical axis at chest level. Against the arms of this crosspiece a man and three boys applied their combined strength and pushed the contraption around. As it picked up momentum their exertions lessened until finally only a slight push now and then was sufficient to keep the thing moving. The little seats, individually sprung, swayed out in a wide curve, and the children were thrilled. In a few moments the smaller carrousel also was ready, and with a boy about fourteen acting as barker was soon in competition with the larger machine. Even this smaller merry-go-round had fourteen seats on it, arranged in seven separately suspended chairs, each wide enough to hold two passengers. Soon it was almost full, and began to turn. The fourteen-year-old, with the help of a boy about nine, furnished the necessary motive power. The chairs swung out in a wide arc and delighted the smaller children who had chosen to ride this machine. The price was 10 centavos, less than a cent.

A clang of 22-caliber shells came from the other side of the plaza, where boys in their teens were taking pot shots at the well-worn ducks and rabbits that served as targets. They were not in motion. Electric power was available but too expensive. The proprietor later confided that he turned the power on when the novelty of shooting at still figures had faded. The marksmanship was nothing to write home about, but it was obvious that these young fellows enjoyed handling a gun. One boy stopped shooting for a moment and allowed his loaded rifle to point into the crowd. The boy next to him gave him a nudge, and he righted the barrel again.

Behind the shooting galleries was a crude motion-picture tent showing cartoons. Its loud-speaker blared forth the program, which consisted of a "colossal series" of "stupendous" cartoons of the most fascinating variety; when the announcer's voice became tired, he put on a record and let the music roar. Serving alternately as disk jockey and movie barker, he kept up a constant din which nearly drowned out every other sound in the vicinity.

Many Mexican towns and villages are noted for a particular product, and on market days this will be prominently displayed in the stalls on the plaza. The countryfolk and merchants of the nearby villages will head for these markets in order to lay in a supply of their specialty. The specialties of Nahualtepec are pottery and black serapes. The pottery is made in every size and shape, the serapes occasionally have designs of white in them, but many are completely black. When a merchant or a farmer needs new pots or a new black serape, he knows that Nahualtepec is the place to go. Many villages make and sell serapes, but Nahualtepec is one of the few that specializes in black ones. These have a particular appeal, as they do not show the dust or grime as the lighter or more varied color schemes do. Furthermore, the black serapes of Nahualtepec are of heavy wool, and offer an excellent protection from the cold night air of the Central Highlands.

All Saturday afternoon burros and human backs unloaded their cargo of pottery and serapes along the sides of the central plaza. Invariably bent nearly double, and invariably moving at that peculiar Indian pace which is halfway between a slow trot and a shuffle, the little brown potters arrived at the plaza, found an empty space, untied the strap which bound the load to their foreheads, and slipped it to the ground. The black serape sellers, men and women alike, carried their goods on their heads as well as on their backs and on burros. If the head bore the load, they walked erect as an arrow, their steps strong and graceful as those of Roman soldiers. Neither the potters nor the weavers were colorfully dressed. This was not real Indian country, although the blood of the community was mostly Indian. The village had been a part of the colonial economy too long to remain true Indian. And the Indian, when he becomes part mestizo, reaches desperately toward the white man's world with that mestizo part. He does not wish to remain completely Indian, though conditions may force him to continue living as an Indian.

The clothes of these people were mostly of the less-vivid colors. The men wore pants and coats of cotton which originally were white, khaki, or blue. They also wore a white sombrero and generally a black serape. They invariably wore leather *huaraches* instead of shoes. A good many of them went barefooted. The women wore cheap cotton dresses of brown, gray, blue, pink, or even red in gingham designs which no longer stood out because of the dust or the fading. They invariably wore a *rebozo*.

I sat for a moment on a bench on the plaza facing the shooting galleries and the movie tent with the blaring loud-speaker. Beside me was a man who had on a reddish coat and faded khaki pants. He was chewing on sugar cane and spitting the pulp out on the sidewalk and grass. On the bench opposite us two boys were eating peanuts, and beside them sat a man dressed in a once-white denim suit, wearing a large white sombrero, with his black serapes draped over the back of the bench. He was eating a package of those little green native pods of edible seeds which had been sprinkled with salt. They were held in a small cone made with a piece of old newspaper. The man threw the green-yellowing hulls on the ground. A couple of benches farther along the walk a mother with baby bundled in a green *rebozo* sat down, undraped her baby and her breast, and gave the child its meal. The bar across the street was doing a good business in tequila, and the huge *panza* (paunch) of the proprietor moved across the bottles on the shelves like an enormous balloon. Potters continued to unload their wares, and black serapes now filled many a bench along the sides of the plaza. I got up and headed home, passing by four steel plowshares which had just been unloaded and lined up for sale beneath the reed castle with its wheels of fireworks.

By Saturday night the town was so packed that it was difficult to walk, even in the middle of the cobbled streets. With my above-average height (six feet two) I felt that I must stick out in the crowd like a sore thumb, but these people paid me no mind at all. They went about their business as if no stranger were among them. Nevertheless, I began to feel again like an odd Gulliver, engulfed by a strange people and a strange culture on some lost planet.

When night came, all the vertical figures seemed almost suddenly to stop moving, then in a few moments they had all found a spot and were stretched out in a horizontal position. It did not seem possible. But there they were, curled up in all kinds of positions, indeed lying practically on top of each other, but each one apparently satisfied with his cobbled bed for the night. There was a thin open line left in the center of the street toward which the mass of brown *huaraches* pointed. By stepping with care one could move slowly along this thin line without treading on a sleeping figure. A thousand dark blankets and serapes heaved rhymically in the dim light. Beside a small fire in the gutter a mother cradled her baby, humming a soft lullaby. On the other side of the street the water bawled cleanly over its dirt and cobbles down to the bend at the corner. If it were a great river, I thought, a Nile or a Ganges, this multitude of unwashed bodies might be cleansed before the dawn. But Mexico has no such river. Its rivers are few and small. When the rains are heavy they may become a raging torrent, but when the rains have passed they are withered basins of dry sand between rugged banks, empty channels serving no purpose for the lands through which they pass.

I retired to my sagging bed and closed the wooden shutters of my window. The steel bars embedded deeply in the thick adobe walls were certainly protection enough, but the night air was chilled, and a faint odor of urine and defecation already permeated the atmosphere. By morning it would become a veritable wave. Mothers and housewives would begin to throw pails of water at the offending piles and puddles, and slowly they would disappear. Others would disappear underfoot. In any case it seemed wise to keep the shutters tightly closed for the night. The patio door could be left ajar, and perhaps the broad-leaved plants would breathe away a part of the noxious air.

Everybody was up early on fiesta day in order not to miss a moment. For breakfast we had the usual wide, very salty, and very fat pieces of Mexican bacon (*tocino*) and eggs. Always there were eggs, although hot cakes (they use the English words) also are popular now. But eggs and sweet rolls (*pan dulce*) are served invariably. Coffee of course, bitter and overroasted as usual. Also preserves of some kind (*conservas*) and occasionally marmalade (*mermelada*). The butter I never touched. Coffee with boiled milk (*café con leche*), about half and half, appealed to me more than plain black coffee. The eggs were always practically floating in heavy grease. No wonder, after you've taken a good look at the ham and bacon.

During breakfast the conversation hinged on the fiesta for a while, then switched suddenly to the colonies of Americans who were living in the towns of Chapala and Ajijic, both of them on the shores of Lake Chapala, Jalisco, the largest lake in Mexico. The Mexican contingent at the breakfast table wanted to know if I intended to retire at one of these favored retreats, and I assured them that I did not.

"Many Americans live there," they told me. "Chapala is full of retired officers from the armed services and Ajijic is filled with artists of all kinds and descriptions. The native crafts have been revived there, and weaving has become a fine art again."

"Yes, I saw an ad in my local paper in the States telling that a person could live well in these places for ninety dollars a month, and on two hundred fifty dollars could live like a king."

"With American dollars, of course," said an old lady who had once lived in San Francisco. "The exchange is all in your favor. But for us it is not cheap."

The principal attractions of these refuges on the lake are as follows: filet mignon at 60 cents a pound, servants at $20 a month, a house for $50 a month, a head gardener for 75 cents a day, and assistant gardeners for 40 cents a day. You can even buy a mansion for $15,000. The climate is mild in every month of the year. Guadalajara, a city of over a million, is only a few miles distant. You will have Americans as well as Mexicans living around you. You will be in the center of thriving artistic colonies.

All the above statements are true. But for some strange reason they sound so much better on paper than they appear at firsthand view. To mention only two slight inconveniences: *filet mignon* that is tough as shoe leather and daily battling swarms of flies are hardly conducive to tranquil, much less to luxurious living. But then if you are simply overwhelmed with the appeal of Lake Chapala, what does it matter? Somehow, I do not feel overcome by that appeal, beautiful though the towns of Chapala and Ajijic are, in a sort of run-down way, in their remote and sleepy mountains, far from the smog and traffic of our urban centers. A recent issue of the *American Legion Magazine* goes much further than this, and baldly states that you can live in Mexico on $90 a month all right if you are willing to live like a peon. Perhaps this is putting it too strongly. In any case, the serious tourist who has retirement in mind can get the cost-of-living figures from the Mexican-North American Cultural Institute, Hamburgo 115, Mexico 6, D.F.

The greatest problem that the North American visitor will encounter in Mexico lies in the drinking water, the milk, and the food. One must be very careful to consume only purified bottled water, or else to see that it is boiled before drinking. Beer or one of the carbonated beverages is a substitute if one likes them. Pasteurized milk is difficult to obtain in most parts of Mexico. Only canned milk is generally safe. The food is frequently upsetting to a stomach that is unaccustomed to it, and improperly washed or unpeeled raw fruits or vegetables often cause painful cramps, extended diarrhea, or even dysentery. The tourist can protect himself temporarily against these things by taking prescribed doses of either Sigmamycin, one of the chlorodine derivatives, Sulfasuxidine, Terramycin, or some other antibiotic. The prescription should be obtained before entering Mexico. Of course, these drugs cannot be taken indefinitely. Only the greatest daily caution will keep the permanent resident in good health.

After breakfast the procession, then the market. Slowly I climbed the hill to the plaza, notebook in hand. It was nine o'clock, and the streets were already lined with people, for the march was about to begin. During the War for Independence the image of the local saint, Our Lord of the Valley, had been hidden in a cave just outside of town, and the fiesta celebrated his removal from this spot and his deliverance from harm. The procession began at the cave, with prayers of thanksgiving. Then the more religious folk of the community, led by the priests and acolytes and with the little image at their head, marched slowly into town and toward the church. They murmured prayers as they advanced, and the air was a great hum of subdued voices as they passed. The women were nearly all dressed in black. Most of the men were wearing black serapes. All the faces were intensely devout.

The Nahualtepec band, fourteen strong, came behind the acolytes, playing strange plaintive airs. The wild notes of reeds and brass mingled with the sound of the little bells rung by the acolytes and formed a weird, almost Oriental music that suggested an exotic temple in some faraway forest. Following the band several sinners, in voices choked with emotion, were begging forgiveness for the error of their way. Every time the procession paused, half a dozen women fell to their knees and clasped their hands in front of their breasts. One little girl, who could not have been more than fifteen, was trying to walk the entire distance, ten or twelve blocks, on her knees. She must have thought that she had committed some dreadful sin, for her face was contorted with guilt and pain, and on her head was a crown of thorns. She had gone only a couple of blocks when her knees began to bleed. A young man of eighteen, a friend or brother, took off his serape and holding one end of it in his hands, let the rest fall on the street. The girl then crawled slowly forward on the cloth. The young man pulled it along the streets in front of her. The girl's progress was pitifully slow. He offered to carry her the rest of the way, but she refused. Finally, she reached the church exhausted, and disappeared inside. The crowd milling in the streets seemed greatly relieved; they had taken her burden for their own.

The moment the image entered the church a great salvo of rockets was fired into the air. Soon after this there was an immense buzz of voices massed in prayer, and then the strains of a religious chant. Fifteen minutes later the church was emptied, and the service was over. The entire religious part of the fiesta had taken barely an hour and a half. Immediately now the crowd took on a different tone. The strained serious expression disappeared from the faces, people broke up into smaller groups and began to chat and laugh. On the plaza the market was already getting under way.

Advancing down the side streets half a dozen pottery vendors were moving toward the plaza, carrying their loads on their heads. These were evidently townsfolk who did not have far to travel: the head was protected with a coil of cloth so placed that it cushioned the cargo of clay that rested upon it.

The visitor who is truly anxious to know Mexico will do well to visit the village markets and to spend some time there, trying not to miss a thing. It is always easier to see the broad strokes of a painting first, then proceed to the finer and thinner lines, to the delicate touches of brush or pen.

The Mexican village market is in its way a thing of beauty, almost a work of art. But like nearly all works of art it must be observed from a certain distance in order to make its keenest appeal. Viewed from too near at hand the imperfections and a certain cluttered effect, not to mention the smells that accompany the market, will have a clumpy and perhaps even an unpalatable aspect, while seen from a distance these same elements will appear to melt into a moving and rhythmic whole which is a live microcosm of the village and of the national life.

The market of Nahualtepec, neither excessively picturesque nor overly regular in its patterns and arrangements, neither flooded with tourists nor packed with wares intended for the world outside, is indeed a village market typical of the Mexican heartland of the Central Highlands. There is no such thing, however, as a Mexican village market without its particular appeal, its particular hue. On the plaza of Nahualtepec, and along the streets emptying onto the plaza, at least two or three hundred persons had already spread out their displays. Twice that number were gathered around to buy or talk. Occupying the largest spaces were the two principal community products: pottery and black serapes. The pots were arranged in dozens of different piles, each size and color in a heap of its own, so that there was a definite pattern in the over-all display. Next to the pottery were the serapes, draped on benches, in high and low piles, or held in the vendor's hands before some prospective buyer, a rhythm of black wings in motion beside the brown-white flowering of the potters' wares. Many of the twenty-eight serape sellers simply wandered about the market, goods on their shoulders, hoping to corner a customer.

Many of the sellers had spread out burlaps or pieces of canvas on the ground and there laid out their wares. In order to give their goods a note of high relief a considerable number had brought wooden boxes or planks which they used as tables on which to lay out burlap and wares. A few of the vendors had placed what they had to sell directly on the ground or on sheets of old newspapers. There were thirty-six stands with canvas canopies to shield them from the sun. One side of these canopies was stretched out on poles, and the other ends were tied to the nearest plaza tree or pole. They sheltered the more enterprising and better supplied stalls.

The pottery stands far outnumbered those of any other product. It was impossible to tell the exact number because they were so crowded together that sometimes a dozen or more *puestos* (booths) formed a single unbroken row. Many of the booths were attended by two vendors. A count of the sellers came to a total of eighty-seven. Perhaps the individual booths totaled fifty. Every conceivable kind and size of clayware was on display: enormous vases, jugs large and small, pots with handles and without, cups, plates, cooking pans, casseroles, storage bins, little animal miniatures for the clay menagerie (lambs, cows, pigs, fowls, birds, burros), and there were also numberless piggy banks, like those which have become so popular in the dime stores in the United States, most of which are imported from Mexico. The pottery was mostly of a light-brownish hue, but some pieces had bands of green, backgrounds of white or cream, and even occasional splashes of red or blue.

A few of the potters had brought in their cargoes that morning on trucks, either loosely packed or in large baskets, cartons, or burlap bags. There were two trucks on duty, which belonged to citizens of the village, one of them to the brother of María Mercedes, and they were making good money by traveling to and from the nearby factories (mostly homes) in order to deliver their loads to the plaza with the greatest dispatch. Some of the larger families had made half a truckload of pots during the past couple of weeks and now offered these for sale.

Most of the vendors were women. Their men had worked hard on the manufacture of the pottery, but now they were taking it easy strolling about the plaza, drifting into the bar, squatting and chatting beside the curbs. However, they did not stray too far away in case their women needed them for some bigger deal. The women were of all ages, from girls in their teens to withered crones far past their sixties. They all stood behind their displays. One girl of sixteen or seventeen wore her blouse so loose that her firm breast was clearly exposed. With Indian obstinacy she left it that way, fully conscious of what effect it was having on the men. Half a dozen boys paraded, with forced nonchalance, to and fro along the path in front of her. She did not even give them a glance. The place was public, and she was safe. Here was Indian requital for many an indignity visited upon her race. Now she could take in the pained excitement of the village blades, and be oblivious to their desire.

The women all wore *rebozos:* black *rebozos,* gray *rebozos* with thin red stripes, dark navy-blue *rebozos, rebozos* that were the color of rust or a dark blending of black and green. Alongside the pottery section were the serape vendors, twenty-eight strong. Their goods were piled neatly on canvas or burlap or lay on boxes on the plaza benches. One of the serape men caught my eye and throwing open a large black item with a slit in the center for the head he came toward me.

"Fifty pesos, señor. Pure wool. The best. All handmade, señor. The finest."

I held one corner of the serape. It was like lead. There was no doubt that it would keep the wearer very warm. I assured the man that I had no need for such a serape.

"Forty pesos," he said, still after me.

I knew what was next, and showed still less interest now.

"How much will you offer, señor?" he asked.

With such an eager salesman it is wise not to make any offer at all, unless you want a quick deal. The last time I had offered 15 pesos for a blanket whose original "asking" price had been 50 pesos, it had been dropped in my hands with the laconic words: "It is yours." That had been many years before. I had shared a Pullman berth with the hairy thing all the way home, then had to leave it in the trunk of the car for use on picnics. It was not allowed to enter the house.

Many of the serapes had slits in the center through which the head would pass so that the four corners might fall evenly and drape the entire body. These serapes, not usually for sale in the tourist markets, were the real thing. Derived from the old Indian *tilma* and the Spanish *manta*, or blanket, they became the poncho of colonial times and of today. The Eskimos have a similar cloak to keep themselves warm in the frigid regions of the north, except that they use thick animal skins instead of wool. But the spacious, loose-fitting style is much the same. When the wearer is in motion the garment bells out on the sides and lets the air enter freely. This allows for the evaporation of perspiration and prevents the storage of too much body heat, so that when the person stops moving he does not suddenly become chilled. Moreover, as soon as movement is halted, the garment drapes itself vertically, hangs tightly to the body, and holds the body heat snugly in, for now there is no generation of excess warmth, and all that is available is needed for physical comfort.

These primitive cloaks of Eskimos and Indians, like the togas of the ancient Greeks and Romans, probably represent the best kind of garment ever devised for human comfort, but the style makers must have their day, and in this epoch of specialists no person would ever dream of wearing a toga. That is, nobody except a poor Mexican Indian who does not know the advantages of tight belts, buttons that pop off, starched collars stiff as iron, and creases that rumple out as soon as one falls into a relaxed position.

In a small open space between the potters and the black serapes steamed a huge iron kettle, the size of a washtub, its high rounded sides thickly coated with soot. It rested on three large rocks which held it above the burning logs beneath. A load of firewood was piled up neatly nearby. The kettle was about half-full of a greasy broth containing huge chunks of pork, which perfumed the air with a heavy smell of boiling lard. It was the "hot portion" of the meal on sale at the market "cafeteria." Customers were served in brown clay pots at 4 cents a bowl.

Not far from the black-bellied kettle were two women slapping out, cooking, and selling tortillas. One of them had worked so fast that she was already ahead of the game and was storing her excess tortillas in a large basket, which she then covered with a cloth in order to prevent the escape of heat. Each of the women had fires going inside little stoves rigged up in large iron cans with one side cut out for a fireplace. They slapped out their tortillas with a rhythmic beat, laid them on the griddles, and then made more. There was no waste motion.

As I stood there watching, one man bought six tortillas, dropped a big dab of beans and chile sauce on them, and ate them like a sandwich, to the accompaniment of occasional slurps from his pork broth. A woman customer arrived and wanted an entire kilo of tortillas to take to her family in another corner of the plaza. The tortilla woman was at a loss. She had no scales to weigh out the kilo (2¼ pounds).

"I'll run over to that vegetable stand," the customer offered.

With this she took a fistful of tortillas and darted across the square. When weighed, it was not enough. The customer hurried back to the tortilla basket. The tortilla woman added a dozen more. The customer ran back to the scales. This pile was too heavy. She returned to the tortilla woman, who took off four or five, and then dashed to the scales again. Now the pile was close enough, and the transaction was closed. By this time everybody was laughing and enjoying the affair enormously, that is, everyone except the purchaser. She was completely out of breath.

"It'll take her a long time to eat all those tortillas," I remarked, glancing at the huge pile.

"Don't you believe it, señor," a nearby vegetable vendor said. "When her kids hit that heap of tortillas, it'll be gone in ten minutes."

The days of the Aztecs all over again. A child's portion then was two enormous tortillas after age thirteen, one and a half tortillas from six through twelve, but the Aztec tortillas were a good foot across. Mexicans today find it more convenient to make them in a smaller size. The cost of that kilo was 1 peso and 20 centavos, 10 cents U.S.

Not too far from the tortilla women four young boys were playing marbles in the dust. In the ring was a five-centavo piece (less than a penny). This was the stake. I heard another boy begging his mother for a coin so that he too might enter the game. He wanted 10 centavos. She refused to let him get away with more than 5.

"That's all you can lose," she said. "And don't grumble, or you won't get that."

The boy, who had already opened his lips, shut them abruptly and went over to where the game of marbles was in progress. In no time at all he had lost his coin.

Stands of fruits and vegetables, twenty-six in all, were scattered about the plaza. They sold tomatoes, cabbages, green peppers, red chile peppers, oranges, watermelons, bananas, peanuts, tangerines, avocados, coconuts, sweet and Irish potatoes, *jícamas, chayotes,* sugar cane, and salted green peas. There were also two sellers of bread, a butcher, four cold drink stands (three of them selling assorted dime-store candies and sweet rolls), two sellers of water, two of tortillas, the vendor of pork broth, and two sellers of dried corn and dried beans (frijoles).

One man sold *jícamas* alone. He had them spread out on a wide piece of burlap on the cobbles. The *jícama* is one of the most popular of the local vegetables, and tastes much like a cross between a turnip and a radish. It has the shape of a turnip, the color of an Irish potato. In a fresh salad it adds a delicious flavor. In the market many customers bought a large *jícama,* peeled off the skin, flavored it with chile, and ate it raw.

Two sellers of potatoes, one specializing in Irish, the other in sweet potatoes (*camotes*), offered the cooked product, boiled rather than baked. The most common fresh vegetable of all was the red tomato, which the Mexicans call *jitomate.* The *tomate* is strictly a small green tomato used only in pickles and for cooking. The *jitomate* is one of the really large crops of Mexican agriculture and is popular all over the nation. In Nahualtepec red tomatoes sold for about 2 cents a pound, in midwinter. Bread was the highest priced food item of all. A loaf of wheat bread was 90 centavos, almost 8 cents. Corn tortillas, of course, take the place of wheat bread in the village diet. The latter is still an item of luxury in Nahualtepec.

The wage scale in Nahualtepec is still very low by North American standards, but it is improving rapidly. A baker makes 180 pesos (about $15) a week. A young seamstress earns half that amount, a stone cutter makes about twice as much, a clerk in a store makes only twenty pesos, less than two dollars a day, a traveling salesman earns about forty pesos daily ($3.25), while the principal of the town school receives two thousand pesos a month, about $160. The average income of a potter or serape vendor is about a dollar a day.

In the very middle of the market, occupying the central position symbolic of the foodstuffs they sold, were two vendors of dried corn and beans, the real blood and sinews of the national menu. These corn-and-bean men were accompanied by their wives, who stood beside the bags of dried produce helping their husbands with the sales. Each man had half a dozen unopened hundred-pound sacks piled up on the ground, and in front of these were two unfolded burlap bags on which were rounded heaps of beans and corn. The beans were of a greenish hue, unlike the redder ones of the northern states. For a nickel you could buy a sizable bag of either commodity.

A truck had backed up alongside one large display of pottery and three men were busy loading it. I inquired about the transaction and was told that the truck had come from a store in the city, fifty miles away, and had driven to Nahualtepec to stock up. Before the day was over I noticed that two other trucks carried away heavy loads. Some wholesale business was obviously going on.

Between pottery row and the sellers of beans and corn was a lone craftsman who had a large display of wooden chairs with straw seats. The wood was painted a bright yellow, and stood out among the other produce of the market like a cageful of canaries in a hen house. His chairs were all cut and tied by hand. They would hardly rival Chippendale's more delicate products, but they were built to endure for years to come. Only two chairs were sold that morning, but before the market closed a truck drew up and took an even dozen. The chair man then closed his booth and disappeared into the saloon.

Three of the stalls were permanent market fixtures. They were open every day, not just on market day. These stalls were made of wood, with little windows and counters in front. They sold cold drinks, candies, cakes, and knickknacks such as combs, small plastic airplanes and cars, whistles, little plastic figures, and charms, et cetera. Bottled drinks outsold all the other products combined. These drinks were brought in on trucks from a larger town, about twenty-five miles away.

The only items for sale which obviously were not entirely of local or regional origin were found among the hardware. The local tinsmith (he might also be called the ironmonger) fashioned many of these items at his forge. At one end of the plaza there were four neatly made plowshares with steel handles, all colored a gray silver to prevent rusting. Everywhere on the farms around Nahualtepec the iron plow was taking, or had already taken, the place of the old wooden plowshare. Indeed, on the group farms, *ejidos*, there were several tractors and harrows, community owned and community operated. The ox and mule were being almost brusquely displaced by the gasoline engine. I found out later that of the total working population of Nahualtepec, 893, there were 457 *ejido* workers, and about 60 more who owned their own plots of land.

The merry-go-rounds were in dizzying whirl, with children screaming their delight. The colors of their clothes flashed in the bright air like a swarm of wings. At the other side of the plaza two men held their heads under the gusher of water, cooling their scalps and rinsing their heads and faces. With fingers they combed their hair. Patiently waiting until they had finished was a caravan of three burros. Their owner took twelve empty five-gallon tins, filled these at the gushing well, then placed them on the burros' backs, four to each animal, two cans to each side in order to balance the weight. Evidently this was the water supply for some farm family for at least a week. After the burros another man carefully loaded two similar cans with water, tied each to the end of a short pole, and resting this upon his shoulders, disappeared down the cobbled street.

Why had they not piped the water into the village homes? Why was the well wasting its precious liquid on the dusty streets? Partly the reasons were social. The townswomen wanted a reason to meet along the gutter where they could wash and talk. Partly it was economic. It would cost a lot of money to lay pipes and install the proper plumbing in the homes of Nahualtepec. Social improvement always bears its price. The people had decided it was not yet time to pay this price. And so the water continued to flow both day and night, caught now at least in one large steel pipe which guided its lifeblood from the inner earth into the parching village.

At the *petate* seller's stand across from the fountain I counted five big rolls of straw mats resting upright on the cobbles. On the other side of the street three *huarache* vendors had their wares spread out both on the ground and on crude vertical racks of wood and reeds. With somewhat of a shock I noticed that most of the *huaraches* had neolite soles.

These *huaraches* were an uncolored dun, and did not have the smell that one often notices in this particular footwear in other parts of the Republic, where occasionally excrement is still used to cure the leather. The Aztecs used urine as a mordant in dying cloth and excrement in fertilizing their fields and in curing their leather. Many of the Indians of today still follow in their steps.

Next to the *huarache* vendors were the sugar-cane men, their tall sticks forming a long green shed resting against horizontal cords. The final booth belonged to a vendor of brooms, which were merely selected stalks of a local brush, purple in color, with thin-fingered, lacy branchings at the end.

In order to make a survey of the entire market picture I sat down on a bench and took a careful count of the vendors then active, checking my figures with a second and slower count in order to make doubly certain. There were 175 vendors of local products (pottery, serapes, foods, etc.) and 13 sellers of manufactured goods from outside. The economy of Nahualtepec, as one can easily see, is largely self-sufficient, in so far as the local market is concerned. The community market imports little, exports little.

Just across the street is the bar, doing a good business in imported alcoholic liquors. Across the plaza is the pharmacy, selling all the sulfas and the newest antibiotics. Alongside the plaza are parked three automobiles, two trucks, a little red bus, and eighteen bicycles. On one of the corners is a *tienda de abarrotes,* selling imported canned goods as well as local produce. The sellers of soft drinks and yard goods were all doing a first-rate business. There was a precarious balance between the local and the national economy. Nahualtepec could survive without the support of the world outside, but it would undoubtedly slip back a notch or two. If we suddenly took away all imports from any United States community of similar size, there would be a toboggan slide, panic, and chaos. Nahualtepec has not gone that far along the road of civilization, but neither is it any longer a community of machineless men. There are trucks and bicycles on its streets, tractors in its fields, new drugs in its pharmacy. The bones and muscles of a new way of life are developing rapidly in the organism that is Nahaultepec.

After supper on Sunday night everybody in our boardinghouse went up to the plaza, which was already jammed with people. This was to be the climax of the fiesta. By eight-thirty the crowd had neatly divided itself into two age groups: (*a*) The young folks who deftly sifted themselves away from the older and began to promenade around the square, the girls walking in one direction, the boys in the other. And (*b*) the older people, with their babies and smaller children clinging to them, who stood on the sidelines to watch.

It was a revelation to see how neatly dressed the young people were, and with what charm they walked. There was no loud talk, no horseplay among them, yet hundreds of voices kept up a constant wave of joyous sound as boys and girls circled the plaza. Occasionally, a boy would drop out and buy a small bouquet of flowers, a handful of pinks, a few gardenias, perhaps even some gladioli, which cost him approximately 8 cents. Then he would rejoin the young masculine contingent in its march, and when he met the girl of his fancy would give her his flowers. If the girl wanted his friendship, she would accept the gift. If she did not, it would be refused. Later, after a few more turns about the square, she would reciprocate and hand the same boy a few of her own flowers. After this, the pact of friendship was securely tied.

For at least two hours the promenade continued, and I have never, anywhere in the world, seen young people having a more delightful time, and at so little expense. No one spent more than a single peso and no one felt that he could not afford the price. There was no attempt to draw off into the dark shadows and paw or kiss. The courting was all open to the public view, but the enjoyment was undiluted. Private lovemaking is reserved for more serious moments, when after many such promenades and a long ritual of courtship the couples are married.

The plaza promenade is a weekly occurrence. These young people all belonged to the decent families of Nahualtepec and comported themselves with a decorum befitting their state. They made up the great majority of the young folks of the community. Beside them the overpainted swarm of prostitutes, who had so invisibly come and gone, seemed but a tawdry, ugly wart on a beautiful face. These youngsters did not push or kick, elbow or rib each other with teasing remarks. They were all out to have a good time, and no one was a wet blanket. I could not imagine a similar crowd of so many young people in the United States, ranging from twelve to twenty years in age, comporting themselves with such graciousness and charm.

By nine-thirty the plaza and all the streets that led to it were swarming with people. It hardly seemed possible that anyone who lived within a radius of twenty miles of town was missing. The number of those present was probably five or six thousand, hundreds more than the total population of Nahualtepec.

On the faded rust-colored façade of the Ayuntamiento, the Town Hall, was an old clock, on which many eyes were now fixed expectantly. On the very second of ten o'clock a match was applied to the reed Castillo, and the fireworks started. The little reed wheels began to whirl around, each in turn forming its circle of moving light. At irregular intervals rockets soared into the air, burst, and sent their multicolored spray out in mushrooming arcs. When all the wheels had gone off, and the top of the Castillo had been reached by the climbing fireworks, a small circular dome lifted itself from the frame and spurted up into the air, reaching a great height, where it floated for a moment like a circle of fire, then faded into the night. This was the end of the Castle; but rockets continued to burst in salvo after salvo. Then a new crackling sound was added to the general bedlam as a long string of firecrackers exploded in such rapid succession that they sounded like a dozen Fourth of Julys.

The fuse of *The Hunt* was now lighted, and soon all the little reed animals were in motion. There were rabbits, foxes, dogs, all bouncing up and down and seeming to race across the frame that held them against the sky. For a good ten minutes the entire scaffolding was a mass of fireworks in motion. It was one of the most spectacular displays that I have ever witnessed, yet had been rigged up with such flimsy materials that it was difficult to believe the results could be so very impressive. The rockets continued to burst all over the plaza, some of them just above the heads of the spectators.

Suddenly a little girl was hit by a falling spark, there was a scream, and people began to mass around her, beating out the flames. A heavy serape was wrapped closely about her little body. The girl's clothes were pretty well demolished, but she was only slightly burned. She began to whimper because she had lost her dress, which was her pride and joy. The spectators immediately, as if with a single accord, began to collect pesos so that she could buy herself a new one. In five minutes they had more than enough. The little girl began to smile. Her parents wanted to take her home, but she refused to leave, so, with the serape still tightly around her, she watched the rest of the fiesta.

Just as the animal chase sputtered and died out, the half dozen long strings of firecrackers hanging in the large church courtyard were all lighted at once, and sounded like a big-time army proving ground. In the meantime the sexton had climbed up into the church tower with a couple of sturdy assistants, and suddenly the three of them began to bang the clappers against the bells. Evidently, ringing them with the usual rope was far too slow, so they stood a couple of feet off, held a yard or so of rope in their hands, and banged away. It was a seven-alarm fire, plus several machine guns and an old-fashioned Fourth of July.

The crowd watched the whole show entranced. There was very little comment, but it was easy to see that this part of the fiesta was a kind of catharsis, a release of tensions, which these poor folk not only enjoyed but needed for their emotional well-being. When the last rocket had been fired, the note of relief on their faces was clear to see. Without getting either drunk or rowdy these people had undergone a vicarious explosion, and now were calm and free. The fiesta is an excellent substitute for the revolution.

About ten-thirty the fiesta was over, and people began to drift homeward. Over by the shell of the Castillo smoke began to spiral into the air. A thatch roof had caught fire and the men had put it out, or so they thought, but suddenly it burst into flames again. Half a dozen men climbed on top of the building and beat at the flames with their serapes. Finally, the fire was under control. This was the last flurry of the fiesta. By eleven o'clock the plaza was almost deserted, and only the small dim lights of the municipal power company illuminated the heart of the town. The littered streets indicated that the big fiesta had come, and gone. On the next day Nahualtepec would begin the onerous job of cleaning up.

There are only two schools in Nahualtepec, one public, the other run by the Church. They both offer work only in the first six grades. The public school, just below the plaza, was so crowded that at least fifty children had to sit out in the patio on the pavement. Every time I walked down the street these children were working calmly at their lessons. The street doors were wide open, and it was impossible to miss them. Occasionally, a teacher would come out and give them a few moments' attention.

The building was dilapidated, with paint flecking from the walls. The classrooms were shabby and the desks were very roughly put together and varnished. I visited the sixth grade, where the school principal had taken over for the regular teacher, who was ill. He was an intelligent gray-eyed man, with great seriousness in his face. He was asking questions about famous Mexican figures. When I entered the room the entire class jumped to its feet, and remained standing until I asked them to be seated. The teacher had not spoken a word. Now he continued his questions. Hands began to go up all over the room, and bright faces looked at me eagerly as they waited for a turn. Their enthusiasm was catching. One boy presented Miguel Hidalgo as the greatest man Mexico has produced, because "he was the father of our independence." Another boy spoke in favor of Benito Juárez as the greatest Mexican, "because, although he was just a poor little Indian *indito*, he became the governor of his state and finally president of the republic. He began the Reform Movement that separated church and state."

They next discussed the Mexican constitution, mentioning several of its most important articles by number, and then went on to the subject of famous Mexican holidays. When someone mentioned the twelfth of October, the teacher asked what this date meant to Mexico besides the discovery of America. A girl said that it was *el día de la raza,* the day of the Spanish race. The teacher corrected her.

"It is the day of our Mexican race," he said. "When the Spaniards came to America our Mexican race, part Spanish and part Indian, began. The twelfth of October celebrates the beginning of our own mestizo race."

I looked about the room and noted that every single child had an Indianist face. They ranged from very brown to mostly white, but the cast of the Indian lay on them all. Their teacher had spoken the absolute truth.

The discussion went on for another hour or so, and the children were still eager to continue. The teacher then turned to me and remarked in a very casual manner:

"I think I ought to dismiss them now. It is twenty minutes past letting-out time."

Not a single restive movement had been made in those twenty minutes. In fact, the pupils did not seem at all anxious to leave their class, even now. They lingered in the patio, watching us with wide bright eyes. We left the room and visited the manual training shop, the kitchen, and the sewing room. In the shop they were making tables for their new library, which consisted of about a hundred fifty paper-backed books in a series put out by the government, which sold for a peso each. The kitchen had a single sink and a small charcoal brazier. On this the girls learned how to cook. The sewing room, which was next to the kitchen, contained two Singer machines, recently acquired, which were the apple of the teacher's eye. None of these rooms was notable for its tidiness. The bathrooms, which I made a point of entering, fell into the same category. Slowly we walked through the other classrooms, and in one I inquired about the size of the classes. The principal said that there were fifty-nine pupils in his sixth-grade room.

"The Mexican teacher can easily handle a class of sixty," he said, "and most of them do. And, as you see, we have no problem of order."

In one of the classrooms I picked up some notebooks that belonged to first-grade pupils and began to thumb through them. The handwriting seemed exceptionally good, and I commented on this. The teacher informed me very frankly that her pupils had not written those paragraphs. The notebooks had belonged to older brothers and sisters and had been passed on so that these first-graders could use the few blank pages that remained in them.

"The parents here are always complaining about spending money on school supplies," the teacher said.

This reminded me of a cartoon that had just appeared in a Mexican magazine, which showed a father standing in front of a bank teller's window drawing out all his money and giving it to his son. He said: "Take this, son, for your textbooks." The poor man was almost stripped; he was down to his shorts. In front of the pawnshop next door a huge line of parents had already formed.

Textbooks are expensive items in Mexico today, but Nahualtepec's secondhand notebooks hardly reflect this problem. They symbolize the deep-rooted poverty of centuries of doing without. In this economy of poverty there is no room for waste. The children who used these blank pages did not mind in the least, and they were learning how to read and write.

On the following day I entered the "Colegio de Nahualtepec." (Nearly all Catholic schools are referred to as *colegios*. The word does not mean college at all. In fact, most of the *colegios* in Mexico are elementary schools.) This particular one had in large letters above its door these words: "incorporated into the state educational system," which meant that it followed rigorously the course of study prescribed by the state.

Outside, the Colegio de Nahualtepec was freshly painted and very trim-looking. It was in a newly remodeled building. The patio, also, was neatly arched and tiled. A sister, dressed in her habit of flowing black, came out to meet me. She wore no head covering of any kind. Her hair was done up like that of any other Mexican woman. We went into her class, which was the third grade. All the students in the *colegio* were girls. This particular class consisted of fifteen girls. The room was bright and clean, the desks were new. It looked exactly like a very choice schoolroom in the United States. Later I visited the other classes, and noted that the entire school was immaculate. So were the girls who attended. They were a cut above the students who attended the public school in their personal hygiene, and no doubt in the economic status of their families. They were also noticeably lighter in color. But the tuition for attending this school was ridiculously low. María Mercedes' mother had told me that she was sending three of her daughters here for a total of 34 pesos ($2.70) a month, hardly enough to bankrupt even a moderately poor Mexican family.

The girls were all scrupulously trained, and their manners were perfect. They could read, write, and calculate considerably better than the children of the public school. When it came to the other subjects I had some reservations. At my suggestion the teacher began to quiz them on Mexican history. The girls all responded quickly, but their language seemed a little heavy and precise. Occasionally they would hesitate, think a moment, and then continue. One girl, obviously the star pupil, was called on two or three times when some other girl had faltered. She talked a mile a minute, the sentences spilling from her mouth, hardly giving her time to catch her breath. After several paragraphs the teacher stopped her and smiled. The girl was telling about the Aztecs, the sacrifices they made, their government, their dress, their customs. She emphasized that the Aztecs were savages who used to go barefooted, et cetera.

At first I did not catch on to what was happening. Then I began to look through the history text and saw that this girl was quoting verbatim from the book. She had memorized the whole text and could recite at random any passage that was called for. No wonder some of the other girls hesitated. It was the old colonial stunt in modern clothes and would certainly produce students of marvelous rote memories. But no number of facts, however impressive, will ever be a substitute for the keen thinking mind.

The children of Mexico are not only bright and well mannered, but they show a charming lack of self-consciousness. In every school that I visited the teacher had but to say the word, and they would recite, sing, dance, or draw as if it were the most natural thing in the world for them, and indeed it was. No one revealed the slightest reluctance to perform before either the group or the stranger. They were both eager and shy, but they were not in the least self-conscious. The writer Charles Flandrau once said that he would like to see all the children in the world born Mexicans and stay Mexican until they were at least fifteen years old. This statement expresses my own feelings perfectly. Of course, we must leave out those poor wanderers of the streets, homeless waifs who make up the very small percentage of Mexico's juvenile delinquents, and we must also leave out the overprotected children of the better homes of the large cities, who can be as obnoxious as any children anywhere on earth. But fortunately the majority of the children of Mexico do not fall into either of these categories. They are uniquely lovable. Mexico can thank its lucky stars that these children will be the country's citizens of tomorrow.

Nahualtepec, one village among 73,000, has one foot in the past and one foot in the present. But it is no statue; it is a breathing, moving organism. A blend of two races, two cultures, with a strong touch from the United States, it represents the Mexico of today and tomorrow, the Mexico of the smaller in-between towns from which are emerging the larger urban centers . . . a symbol of the Mexican village which is transforming the hinterland, absorbing the Indian. Nahualtepec is a microcosm of Mexico's mestizo culture today. The rounded hills, the shining lake, the low-flung plaza, and the single-towered church may not show much change, but man himself has changed, inside. His energies are now fixed on a different perspective. He has hope and pride and strength, he has new wants, and he will grow and ultimately he will transform even the hills and the valleys.

XX

MEXICO CITY

Traveler: you have reached the most transparent region of the air.

—Alfonso Reyes, from *Visión de Anáhuac*

The city is unbelievable! Crevasses of towering stone, surrounded by denuded hills. Dotted with lakes of trees, and sprinkled with flowers. Fifth Avenue, Wilshire Boulevard, and Chapultepec, with a good peppering of California modern, and more than a good peppering of the Mexican slums of San Antonio, Texas. In its newer parts a smell of freshly washed and perfumed bodies; on its older streets a smell that is Mexico, a faint odor of must and urine that does not disappear. Fabulous, powerful, imposing . . . or miserable beyond compare . . . all depending on where you start. But everywhere stuffed with buildings of concrete, brick, and *tezontle*, tall creeping scaffolds of reeds and hemp, nervous folk that hive the stores and markets, all pouring themselves into this megalomania that is hardly Mexican, but which from sheer wealth, power, and drive has made itself into the heartbeat of the country.

The city cannot keep pace with its growth. Crammed in this filled-in lake bed, once a blaze of floating gardens, vast hordes of Mexicans pound wildly up streets and boulevards, all at the same hour, then as suddenly disappear, like water in the sand. The city is an overcrowded beehive which disgorges itself at sporadic intervals. It is not homogeneous, but it is all Indo-mestizo Mexican, not of one pattern, but of many patterns commingled. Start at the *zócalo* and walk two blocks in any direction. Look at the buildings, look at the clothes, look at the faces. Aztec, Renaissance, plateresque, red man, white man, mestizo, modern. These are leaves on a great tree whose roots dip into the bottomless well of the past. The leaves are trembling in the clear blue light. The history of Mexico is the pageant before you.

It is the end of January as I write this. In Mexico the schools will soon begin their second semester. In Mexico City enrollment is about to start. The schools of the capital are crowded, very crowded. The tremendous growth of the large urban centers has caused a great overload in the schools of all Mexican cities, but the capital is perhaps worst hit of all, for its increase in population during the past few years has been phenomenal. The metropolitan area now has about eight million inhabitants, with more pouring in every day. Industries are humming, the city is teeming, and the schools are bulging with students.

I walk down the streets of the city, and on one of the sidewalks a line has formed. There are perhaps forty or fifty people in the line, mothers and fathers, but mostly mothers. One of them has a baby wrapped in her brown *rebozo*, carried in front as Mexican women usually carry their babies, and forming a big bulge over her stomach. You cannot see the baby, but you know it is there, closed in completely from the night air. It is nine o'clock, and the streets are dim. Mexico does not believe in wasting electricity. The streets are also cold. A blast of chilled air seems to be moving down from the snow-covered mountains. It penetrates the skin, hits the bones, chills to the marrow. The people in the line are not heavily dressed. Two of the men have old serapes flung over their shoulders, one gray, one brown. They are hooded figures, shrinking from the wind. The women all wear *rebozos* of dark tones and little design. It is not a well-to-do crowd, although some of them are not poorly dressed. As I stroll by, five or six additional persons fall in at the end of the line. I stop to ask what is going on.

"The school, señor. It is the school," a fat Indian-looking woman with a warm round face tells me. She looks out of the blue *rebozo* that is wound around her head and continues, vigorously moving her hands as she speaks.

"The schools are all crowded. This is one of the worst."

"The very worst," chimes in the man with the brown serape.

"They say they will not take any more students after the classrooms have been filled. They will not have students without seats," the chubby round-faced woman added.

"They ought to let them sit on the floor. It won't hurt them," the man continued. "Plenty of them sit on the floor at home."

"Plenty of them sit on the streets, if you let them," the plump Indian-looking woman went on.

"And if they can't get into school they will be sitting on the streets again," the woman with the baby put in, cradling her small burden as she spoke.

As this conversation was going on, several of the people in line had squatted or sat down in little groups near the wall, one of those thick plaster-covered walls that line so many Mexican streets. One group was hovering around a charcoal fire in an old iron brazier. Another group of four had made a fire of old kindling and scraps of branches in a worn-out washtub. Two other groups had tin buckets burning with low flames, which reminded me of the California smudge pots. They were using cheap fuel oil, and carried an extra supply in an old vegetable-oil tin. Before long they had settled down for the night, sprawled out in all kinds of positions, but mostly sitting all humped together, muffled to the ears. One enterprising woman brought forth a large piece of burlap and threw up a windbreak, a kind of improvised tent. The men graciously helped her hook it to a piece of broken bottle embedded in the top of the wall to keep climbers out.

"When does school start?" I asked.

"Day after tomorrow," the man in the brown blanket said. "It's first come, first served, and we want to make sure that our children get into school." He pulled out a cigarette and rubbed the back of his hand across the stubble on his face. He offered me a cigarette, and I refused. As we talked, the crowd grew silent and began to go to sleep. Faces disappeared behind heavy serapes, *rebozos*, and blankets. The fires burned dimly in the night.

These people would wait on the street, through the long cold of a plateau night, huddled around makeshift fires, so that their children might enter school. The desire of these people to better themselves is so intense that it almost brings the tears. The Church was the heart of the old Mexican culture system; the school is the heart of the new.

This new culture is not all good. Some of the finest of the old values are being lost; but the new culture is vibrantly alive, sincere, intense. And it is expanding all over the Mexican countryside with fruitful seed. The Mexican parents of yesterday were afraid of the schools. They broke too many taboos of the old culture. Often, in the smaller villages, they drove the teacher out of town. Now they have taken the schools to their hearts. Good, bad, or indifferent as the schools may be, they realize that the children of today live in a mechanized world of which book learning is an integral part. In this world their children *must* at least know how to calculate, *must* know how to read and write.

All of this should be remembered when mention is made of the various poverties of Mexican daily life, no scabrous accumulations of which can possibly efface the progress that education has made, that further education in more and better schools will surely make. The Mexico of today and tomorrow rests securely upon this base.

In Mexico City the streets have a way of changing their names with exasperating frequency. The main thoroughfare downtown which is called Madero Street as it runs by Sanborn's House of Tiles, a block or so farther on becomes suddenly Avenida Juárez. Finally, it changes to the Avenida del Ejido. No Mexican patriot or ideal must be left out. On Avenida Juárez, in the very heart of the city, stands the Palacio de Bellas Artes, the Fine Arts Theater, in its casing of white marble. The building is not even faintly Mexican; it resembles more closely the Paris Opera House, or a theater of Italy. A large sign tells you what the building is. Under the letter "B" of the phrase "Bellas Artes" is the white statue of a naked woman. She has one leg slightly raised, and her right arm is held over her head. In front of the building are two statues of Pegasus, the flying horse. Today above the entrance of this gleaming structure of Greek figures, Italian marble and architecture, another sign indicates that the Moscow Philharmonic is playing. Scheduled for later were the Prague Chamber Orchestra, the Israel Philharmonic, the Russian Classical Ballet, a piano concert by Ashkenazy, and a series of operas with world-renowned singers.

On the other side of the street, not far from the Hotel del Prado, three sturdy boys in their late teens are throwing toy helicopters into the air, watching their flight anxiously, then dashing out into the heavy traffic to rescue their machine before it is crushed. Frequently, a helicopter strikes a passing car with a sharp thump. Sometimes a machine will come to rest on the top of an automobile. It does not matter; the boys race everywhere and grab their little contraptions before they are broken. I never saw one destroyed. On the sidewalk, in complete safety, stood the man who was selling these machines. He was the boss. The boys were his advertisers, and they kept the air so full of helicopters that the passers-by could not help seeing them.

The crowds are well dressed. The shops are full. The motion-picture theaters are packed. Traffic on the streets is indescribable, but it flows smoothly, without noise. The frequent sign *No use el claxón* ("Don't use your horn") has had its effect. The policemen, who stand on nearly every corner, are efficient and polite.

The streets are always full of Americans. It gives one a twinge of shame to compare the walk of the Mexican women with that of the American girls. Why does the American woman walk with such ponderous awkwardness? I had never noticed it in the United States, but here in Mexico it stands out like a sore thumb. Another question: why not do more Mexican men shave their faces, and why do not more Mexican women shave their legs? Several of my Mexican friends, men friends, of course, told me frankly that they like their women to have hair on their legs. And that stubble on the men's faces? Laziness perhaps, or perhaps it is the part-Indian who wants to display as thick a growth as he can muster.

Across the Alameda from the Del Prado is the Hotel Cortés, in an old colonial mansion of rose *tezontle*. It is one of the most charming hostelries in the city. Move on down the Alameda on Avenida Juárez past the mounted statue of King Charles IV, which is always referred to affectionately as "El caballito," the Little Horse. At this point the street changes its name for the second time and becomes Avenida del Ejido which leads to the Arched Monument to the Revolution, with its squat Indian statues put up in the days when the Indian was exalted above all others.

The famous promenade, the Paseo de la Reforma, branches off to the left from Avenida Juárez. The very name is an anomaly. This promenade was opened up by the Emperor Maximilian so that there would be a direct and beautiful route to Chapultepec Castle, his residence. The Aztec called this "Grasshopper Hill," and a statue of the grasshopper commemorates the old name. When Benito Juárez and his Reform Movement finally overcome Maximilian, it was clear that the promenade must be given a name that fitted in with the new turn of Mexican history, and it was called Paseo de la Reforma.

The *paseo* is lined with beautiful buildings and flower gardens. Here modern architecture, with towering glass-enclosed buildings, looms magnificently above the Paris-like structures of an older date. Everywhere there are flowers. The head beautifier of the city is called Don Florindo Fuentes, Mr. Fountains and Flowers. He has kept the roses blooming, the grass well trimmed, the trees and shrubs all green and growing.

Visit Chapultepec Park on Sunday. Everyone goes. The children love the Zoo and the little train with its cars all enclosed with meshing so that no one can fall out. Fathers, mothers, and children jam the paths and sidewalks. In a grove of towering trees the band plays the *Egmont Overture*. Then on to Chapultepec Castle and Grasshopper Hill, which affords a beautiful view of the city. The castle now houses a museum.

On Sundays it is flooded; the crowds go through, see the flag of Father Hidalgo, the decree of Mexican independence, the collection of pre-Columbian art and colonial displays. There are several Spanish coats of mail, some of them covering even the fingers with steel. Spanish shields also were of steel, and their lances were tipped with steel. The

Indian shields of cloth, leather, and wood hadn't a chance against them, man for man. Yet in the end these Indians overwhelmed the men from Spain, not with the blood of the battlefields, though these ran scarlet, but with the blood of fertile lovemaking, which no soldier could resist.

Go out on the balcony and observe the city, which straddles the old lake bed and almost covers the valley. In summer it is huge and green, with a gray mist often hanging above the buildings and the trees. In winter it is shining and bright, luminous as a painting dipped in sunlight. Walk down the hillside and under the tall *ahuehuete* trees where Montezuma once strolled. (The Indian word *ahuehuete* means "old man by the waters.") These ancient trees, which resemble the cypress, soar above the pathways with gracefully arched branches. Many of them reach a majestic height. One, in Santa María del Tule, is over 120 feet tall and even more than that in circumference.

Walk slowly through Chapultepec Park. The crowds are gay, content. The people are all neat and well dressed. They are Mexico's new middle class. Mr. Fountains and Flowers has done a fine job, and the city is trim, the gardens filled with color to the farthest rim of hills that edge the valley. Mexico, like the butterfly, is about to emerge from the chrysalis. There are strange comparisons: the airport is just about the most modern and the most beautiful in the world, but the railway station would be a disgrace in a city of ten thousand. The new skyscraper apartment houses are magnificent, but in the vacant lots beside them families often live in hovels. These lots are all walled off, but the poor devils dig under the walls, slip in, and establish their homes until they are driven away. The new university campus is one of the most impressive in the entire world, but its library is extremely deficient for serious research.

Mexico is made up of such contrasts, and in the capital these contrasts may be seen on a vast scale. I get the strange feeling that this is not a Western country. In spite of its skyscrapers, its factories, its great city, and its beautiful parks, this is not a Western country. It is not Indian, of course, but it is mostly Indian. It is something unique, apart. The Spanish bud on the Indian root-stock has produced an exotic civilization. The air and colors diaphanous, the language Spanish, the culture, like the people, mestiza. Mexico has a facile, picturesque appeal, but it is not an easily understandable culture. It is not a Western country.

Take a first-class bus back into town; the fare is one peso, or approximately eight cents. First-class buses will take in only as many passengers as they can seat. No standees allowed. As you drive down the streets you will pass many neat, up-to-the-minute *super-mercados*, United States style supermarkets, with canned music, attendants in white aprons, foods attractively displayed, and all the rest. You will also pass Sears, Roebuck, and a dozen *fuentes de soda*, soda fountains, also American style. Huge office buildings of many shapes and designs, with wide glass panels taking the place of solid walls, follow the changing contours of the street. New buildings are going up on every side. The capital is in a fever of construction, in which Indians carrying excavated dirt in small baskets work alongside monstrous machines that drive down the piles, mix the cement, or shovel out the earth. A few years ago every heavy building in the city was sinking into the subsoil. The lake bed has never completely settled, and the entire city is raised upon a fill. Even the Fine Arts Theater sank into that quagmire so fast (one side went down fifteen feet) that it threatened to crumble. Many buildings still stand at uneven levels as reminders of that treacherous subsoil. But young architects have now licked the problem. They drive pylons deep into the earth until these either rest on a firm bedrock or "float" evenly in the mud. Some structures resting on bedrock were left high and dry when the valley floor settled as a result of increased drainage of the watery subsoil. Steps had to be added so they could be entered. Now many such structures are placed on great jacks so that they can be lowered as the ground level sinks beneath them. Buildings, which used to be limited to five stories by law, may now soar to any height. An immense skyscraper built by the Latino-Americana Insurance Company, reaches over forty stories into the air. The Paseo de la Reforma is lined with other structures almost as high. Modern architecture is now having a field day in Mexico's capital.

Mexico City has many residental districts where the homes of the wealthy have set an imposing pattern: Lomas de Chapultepec, Polanco, Barrilaco, and especially the Gardens of the Pedregal, carved out of the lava beds beside the new university campus, where lie the city's smartest homes. A few years ago the Pedregal was an ugly tract of wasteland, dotted only with native weeds and broken mounds of gray and black lava which overran the area some five thousand years ago when Mount Ajusco erupted and, incidentally, destroyed itself in the process. Yet this desolate area did contain pockets of rich virgin soil, and the underground water was not hard to reach. A group of young architects and engineers, headed by Luis Barragán, saw the possibilities of the place, and invested their last penny in developing it into the paradise that it has become today. Trees and flowers were put in, streets were laid out, fountains installed, and as a final eye-catcher they planted a beautiful garden which the public was invited to visit.

At first, sales were few and far between, but as more homes went up it was soon clear that here was a new and fashionable kind of residential area. Houses all had to be in the modern tradition, with flat roofs and walled lots; careful landscaping was an integral part of the construction of every dwelling. Lava mounds and rich soil pockets lent a fascinating variety to the yards, and the whole area took on an exotic, spectacular appearance which is quite unlike anything anywhere else in the world. Many of the homes have swimming pools; all of them have beautiful lines, and spectacular gardens. The wealthy Mexican now feels that he has something which he can call his own in residential building. No longer is he limited to pale imitations of the so-called "California" architecture, which was on the way to making Mexico City a replica of Los Angeles. The fabulous City of Palaces of colonial times is now fast becoming a metropolis of modernistic mansions with a unique Mexican charm. Like the people of Mexico, these dwellings seem rooted in the soil. But how different, how vastly different, from the baroque palaces of an earlier day!

Not far from the Pedregal is Mexico's University City. The Spanish language has no word for "campus," and the Latin Americans have invented the term "University City," which sounds much more impressive, to take its place. There are several of these university cities in Latin America, but the one in Mexico outstrips them all. Rising majestically above the lava fields that adjoin the Pedregal, its strikingly designed, fresco-adorned buildings, several of them many stories in height, represent a new achievement in campus architecture.

The National University is the oldest in America. It was chartered in 1551, opened its doors in 1553, and was the great educational center of colonial days. Maximilian closed it in 1865 in order to protect his regime from student protests and to build up the extremely backward lower educational system.

Up until the year 1910 the university was a semimedieval institution, clinging tenaciously to the colonial concepts of education. But in that year, which was the centennial of Mexico's independence movement, Justo Sierra, one of the really great figures of the Díaz regime, reorganized and reopened the ancient institution and gave it modern form. The university has continued to grow and to improve from that day to this, but the project for an up-to-date plant remained a dream until four more decades had passed. Under President Ávila Camacho a huge acreage was acquired on the outskirts of the city among the lava fields. The arable soil of these fields was then being worked by several *ejido* families who broke up the lava rocks, sold them as building materials, and then used the fertile soil beneath for their crops. When the government bought this land it moved the *ejido* workers en masse to another place nearby where they were provided with new two-story houses, all with kitchens, wells, and nice yards.

By 1950 the university was ready to begin construction of its new plant. The institution at that time was scattered all over the city in several localities, and occupied a heterogeneous series of monasteries, convents, and colonial mansions, which the government had provided from time to time to take care of the growing student body. Each branch occupied a separate location, and there was little unity to the institution as a whole. In 1950 President Miguel Alemán's administration appropriated 200 million pesos, an incredible amount in a country the size of Mexico, and the ground was broken.

The young dynamic architect Carlos Lazo (killed in an airplane crash in 1955) was appointed general co-ordinator of the project. Lazo assembled as members of his team 150 architects, engineers, and artists, nearly 100 contracting companies, and 10,000 laborers, the largest labor force ever assembled in Latin America for a single building project. Under Lazo's able and inspirational direction this immense group was soon welded into a single great team with a marvelous *esprit de corps.* A kind of mystic fire drove them day and night to dream, think, and build University City until, three years later, the campus was ready for occupancy. The whole vast project was a miracle of organization, planning, and achievement.

Exciting new architectural ideas were brought forth to make the best use of the terrain, artists were chosen to decorate them with huge glass, oil, and stone murals, and interiors were so designed that they would be both functionally modern yet completely Mexican. The library was constructed almost entirely without windows so that the unbroken wall space inside might be used for bookshelves and the exterior walls for vast mosaic frescos. Space was provided for two million volumes. Ball courts were built in the shapes of pyramids, and the stadium, with its great relief fresco of natural stones by Diego Rivera, was so constructed that most of the seats were along the fifty-yard line. Rivera's mosaic represents the Eagle and the Condor, symbols of the university, and below these are the Indian mother and father from whom stems the racial vigor of the Mexican people. There were two seating levels, one directly above the other, and in this manner the usual number of center seats was doubled, with no obstruction of the view. This stadium, which seats close to 100,000 persons, is perhaps the finest in the world. Just beside it is a magnificent swimming pool, one of the largest in the Americas. As I walked up to the entrance of the stadium to have a look inside, I saw an announcement on the Bulletin Board with the heading: *¡Alegría—Optimismo—Dinamismo!* "*Joy—Optimism—Dynamism!*" No better characterization of the magnificent new university could be made.

Now come the buildings themselves. The exterior walls of the huge library building are covered with mosaic murals by Juan O'Gorman, depicting the history of Mexico. They are composed of small stones of natural color brought from different regions of Mexico. Yellow, bright rust, green, and blue are the principal colors used. The north wall, containing the main entrance, represents the pre-Spanish epoch with its pantheon of Aztec gods. The south wall shows the colonial period of Mexican history, with many details of the conquest by soldiers and church. The west wall represents modern culture, with the university seal above, and the east wall shows the agrarian Revolution and the modern industrial period of Mexican history. The Rectoría, or Administration Building, has translucent onyx windows on the lower floors, and several large murals by Alfaro-Siqueiros; one of them jutting outward from the east wall marks the space occupied by the stage inside. This mural represents culture. The low-lying Humanities Building (it is only four stories high) extends for a length of over 1,000 feet, held above the ground by a long row of low rounded columns. This is one of the longest colonnades in the world. The Medical School, appropriately enough, is marked by long bands of red, which suggest the trim efficiency of a fine surgical incision. The large mural on the façade of the Medical Laboratories is by Francisco Eppens, and represents "Life, Death, and the Four Elements." In this fresco water is symbolized by red circles and the god Tlaloc as in the old Maya codices, Maya suns represent fire, the snake-goddess Coatlicue represents the earth, and life is symbolized by an ear of corn, which is being devoured by Death. In the center of the mural Mexico Today is seen emerging from its Indian mother and Spanish father.

The School of Science occupies a rectangular tower decorated with two fine frescoes by Chávez Morado. One represents the "Evolution of

Energy," the other is entitled "The Return of Quetzalcoatl," who is shown riding his raft of coiled serpents, and bringing back to America with him the Egyptian, the Assyrian, the Chinese, the Hindu, the Roman, and the Greek, symbolic of the world's great civilization. These two murals appeal to me personally more than any of the others at University City.

There are numerous other buildings on the vast campus, too many to mention in detail: the Schools of Commerce and Dentistry, the Chemical Sciences, Veterinary Medicine, the Laboratories for work in Nuclear Energy and Cosmic Rays, the School of Architecture, the Student Union with its restaurant, a huge apartment house for the professors, and several student dormitories, which are still in process of construction.

This great University City lies just outside the capital on the road to Cuernavaca and Taxco. A rounded rim of mountains stands beyond it, the Gardens of the Pedregal lie off to one side. There is space to spare; great open space, and on a clear day the snow-capped peaks of Popocatepetl and the Sleeping Lady float above the soft curve of the landscape. At first the students complained of the long trip out to the campus, but they no longer grumble. It costs the ordinary passenger ten cents to get into town; the student pays even less. Summer school, also, is held at University City, and is attended by hundreds of Americans.

I went into the library and examined the card catalogue. Many famous Mexican books were not listed at all. The great library building, supposed to hold 1,200,000 volumes, scarcely contains one-tenth that number today. There was talk of moving the excellent but spotty collection of the National Library to the university campus, and at one time these books were packed and ready to go, but a great cry was raised by citizens who preferred the downtown location of their National Library, so the books were unpacked and replaced in the remodeled old building. Advanced students are now obliged to use this poorly catalogued collection. Scholar and student alike would be prone to say that a huge university without an adequate research library is somewhat of an anomaly.

The professors? Some of the finest, but their pay is so ridiculously low that they all must take at least two or three additional jobs in order to make both ends meet. One professor I know teaches, writes, works at the University Press, edits a series of books, edits a magazine, teaches at night, and has a regular weekly radio program. By putting all these salaries together he makes enough to live on, precariously. In Mexico the professor and the schoolteacher are both miserably underpaid.

What do the Mexicans think of their great new university? Most of them are inordinately proud of it. The foreigner, too, is awed by the tremendous size and the vivid coloring of the buildings. But not everyone has words of praise. The Mexican José Vasconcelos, the former Minister of Education who started his country on the road to education in the 1920's, had this to say:

"*La Ciudad Universitaria es grandota, pero sin grandeza. Podría ser fábrica, podría ser cuartel. No habla, carece de espíritu.*"

("The University City is huge-looking, but it lacks real greatness. It might be a factory; it might be an enormous military barracks. But it doesn't speak, it lacks spirit.")

Another Mexican writer, Fernando Benítez, counters with this very personal opinion: "José Vasconcelos doesn't know it, but he died twenty years ago." [1]

Whether or not one shares either of these opinions, many observers do feel that some of the university buildings are overly ornate. In their desire to impress and to achieve a quality that is truly Mexican, the architects, and especially the mosaic artists, have at times let their imaginations run away with their good judgment. The library is a particular example of this. The campus of today is the present moment's answer to the baroque urge which still runs deep in the blood of the Mexican temperament. It is an example of the contemporary baroque in Mexico today.

Enrollment in the university (called Universidad Nacional Autónoma in Mexico) has grown rapidly. In 1954 it was only 5,000; by 1957 the total was 20,000, and by 1970, 100,000 students. This makes it the largest single-campus university in the world. Tuition is $16 a year for Mexican citizens; foreigners pay $175 a semester. The rival technical college, the *Politécnico*, has an enrollment of 78,000. It has branches in both Monterrey and Guadalajara.

Although books are at present lacking in its library, the university has a fine closed TV circuit for the use of advanced students, and its other laboratory facilities contain many items of up-to-the-minute equipment. The National Heart Institute, which is not a part of the university but which does embrace the most advanced medical knowledge in Mexico, is probably the finest institute of cardiology in existence anywhere. We have nothing like it in the United States. Competition among the doctors here is so intense that only the very best are able to survive, and these must produce constantly. Research of outstanding quality is coming out of this institute. The Medical School of the university also has the highest standards. Less than one-fourth of the entering class eventually graduate with the degree of Doctor of Medicine. The training is more rigorous than in many schools of medicine in the United States.

On the cultural side of the ledger the university publishes a periodical called *Universidad de México*, which is one of the best literary organs in the country. Instead of carrying stories about the latest football victory, this journal contains articles of the finest quality by internationally famous authors. One of the recent issues, for example, had an article by E. M. Forster on "The Tower of Ivory"; it contained a poem by Ezra Pound and an essay on that poet; Alfonso Reyes, Mexico's best-known literary figure, appears in a posthumous work; there is an article on anthropology, another on the drama, one on economics, et cetera. The magazine is beautifully illustrated and is widely circulated.

At last Mexico is combining the best aspects of contemporary science with her long-recognized superiority in the field of humanities and in the cultural arts. The National University is one of the most powerful influences in helping to bring about this fusion. It is an institution of which any nation in the world would feel justly proud. It is the outward and visible sign of that new inward and spiritual grace which is the essential quality of Mexico today.

Mexico City, which has mushroomed in all directions during the past ten years, now covers an urban area twice that of Paris. People continue to pour into the great metropolis in an ever-growing stream. The city is experiencing an unprecedented building boom and land values have rocketed sky high. Some of the most exciting modern architecture in the world is going up in Mexico City today, and it is an architecture strongly colored by Mexican geography and the Mexican cultural past. This architecture has yet to be discovered by the world at large.

Richard J. Neutra, one of the outstanding architects of the United States and of the world today, praises the Mexican achievements in unstinting words:

> Mexico is to my mind the most vital native country of the Americas, where the most modern innovations in architecture and the arts are wedded

to indigenous trends of an indigenous people. . . . The early works of Frank Lloyd Wright, Louis Sullivan and certainly of myself can be called immigrant in nature when compared with the works of those Mexican architects who stem from long resident families. Mexico no longer follows. In the modernization of public buildings, from hospitals to schools, Mexico is in the lead. Officials of many countries, our own United States included, have been asleep while their opposite numbers in Mexico have been saying an open-eyed "yes" to a new architectural expression of a new situation.[23]

This new architecture of Mexico began in the 1920's as a result of the Revolution which had upset all the existing upper-class values. In the latter part of that decade the introduction of steel and concrete construction afforded the means of expressing the new ideas with the techniques of contemporary building. The development of mural painting in Mexico, also as a result of the Revolution, gained tremendous impetus in the same decade and added to architecture a colorful, deeply Mexican note. In 1923 José Vasconcelos, Minister of Education, turned several public buildings over to the fresco artists, who decorated them with vast murals depicting the country's hopes and the country's history. In the 1940's and 1950's an additional element was added: the mosaic fresco. All these influences were blended together to produce the modern architecture of Mexico today.

This new architecture of straight, clean lines, spaciousness, and great areas of glass has produced a geometric beauty of almost classic quality. It may be found in almost every possible kind and size of building: the skyscrapers of University City, towering office buildings, public buildings of many kinds, hospitals, schools, private homes, apartment houses, service stations, multifamily dwellings, stores, factories, dairies, churches, new housing developments, swimming pools, multilevel parking lots, and others. Wherever one goes in urban Mexico today, one will find some of these buildings, but it is in Mexico City that the new trends in architecture have taken root and spread like fire. The wealth of the country is concentrated in the capital, and architecture in general is a costly commodity.

The frescoes in mosaic, one of the most distinctive characteristics of contemporary Mexican architecture, have had a phenomenal development in the past ten years. Within a single decade Mexico has achieved pre-eminence in this extremely difficult medium of artistic expression. The fresco mosaic is not exactly a new idea, for it was employed in Greek, Roman, and Byzantine art. But nowhere did the mosaic ever attain the vast proportions that it has in Mexico, becoming an integral part of architecture itself, indeed creating a new architectural style. Dozens of buildings in Mexico today have walls which display great sweeps of pictorial color, sometimes by the hundreds of square feet. There are vast mosaics in native stone, glass, ceramics, concrete, tiles, and bricks, which have turned whole buildings into beautiful Oriental tapestries.

Diego Rivera used the stone mosaic to decorate his own pyramid which was designed to house his art collection. Later he applied the same technique at the Lerma Waterworks and on the University City Stadium. Juan O'Gorman decorated the entire exterior walls of the huge University City library with stone mosaics, and Pérez Palacios used the same Persian-carpet style in the amazingly beautiful Ministry of Communications Building. Carlos Mérida developed and became the outstanding master of the ceramic fresco, now widely used in commercial construction. Numerous other fresco artists have added their own personal touches to these new fresco mosaics: "frescoes which *are* a wall, not frescoes which are on a wall," as the Mexicans so aptly put it.

The fresco mosaic fits in ideally with climatic needs, for it gives the buildings color and finish which will not be affected by the weather. These frescoes do not fade or chip or peel. The new art also fits in perfectly with the strong plastic tradition of the Mexican stonemason, who has lived in close contact with mural art since the days of the Mayas. The ancient Indian past of Mexico has merely re-awakened in these vast frescoes of today. The humble stonemason often contributes his own shadings and variations as he applies himself to his task, which is also his joy. The cost of these fresco mosaics, calculated as they are by the square yard, is very little higher than that of ordinary tile facing. But they afford a range of design and use of color which are far more effective and far more beautiful. And they appeal strongly not only to the plastic temperament of the Indianist worker, but to the mestizo occupant and landlord as well.

Although the mural, and especially the mosaic mural, is perhaps the most distinctive feature of Mexican architecture today, many other elements have blended together to produce the Mexican modern style. Take, for example, the dwellings of the smartest suburbs of Mexico City. Here the architect has glorified the plain, unbroken geometric line, and has achieved an admirable simplicity and restraint in expression. Most of these dwellings have frames of reinforced concrete, flat or only slightly slanted roofs, large wall areas of glass paneling, metal-framed windows and doors, cantilevered balconies or terraces, overhanging eaves, contrasting areas of glazed tiles, clay bricks, or native stone, either rough or polished to a soft luster. The dwellings are white or painted in warm earth colors: terra cotta, brown, yellow, green. The outside walls may be of reinforced concrete, brick, adobe blocks, tile, stone, or rubble. Fencing of these same materials often continues right on into the house, interrupted only by the fireplace. On the roofs is always one bulky object which the architect must conceal or disguise as best he can: the water tank, which is made necessary in order to have sufficient pressure for easy flow. These tanks are covered up or incorporated into the roof lines in many ingenious ways.

The private swimming pool is another characteristic of the contemporary homes of the wealthy in Mexico today. These pools are frequently made in shapes which utilize graceful flowing curves and follow the contour of the land, the lava pockets, or else carry out and extend the contours of the house itself. One home had a pool which was an integral part of the house; it was simply an additional room, the swimming room. One complete wall of this room was of sliding glass panels, leading outside. There was a large fireplace in the room before which the bathers could lounge and warm themselves or read and drowse. Here was a pool that could be used comfortably any day of the year. Another house had a pool built beneath the structure itself, which bridged over the water in a low-flowing curve. One could look from the windows of this home directly into the pool below and the garden surrounding it. In another home a small tip of the pool entered the living room, making a little interior pond that literally abolished the wall between home and yard.

Furnishings are in modern or contemporary style, with a great use of the rich native woods. Many walls are also paneled in wood or stone. The sway-backed, woven-leather chair is common. Heavier chairs and sofas of simple lines and thick padding also are popular; these are often contrasted with clean-cut, light-looking tables and chairs, and cabinets of restrained rectangular design. Much exciting contemporary furniture is being manufactured in Mexico today.

On the interior these houses are light, spacious, and every inch functional. For decorative purposes they often make use of the marbles of Puebla, the stone of Oaxaca, the precious woods of the Yucatán jungle, statues, murals, mounds of lava rock, and natural landscape pockets for pools. The formal garden has been banished, and in its place is the outdoor patio garden onto which open large sliding glass panels, which bring the outdoors into the house. Flaming coral trees, bougainvillaeas, and other native trees and flowers are so placed that they too become an integral part of the home. But most important of all, every line, every wall is simple, clean, unbroken. There are no edgings or protruberances to destroy the geometric continuity of line.

Architecture is not the only item which gives Mexico City its unique appeal today. Despite the unprecedented "citification" of the Mexican metropolis during the past decade, many survivals of the historic past still stand forth and link the living with the dead. On the physical side are the numerous colonial buildings reminiscent of the viceregal "City of Palaces." On the human side are the native markets, which are as much alive today as they were in the times of the Aztecs of Tenochtitlán. The Spaniards marveled at the *tianguis* (market places) of the Aztecs, so picturesquely described by Bernal Díaz. Thousands of people congregated in the great market place in Tenochtitlán to buy and sell. Each type of merchandise occupied its street, the market was efficiently policed, orderly, and clean. Almost every product of the Aztec Confederation was for sale here. The market in those days was at Tlaltelco, about a mile north of the Zócalo.

During colonial days the central plaza of Zócalo became the economic heart of the city. The Municipal Building was erected here, and many stores were built and rented to town merchants by the city government. Other vendors occupied wooden stalls known as *cajones*, or boxes, because they were constructed of boards from the boxes in which clothing had arrived from Spain. The market was anything but clean during most of the colonial epoch. Great heaps of garbage and filth accumulated, and the Viceroy Revillagigedo complained that he was unable to cross the street without stepping in muck halfway up to his knees. This was a far cry from the Aztec market, kept constantly clean by the labor of the hundreds of streetsweepers who were on daily duty in Tenochtitlán. The mounds of refuse had to be cleared away at each colonial celebration, for the state occasions were always celebrated on the Zócalo. Revillagigedo in 1789 was so irked at the mammoth task of cleaning the place up that he prohibited the market's return to the central plaza, and it was then moved to the Volador Plaza, now occupied by the Supreme Court. The Volador Plaza was the place where the Aztecs originally held their "flying-pole" ritual.

This celebration was especially impressive at the end of each 52-year cycle (the Aztecs' century), when priests bore flaming torches from the hill temples into the city and thus began the grand fiesta, of which the dance of the "flying men" was the climax. Five of these *voladores* dressed in the feathers of the eagle, climbed to the top of a high pole, and while one remained above on the lofty perch to dance, the other four, their feet roped to the pole, "flew" downward as they unwound themselves in exactly 13 circles. Four times 13 adds up to the 52 years of the religious cycle. The Aztecs believed that at the end of one of these cycles the world would come to an end, so each occasion when it did not end was cause for tremendous jubilation and thanksgiving.

Santa Anna built a permanent market building on the Volador Plaza in the 1840's and the building stood until 1935, when the present Supreme Court replaced it. But the Volador Plaza was not the only market place in Mexico City during the nineteenth century. It was soon outgrown, and specialized markets were established at the old Convent of Merced (wholesale fruits and vegetables), and at la Lagunilla, northwest of the Zócalo (clothing, furniture, general accessories). When the Volador became a bazaar in 1890 a third market was set up at the Plaza of Mixcalco, northeast of the Zócalo.

The Merced is still the largest market in Mexico, and each year further units are added; la Lagunilla is also still one of the most exotic markets in the city. Pauline Kibbe, in the fascinating magazine *Mexico This Month,* lists and describes in detail six other markets in Mexico City. All these markets are now open seven days a week, but one day is still known as "market day." "In the Coyoacán market, for example, some 336 vendors are permanently housed in the new market palace; but on Friday, Coyoacán's 'market day,' the total number of vendors rises to more than 1,500, the transients establishing themselves in concrete stalls provided for that purpose in the courtyard of the market building. These mobile merchants move from one market to another on the respective market days. This is the system in operation throughout the country."

Many of Mexico City's markets now occupy modern concrete buildings with great areas of glass and mosaic tiles, and containing trim brick or tile stalls. There are uniformed vendors, the most modern refrigeration devices, even nurseries for the children. Sixteen such plants are now in operation, and additional units are already under way. The color, orderliness, and neat functional beauty of these modern markets of today recall the *tianguis* of the Aztec more than they do the dirty and cluttered markets of colonial times. In them Mexico's Indian heritage is coming again to the fore to blend with the most advanced techniques of supporting life.

How does the ordinary family live in Mexico City today? This is a question to which many visitors would like an answer. It is, however, a question which has no answer. In the first place, there does not exist, even in Mexico City today, such a thing as "the ordinary Mexican family." Despite the rapid growth of the middle class during the past twenty years, most Mexicans are still relatively poor. Would the poor family, therefore, be representative of the "average" Mexican of today? It would be very unwise and very unfair to say this, for while relative "poorness" does characterize most of the population of Mexico, *improvement* year by year, even month by month, is the most marked characteristic of the urban middle class.

Let's be specific. The average family in the United States will possess these things: at least one car, an automatic refrigerator, a washing machine, a modern gas or electric stove, a modern heating unit in home or apartment, a TV set and a radio, an income of at least $500 a month. This family will live in a five-room house, with hot and cold water, sewage disposal, water pure enough to drink as it flows from the tap. The family will have no servant.

Most Mexican families, even in Mexico City, do not have all these things. Most middle-class families do not own a car, they lack many of the automatic appliances mentioned above, and have neither the heating nor water facilities of the American home. On the other hand, most of them have domestic servants, which are comparatively cheap. Consequently, the Mexican middle-class housewife does even less work than her counterpart in the United States. The wealthier Mexican families, of course, not only have all the things listed above for the middle class of the United States, but in addition have a whole corps of domestic servants, as well as every automatic appliance, and the most expensive furnishings and automobiles.

It would be senseless to carry the comparison any further. One thing, however, is certain. The growing middle class in Mexico today constitutes an immense market potential for tomorrow. The wants are already there, so is the drive; all that is lacking is the increased purchasing power, and that too is growing at an incredibly rapid rate.

The most disappointing characteristic of the Mexican middle class lies in its desire to imitate, almost blindly, its United States counterpart. Already thousands and thousands of homes in Mexico are filled with the useless knickknacks and atrociously designed furniture of the United States middle-class home. Instead of leaning toward the artistic designs arising from the Indo-mestizo tradition or toward the trim lines of Mexico's modern architecture, the middle-class Mexican family lingers before every furniture show window looking with hungry eyes upon fat and ugly overstuffed red and green sofas and chairs or cheaply manufactured chrome work for dining room and kitchen. Only rarely do the families of the Mexican middle class show that flair for color and design which has come to characterize the Mexican of education and the Mexican of wealth. Good taste in the United States is hardly known as a national characteristic, but it is present in our middle as well as in our wealthy class. Our poor folk, unfortunately, show very little taste indeed.

In Mexico the picture is not the same. Taste is present among the poor classes, who still cling to their great plastic traditions, and is also present among the well-educated and well-to-do, who have made almost a religion of getting behind every manifestation of contemporary art. In the Mexican middle class artistic good judgment is slipping, but there is one great saving grace. While the Mexican middle class in its *private* life strives blindly to imitate the United States, in its public life it has the wisdom to support the government and the artists who have linked themselves together in order to foster publicly the native arts.

One absolute "must" for every visitor to Mexico City is the unique new Anthropological Museum designed by Pedro Ramírez Vázquez to house the marvelous collection of pre-conquest art. Its wide façade, countless halls and open-air exhibits, huge patio sheltered by a great cement canopy supported by a single carved pillar, make the structure as striking as its collection. One exhibit is an entire Maya temple, another is the 167-ton statue of the rain god, Tlaloc. Within easy walking distance is the Museum of Modern Art with its fine collection of paintings.

The city's new subway system uses tubes that float in the muddy subsoil bearing trains with rubber tires. Fare is one peso. Excavations for the subway brought forth many tons of ancient art objects. In 1968 Mexico City hosted the Olympic Games, and in 1970 the world championship soccer finals. Soccer, called *futbol* in Latin America, is the most popular of all international sports.

XXI

MONTERREY

A world pallid with dryness, inhuman with a faint taste of alkali. Like driving in the bed of a great sea that dried up unthinkable ages ago.

—D. H. Lawrence

Monterrey is Mexico's answer to Pittsburgh. It is a great industrial center with a population of over a million. It is the most Americanized city in Mexico. You can drink the water that comes out of the tap in Monterrey, for it has a lower bacteria count than that of many cities in the United States. On the streets the people even seem to walk faster in Monterrey, and everybody speaks English or is learning it. Here is a bustling, hard-driving, hard-working, wealthy city, which for all that boasts an opera season longer than in any center twice its size in the States. Monterrey also has one of the finest technological institutes in North America. It is often referred to as Mexico's M.I.T.

But drive into Monterrey from Texas and you see only the mountains, the rocks, and the desert. The highway is straight as an arrow; it almost seems to race across that flat and barren land. Drop into Monterrey on the plane, and you land in the center of a wilderness of mesquite and cactus. There is no town, but only the desert, and the pale dry earth, baked to a powdery loam under the withering sun. A few scrubby plants push up their dusty bending leaves. The airport lies in the midst of this baked desolation. Once, on the way into the city, I saw a scrawny coyote bound across the road in front of the car, then disappear in the sage and mesquite. Unlike the magnificent airports of Mexico City and Guadalajara, Monterrey has a scrubby-looking station which looks very much like those in most United States cities. It was built for use, not beauty, but it has long since outgrown its original facilities and is now (like our U.S. airports by the dozens) a disgrace to the community and a pain in the neck to the passengers.

The taxi driver does not look like a Mexican; he does not even look like a Spaniard. He might be a cabbie in New Orleans or Dallas. It is a long ride into town across the dusty desert; it is midsummer. Over the earth a sky of powder blue, flecked with gray dust. There is an alkaline aridity in the air and in the land. There is almost a smell and a taste of alkali in the air that hangs over the soil. The sun sprays down its fire unceasingly. To a Californian or an Easterner it is a scorcher; to a Texan it is a cool day, in the low nineties. The air is hot by any man's measurement, but it is dry and not oppressive. Monterrey is definitely more pleasant than Houston, Fort Worth, or Dallas. To me the summer weather was absolutely perfect.

There is little growth in the fields. Where are the orchards and the gardens? "Over there," says the driver. "In that direction," adds another passenger, nodding toward the southern side of town. I see them later, beautiful groves of green, but here the earth is a poor crust of parchment. It has been written that the world's great religions have all arisen in the desert. The defiant barren earth, unyielding to man, called forth the seed in his soul, for no seed came from the baked and fruitless fields. It is an interesting hypothesis. But no religion has arisen in this part of Mexico. There is no great aloneness in these fields, which are but the pretext for the city. They surround it with their poor ugliness and make it appear all the more abundant, all the more wealthy, all the more progressive. We enter the outskirts of town. Tourist courts, houses, factories. The factories are better than the houses. Business before pleasure! There are slums in Monterrey, just as there are in San Antonio or Chicago, but there is also plenty of business, good business, and there is plenty of money. The people of Monterrey are often called "tight" by the inhabitants of the other parts of Mexico, but in Monterrey this is simply called "good business." What these people want they are willing to pay for, through the nose, if necessary. And they always get it.

Mexico makes some of the best beer in the world, and Monterrey is a great beer-manufacturing center. The huge *cervecería* here (which makes *Carta Blanca* beer) is proud of its product and proud of its achievements in social and worker welfare. Visitors are welcomed. There is an infirmary, a large clubroom, a playground for children, a fine dining room (a meal costs less than 50 cents), a commissary where goods are sold at wholesale prices. The workers receive all kinds of safeguards and compensations. Labor conditions are excellent. The *cervecería* even provides a library and theater for its workers, and a special school where they can take free courses in office work or the practical arts.

Monterrey is also a big steel-smelting center. Its *fundidora* employs perhaps five thousand workers. Towering stacks belch fire and smoke into the tile-blue air. The plant's appearance is certainly not anything to boast of, relations between management and workers are often taut, visitors are not welcome. But steel ingots are poured forth in an ever-growing stream. The slogan *hecho en Monterrey* (made in Monterrey) appears in dug-out letters on thousands of articles in Mexico, from locomotives to small steel tools. Mexico has also recently taken up the cry of the Texans, and one now sees on automobiles everywhere the words "Made in Mexico by Mexicans!" Texas megalomania has crossed the border and found a comfortable home in this part of Mexico.

Monterrey is not a beautiful or a charming city. It is a businessman's town, and for the tourist is simply the gateway to Mexico. From Monterrey one either goes farther south or heads off into the mountains, perhaps to Saltillo, only a few miles distant, but at an altitude of 5,000 feet in an entirely different geographic setting. They say Saltillo is "one hour and three centuries away."

Downtown Monterrey is always full of traffic, which even a six-level parking building has done little to lessen. There are many excellent hotels, huge stores selling farm machinery and appliances, a fine North American library (Benjamin Franklin Library) which is always full of Mexicans reading books and magazines from the United States. There is also a large branch of Sanborn's, a huge combination of store and restaurant in the American style. Nearby is the Carapán store and inn, one of the most charming spots in the city, which is owned and run by Humberto Arellano Garza, a nationally known specialist in the Mexican folk arts. One could not find anywhere a more modern hotel than Monterrey's Ambassador. It is as trim and clean as the best in New York or Los Angeles. For 100 pesos a day ($8.50) you can get a room and bath. The dining room is neat and pleasant; the only Mexican touch is a flock of parakeets which constantly fly out over the diners from their perches under the staircase. The dining-room is filled with American businessmen anxious to close some deal in Mexico. Branch plants are going up by the dozens. John Deere is one of the latest.

Monterrey is the capital of the state of Nuevo León. It is outstanding in the production of steel, glass, cement, furniture, tiles, and electrical equipment. It also makes beer, candy, shoes, flour, and perfumes. Many natives are proud to point out that in atmosphere it more closely resembles San Antonio than the other cities of Mexico.

Monterrey also has an excellent up-to-date hospital, one of the best vocational schools in the country (Alvaro Obregón Vocational School), and several outdoor swimming pools. Its municipal transportation system is cheap and convenient. There is a large workers' colony where modest but well-constructed houses have been built by the city and sold at cost. There are more Texas newspapers for sale on the streets of Monterrey than there are papers in Spanish. In spite of its location in the midst of the desert it has already become the great industrial center of northern Mexico, the gateway to the south, and the most dynamic city in the country. In many areas that surround the town there are orange groves and truck gardens. Here the desert has truly been made "to blossom as the rose."

Monterrey's pride and joy is the new Instituto Tecnológico, located on a brand-new campus just at the outskirts of the city beneath the long shadows of Saddle Mountain, which towers above the flat terrain of metropolitan Monterrey. The institute is an oasis of emerald green shimmering in the stark aridity that surrounds the city. It has a swimming pool of clear blue glowing in the sun, a campus of green grass and trees and flowers, many modern dormitories, a fine dining hall (cafeteria style), an excellent staff of well-paid professors. The institute is a tribute to the wealthy businessmen of Monterrey who decided they needed a first-rate place to train technical specialists and then set about building one. Training is given in all the technical fields: engineering, chemistry, architecture, and so on. Many of the texts used are in English. The hand-picked staff is the best paid in Mexico, the minimum professor's pay being about $600 a month (in purchasing power the equivalent of $900). The institute also has a priceless library of old and rare books, many of them being incunabula.

In the winter this school has an enrollment of about 7,000; in the summer months there are 300 Americans studying here, and perhaps twice that number of Mexicans. It is an ideal place for the young high school or college student of Spanish to spend a pleasant, profitable, and cheap few weeks in Mexico. The school is clean as a pin, students are carefully chaperoned, and there is always a doctor in attendance. The school has its own buses which take students into town free. Monterrey also has a University of Nuevo León and a branch of the *Politécnico* of Mexico City. The state of Nuevo León spends 59 per cent of its annual budget on education.

Modern architecture has also come to Monterrey, as it has to every urban center in Mexico today. The six-story *estacionamiento*, or parking building, in the midst of the downtown area, is one notable example. It rises on graceful columns, apparently lifted effortlessly into the air. The downtown area is full of trim-looking pharmacies, ice-cream parlors, restaurants. But the supreme example of contemporary architecture in Monterrey is the brand-new Church of the Virgin of the Immaculate Conception, who is the city's especial patroness. This is the first modern church to be constructed in Mexico, and it is fitting that it should have been built in Monterrey, which makes most of the country's concrete, steel, and glass. All these materials are embodied in the structure, which is a fusion of straight lines and graceful curves suggesting a kind of "modern Gothic." The rectangular-shaped tower soars to an immense height and is topped by a simple stone figure and a cross. The tower itself is unadorned, its rough stone facing contrasts sharply with the smooth gray concrete walls, all of which flow upward in a narrowing oval curve which to me suggests a functional simplification of the pointed Gothic ogival. The façade, with its great curve of enfolding cement, contains in its center a figure of the crucified Christ, and below this statue are the twelve apostles. On the left of the façade rises the rough stone tower. The structure is well conceived and integrated and has achieved an undeniable spiritual quality that is in keeping with today's feeling for form and space. There is no reason in the world why a beautiful religious architecture cannot emerge from the contemporary style.

Monterrey is a city of many beautiful homes which reach up onto the slopes of the mountains behind it. These smart residential districts are called *colonias* in Mexico. In Monterrey there are several of these wealthy suburbs: El Obispado, Vista Hermosa, Colonia del Valle, Chepe Vera, Roma, and Las Mitras. Homes in these zones are comparable to the better residences in the United States, but there is more emphasis on modern architecture and functional design. Monterrey also has its *Ciudad de los Niños*, or Boys Town, which was begun after Father Carlos Alvarez had seen some motion pictures of Father Flanagan's Boys Town, Nebraska. Approximately a hundred boys now live here, but plans call for expansion to take care of an eventual two thousand.

Despite its stress on business, Monterrey is also proud of its cultural activities, and among these the yearly opera season is noteworthy. Top-flight singers appear in these performances, which are always filled with the city's best families. During one recent season Victoria de los Angeles sang the leading role in *Manon*, which was followed by *La Bohème*, *Faust*, *Madame Butterfly*, and several others.

Although the working class of Monterrey is certainly not the worst paid in Mexico, wages (with some notable exceptions) are relatively low. The daily wage at the steel plant is supposed to be 60 pesos daily (about $5). A tortilla maker gets only 20 pesos a day. A bookkeeper in a bank to whom I talked made 1,000 pesos a month (about $80), a girl clerk in a store earned 800 pesos, a domestic servant 400 pesos, a carpenter 800 pesos. You can get a fine haircut for 70 U.S. cents.

Unions are not strong in Monterrey. The wealthy tycoons have been able to keep their workers satisfied or have been able to buy them off. Unions are divided into two kinds: the Sindicato Rojo (Red Syndicate), which is the leftist trade union, and the Sindicato Blanco, which is the company union. The steel plant has the "red" union, the beer factory the "white" one. Neither union truly represents the workers, yet working conditions and wages are so much higher than they were a few years ago that the working class is not about to rebel and kick over the traces. The future, however, is certain to see a growing friction between worker and employer as Mexican industry continues to expand. At present the average worker is disgusted with the politically leftist union, which many workmen to whom I talked in Monterrey called "corrupt and purely opportunistic for the labor bosses." They are equally disgusted with the company unions, which have a spy system that keeps tabs on their political activities and sees that they stay in line with the management.

Being essentially an industrial city, Monterrey has its problems of juvenile delinquency much like those of our own "mill town" variety. The most unpleasant experience that I had on my latest visit to Mexico took place on the main plaza in Monterrey. I had sat on the bench and observed the promenade of the young boys and girls, which broke up promptly at ten o'clock at night. A couple of the boys then sat down beside me and began to converse, first in Spanish, then in broken English. One of them planned soon to leave for Detroit, where his brother was living and working. Both of them were students in the local equivalent of our high school. They were about seventeen years old, and had been studying English about two years. They were neatly dressed, attractive young fellows, and it was a pleasure to chat with them. We had been talking about ten minutes when I noticed a group of very different-looking boys gathering around the bench opposite us. These boys wore their hair long, had on loose-fitting baggy pants, and kept a perpetually defiant sneer on their faces. One of the largest of them finally came over and said to the boy sitting beside me: "This kid here," pointing to a ten-year-old, "said you were talking about us. He said you called me a gorilla. What about it?"

"We were not talking about you at all," my companion said. "We called you no names at all. Ask the señor sitting here."

He did ask me and I assured him that the boy had told the truth. But the other boy was not satisfied. He sat down on the bench opposite and began to throw clods of dirt at the two lads on my bench. We got up to leave. He came over and grabbed one of the boys around the neck and twisted it, hard. The boy made no effort to resist. Finally, the big lout let the boy go and then pulled out a knife with a blade at least six inches long. By this time we were moving away. The big fellow came at the boy he had tackled before and swatted him in the jaw with all his might. We walked faster and in a moment were among people, where the gang left us. The boy beside me had a welt on his neck and chin, and was extremely upset. I asked why he had not shouted out or hit back. He said that if he had he would have gotten the knife in his back or side.

"It happens all the time," he said. "The cops always get there too late."

We walked on to my hotel, chatted awhile in the doorway, then said good night.

Hoodlumism is not limited to any country or to any city. Mexico has less of it, I believe, than the United States. But this particular incident, which took place on the Plaza de Zaragoza at about ten-fifteen at night, left a very deep impression on my mind. The following day, while I was reading the local paper, *El Norte*, my eyes fell on a column headed *PESQUISAS* (INQUIRIES). It contained pictures of three children who had disappeared from their homes and had not been heard of since. Four additional children were listed in the column without benefit of photographs. For one reason or another these seven teen-aged children had all disappeared from their homes in Monterrey and had not come back. Perhaps they had been swallowed up by that dark whirlpool of anonymity which surrounds every industrial city, either to make their own living, to join a gang such as the one I had just seen in action, or to leave for parts unknown in an attempt to make their fortunes. It was truly heart-rending to read about so many of them in a single issue of the Monterrey *Norte*.

When I was in Monterrey in 1965, last year of the *bracero* program, I tried to take the train home but found the station overflowing with disappointed passengers. Thousands of *braceros*, farm laborers, were returning from the United States, and every train south was packed and jammed. The people in Monterrey who wanted to get anywhere found it impossible to do so. While I was in the station a train came in, and at least a dozen men ran toward it trying to climb in through the open windows. But even this was not possible, for every available inch of space was taken. The lack of equipment on this particular run was simply tragic. I spoke with some of the people and found out that not only were coaches lacking, but that many of the so-called first-class trains were using box-cars to transport passengers, and that some of these were packed with as many as three hundred people. Of course, they had no water or sanitary facilities. Some of these trains, in order to prevent additional passengers from crowding aboard at intermediate stations, were making a habit of stopping out in the country, a couple of miles away, and forcing those who wanted to get off to do so there. The women and children were suffering greatly from these enforced unloadings and the consequent long walks into town in the broiling sun.

The rail fare to Mexico City from Monterrey was only 83 pesos first class, with an additional 22 pesos for a reserved seat. A lower berth was 53 pesos. (Fare approximately $7, seat $2, berth $4.) The distance is 1,022 kilometers, approximately 625 miles. The bus fare, first class, is about $8 for the same trip, and the plane costs $26. I finally went on the bus, making one overnight stop in order to avoid riding all night. The first-class buses in Mexico are generally very comfortable, and on the main runs are as good as our own. But never take it for granted that you will be able to ride a first-class bus, for there are many places to which they do not go, as many a tourist has learned to his great discomfort.

My visit to the railway station paid off in more ways than one, for after getting complaints about the train service off their chests, many of the men were eager to talk of their experience in the United States as *braceros*. When they found out that I was a teacher and not a farmer or businessman, they opened up. Several of them had heard reports of bad treatment in the States, and three of them complained bitterly of their own personal experiences. They felt that their food had been bad, that they had been unnecessarily pushed around and discriminated against, and that the manner in which their wages had been calculated left much to be desired. This is a mild statement of their case. The majority of the workers felt that they had been treated fairly, and were glad that they had gone. They had been able to save a considerable sum to take back to their families, sums which would represent several seasons' profit in Mexico.

After the most vigorous complainers had withdrawn, one of the more satisfied workers leaned over and said:

"Señor, there are always those who complain. I do not know the facts, but I am willing to bet that those men were poor workers. They wanted something for nothing. I and my friends worked hard, but we were well paid and well treated. After all, we did not go to Texas for a vacation."

A pal of his added, as a rejoinder:

"What my friend says is true, señor, but I am sure that there are places where the *bracero* is not well fed, well housed, or fairly paid. But things are much, much better than they were three or four years ago. My brother spent two months in Texas then, and he came back saying that it was terrible. He tried his best to keep me from going, but I am satisfied that I went. Now I have a better opinion of the whole exchange. There is only one complaint that I can truly make, and it is that in Texas many people still look down on us as if we were some sort of lesser human beings, not really belonging to their race. Frankly, señor, I did not like that at all. I do not believe they will treat an American like that in Mexico, señor."

His hard-working friend agreed that this was true.

The one whose brother had given the bad report said:

"Our own government is doing plenty to push the *braceros* around. Those who want to leave the country now are first made to work several days in the cotton fields along our side of the border for fifteen pesos a day before they will be given a permit to cross the border."

"That's hard," his friend agreed, "but it may be necessary. There is a one billion peso crop of cotton in that area which would otherwise go to waste. If Mexico needs us, isn't it fair that we work for our own country first?"

"I suppose so," the other added. "But at least we ought to remember that the wages we get and the food and lodging that are given us in Mexico are certainly worse than anything we find in the United States. That is what I meant."

Both men wanted to make it plain that they felt complaints had been exaggerated and, if there had been misunderstandings, were anxious to admit that the Mexicans were as much to blame as the Americans. They were overforgiving and overgenerous, for this is not truly the case. No matter how many wetbacks have crossed the border illegally, there is never any excuse for the unjust treatment of an honest Mexican citizen. And the feeling that Mexicans are second-class human beings is, I am very much afraid, still prevalent among many of the more backward, more fanatical, and more ignorant communities of Texas. I lived in several different parts of this state for over twenty years, and ought to know. The other border states have solved the problem, and at last the intelligent people of Texas are really trying to do something about it.

The Second World War was the beginning. The Good Neighbor Policy was very much in the public eye, and the state of Texas did not want to be the irritant. The Chambers of Commerce, the Rotarians, and other business clubs of the state decided to stop using the word "Mexican," and to employ instead the term "Latin American." Every public newspaper or radio reference then began to substitute the adjectival phrase "Latin American" for "Mexican." This was certainly a peculiar way to go about combating anti-Mexican prejudice, but it seemed the only immediately effective method open to the good businessmen of Texas. Ethically, it was just plain silly, but realistically it did pay off in a softening of the intolerance so widely shown Mexicans in the Lone Star State. It now remains for the parents and schoolteachers to take up the struggle and restore tolerance to its proper ethical base. The only acceptable moral basis of human conduct is to take a man for what he is and not to prejudge him because of some incident which does not apply to him at all or because of idiotic casuistry or some old wives' tale which has been handed down for decades or centuries.

The history of the *bracero* program is a capsule synthesis of the primary problem in U.S.–Mexican relations. The program began during World War II when the United States desperately needed additional manpower on its farms. Mexican farm workers were allowed to cross the border and work in the states for a limited period. The number of *braceros* averaged around 400,000 a year. With the war's end resentment grew among U.S. workers at the intrusion of these thousands of Mexican farm hands who were willing to work for less pay than they. In a great many cases, too, the Mexicans did a better job, so envy certainly contributed its portion. In any event, the *bracero* program was terminated in 1965 in response to strong political pressure. Today, however, in 1970, between two and three million Mexican nationals still work in the United States, some of them with border-crossing cards, others holding green-card immigrant visas, and still others who are here illegally.

Now that the word *bracero* has practically disappeared from our vocabulary, we are constantly bombarded with the word "Chicano," which was for years a pejorative term for "Mexican-American." The *bracero* was never a U.S. citizen, or even a permanent resident; the Chicano almost always is. The total number of those now referred to as Chicanos may be over five million, the vast majority of them residing in the states bordering Mexico. In the late 1960's, inspired largely by the Negro struggle for civil and economic rights, there began a widespread pro-Chicano campaign with speeches, articles, books, television appearances, public demonstrations, and group political activities. "Chicano power" became an obsession with many leaders of the movement. In Denver, Rodolfo "Corky" González and his followers came up with the *Plan de Aztlan*, which asked for nothing less than the restoration of the Southwestern United States to the Chicanos. "Chicanos are already a nation," was one of the policy statements of this group, which demanded an "independent Chicano school system" for the "independent nation of Aztlan." Aztlan was the old Aztec name for this territory, and some Chicanos called for a plebiscite feeling that they were now in the same position as the Jews before the establishment of Israel.[48]

Other leaders of the movement demanded that "Chicano studies" be added to the curricula of our schools, especially our colleges, and these demands were met. Unfortunately, many of the Chicano leaders themselves do not know Spanish, which is a great pity if they really wish to help their Spanish-speaking brothers. On the other side of the spectrum, large numbers of Americans of Mexican descent detest the very term "Chicano," which exemplifies for them a kind of segregation in reverse. Would it not, they say, be utterly ridiculous to insist on exalting such terms as Bohunk, Polack, Nigger, Wop, or Kike? These Americans of Mexican ancestry want more opportunity, more education, more justice, of course, but not based on the use of a specious term which encourages the overzealous opportunist to make his own political hay out of their disadvantaged position.

XXII

MEXICO TODAY

A revolution is fought by men of flesh and blood, not by saints, and every revolution ends with the creation of a new privileged class . . . the ruling class in Mexico, alias the Partido Revolucionario Institucional, alias the President of the Republic, equals: the nation, the Revolution, the glories of the past, the Aztecs, everything. So they have to promote a revolutionary rhetoric that strikes deep chords in Mexico, because it is the source of political power. Mexico is not prosperous enough to be governed without a revolutionary rhetoric.

CARLOS FUENTES, Mexican novelist

THERE is a tremendous economic boom in Mexico today. It began during the Second World War, when the pace of industrialization commenced to quicken. Mexico City, Acapulco, Monterrey, Guadalajara, and many other urban centers have taken on an air of modernity, neatness, and wide-awakeness which was utterly lacking twenty years ago. The government is stable, the peso is solid and steady, foreign investments are pouring into the country, there has been a rapid increase in commerce, and transportation, particularly by air and highway, has soared to unprecedented heights. Within the past decade the national production has increased by approximately 70 per cent, while the population growth was only 33 per cent. Per capita income has increased steadily. The people of Mexico are living better, eating better, feeling better than ever before in their history.

The signs of this rejuvenation are visible on every hand. New parks are being laid out; existing ones are trim and green; there are flowers everywhere. Attractive modern airports cover the territory of Mexico, which would shame those of most United States cities of comparable size. Factories are springing up all over the country. Beautiful new buildings, homes, schools, offices line recently widened and freshly paved streets. Sparkling and commodious supermarkets, with white-aproned vendors and piped-in music, are being opened, and big new fleets of trucks are carrying goods for hundreds of businesses and industries. There are tractors in the fields, planes in the skies, and automobiles on the highways. New housing developments are mushrooming in all directions, and in the capital they reach out to the very slopes that rim the valley.

This tremendous spurt of development is, percentage-wise, one of the greatest in the world today. It cannot satisfactorily be explained in terms of mere economic expansion and big investments. Education, good government, and improved social conditions have had an even greater share in laying the basis for what is taking place in Mexico today. Only during the past ten years has Mexico begun to reap the benefits of the efforts toward education and an equitable solution of the social problem which were made forty years ago. These efforts are now having a cumulative effect. Education and social justice are suddenly paying off in the tremendous returns of greater output per worker. Good conditions have made him willing to work harder; better tools and a better education have made him able to produce more. An expanding economy has made him able to buy more. All these things, plus the revolution in social and cultural thinking, have made him as alive culturally as he is economically, with a vitality, drive, and spirit which the people of Mexico have not had since preconquest days.

It is impossible to separate this dramatic growth from the political structure of Mexico embodied in the Mexican Revolutionary Party which has run the country since the 1920's. Therefore a brief political survey is appropriate at this point.

The foreigner is apt to be deeply puzzled by Mexican politics. There is nothing like it anywhere in the world. A system of one-party rule which by definition would appear, especially in a Latin country, to be incompatible with tolerance and good government, if not downright irrational and unworkable, has been operating in Mexico for fifty years, and for forty of those years with impressive effectiveness. It has brought the country a longer period of stability and progress than that enjoyed by any other Latin American republic.

The Mexican Revolutionary Party, now known as the PRI (Partido Revolucionario Institucional, or Institutional Revolutionary Party) is mainly responsible for these results. The Party is something unique in Latin American life. It also presents somewhat of a paradox, for it is a revolutionary party that is no longer revolutionary. It is not, however, monolithic, but has been flexible enough to change with the times, and this has insured its survival. The Party does not choose its candidates openly, as is the practice in most democratic countries. Its crucial decisions are made behind closed doors and after a period of give-and-take which is strictly *tapado*, that is, under a tight lid.

The history of the Party and the history of Mexico have been closely intertwined since the end of the Revolution. In the early chaotic post-Revolutionary years (1920–1928) Obregón and Calles saw the need for a closely knit political organization which could give a permanent structure to the revolutionary government of Mexico. Envisioned as a representative political party composed of all the elements of the Revolution, such an organization would have to include generals, politicians, workers, labor leaders, peasants, and businessmen. Nothing concrete was achieved until Obregón was assassinated by a Catholic fanatic in 1928. After Obregón's death Calles appeared before an assemblage of the Congress and state governors and made an impassioned speech in which he referred to Obregón as "the last caudillo." He then called for the continuance of the Revolution by peaceful and democratic means. There were those who thought that Calles was more interested in his own charisma than he was in democratic government, but in any event, in 1929 a cross-section of revolutionary elements did gather and organize themselves into the Partido Nacional Revolucionario, or National Revolutionary Party. The name has been changed twice since then: in 1938 to Partido de la Revolución Mexicana, Party of the Mexican Revolution, and in 1946 to Partido Revolucionario Institucional, Institutional Revolutionary Party, or PRI. The change in name is indicative of the change in character from early revolutionary zeal to present-day middle-of-the-road institutionalization, representing essentially an alliance of business and political leaders in the maintenance of political and economic control.

The organization of the Party was a stroke of genius, and its success in curbing individual political rivalries has made possible the miracle of Mexico, enabling a backward semi-Indianist society to become the most productive nation in Latin America. The original organizers saw the danger of a breakup into many antagonistic splinter groups, which would lead to political chaos if there was an open fight for the presidential candidacy every time elections were held. Their main idea, therefore, was to keep all discussion of presidential candidates under rigid party discipline and behind closed doors. The Party would permit, even encourage an opposition, but would never allow an opposition candidate to be elected President. (The conservative Catholic opposition party is the Partido Acción Nacional, or *PAN*, whose initials spell the word "bread.") Some regional officials, however, do belong to this opposition. The Revolutionary Party (PRI) has been flexible enough to back down if the imposition of one of its own local candidates aroused too much grumbling, as happened in the governorship of Oaxaca in the 1950's. The most important point of all, was the Party's gradual swing away from military control toward a civilian leadership as younger men replaced the older generals.

The last five Presidents of Mexico have all been moderate civilians. Without this *sine qua non* of freedom from military domination, the expansion of Mexico in an economic sense, and her very good record in the area of civil rights would not have been possible.

Those who criticize Mexico for holding national elections in which the opposition presidential candidate has no chance of being elected see only half the picture. The Party (PRI) very simply regards it as nonsensical to allow the Revolution, which cost the country nearly a million dead and untold economic loss, to be undone at the ballot box. Hence, its insistence on one of its own as President of the country. On the other hand, plenty of discussion goes on inside Party ranks before their candidate is chosen, and this, say the Party leaders, is all the democracy that Mexico can at present afford. A comparison of Mexico's progressive political history in the last fifty years with that of any other Latin American country gives considerable substance to their view.

General Álvaro Obregón, a *ranchero* who had defeated Villa and then run Carranza out of Mexico City, became President of the country in 1920, the year which is generally regarded as marking the end of the violent phase of the Revolution. Obregón was not himself a very revolutionary figure. He aligned himself mainly with the old land-owning class, but he did make a few impressive gestures in the direction of the peasantry. The Revolution had by now become "official" in Mexico, and Obregón could no more turn his back on it than could any of the eleven Presidents of the country who have succeeded him. Under Obregón the direction of government began to change in Mexico with a clear move toward political and agrarian reform. In the following decades it was to swing to and fro several times between left and right, finally to come to a halt somewhere just left of center.

The outstanding contribution of Obregón as President was that he held sufficient power in his hands to give Mexico relative peace, the prerequisite to economic progress. He also used brilliant judgment in appointing the intellectual, José Vasconcelos, as his Minister of Education. Vasconcelos, who regarded the Spanish heritage as the bedrock of civilization in Mexico, became the impassioned messiah of education as a panacea. During his brief term as head of the educational ministry he established almost a thousand new schools in Mexico. Obregón helped by allotting to him an unprecedented portion of the very limited national budget for this essential work. Although it was contrary to the constitution for Catholic schools to exist in Mexico, both Obregón and Vasconcelos winked at the already existent Catholic schools believing that "illegal education was better than no education at all." Vasconcelos was also responsible for turning over the walls of so many public buildings to the artists of Mexico with the notable flowering of the great mural art. If Vasconcelos had died at the height of his fame he would have gone down in Mexican and Latin American history as one of the greatest figures ever produced in that part of the world. However, he outlived his usefulness as well as his ideals and soon became the leader of the reactionary forces in Mexico.

We might say that under Obregón a prostrate Mexico picked herself up and began to move again, but the reconstructive aspect of the Revolution began with Calles. Elías Plutarco Calles, President during the period 1924–28, was a schoolteacher, farmer, and tradesman from Sonora. He had risen to the rank of general in the revolutionary army. He did not have Obregón's geniality or tolerance, but it was Calles who gave Mexico the basis of a revolutionary society. In his early years he pushed vigorously a program of economic and social reform, and he also applied much more rigorously than had Obregón the anticlerical laws of the Constitution of 1917. He deported 200 foreign priests and nuns and ordered the registration of all others. The Church retaliated by refusing to hold any services, and the deadlock lasted for several years. An antigovernment rebellion among the Catholics of Jalisco and neighboring states resulted in thousands of deaths on both sides. The government generals treated as pawns in a game the rebellious Catholics, called *cristeros* because of their battle cry, *Viva Cristo Rey*, "Long live Christ, the King." The revolt was not finally suppressed until 1930, after three years of bloodshed.

Calles got Mexico's economy moving again. He initiated large irrigation and sanitation projects and began to construct a vast system of highways which would eventually link Mexico with the United States and also connect the various isolated regions of the country. He helped to build up organized labor, speeded the distribution of lands to the landless rural population, created agricultural banks, and encouraged the growth of a neo-capitalist industrial expansion. He threatened to expropriate the foreign-owned oil lands of the country, and oil interests in the United States immediately rose in protest. At this stage President Coolidge sent Dwight Morrow, a partner in the J. P. Morgan and Company banking house, to Mexico as North American Ambassador (1927). Morrow, a man of great personal charm, at once ingratiated himself with the Mexican people. He sincerely loved the country and its culture, and he became the very close friend of President Calles, who soon began to see the wisdom of having the United States as an ally rather than as an enemy. Under the suasion of Morrow, Calles put the brakes on his land reform program, and soft-pedalled talk of expropriating the foreign-owned oil lands. Morrow invited Will Rogers and Colonel Charles Lindbergh to Mexico on good-will tours, and as a result of the latter's visit his daughter married Lindbergh. Morrow also reconstructed for his family an old mansion in Cuernavaca, and he paid Diego Rivera to paint murals on the walls of the ancient house of Cortés in Cuernavaca as a gift to the Mexican people. His three years in Mexico were well spent insofar as United States interests were concerned, but they had a very noticeable dampening effect on Calles' revolutionary zeal.

During Calles' term as President federal policy was "give a little and take a little." The generals still ran the country, and Calles was simply the most powerful general. He was known as the *jefe máximo*, or "big boss," because he personally controlled everything. There was one general to every 350 soldiers in the Mexican army, and these relatively well-paid officers paraded up and down the streets of Mexico City in their Cadillacs and Rolls Royces, displaying their young mistresses and invariably wearing their pistols, in order to intimidate the citizenry. At the top, Calles and his friends were clearly enriching themselves while they paid loud public tribute to the ideals of the Revolution. For a time the national treasury stood on very shaky ground, and I remember well the chagrin of an old professor from Virginia who had been invited to teach in the summer school of the University, when he was paid with an enormous canvas sack full of silver pesos. There was little faith in the paper currency, because of lack of solvency at the base.

Obregón was elected for a second term to succeed Calles on July 1, 1928, and it appeared to many that the dominant power in Mexico might alternate between these two friends for some years to come. But seventeen days later, as the President-elect sat in a café in San Angel, he was assassinated by a young Catholic cartoonist who said that he wished to sketch his portrait. Many Catholics applauded the deed, and a book came out praising it, with the title, *El santo que asesinó, The Saint Who Assassinated.*

It was at this point that Calles rose to the level of real statesmanship and called for an end to *caudillo* rule. However, he had no intention of relinquishing his own personal power, and the three men who served brief interim periods as President during the next six years were all hand-picked by him. The *jefe máximo* thus stretched to a full decade the period of Callista domination.

Things began to change with the election of General Lázaro Cárdenas, in 1934. Calles was largely responsible for his selection as candidate of the Revolutionary Party. Cárdenas, governor of Michoacán, was a good friend of Calles, and the "big boss" thought that he would prove as manageable as his three predecessors had been, but such was not to be the case. To avoid cluttering the text with names, we give below a complete list of the Presidents of Mexico since 1920; the decade of the Calles dictatorship is clearly marked:

Álvaro Obregón	1920–1924
{ Plutarco Elías Calles	1924–1928
{ Emilio Portes Gil	1928–1930
{ Pascual Ortiz Rubio	1930–1932
{ Abelardo L. Rodríguez	1932–1934
Lázaro Cárdenas	1934–1940
Manuel Ávila Camacho	1940–1946
Miguel Alemán	1946–1952
Adolfo Ruiz Cortines	1952–1958
Adolfo López Mateos	1958–1964
Gustavo Díaz Ordaz	1964–1970
Luis Echeverría Álvarez	1970–

Lázaro Cárdenas (1934–1940) was the conscience of the Revolution. When he retired from office he was the most loved Mexican President after Benito Juárez. He began by campaigning vigorously and effectively, traveling thousands of miles in order to speak before people in all parts of the nation. He was a man of great affability, integrity and political acumen, so it was not long before he was widely known and deeply respected. Cárdenas unstintingly supported all the reforms embodied in the constitution of 1917. During his term he distributed more land than all his predecessors combined, thus making economic survival possible for millions of rural citizens and at the same time creating the basis for a growing market for the national productivity. He was also the first President who did not govern from Mexico City. Cárdenas went into the outlying provinces to meet with the humble villagers and to hear their problems first hand. He was strongly pro-peasant, pro-labor, pro-Indian, pro-Revolution, not only in word but also in deed. He had no intention of allowing people in the government to exploit the poor for the benefit of the well-to-do.

Once Cárdenas was firmly established in office and had revealed his true sympathies, a showdown between him and Calles became inevitable. Cárdenas hastened the confrontation by closing the illegal gambling houses, owned mainly by wealthy Callistas, who were thus draining off the capital so desperately needed for the development of Mexico. When strikes broke out he at once expressed sympathy for the strikers, whereas Calles was anxious to suppress them because his big business friends were being hurt by the work stoppage. Finally, in April, 1936, the "big boss" made his move to organize an anti-Cárdenas bloc, but he was unable to gain any support because the majority were already either on the side of the President or were convinced of his overwhelming popularity. Masses of workers actually demonstrated demanding death for Calles. When Cárdenas was apprised of the complicity of the "big boss" he sent messengers to Calles' home and had him put on a plane bound for the United States. The "big boss" spent six years in Southern California before returning to Mexico where he died unmourned and almost unnoticed in 1945.

In 1938, when he was firmly ensconced in office, Cárdenas decided to expropriate all foreign-owned (U.S. and British) oil properties, and to pay for them a sum set by the Mexicans themselves. The companies shouted that this was highway robbery, and their lobbies did everything possible to bring about U.S. intervention in their behalf. Fortunately for Mexico Franklin Roosevelt was President of the United States, while Britain was on the verge of World War II. Mexico was tense when Cárdenas went on the national radio hookup to announce the expropriation, but when he got away with it, a surge of patriotic zeal and pride swept across Mexico. One extremely important result of Cárdenas' administration was that he consolidated the state's control of the working class. The Mexican economy expanded during the Cárdenas years, but the rate of growth was less than one per cent a year. Cárdenas gave new dignity to the working man, and the main burden of his period in office was to affirm and stabilize the Revolution.

Cárdenas was perhaps better known in the small villages and rural areas of Mexico than any other President. I can remember witnessing his visits to some of these hamlets, where the townsfolk turned out en masse and greeted the President with enthusiastic shouts and hand-painted signs which read: *Bienvenido, Tata Cárdenas,* "Welcome, Daddy Cárdenas." Those signs embodied much of the mystique of the Mexican presidency, a mystique which makes the position quite different from that in this country. The President of Mexico holds infinitely more power in his hands than does the President of the United States. He is not accountable to anyone. He is a combination of tribal chieftain, modern dictator, and democratic president, all rolled into one. He decides what laws are to be passed, which programs are to be pushed, how to obtain and how to expend the federal budget. Nothing of national or of great local importance from Indian affairs to the newest engineering projects escapes his attention. Even the Supreme Court is amenable to his will. That this power has in the main been exercised with both tolerance and flexibility for over forty years is one of the wonders of modern Mexico.

Carlos Fuentes, Mexico's best known and most widely translated novelist, characterized the Cárdenas years very accurately in the following words:

> Mexican capitalism is indebted to two men: Calles and Cárdenas. Calles laid the foundation. Cárdenas brought it to life by creating the possibility for a large internal market. He raised wages, gave labor every conceivable guarantee, protected workers so there was nothing for them to agitate about; he established once and for all the policy of Federal investment in public works; he broadened credit, broke up land holdings and on all levels tried to stimulate a vast circulation of stagnant wealth. These were permanent accomplishments, still living. If Cárdenas had not given the labor movement an official character, the administration that followed would not have been able to work peacefully and to increase the national production. And above all, Cárdenas ended Mexican feudalism. Mexico might become anything, but never again a kingdom of great absentee landlord estates ruled by a perfectly useless agrarian plutocracy. Plutocracy we may have, but thanks to *this* plutocracy, markets are created and jobs are provided and Mexico moves ahead.

This statement is made by Cienfuegos, who is a character in one of Fuentes' novels, *Where the Air Is Clear,* but the views expressed coincide with those of the author except for the concluding favorable evaluation of the contemporary Mexican plutocracy. Fuentes holds no such opinion.

Ávila Camacho (1940–1946) succeeded Cárdenas. With him the

Mexican Revolution took a definite turn to the right. Ávila Camacho made his peace with the Church by affirming that he was a "believer," but he could not hold a candle to Cárdenas personality-wise. He was widely known among the people as "the unknown warrior" and as "the knight of the virgin sword," because of his insignificance in the military phase of the Revolution. He continued the programs initiated by Cárdenas, but with greatly diminished enthusiasm. During his term, World War II gave Mexico an unprecedented opportunity for increased profits and for rapid economic expansion. Mexico began to industrialize and the Gross National Product expanded at the rate of seven per cent a year between 1940–46. Ávila Camacho slowed down the program of land distribution, doling out only one-fifth as many acres as his predecessor. It was not necessary to be very revolutionary any longer. The Revolution was on the way to becoming a bonanza.

Miguel Alemán (1946–1952) was the next president of Mexico. He was a young, personable man, very proud of his *machismo* (maleness) and his exploits with the ladies, a forceful representative of the new generation of entrepreneurs, and clearly out to make a nest egg for himself and for his friends while he was in office. On the other hand, Alemán was a great builder. He knew that if he did not make he could not take. He stepped up the pace of industrial expansion, erected dams to irrigate the land, built the University City, extended the highway system, and constructed airports from one end of the country to the other. In the first year of his term an epidemic of the dreaded *aftosa*, the hoof-and-mouth disease, hit Mexico, and before it was wiped out by U.S.–Mexican collaboration, 680,000 cattle, sheep and goats had to be slaughtered and then buried by bulldozers.

Alemán profited from land speculation in Acapulco, which was just beginning its growth as a tourist Mecca, and he agreed to a deal with the British El Águila oil company (a subsidiary of Royal Dutch Shell) which was much more favorable than that made with any U.S. company. El Águila owners received payments totalling approximately $131 million, whereas the total paid to U.S. companies was about $24 million. Mexico agreed to make these payments in dollars, so when the peso was twice devaluated, she paid a truly exorbitant amount.

Alemán also headed the campaign which led to the alteration of article 27 of the constitution, increasing by fifty per cent the number of allowable acres in irrigated private farm properties if the land was planted in cotton. If the farms were planted in sugar cane or in grapevines the permissable total was tripled. (Article 27 set the limit at

100 hectares.) This meant that a man might own 150 hectares of land (370 acres) if he had an irrigated cotton farm, and 300 hectares, or nearly 750 acres if his fields were in sugar cane or in vineyards. With the man's wife, son, daughter, and son-in-law each being allowed the same number of acres, this actually meant the buildup of several large haciendas of many hundreds of acres off which the wealthy owners could live almost as luxuriously as in the days of Porfirio Díaz. The process of judgment here appeared to be "the more remunerative the crop the bigger the allowable farm."[37]

Alemán left office a multimillionaire, but it must be said in his favor that he laid the groundwork for Mexico's full-fledged entry into the twentieth century. His term as President represented a strong swing from agriculture to industry and from the *ejido* to the factory. New superhighways stepped up the tourist trade during the term of Alemán, and tourism soon became one of the most profitable "industries" in the country. The Korean War, however, put a crimp in this source of income, and also caused a big cut in the sale of many Mexican products. When Alemán turned the presidency over to Ruiz Cortines the national treasury was in anything but a hale and hearty condition, whereas many wealthy Mexicans had skimmed sizable portions of cream off the top.

It was precisely this aspect of the Alemán administration which his successor, Adolfo Ruiz Cortines (1952–1958) criticized so vigorously. Ruiz Cortines claimed that the enrichment of the few to the detriment of the many was causing Mexico to head in the wrong direction, and during his own term he placed his main emphasis on more corn and beans for the indigent Mexican masses. He put the brakes on industrial expansion, and also demanded absolute honesty from all government officials. The President himself set the example by making a complete public statement of his financial assets. Ruiz Cortines was not Mexico's most colorful President by any means, but he was an honest man, and in the end his honesty and hard work, plus the hard work of the Mexican people, paid off.

With tourism way down because of the Korean War it was difficult for Mexico to make up the deficit, but make it up she did. When Ruiz Cortines delivered his State of the Union message shortly before his retirement from office in 1958, he could claim the following dramatic results:

Mexico had completed a new hospital each week during the past six years.

There had been a 95 per cent reduction in the incidence of malaria during the same period.

In 1953 Mexico had needed to import 400,000 tons of wheat, but in the years 1955–58 she had been able to export an average of 300,000 tons a year.

Rural social welfare centers had grown from four in 1953 to a total of 4,600 in 1957, aiding seven million people.

Mexico had completed a new school each day during Ruiz Cortines' term in office. More than one fifth of the federal budget was being spent on education.

Three million acres of land had been put under irrigation.

Five thousand miles of "farm to market" highways had been constructed and over fifty airports had been built in all parts of the country.

While the rapid pace of industrialization set under the Alemán administration was deliberately slowed down by Ruiz Cortines, there is no doubt that the Mexican people as a whole profited from his stress on public works and rural development. During his term Mexico's Gross National Product continued to increase at twice the rate of the increase in population, and that rate has been maintained ever since.

Adolfo López Mateos (1958–1964) took off all brakes and pushed for more productivity in Mexico. When the railway workers struck in 1959 slowing down economic activity, he suppressed the strike with the army, claiming that the stoppage was Communist inspired. Those charged with illegal agitation were summarily jailed. The famous mural artist, David Alfaro Siqueiros, was also slapped into jail for insulting the President. López Mateos completed the nationalization of the electric power industry which had been 70 per cent privately owned when he assumed office. He also distributed 25 million acres of land, but most of it went to private farmers. The *ejido* had reached a point of no return. Many *ejidos* were inefficiently run, and many others were subject to corruption. When López Mateos retired from office it was clear that Mexico's underdevelopment could not be solved by land distribution, for most of the good lands of the country had already been distributed. The problems of poor working conditions and poor productivity would have to be solved in the cities, in factories, in business, and in the supporting trades.

Gustavo Díaz Ordaz (1964–1970), a lawyer, was elected by 89 per cent of all votes cast, an indication of how the national elections are run in Mexico. He was the first Mexican President to call himself a conservative. During his administration Mexico was clearly in the hands of the new post-revolutionary business class: the industrialists, bankers, businessmen, entrepreneurs, big farmers. Díaz Ordaz maintained a middle-of-the-road political stance, and encouraged the further industrialization of the country. Under him student demonstrations were violently suppressed, the 1968 Olympic Games were held in Mexico City, the magnificent new anthropological museum was completed, and the construction of a subway system was begun in the capital.

Díaz Ordaz has pointed with pride to the record 57 million acres of land that were distributed during his presidency, but the mystique of land ownership was no longer satisfying to the people. In many rural areas thirty to forty per cent of the peasants were unemployed, and tens of thousands of families were trying to eke out an existence on tiny unproductive plots of two or three acres. One half of Mexico's exports are agricultural products, a great part of them coming from *ejido* lands farmed in direct violation of the law. In these cases entrepreneurs rent the land of an entire village, hire the owners as contract workers, and provide seed, tools, and expertise of a quality and quantity that the individual peasant could not possibly afford. The entrepreneurs keep the profit. Furthermore, many cattle ranches, especially those along the U.S. border, exceed the acreage limits set by Mexican law. A large number of these are "owned" by U.S. citizens and have become a source of great discontent among the land-hungry peasants of the area. Government officials turn a blind eye toward these cankers in the national agrarian life. They have no wish to stir up trouble with the United States, or to take any action which might have the effect of decreasing productivity. The crux of the matter is very simply the shortage of available good land in Mexico. Out of a total of approximately 487 million acres in the country only 72 million acres are considered as good arable land. But 200 million acres have already been redistributed by the government, and there still remain two million landless rural Mexican families.

In 1964, when he assumed office, President Díaz Ordaz named Carlos A. Madrazo, an ardent and brilliant Party member, as president of the Mexican Revolutionary Party, the PRI. Madrazo was told to reorganize and to reform the Party, a job that was long overdue. He took his work seriously, and at once announced open, unrigged primaries; he also promised more student participation in the Party, requested a Commission for Honor and Justice which was to expel racketeers from the

Party, called for a closer scrutiny of patronage, etc., etc. His promises appealed greatly to Mexico's youth and intellectuals, but they met immediate resistance from the entrenched Party leaders, who were unwilling to yield one iota of their power, however unjust or inequitable. The following year (1965) Madrazo was forced to resign. He continued to stump the country, however, still pleading his case, and he sent a letter to 3,000 leading citizens pointing out that Party rigidity and the indescribable poverty of many rural communities made intelligent administration impossible. But Madrazo's campaign for more democracy within the Party only had the effect of further infuriating the establishment, and in 1968 he was killed in a plane crash near Monterrey, the nature of which many Mexicans regard as suspicious.

Díaz Ordaz plainly showed his colors as a protector of the establishment when he forced Madrazo's resignation. The youthful elements in Mexico were deeply resentful, and student frustration exploded. The students demanded both Party reorganization and a reform of the university and other institutions of higher learning. There were various angry demonstrations described officially as riots, the rector of the university resigned, and Díaz Ordaz announced that his government would not tolerate "anti-social acts," and that if the students did not want to study he would see to it that the millions of pesos earmarked for their education would be used to improve the lot of the peasant on whom it would not be wasted. Mexico was beginning to act and to react very much like the United States.

Relations between students and government continued to deteriorate, and on October 2, just a few days prior to the start of the Olympic Games, 6,000 persons gathered in Tlatelolco Plaza of the Three Cultures in front of a large housing project in order to march to the National Polytechnic Institute to protest army occupation of the campus. The government, afraid that Mexico might lose face before the world, sent army troops with tanks and machine guns to quell the "disturbance." Trigger-happy soldiers sprayed the crowd with bullets, killing many residents and bystanders, among them several people, old women and children, as well as young demonstrators. The number of dead was reported officially to be thirty-eight, but there is good evidence to indicate that many more were killed, perhaps ten times the official estimate. Dozens more were critically wounded, and 1,500 were imprisoned. It is reported that about 200 of these are still being held in jail with a total disregard for the due process of law.

The Olympic Games began as scheduled. Hundred of white pigeons were released to mark the opening ceremony, and athletes from all over the world turned in some remarkable performances despite the altitude. More records were broken than at any previous Olympics, and for the first time not a single athlete died during the games. But the shootings on Tlatelolco Plaza had been a traumatic experience for Mexico. Mexicans thought their country was beyond this kind of violence, and there was bitter condemnation of the government from many quarters.

President Díaz Ordaz assumed "full responsibility" for the bloody clash. He implied that "foreign elements" had helped to stir up trouble and that there was a concerted effort "to push the nation to anarchy. We know that some persons are confused," he went on. "They labor under the belief that we live in a country where all doors are closed to them. They exaggerate imperfections—which we do not deny—and refuse to recognize the progress achieved, which is exceptional."

One of the strongest critics of the government action was the grand old man of Mexican letters, Octavio Paz, who was at the time ambassador of his country to India. An interview with Paz came out in *Le Monde*, a Parisian paper, in which the famous poet and essayist said that the governmental political party, the PRI, "revolutionary in its origin, has now become merely an administrative organism, which constitutes from today forward an obstacle to the progress of Mexico." Paz then went on to defend the demonstrators and their right to protest. He vilified the government by saying that the sending of trigger-happy army troops to suppress them represented a return to "the black myth of Mexico's pre-conquest past," and was a re-enactment of the Aztec ritual of blood sacrifice. Paz admonished the Mexicans to stop complaining about the trauma of the Spanish conquest, and to take a good look at their country's earlier history. "It is no accident," he wrote, "that in our great anthropological museums the center is always dedicated to the Aztec Hall, that is, to the oppressors of pre-Columbian America, those who terrorized the Mayas and the Zapotecs. It is not mere chance that the young Mexicans who were slain on the second of October fell on the Plaza of Tlatelolco, where there used to rise an old Aztec temple in which human sacrifices were made. The death of these students was a ritual sacrifice, for there was no political reason to justify the action. The only possible cause was to terrorize the people." In public protest against his government Paz then resigned his post and returned to Mexico where he was officially *persona non grata.*

Paz is the author of one of the most perceptive and most scathing analyses of Mexican character in a collection of essays entitled, *The Labyrinth of Solitude.* "We Mexicans," he says, "oscillate between violent life and violent death, between intimacy and withdrawal, between a shout and a silence, between a fiesta and a wake, without ever truly surrendering ourselves." Mexicans are a hermetic people, filled with suspicions, hostile loneliness, and an exaggerated need for self-protection. "We cannot bear the presence of our companions. We hide within ourselves." The Mexican male is obsessed with the necessity to protect his quality of maleness by never "giving in." He is constantly on the defensive, and values more highly fortitude in adversity than victory itself. History has taught him never to trust, never to open himself up to anybody. The quality of "maleness" (*machismo*) is an obsession with him. He regards himself as a descendant of Hernán Cortés and Malinche, his Indian mistress, founders of the Mexican race. He is unsure of his own identity, but he refers to his enemies as *hijos de la chingada,* "sons of the violated woman," considering this as the final and irrefutable insult. But the insult also applies to him, for he cannot escape his own history. He is convinced that if he does not violate others they will certainly violate him. His life, therefore, exists in a continuous labyrinth of solitude into which the exterior world is never allowed to penetrate. He lives on the margin of contemporary history, weakened and made hostile and guilty by traditional resentments which he is unable to overcome. In a word, "the history of Mexico is that of men in search of their origin, their affiliation, their identity."[38]

Paz is not the only well-known Mexican writer who has dissected the character of his countrymen. Juan Rulfo and Carlos Fuentes, the two best contemporary novelists of Mexico, have done the same thing in fiction. Juan Rulfo in his novel *Pedro Páramo,* 1955, described the life and death of a Mexican landowner and political boss (Pedro Páramo) and his son (Juan Preciado) by telling their stories from the graveyard. The reader does not realize that all of the characters in the novel are dead until the middle of the book, when Juan Preciado, remembers his own death in the ghost village of Comala.

Comala had once been a Paradise surrounded by fruitful green fields, but by the time Juan reached it searching for his father and for his lost childhood it had become a veritable hell inhabited by dead people. Paradise always lies behind us; it is a lost Eden, alive only in memory. The cult of death rules life, at least Mexican life, for in Mexico the dead determine the fate of those who are to follow them.

Juan's search for his father reminds us of the search in Homer's *Odyssey* and in James Joyce's *Ulysses*. In Mexico that search takes on a national significance, for there are thousands of Mexican children who are fatherless in fact, if not in blood. They must all seek to reconstitute their lives out of whisperings, out of hearsay, as does Juan when he arrives in Comala, which is a village of *ánimas en pena*, of grieving ghosts. These Mexican villages, says Rulfo, are "dedicated to the cult of death. A Christian respect for the dead has mixed with pagan ancestor worship." Death is present in Mexican games, fiestas, in Mexican loves and thoughts. "To die and to kill are ideas that rarely leave us," wrote Paz, in the same vein as Rulfo. "We are seduced by death. The fascination it exerts over us is the result, perhaps, of our hermit-like solitude, and of the fury with which we break out of it. The pressure of our vitality, which can only express itself in forms that betray it, explains the deadly nature, aggressive or suicidal, of our explosions." Rulfo, more personal, probes for some reason for it all. "Why does the world press in on us from all sides," he asks, "and break us into pieces, and water the ground with our blood? What have we done?" [39]

Rulfo feels that the Revolution unleashed passions that have become habits in these Mexican villages, engendering an all-pervading "hate-death" syndrome. While in the cities the Revolution soon became a political and economic bonanza, in the small isolated villages it was synonymous with violence, destruction and death. Thousands of villages were abandoned en masse by people in flight from the seemingly endless waves of the holocaust, people who carried much hatred in their hearts.

Pedro Páramo was a *caudillo* who, like the revolutionists that he personified, believed that anything could be won by force. He took his village, Comala, in this way. But when Pedro in his personal life was denied by love and beauty he became hate and violence incarnate. He destroyed what he could not possess, leaving only a dead Comala behind him. He embodies both poles of his country and its Revolution, swaying between violence and the search for beauty. Rulfo tells us that desolate, dead Comala is symbolic of much of rural Mexico. These dead villages were never reinhabited. The process was irreversible. As they disappeared the cities continued to grow until they burst. Rulfo did not realize it at the time, but his words were tragically prophetic.

In an interview Rulfo pointed out that the Revolutionary land program was a great failure in his state of Jalisco. "The land was distributed among small tradesmen instead of farmers. It was given to the carpenters, brick layers, barbers, shoemakers. They were the only ones that formed a community. To form a community you needed twenty-five people. All those twenty-five people had to do was get together and ask for the land. The country people never asked for it. The proof is that until this day they have no land."[43]

In another outstanding novel, *The Edge of the Storm*, by Agustín Yáñez, the love-death theme is presented with consummate artistry. This is perhaps the most beautifully written novel to come out of Spanish America. Yáñez, at one time governor of the state of Jalisco and then Mexican Minister of Education, takes an isolated village in Jalisco and by deftly probing into the psyche of its inhabitants at several levels he depicts it as a composite Hispanic village spanning the centuries. Saint Augustine's war on sex is an obsession in this village, which is dominated by the Church much as the medieval towns of Europe were dominated by theirs. But there is no great church building going on here, no sublimation of instinctual desire; everything is now turned inward and festers in repressed feelings of guilt, hostility, violence. Such was the vengeance of the Counter-Reformation. In his opening pages, which serve as a kind of overture to what is to follow, the author writes:

> *The women have gaunt faces and abstemious hands. Cheeks without makeup. Compressed lips. Pale skin. The men are weathered and browned by the sun. The hands of the women, hands that draw water from the town's deep wells, are rough. The hands of the men are also hard, for they work the soil, rope the cattle, bundle the hay, thresh the corn, haul stones for the fences, ride horses, tame steers, milk cows, make adobe bricks, haul water, hay and grain.*
>
> *Among black-robed women life passes by. Death comes. Or love. Love, which is the strangest, the most extreme form of death; the most perilous and dreaded form of living death.*[40]

The novels of Yáñez are in the mainstream of present-day fiction which lives under the omnipresent Freudian shadow. This linking of love and death, of course, is not new in history. The Greeks created their mythic Eros who impregnated the Earth with arrows, and Dionysus was both the creator and the destroyer. The ancient Chinese had a proverb which said: "Sexual intercourse is the human counterpart of the cosmic process." Life leads to death and out of death new life emerges. The process is unending. "The fundamental paradox of love," writes Rollo May, "lies in the intensified openness to love which the awareness of death gives us and, simultaneously, the increased sense of death which love brings with it. We recall that even the arrows with which Eros creates—these life-giving shafts he shoots into the cold bosom of the earth to make the arid surface spring up with luxuriant green verdure—are *poisoned*. Here lie the anxiety-creating elements of human love."

This oscillation between the search for love and beauty on the one hand, and on the other, the explosion into violence, is the fundamental rhythm of Mexico. The novels of both Juan Rulfo and Agustín Yáñez emerge from the same taproot, but it is a younger novelist, Carlos Fuentes, who focuses the love-death theme on Mexico's economic and political state. Fuentes is the gadfly of the Mexican intellectuals. His novels, which have been widely translated, are a new form of social protest. They are no longer merely regional in outlook, but are an attempt to break through his country's hermetic shell and open it up to the world, thus linking Mexico to humanity at large, whatever its region or nation.

In *The Death of Artemio Cruz*, Carlos Fuentes presents the life of a man who had taken part in the Revolution and who then had become one of the post-revolutionary millionaires. In every key decision of his life Artemio Cruz had followed the path of self-benefit and self-aggrandizement. His biography symbolizes the Revolution itself, its idealism lost in violence, its opportunism, its wrong turns. Artemio, a dying man of seventy, remembers with nostalgia his lost youth, lost love, lost hope, lost beauty. As he had rejected others now they rejected him. His final gesture was to send his son off to fight and to die in the Spanish Civil War. He held the vicarious hope that this part of his flesh might be able to recapture some of the magic idealism and pure love on which Artemio himself had so often turned his own back. But Artemio was not all evil; he had never ceased to long for warmth and forgiveness from his wife. He repeatedly begged for her love, but she was unable to feel any real tenderness for him. Only her body belonged to him. He died a beaten and a broken man, much like Mexico itself, which Fuentes calls "that twisted mass of blood and hate."

Carlos Fuentes believes that every revolution ends with the creation of a new privileged class. In Mexico there is the class of new and crafty industrialists, politicians, and entrepreneurs who still use the old rhetoric. "Today nobody tyrannizes the Mexicans," he writes in *Where the Air Is Clear*. "They do not need to. Mexicans are tyrannized by what they are. And for thirty years there has been no other tyranny. . . . In Mexico no one is more admired than a perfect son of a bitch." All this is very bad, but Fuentes realizes that "Mexico is not prosperous enough to be governed without a revolutionary rhetoric." [42]

He goes on to say that "in Mexico the defeated are glorified, and the only saving fate is sacrifice. All our heroes are dead heroes. . . . If Madero, Zapata, or Pancho Villa were alive today, each with his finger in profiteering and graft, he would no longer be a hero."

Fuentes is appalled and obsessed with the ever-present murderous instinct of mankind. In the relations between nations, between governments and their peoples, and between individuals among these peoples he sees reflected the cannibalism of nature. In *A Change of Skin* he depicts the murder of an ex-Nazi in Cholula, city of ancient Indian sacrifices and site of the blood bath visited upon the indigenous inhabitants by Cortés, but the entire novel is a pondering "over mankind's astonishing capacity for rationalizing blood sacrifices at every level of cultural development and under every form of social organization." It appears that men feed upon other men as did Saturn upon his own children. The question arises: is this the inevitable and irreversible course of history, or is there some iota of hope that we may some day, in some way, be able to change it?

Fuentes's loss of faith in the Mexican Revolution is almost absolute, but he recalls its early years as a beautiful dream. "The Mexican Revolution was the first great movement of this century to face the basic problem: how to insure the community welfare without sacrificing personal dignity. But why, then, did we not develop the idea? Why did we stop with half solutions? The Revolution has stopped being a Revolution; both intellectuals and workers have discovered they have become official. . . . Mexico's cultural and political life is now a continual marking time. . . . The intellectuals, who could be a moral counterbalance to the force that is overpowering us—well, they are deader than the fears of a raped virgin." Through Zamacona in *Where the Air Is Clear* he implies this dictum: "The only concrete result of the Revolution was the rise of a new privileged class, economic domination by the United States, and the paralysis of all internal political life."

Fuentes feels an intellectual and emotional kinship with the North American writer, Oscar Lewis, author of *The Children of Sánchez,* which is a book of tape-recorded statements describing in graphic detail the life of a poverty-stricken family in the slums of Mexico City. The book was translated and published in Spanish, but it was denounced by the Mexican Geographic and Statistical Society, which called its picture "obscene and slanderous" and degrading to the country. Fuentes came to the rescue of Lewis, and said: "In defending Lewis we are defending ourselves." He decided to make a film version of the book. Fuentes, like Lewis, feels the necessity of telling the complete truth about Mexico. He believes that a chauvinistic nationalism leads nowhere "because of its dehumanized and blind mystique."

On the other hand, Fuentes wants to continue the Revolution, to nourish and develop its human values, to make Mexican nationalism progressive and great and an example before the world. In candor, it must be stated that he is a prophet almost without honor in his own country. *Sic transit gloria mundi.* Nevertheless, he is the conscience of his country. The writer can be a thriving part of a society and still condemn that society for its faults and its weaknesses. This is the role of Carlos Fuentes, who cannot properly be criticized for ever allowing social protest to override his artistic integrity as a novelist. And fortunately the world is never finished; something always remains to be said.

The novels and short stories of Fuentes, Yáñez, and Rulfo indicate clearly how Mexican and Latin American literature generally have changed in perspective during the last twenty years. In the preceding generation literature had been epic in scope, and had expressed regional ideals embodied in regional heroes: *Don Segundo Sombra,* of Ricardo Güiraldes, which evoked the mythic essence of the Argentine pampas; *Doña Bárbara,* of Rómulo Gallegos, which told of the struggle between law and barbarism on the Venezuelan *llanos; La Vorágine* (*The Vortex*), by José Eustacio Rivera, which presented the conflict of man against nature in the jungles of Colombia and Brazil, where neither society nor law existed; *Los de abajo* (*The Underdogs*), of Mariano Azuela, in which the Mexican Revolution is pictured as a hurricane which simply sweeps men before it, reducing them to a bestial *machismo.*

These novels, and others like them, were all based on the epic struggle between civilization and barbarism during the earlier years of Latin American nationhood, and the solution, stated or unstated, was very simple: civilization must win. Peoples must have law, schools, industries, construction, communications. But in the present generation of writers civilization has already won, at least a material victory, and it is here to stay. The question now is: Where do we go from here? There is no longer a simple answer. The novelist has moved from a position of ebullient optimism to one of uncertain anguish. Justice is no longer a naïve concept. The search for human values transcends the search for national values. The new Mexican writers know perfectly well what it is to be a Mexican; they want to find out fully what it is to be a man.[43]

Mexican art has kept pace with Mexican literature and the various folk arts. If the Revolution gave it a sudden burst of fervor and life, the post-revolutionary economic development with its flowering architecture and art-conscious millionaires have kept it alive and stirring with a continuous competitive demand. Of the three great original artists of the Revolution: Rivera, Orozco, David Alfaro Siqueiros, the first two are dead, while the last, now an old man, is still at his dramatic oils and immense murals which today sell almost by the square yard. His huge "March of Humanity," commissioned by the Mexican millionaire, Manuel Suárez, to adorn a hotel in Cuernavaca, is 169 feet long and 33 feet high.

Rufino Tamayo, born in 1899, has always been a kind of lone wolf who follows his unique non-political path despite every fad and fetish of both the old and the new generations. Tamayo has an instinctive, congenital affinity with pre-Hispanic art. His murals, canvases and lithographs are at once modern and native in form and coloring. He is noted for his glowing pinks, and for his carefully wrought designs. Tamayo and Carlos Mérida have inspired a younger generation of artists: Ricardo Martínez, Juan Soriano, Pedro and Rafael Coronel. José Luis Cuevas continues the graphic tradition of Orozco, and at times suggests a Mexican Goya with his famed grotesques. A recent folder of twenty lithographs by Cuevas quickly sold out at $1,800 a copy; even at $90 apiece these lithographs were considered an excellent buy. Among the many celebrated foreign artists who have become identified with the Mexican school are Juan Charlot, Wolfgang Paalen, Pablo O'Higgins, Leonora Carrington, Alice Rahon, Remedios Varo and Vlady, whose father, Victor Serge, was a famous Russian novelist who escaped from Siberia. Under the aegis of this host of painters, sculpture has also flowered in Mexico. Francisco Zúñiga, Germán Cueto, Mardonio Magaña, Bracho and Monasterio, are all well known in this field. They, too, are rooted in the popular art and mythic rhythms of Mexico.

There is a kind of Renaissance feeling in Mexico City today linking the artists and those of the wealthy class and in the government who support and encourage them. Mexican society, while building itself factories, industries, opulent mansions, and great public buildings, gives a pre-eminent place to the creative artist, who therefore enjoys in Mexico more emotional and more financial security than in most other countries.

If a Mexican artist, even an openly avowed Communist, wishes to have a talk with the President, a Cabinet Minister or a leading banker, he has merely to pick up the phone. He is very much of a VIP, respected by every member of the ruling elite.

In the past two decades there has been a swing away from revolutionary and nationalistic themes toward a more universal kind of art. Cuevas dramatized the swing when he said: "I represent the definitive break with superficial nationalism. What I want in my country's art are broad highways leading out to the rest of the world, not narrow trails connecting one adobe village with another." And Juan Soriano affirmed: "I don't have to remind myself every day that I am a Mexican. I am not concerned with my nationality and I don't carry it like a chip on my shoulder. I am a Mexican and without worrying about it. But it wouldn't bother me at all if I was of another nationality. For me, the only important revolution is that of taste." This liberation of the artist from the original source of modern Mexican art has resulted in a generation gap among those in the art world as well as among the people of Mexico. The younger artists carry on a constant battle against their older mentors.

In 1966 the feud between conflicting opinions reached a point of no return, and then simmered down. Mathias Goeritz called Mexican artists generally "a bunch of hysterical and bad-mannered children; which would be perfectly acceptable if the *art* they produce were something of service to God or humanity." The Goeritz doctrine is that "art in our time is finished, for the reason that artists believe in nothing and care for nothing; are without commitment and without faith. With this insistence many artists agree, including poets, philosophers, playwrights and composers. Art being essentially a function of loving giving, how can it be practiced, many contemporaries cry, unfocussed and pointlessly?" Cuevas refused to take part in the feud and exclaimed that this proved he was the only independent artist in Mexico. And Tamayo said: "Siqueiros and I are the heads of the two main pictorial schools in Mexico, so we are the only ones capable of judging who's who."

Despite this confrontation, which was more verbal than artistic, one who is objective is deeply impressed with "the underlying kinship, the characteristic wild vigor of color, the freshness of approach, the violent sincerities" of contemporary Mexican art. And suffusing it all is an indefinable quality which is uniquely of Mexico. Mexican artists have become universal without losing that intangible uniqueness which makes them Mexican.

In 1930 the population of Mexico was 16 million. By 1950 it had reached almost 26 million. Today (1970), it has increased to 50 million, and is growing at the rate of 3.3 per cent a year, thus adding a million and a half inhabitants annually to the national total. If the present rate of growth continues, by 1980 the country will have 66 million inhabitants, and by the year 2000 it will have a population of 100 million. Chances are that the growth rate will gradually slow down and that the total population will finally level off at something less than that final figure. The Federal District alone now holds more than 7 million people. This area is increasing at double the national rate, and other urban areas show a similar rate of growth. Within a radius of 125 miles of Mexico City live 20 million people. One out of seven Mexicans lives in the capital city, which pays 70 per cent of all wages earned in the country, has 35 per cent of the retail sales, half the nation's telephones, radios and television sets, 18,000 taxis, 400,000 other vehicles, and almost all of Mexico's industrial smog. The most noteworthy aspect of Mexico's population is the high percentage of young people. Today 60 per cent are under twenty and 72 per cent are under thirty. It is a young, driving, dynamic country.

The present rate of population growth means a rapidly expanding market; it also means more mouths to feed. So long as the economic development of Mexico exceeds the increase in population, the country will continue to improve economically. Mexico is still a relatively underdeveloped but rapidly developing country. The items below indicate a few of the more spectacular areas of recent economic progress:

Item: Mexico's rate of economic growth during the past two decades has been phenomenal. Gross national product has increased 7.1 per cent a year between 1963 and 1970, more than double the rate of population growth. In 1970 the GNP was close to thirty billion dollars annually, more than that of any other Spanish-speaking country, and triple that of Mexico only fifteen years ago. Per capita income has increased to $550 in 1970; it was only $100 per person in 1930. Unfortunately this is still barely one-fourth that of the more industrialized nations of Western Europe.

Item: Just prior to the Revolution the life span of the average Mexican was a mere 28 years, less than that of a person living centuries ago in the Roman Empire. By 1970 the life span had increased to 65 years. Many dread diseases have been wiped out: smallpox, malaria, typhus, yellow fever.

Item: In the days of Porfirio Díaz only 15 out of 100 Mexican children had access to primary schools. In 1970 actual attendance was 80 out of each 100. A quarter of a million young people are now being trained in institutions of higher learning, and 2.9 per cent of the national budget (the military gets only 10 per cent) is being spent on education. Total school enrollment is over eleven million, and in 1970 showed an increase of 400,000 over 1969.

Item: Since 1930 agricultural production has increased seven fold; for many years it grew at almost twice the rate of increase in population. In 1970 corn, wheat, and beans, the essential foodstuffs of the Mexican people, were all in surplus supply, having exceeded internal consumption. Per diem calories consumed by the average Mexican totalled 2,640, considerably more than in most of the world's other developing countries. Total agricultural production for 1970 was worth 34,197,000,000 pesos.

Item: In 1928 there were only 695 kilometers of highways in the entire country. In 1970 the total highway system was 75,000 kilometers in length. Mexico is now spending 100 *times more each year* on her highways today than she did in 1928.

Item: Tourism which was only a dribble just after the Revolution, now brings two million visitors a year into Mexico, not counting Americans who cross the border for one-day visits. (*Fifteen million* one-day visitors go to Tijuana each year.) These tourists spend almost a billion and a half dollars annually in Mexico. They bring into the country an amount which approximates the total value of Mexico's exports.

Item: Close to 25 per cent of the national labor force is now in industry, compared to 12 per cent in 1940, and the industrial worker produces 4.3 times as much as his counterpart in the 1920's. Industry contributes 28 per cent of the gross national product, having exceeded agriculture, commerce and services.

Item: Oil production, which was 240,000 barrels a day in 1957, has increased to 475,000 barrels a day in 1970.

Item: Electric power in 1970 generated 21 million kilowatt hours, four times that of ten years ago. Mexico's expansion of her electric power resources will give her great new sources of energy.

Item: Mexicans with money, unlike wealthy Argentines and Brazilians, do not send their capital out of the country for investment and safety. Approximately 80 per cent of all funds invested in Mexico originate within the country, and 80 per cent of all savings in Mexican banks represent Mexican savings.

Item: Savings deposited in Mexican banks totalled 170 billion pesos in 1970, ten times the deposits of ten years ago. Financing granted by the country's banking system reached a total of 150 billion pesos in 1970, of which more than 75 per cent was allocated to economic expansion.

Item: During the two years 1969–1970 Mexican imports increased by only 10 per cent while exports were up by 30 per cent. In 1970 imports were in excess of two billion dollars, four-fifths of it for capital goods. Half the exports were in farm products, with cotton and sugar in the lead. The United States bought 53 per cent of Mexico's total exports. During the same two-year span manufacturing rose by 17 per cent, electric power by 16 per cent, and trade by 15 per cent. The Mexicans were trying to solve all problems by industrialization. As José Hernández Delgado, director of the Nacional Financiera, said: "We are latecomers to the world economic scene. When Mexico was invited to the banquet of civilization the main course had already been served. We have no choice but to industrialize as rapidly as our human and material resources permit."

None of the above imposing statistics would have much validity if inflation had eaten up the increase in income and made national productivity figures meaningless. But Mexico, during the period 1960–1970 underwent an average annual inflation of only 2.5 per cent, a total of 25 per cent for the decade, about that of the United States. Compare this, for example, with the figures for many other Latin American countries: inflation in Brazil during the decade was 2,900 per cent, in Uruguay it was 1,130 per cent, in Argentina 920 per cent, and in Chile 532 per cent.

The growth of specific basic industries indicates even more clearly Mexico's rate of expansion in the past ten-year period. In 1960 iron production (first fusion) was 777,000 tons, but by 1970 this had jumped to over two million tons. In 1960 the production of steel ingots was 1,539,000 tons, and by 1970 it had increased to 3,800,000 tons. During the same ten-year span, production of cement rose from 3,086,000 tons to 7.2 million tons. Plate glass increased from 4,499,000 square meters to 16.6 million square meters. Automobiles produced rose from 28,121 cars in 1960 to 128,000 cars in 1970, while production of trucks and buses rose from 21,686 to 53,000 units during the same period. Production of sulphuric acid increased from 249,000 tons to nearly a million and a half tons during the decade, with a 94 per cent increase in the three years 1968–1970. Anhydrous ammonia rose from 19,000 tons to nearly

500,000 tons, or twenty-five times as much. Aluminum ingots jumped 103.5 per cent in the two years 1968–1970, reaching a total of 46 million tons, and in the same period artificial fibers rose 35 per cent, from 63.7 million tons to 86.4 million tons.[49]

The production of petrochemicals more than doubled during the five years 1966–1970, and construction also continued its spectacular rise with a growth of 33 per cent during the same brief period. On the other hand, agriculture and livestock production have apparently levelled off and now have a very slow rate of growth. Sugar cane, with the Cuban market shut off from the United States, has made an impressive advance, having jumped from 19,542,000 tons in 1960 to almost 30,000,000 tons in 1970.

Stability is the mainstay of this phenomenal economic progress. Four decades of peace plus continuous government stimulation of economic development have combined to make Mexico unique in this regard in Latin America. Today half of the direct federal expenditure is for economic expansion. Mexico's foreign debt is only $2.59 billion dollars, of which less than one-fifth, or $500 million dollars, corresponds to the debt of the federal government. The remaining four-fifths of the total is the debt of government-owned businesses and agencies, most of which are profit making. The federal government is completely solvent, and the peso is one of the most stable currencies in the world today. In 1970 the gold and foreign reserves of the Bank of Mexico totalled $762 million, $111 million more than in 1969, and considerably more than the debt owed by the federal government. Besides this, Mexico has $500 million dollars through drawing rights with the International Monetary Fund. This Fund has recently been selling Mexico gold in order to use the peso in support of currencies in other countries. The federal government and the Nacional Financiera have recently floated bond issues in the European market, one issue for Swiss francs, and three issues for deutsche-marks. These issues take on great importance because they are the first in currencies other than the dollar.

New and valuable sources of mineral wealth have been discovered in Mexico, and more than 90 per cent of the mining and metallurgical production of the country is by companies that are totally Mexican or which have a majority of Mexican capital. Immense new sulphur deposits have been found on the Isthmus of Tehuantepec, where proven reserves now total 78 million metric tons. In less than five years known sulphur reserves have risen 320 per cent. Recent uranium discoveries have increased the reserves of that mineral to a total of 4,366,248 tons of ore.

A huge copper deposit was recently located in the state of Sonora, containing an estimated 200 million tons of ore, more than ample to meet all domestic needs. Total copper reserves are 1½ billion tons, and iron reserves are 730 million tons. Mexico continues to be one of the leading silver producers of the world, and in 1970 was second only to Canada in this regard. Production was 42,900,000 Troy ounces in 1970. Total silver reserves are 15½ million tons.

The industrial development of Mexico has promoted the growth of a powerful class of businessmen who have a proud nationalistic point of view. They willingly adopt the most advanced international technical processes and improvements but have no wish to be dominated by foreign capital. There has also been an impressive growth of the Mexican financial system, which is solidly based and intelligently administered. In the rapidly expanding economy a profit of 10 per cent on gilt-edged securities is considered minimal.

The February-March 1970 issue of the magazine *Mexico This Month* presents details of Mexico's investment potential, and gives this judgment in the words of Eugene Latham, a well-known investment consultant: "The Mexican money market has continued to attract investment capital in unprecedented amounts, due primarily to the high interest rates available in fixed-income investment forms and the ever-increasing awareness in international money markets that Mexican economic growth is both rapid and secure. It is our feeling that Mexican fixed income investments presently offer unequalled opportunities for the placement of funds with complete security and most attractive yields."

Mexican investment banks, or *financieras* as they are called in Spanish, are the main sources of these high-yield investments. The *financieras* are under the control and close scrutiny of the national Treasury Department and the nation's central bank, the Banco de Mexico. Funds on deposit are *not* insured as in the United States, but the federal government has never allowed any *financiera* to default on its obligations. In order to obtain the highest yields a minimum of $2,000 (25,000 pesos) must be deposited. If this amount is left untouched for one year, interest paid after that time totals 11.45 per cent net, after taxes. With interest withdrawn periodically but with capital untouched the yield is 11 per cent. If the total amount is left for two years, the interest paid rises to 12 per cent net annually. Demand accounts in lesser amounts yield approximately 9 per cent with complete liquidity. The retired person living in Mexico may thus obtain a ready and very secure high-income yield on his investment bank deposits, over either the short or the long term, provided that he has the capital to begin with.

The Mexican peso, in which these investments are made, has had a hectic history, partly because of economic conditions within the republic during years of political unrest, partly because Mexico borders the United States, whose industrial plant capacity dwarfs that of her smaller neighbor. For many years the peso was worth approximately 50 U.S. cents, and Americans took it for granted that you got two pesos for one dollar. But a black market began to grow up, and in 1933, when the United States reduced the gold content in the dollar, Mexico "stabilized" her peso at 3.60 pesos per dollar. Further "stabilizations" have followed: In 1941 the exchange was set at 4.85 pesos per dollar; in 1949 it rose to 8.65 pesos per dollar, and in 1954 it reached 12.50 pesos per dollar.

The ideas back of these devaluations were to (a) help Mexico develop her economy and thus become more nearly self-sufficient, (b) keep imports down, (c) increase exports of agricultural and manufactured products by making their prices more attractive, (d) encourage American tourists to visit Mexico and spend money there, (e) and stimulate the repatriation of Mexican capital and the investment of Mexican savings in the national economy.

There was a great hue and cry in Mexico every time the peso was devaluated, and this was especially loud and sharp in 1954. But the federal government, which had the benefit of the country as a whole at heart, was absolutely correct in its analysis of the situation, and the national economy has expanded phenomenally within the past few years. The peso is now the most stable currency in Latin America. Of course, such luxury items as automobiles and electric refrigerators cost enormous sums in Mexico today, but by keeping Mexicans from buying these things on a wide scale the national government has more or less forced them to invest their funds in Mexico's own expansion program. The decision to devaluate the peso was not an easy one to make, but it has certainly paid off magnificently.

Devaluation alone, however, would not have been enough to cope with the critical economic problems.

> When an underdeveloped country is faced with low industrial production and a situation of rising prices lingering for five years after the second of two monetary devaluations in five years also, the government has two choices about future progress.
>
> Either it can do nothing to break the recurrent inflation-devaluation cycle, or it can take hold of the reins of the economy and definitively guide its development.
>
> Just as Mexico has a *guided democracy,* so does it have a guided economy

where government is decidedly the leader and private enterprise is sometimes obliged to take a back seat in major production decisions. (Basic petrochemicals, a government defined term, is one example; the sugar industry may become another.)[50]

The country's uninterrupted industrial expansion in the past decade indicates the success of the government policy. This success is reflected in the national budget as well as in the national economy. There is no budget deficit in Mexico currently. All budgets are balanced; indeed, there is usually a surplus at the end of each fiscal year. Few countries in the world today can boast of such fiscal stability.

The preceding comments and statistics on Mexico's spectacular economic growth during recent years should not lead one to conclude that the country has achieved a standard of living comparable with that of the United States or the more industrialized Western European nations. As the last two Presidents of Mexico have stated in addresses to the nation, approximately one half of the people of Mexico still lack safe drinking water, and close to half of them must still be classed as essentially illiterate. Almost thirty per cent cannot read or write, and an additional twenty per cent are not well enough educated to read or write anything beyond the simplest materials. A third of the population lives in shacks, without sewage, without medical care, on a diet of beans and corn.

A brief comparison will make the situation clear. Mexico, for example, has approximately the same number of inhabitants as France, about 50,000,000, but the gross national productivity of Mexico is only one-fourth that of France, and it is just equal to that of Holland, which has a population of only thirteen million. Mexico's productivity is one-third that of Italy, which has the same population, and compared with the United States on a per capita basis (that is, if we divide U.S. productivity and population by four, thus giving the productivity of 50 million persons, which is Mexico's population) we find that Mexico produces only one-eighth as much per person as is produced by the much more materially advanced economy of the United States. This means that while there are quite a few wealthy families in Mexico, and a rapidly growing middle class, the great masses of Mexican people, especially in the rural areas, still live at the bare subsistence level. The critical problem of these millions of undernourished, uneducated, unproductive citizens has yet to be aggressively tackled by the Mexican government.

U.S. investments in Mexico have continued to grow since the stabilization of the economy during the Cárdenas presidency, and in 1970 totalled a billion and a half dollars in direct investments. Another half a billion dollars is in indirect and hidden investments. About thirty thousand Americans are working in Mexico today, and many thousands more, mostly retirees, are living in various parts of the country on a permanent or semi-permanent basis.

Among the American businesses which have branches in Mexico are General Motors, Ford, Monsanto, Dow, several ethical drug companies, Burroughs, Kodak, Motorola, John Deere, Celanese, Pepsi-Cola, Coca-Cola, Sears and Roebuck, Goodyear, American Metals, Anaconda, Gulf Sulphur, American Smelting and Refining, and dozens of other concerns well known in United States business circles. A purely U.S. touch, Mother's Day, has been eagerly taken up by the Mexicans, and each May sends retail sales to record heights. Christmas decorations and Christmas cards, U.S. style, hardly known in Mexico a generation ago, are also big business today.

Mexico today is undoubtedly a country of great opportunity. She stands now about where the United States stood at the end of the Reconstruction period after the Civil War. The government of Mexico looks favorably on the entry of private foreign capital into the country, particularly if it is invested to increase production, improve the utilization of the natural resources, or provide new techniques of production, organization, and distribution. The principle of mutual benefit is the keystone of the government policy, whose main object is to expand the economy and raise the standard of living of the Mexican people. In many instances the combination of native and foreign capital has worked very well in producing two-way benefits.

One striking case is the development of the vast sulphur deposits on the Isthmus of Tehuantepec, where American capital and efficiency, aided by Mexican labor and capital, have achieved not only excellent profits for the investors, but a much higher standard of living for hundreds of Mexican workers. Mexican businessmen recently bought a majority interest in this enterprise. This is the kind of development that Mexico is seeking; the day of exploitation is over.

The U.S. and Mexican governments have also set an example of what may be achieved through cooperation in their joint $80 million Amistad (Friendship) Dam project upriver between Del Rio, Texas, and Ciudad Acuña, Mexico. This six-and-one-half-mile-long dam provides flood control and will create a vast source of hydroelectric power besides impounding a reservoir more than 85 miles long for purposes of irrigating adjacent farmland. Both countries will receive the benefits of this new dam.

In another and very different way American inspiration also has aided Mexico. One noteworthy example of this is the story of William Spratling, who arrived in Taxco in 1930 and decided to settle there because of the charm and beauty and low cost of living in the town. In former years Taxco had been a great silver center. Borda had made his fortune there, and left the beautiful Church of Santa Prisca as a monument to his name. Silversmiths had wrought lovely patterns in this precious metal in years gone by. But in 1930, when Spratling arrived, silver jewelry had fallen into disfavor, and Taxco was a ghostly village, with only a single silversmith. Spratling set up a small shop, gathered the best craftsmen he could find, taught them what he knew, inspired them to go on—and the Mexican silver industry took a new lease on life. By concentrating on quality rather than quantity Spratling revitalized the ancient plastic instincts of the race, and before long competition among the Taxco silversmiths was keen. Spratling was regarded as the master, but many of his apprentices later left his employ and set up their own shops. Taxco today is a hive of silver shops, which line every nook and cranny of the hilly town. And the making of silver jewelry is again one of the great arts of Mexico.

"Folk art here," Spratling writes, "is an integral part of daily living—not simply an attempted revival of neglected arts. Only in Mexico will you find today the happily uninstructed little people, even in remote villages, busily producing new forms and giving virile and charming new expressions to old needs." In weaving, embroidery, pottery making, in furniture and in hand-blown glass, this revitalization of the old folk arts is very much alive in Mexico today. The government awards annual prizes to urge the artists on, but there is no huge government program to regiment their talents. Among the outstanding silversmiths of the past three decades are Spratling, Antonio, los Castillo, and Salvador. Their work is very different, but they all produce pieces that are exquisitely designed and wrought, as fine as one can buy, and at a cost far less than one has any right to expect. Indeed, a person or family wishing to purchase a silver service may well save enough by buying this item in Mexico to pay for the complete trip.

What about retirement in Mexico today? Many thousands of North Americans have done just that, and hundreds more are joining them every year. Of course, there are also some among these who, disenchanted with life in Mexico, return to the United States, but the number who remain continues to grow. A part of this disenchantment may be attributed to the exaggerated reports that a person can live in luxury in Mexico on one or two hundred dollars a month. Actual costs are considerably more than this, if one wishes to have the ordinary comforts of home: electricity, hot water, sewage disposal, etc. We take these things for granted. Many Mexicans do not. The actual cost of living in Mexico would be something like this: in Mexico City a couple might scrimp by on about $350 a month, but there would be no frills. A reasonable monthly expenditure of $400 to $650 for comfortable living would be more like it. In the provinces things are cheaper. The same minimum, $350, might allow a couple to get by quite adequately in Guadalajara, or in one of the neighboring towns. Acapulco would be much more expensive. Morelia and San Miguel de Allende, two other favorites, would approximate the minimum. Puerto Vallarta, bursting at the seams with tourists, would be a little higher. If one wishes to keep a car and do a lot of driving, the cost would increase, of course.

What are the difficulties and categories of permanent or semipermanent residence in Mexico? The *Visitante-Rentista* (income-holding visitor) may obtain a visa good for six months, with the possibility of three six-month renewals, for a total of two years. This is the simplest way of giving Mexico a try. The income-holding visitor must prove that he has a minimum income of 2,000 pesos ($160) a month, and an additional 1,000 pesos ($80) for each member of his family over fifteen years of age. The visitor with a tourist card may change this card to a *Visitante-Rentista* document while in Mexico.

The second category is that of *Visitante* (visitor) which is a flexible and easy way for the foreigner to transact business on a temporary basis in Mexico. On this card, which costs about $4 at a Mexican Consulate in the United States, one can even work for a limited period of time, but he must prove that some concern in Mexico directly needs his help.

The permanent resident must enter Mexico as an *Inmigrante* (immigrant), in which category he must either (a) prove that he has an income of $240 a month for himself and $80 for his wife and each dependent over fifteen or (b) he may be a capital investor *(Inversionista)*, in which case, if he wanted to reside in Mexico City, he would have to invest $48,000 in a business owned partly or entirely by himself. If he planned to reside in some other part of Mexico the capital investment would be only $16,000.

There are other categories for professional men and women, specialists and students, each of which have their own requirements. It is very easy to obtain a student visa, if one has sufficient funds to support himself, but professionals and specialists must offer a type of training specifically requested by some concern in Mexico and they must provide skills in which *no available Mexican nationals are properly qualified.*

Owning property in Mexico presents several special difficulties for the foreigner. In the first place, the foreign national may buy Mexican property only if he is in one of the immigrant categories. The shorter range visitors or residents have no legal right to enter into a contract and are specifically prohibited from buying real estate. In addition, no foreign citizen, not even a permanent immigrant, may buy property within 100 kilometers (62 miles) of the land borders of Mexico, or within 50 kilometers (31 miles) of any seacoast. Indeed, the foreign immigrant may not even lease real estate in these prohibited areas for longer than ten years.

Of course, there are many real estate development projects which have found ingenious ways to circumvent these laws, but one should be extremely wary before making any deal with such concerns for property in Mexico. The most common practice is for the real estate company to ask the prospective buyer to invest $10,000 or so in a "club," with the understanding that this outfit will build a house for him to his own specifications. The house is constructed on a lot which is club property, and it is then "leased" to the tenant for nine years and 364 days.

Cost of building a house would *begin* at around $12,000 in the area of Guadalajara, and would range up or down from that figure in other parts of the country. The refugee from Los Angeles, New York, or Mexico City immediately notices how much less crowded the streets of Guadalajara are, because of the greatly reduced number of vehicles. These total around 100,000 automobiles of all kinds in a metropolitan area of a million and a half inhabitants.

Guadalajara's suburbs are a delight, and many thousands of North Americans and Canadians have already ensconced themselves therein. One impressive new real estate development, at Santa Anita near Zapopan, sells luxury houses to foreigners for about $40,000, and membership in its "club" for another $3,000. In return for this investment the concern agrees to keep up all the grounds, to help rent the houses when the owners are gone, to provide an eighteen-hole golf course and clubhouse, etc. Many of Guadalajara's leading citizens are involved in this development and a considerable number of them will own homes here. Close to 100 million pesos have already been invested in the projects, and in order to make the golf course absolutely top-flight forty carloads of the best loamite were imported by rail from the United States. Streets will be promenade style, with trees, grass and flowers in the middle. There is no smog. A more modest housing "club" is Rancho Contento, a few miles out of Guadalajara on the Nogales highway. Here lots cost $10,000, houses $20,000, and club membership (shareholding) $1,600 a year. Other attractive communities are Cocoyoc, near Cuernavaca, Las Brisas in Acapulco, Jurica in Querétaro, and Atascadero in Guanajuato. For details see 1969–1970 issues of *Mexico This Month* magazine.

Good servants in Mexico earn roughly 350 to 450 pesos (between $30 and $40 a month, but one must speak Spanish in order to get the best from them. In the provinces these servants are in general hardworking, honest, devoted, and it is a delight to have them around. The high unemployment rate in the rural areas makes it much easier to find good servants in the smaller towns than in the large urban centers. Another advantage of living in Mexico is that if one rents or leases a house and wants it remodeled or redecorated, workmen can be found who will do a very good job at prices which are ridiculously low by U.S. standards. There is a carpenter in almost every block, and nearly any neighbor can recommend some plasterer, plumber, electrician, or bricklayer who has given him good service. Furniture can easily be made to order, and the best *ebanistas*, cabinet makers, turn out first-rate pieces. The worker still takes a pride in his job, and if one exercises a reasonable amount of caution the annoyances of broken promises, delays, inferior workmanship, and a general air of unpleasantness which make almost any repair, no matter how small, painful in the United States, need not be experienced in Mexico. But again, the necessity to understand the native psychology and to be able to express oneself clearly in Spanish is obvious. Otherwise, grievances due to misunderstandings are almost inevitable, for two completely different life styles are involved.

Nearly half of the people of Mexico still depend on agriculture for a living. In 1970, out of an estimated 16 million workers, 46.1 per cent or nearly 8 million of them were engaged in farming. A very small proportion of this number is economically well off, but the majority of Mexico's agricultural workers live in constant poverty and a high percentage of them are unemployed or underemployed at any given moment. In the central and southern parts of the country unemployment of rural workers often reaches 40 to 50 per cent. These people eke out an existence somehow, but their work is never secure, they have no savings whatsoever, and almost no income. Perhaps 50 per cent live on less than $60 a month. When unemployment hits them, they simply depend on the charity of some other member of the family who is working at the time. It is a precarious, almost hopeless way of life. The fundamental problem of Mexico today is how to raise the standard of living of these millions, for when they are able to buy more the national market will be doubled, and the country as a whole will surge forward. The wage scales given below show the depth of the problem.

MINIMUM DAILY WAGES IN SELECTED REGIONS

	1960–1961		1970–1971	
	Urban	Rural	Urban	Rural
Mexicali	$2.00	$1.75	$3.85	$3.00
Monterrey	$1.10	$1.05	$2.50	$2.35
Guadalajara	$1.05	$1.05	$2.35	$2.20
Puebla	.95	.75	$2.20	$1.85
Federal District	$1.16	$1.12	$2.55	$2.40
Oaxaca	.60	.45	$1.50	$1.32

These are the official minimum wages as reported by the Banco Nacional de México. Actual wages received may at times be less. On the basis of the above scale, however, if a worker is employed steadily his *weekly* wage (in 1971) would range between a low of $7.92 in Oaxaca to a top of $23.10 in Mexicali, if he worked *six days a week*. Given the high rate of unemployment in all rural areas his real income would, of course, be much less than this on a yearly basis if he worked outside the city. These official figures indicate how critical the problem of income is in rural Mexico.[44]

A few pointed comments in regard to Mexican agriculture, therefore, are now in order. First, corn is the basic crop of the Mexican farmer. Corn was cultivated by the indigenous people of the land before the conquest, and it is still by far the most important single crop in Mexico today. In some ways, it is more important than all other crops together, not money-wise but because so many millions of lives depend directly upon the corn crop for their very survival. "Corn," writes the economist Edmundo Flores, "is the most important single item in Mexico's diet, cuisine, mythology and politics. It is a basic need, a dietary obsession and a nightmare for the minister of agriculture." The significance of corn in the national life may easily be seen if we bear in mind that in

1970 out of a total of approximately 40 million acres of crop-bearing lands, approximately 20 million acres were in fields of corn. In other words, one out of every two acres of cultivated farmland in Mexico is planted in corn.

For many years Mexico was unable to supply enough corn to meet the demands of her population, and considerable quantities had to be imported. As recently as 1966 the Bank of Mexico predicted that by 1970 it would be impossible to feed the fast-growing population of the country and the specter of widespread famine loomed. However, since 1966, with the help of Rockefeller funds, new strains of seed corn have been developed, the use of fertilizers and irrigation has been greatly extended, and consequent yields per acre, not only of corn but of nearly all farm crops have doubled, tripled, even quadrupled. Land that produced only 700 pounds of wheat an acre in 1965 now yields five to six times as much. The production of corn, wheat, and beans is in excess of the amount needed for internal consumption, and large quantities of these items are being exported. One million tons of corn were sold in the export market in 1968. There is no short-term fear that Mexico will be unable to feed its people if efficient production *and equitable distribution* go hand in hand.

A brief survey of production for the three basic foods, corn, wheat, and beans, during the decade 1960–1970 will show what the picture is in this regard. In 1960 Mexico produced 5,420,000 tons of corn, but by 1967 production had risen to 9,264,000 tons and in 1968 it reached a peak of 9,412,000 tons. Corn then began to glut the market and to rot in storage before it could be sold. As a result in 1969 production declined to 8,496,000 tons, but in 1970 it rose sharply again to 11.1 million tons. Beans jumped from 528,000 tons in 1960 to their peak of 1,008,000 tons in 1967, and then declined, but 1970 production was 1.3 million tons. Wheat is the only one of the three basic commodities which has continued its dramatic climb without interruption, increasing from 1,180,000 tons in 1960 to 2,377,000 tons in 1969. The rise in wheat production also indicates that in his daily diet the average Mexican is gradually moving away from corn as the staff of life, and moving toward wheat, which is widely regarded as a more sophisticated food. Nevertheless, Mexico's poor rural population still lives primarily on corn and beans, a high-caloried but lopsided regimen which is neither good for the health nor comfortable for the bowels. Unfortunately, the "green revolution" of bigger crops, heavily subsidized by the Mexican government, is already leading to distortions in the economy.

An ideal, but at present theoretical, solution to the problem would be to utilize only the best corn land for corn and to cultivate this intensively, according to the latest scientific methods. The remainder of the corn land could then be used for other diversified crops and for cattle raising, and gradually the rural population would become meat and vegetable eaters. This would balance and add more much-needed meat protein to their diet, would help curb the omnipresent diarrhea and enteritis, and would add an extra margin of safety to the present subsistence diet. Although the rural population of Mexico is not by tradition meat eating, these people will eat meat when they can get it. The main problem is to obtain meat at a price they can afford to pay.* The corn lands in question, if converted to cattle raising, would be almost ideal for this purpose. The production of better strains of beef cattle would obviously also be a part of the picture. This solution, unfortunately, is merely theoretical under present conditions, because most Mexican farms are too small to produce cattle efficiently. The small farmer has no money to buy the meat even if it were produced and so he is condemned to produce corn and beans on his small plot of land in order to live. It is a vicious circle, which only the national government can break.

Another potential source of more good protein food which could be developed without changing cultivated acreage in any way may be found in Mexico's present underdeveloped fish industry. The country is bordered by vast stretches of ocean teeming with marine life, and it has been estimated that one acre of ocean contains fifty times as much food as can be produced on one good acre of cultivated land. Three dozen kinds of excellent seafoods are being produced today by Mexico's ocean water, but these are seldom consumed by the rural population, except right along the coasts. The Bank of Mexico's recent official report on the nation's economic development expressed this succinct judgment: *Mexico's waters abound with fish, but the lack of a fishing tradition keeps exploitation low.* With the country's present excellent transportation system and a wider use of refrigerated cars and frozen foods this need not continue to be the case.

Need not, but doubtless will. Traditions are hard to change in Mexico. A young Mexican known to the author, after graduating from college in the United States, returned to Mexico and offered capital and know-

* Mexico is in thirty-sixth place among the world nations in consumption of meat per capita at thirty-seven pounds a year. Uruguay occupies first place with 227 pounds per capita. The U.S. is in fifth place. Japan, a well-fed fish-eating country, is in thirty-ninth place.

how for expansion to a member of his family who was the biggest fisherman in Vera Cruz. He saw great profits in shipping refrigerated and frozen seafoods to the cities of the interior, but his uncle was not interested. This man and his many fishermen never brought in more fish than would be consumed in Vera Cruz in a single day. They could easily make this catch in three or four hours, so they were not interested in better boats, better nets, or longer trips. But this was not all. The old fisherman said to the young graduate: "I would not consider such a thing. You, a college graduate becoming a fisherman! It is unthinkable! You can't work with your hands. And besides, why should I expand? Just to work harder, have more worries? I do not need any more money than I am making. And I now have time to enjoy life on what I earn. I do not want to be big just to have less time and more troubles." And he did not change his way of life.

The further diversification of Mexican agriculture is also a critical problem. Corn, while it actually does feed many millions of people in Mexico, has also held these same millions in bondage for centuries. Corn is the bane as well as the benison of the rural Mexican population. Even on their small farms if these rural families could break away from the corn habit they would be better off. The present average income per acre of corn is approximately 628 pesos. However, the avocado crop averages 4,120 pesos per acre, oranges yield 2,340 pesos per acre, Irish potatoes bring in 1,800 pesos per acre, and many vegetable crops (tomatoes, eggplant, lettuce) can bring in over 6,000 pesos an acre. The yields in poultry, eggs, or fruit would be similarly high, from ten to twenty times the yield per acre of corn, for these products are in constant demand in Mexico today. Yet in the immediate vicinity of Mexico's largest urban centers, including the capital itself, hundreds of acres are still given over to the production of corn. On a recent jaunt I mentioned this to a corn farmer near Mexico City. He looked me in the eyes as he said, "I and my family *eat* corn every day, señor."

Now we are back again to the problem of land. For a century and a half land has been the great Mexican problem: how to distribute the land, how to use the land, how to save and how to improve the land. Since the lives of 46.1 per cent of all Mexicans depend directly on the land, this problem is certain to be a fundamental one for many years to come.

Two facts must be borne in mind. First, the corn economy has kept the rural population in bondage for centuries. Second, the Mexican

Revolution, with its battle cry of "Land and liberty," made people believe that if only the concentration of land ownership were broken, and if the land of Mexico were redistributed equitably among its people, the national economic problem would be almost solved. The government has zealously carried out a good part of this program of agrarian reform, but with results which have been very spotty indeed. The program has now reached a point of no return. Just to give a family land to grow corn on is simply to continue to tie that family's life to hopeless poverty. At present the *ejido*, the small private farm, and the large estate all exist side by side in Mexico, but emphasis is on the first two. Individual land parcels allotted to heads of families now average 90 to 100 acres per family. On the other hand, 46 per cent of the rural landowners have received no lands at all as a result of this process of distribution, and their small plots, *if they own any land at all*, average only three to four acres each. They are an economic disaster.

A total of 200 million acres have been distributed since 1917. This is approximately 43 per cent of Mexico's total area. During the term of President Díaz Ordaz (1964–1970) the land distribution program was speeded up, and a total of 57 million acres were doled out to rural families, some of it reclaimed swamp land.[49] With considerable fanfare over ten million acres were distributed during the President's last year in office. This amounts to an incredible 27,000 acres distributed *every single day* of the President's six-year term.

As F. M. Foland writes in *Foreign Affairs*, October, 1969, "Mexico's agrarian reform is an irregular program with significant successes to show in some geographic regions and abject failures in others; with ultramodern agricultural techniques on some farms juxtaposed with oxen and wooden plows on others; with the idealized *ejido* system disintegrating into individual plots, yet instilling the *ejido* farmers with prestige and a sense of dignity; with spurts of governmental enthusiasm followed by conscious attempts to suppress the whole concept."[45]

In any event, Mexico's land reform is an already mature program, unlike that of Bolivia, Chile, Colombia, Brazil, and other Latin American countries where it is barely beginning to make a dent in the national life. Mexico long ago came to realize that credit, research, crop advice, marketing controls, seed improvement, irrigation, and farm insurance were absolute essentials if the whole plan was to be saved from bankruptcy. The net result of Mexico's program is that it has benefited over two and a half million families, from twelve to fifteen million citizens, representing 54 per cent of all landholders. *But* there still remain an estimated two million rural families wanting land, and there is only enough for about 300,000 more families. In land reform, therefore, the moment of truth has already arrived for Mexico. Here is a picture of the present status of how the country's total area is divided:

Mexico's total area	487,000,000 acres
Arable land	72,000,000 acres
Actually harvested (1970)	40,000,000 acres
Pastures (mountainous)	172,000,000 acres
Pastures (plains, hills)	41,000,000 acres
Forests	165,000,000 acres
Deserts, useless rocky areas	37,000,000 acres

The Mexican Department of Hydraulic Resources in a recent report made this further breakdown of Mexico's arable land:

Wet tropical land, abundant rainfall	5,000,000 acres
Land needing irrigation	22,000,000 acres
Land irrigated (1970)	8,200,000 acres
"Seasonal" land, *temporal*	37,000,000 acres

The lands referred to as "temporal" in Mexico are those which receive an undependable rainfall. These lands average one good crop every three years. On the other hand, about one-fifth of the more than eight million acres of irrigated land can produce two crops in a single year. The irrigated areas produce about 33 per cent in value of the total agricultural output, which is 34 billion pesos a year.

The agricultural land of Mexico is not rich. The further extension of irrigation and a wider use of fertilizers, crop rotation, erosion control, and more scientific methods of farming are a desperate necessity in Mexico today, especially in the depressed central and southern parts of the country. According to the calculations of H. H. Bennett, former chief of the Soil Conservation Service of the United States, because of improper use over 28 million acres of good agricultural land have been ruined or severely damaged by erosion. Approximately 700 million tons of soil are washed away in Mexico every year. This loss is of incalculable importance in a country where half the population still depends on farming for a living. It takes nature five hundred to a thousand years to make one inch of good topsoil, but man can destroy it in one moment of recklessness.

Recognizing that erosion is a national calamity, the government has taken vigorous steps to combat it. For example, 300,000 maguey bushes and 600,000 nopales (prickly pear bushes), were recently planted in the state of Tlascala in order to hold the soil. These plants are native to the area and have taken quick root. The federal government's Division of Soil and Water Conservation has motorized divisions in every part of Mexico working constantly to control erosion. A total of 70 million trees were planted during the six-year term of President Díaz Ordaz. Thousands of acres have been tested, terraced, drained, banked, fertilized.

Agriculture stands at the crossroads in Mexico today. As the land goes, so go the people. Further industrialization may be the answer to many of Mexico's problems, but the critical situation of the rural masses is a concern of urgent and immediate necessity. Fortunately, the percentage of rural folk has been continuously decreasing. In 1930 those engaged in agriculture constituted 71.6 per cent of the total population; by 1940 this had declined to 65.4 per cent; by 1950 it stood at 58.2 per cent, and in 1970 it was approximately 46.1 per cent. Meanwhile, the urban centers have grown apace. Hundreds of thousands of agricultural laborers have been turned into industrial workers. Other thousands have entered the service industries. The problem of the poor rural population of Mexico will be solved not only in the fields, with better farming methods, but also in the cities, with expanded business services and with machines inside factories.

A comparison of the productivity of workers in each of these three main branches of the economy will show the picture more clearly. The output per worker in primary activities in 1970 (agriculture, livestock, forestry, fishing) was only $467 a year. In industry (manufacturing, construction, electricity, petroleum, mining) productivity per worker was $2,669 a year, and in the services (transport, commerce, government) it was $3,734 a year. Little wonder that nearly every farm laborer wants to come into the city even if he winds up living in a shantytown just one jump ahead of starvation. To the farm worker urban life is today's only true El Dorado. In his mind's eye the magic of the big city turns every effort to gold, gives him and his wife security, and holds the promise of a better future for his children. Great mushrooming clusters of hovels about the cities, even on the roofs of swank apartment houses in the capital where so many servants live, prove only too clearly that this is not always the case. Still, the glitter of the city goes on luring the farm boys, and Mexico which was only 35.1 per cent urban in 1940 was 60 per cent urban by 1970.

During the decade 1960–1970 U.S.–Mexican relations, despite a few notable rough spots, have been those of *buenos vecinos*, good neighbors.

In July 1963 the long-disputed Chamizal strip was officially returned to Mexico, and the settlement was considered as a feather in the cap of President López Mateos, who had engineered the final negotiations. The dispute went back to 1864 when the Rio Grande changed course and 437 acres of Mexican territory between El Paso and Ciudad Juárez was shifted to the American side of the river. Several decades later the United States agreed to arbitrate, but then refused to abide by the decision when it went against them (1911). When restoration was finally made to Mexico in 1963 the United States reimbursed the 3500 Americans living on the strip for their properties, and aided them to resettle elsewhere.

Another sore point between the two countries concerned the Colorado River between Arizona and California, the source for irrigating many thousands of acres of Mexican farmland. In 1965 the United States earmarked five million dollars to stop the flow of salty waters into the river, which had caused the loss of many crops in Mexico.

In inter-American relations Mexico has maintained a very strict independence of U.S. policy. In the various confrontations between this country and Cuba, Mexico took a neutral position, which she affirmed was based on the policy of non-interference in the affairs of another American state. Firmly rebuffing her stronger neighbor, Mexico was the only country to vote against the U.S. proposal to oust Cuba from the Organization of American States. This stand was loudly applauded in Mexico. It was a case of eating your cake and having it too, because of the unconstrained certainty of U.S. support should Mexico herself ever be threatened by a foreign invader.

The United States more than evened the score in the fall of 1969 when Operation Intercept brought to a halt nearly all travel across the U.S.–Mexican border by causing every single vehicle to submit to a rigorous search for drugs. Long lines immediately formed, there was interminable waiting, and prospective travelers at once called off their trips, thus creating near ghost towns along the border. On the Mexican side business dropped 70 per cent and losses were heavy. A well-known Mexican magazine editorialized: "Down here nobody is *for* marijuana, but at the same time nobody seems to be *for* the way the U.S. government has acted in attempting to cut off the flow of the weed from south of the border to north of same. In fact, most Mexicans, both highly-placed and man-in-the-street types, are dumbfounded by the massive search-and-seizure operation instigated by U.S. border guards and customs officials."

The Mexican government protested vigorously and Operation Intercept was called off after a couple of weeks. Still, the prevailing but mistaken belief this side of the border is that Mexico holds a very permissive attitude toward drugs, and that she has refused to do anything to stop the drug traffic across the border. The fact is that in the period 1969–1970, with the aid of U.S.-lent helicopters and airplanes, two million acres of marijuana was burned down in Mexico, and a comparable area planted in opium poppies was also destroyed. More than 1,300 persons were arrested, and 175 tons of marijuana and 100 pounds of hard drugs were seized.

Mexico was never the marijuana or heroin Mecca many Americans have thought it to be. Those arrested on a narcotics charge in Mexico cannot obtain bail, and often spend over six months in jail before coming up for trial. Conviction carries heavy penalties. Even relatively remote Oaxaca, renowned for its hallucinogenic mushrooms, which thus attracted sizable numbers of hippies from the United States, is now widely known as a place to avoid. Federal police patrol the backroads and any strangely groomed or strangely garbed youth may find himself suddenly behind bars.

On the other hand, it is certainly true that many U.S. drug companies have made big profits by selling large quantities of drugs to non-existent companies in Mexico. These shipments were received directly by the big-time dealer with a fake letterhead in Mexico, who in turn resold them to the illegal market in the United States. In such cases the American drug company who sells is at least as much to blame as the dealer in Mexico who buys. The real world center for the illegal drug trade, however, is Marseilles, France, and until the French government does something to stop this Mafia-dominated traffic, all other efforts at drug control will be ineffective.

One final reflection: President Nixon's administration in the United States, after a big initial gesture toward Latin America in Nelson Rockefeller's 23,000 mile trouble-shooting hegira and report, pigeonholed most of the recommendations made in that report because of increasing preoccupation with domestic problems, the Near East and southeast Asia. Rockefeller's visit elicited official approbation in Mexico, but there were wry comments in the Mexican press. An editorial in *Excelsior* pointed out that the trip was "marked by deaths and tensions mounting to impressive levels, and disturbances of previously unseen dimensions." Obviously a redevelopment of relations between the U.S. and Latin America was needed. The editorial concluded: "None of this—it must be underlined—has anything to do with philanthropy or with the price of raw materials. It seems paradoxical that this must be proclaimed so energetically at a time when the communications media are so prodigiously developed. The fact is that we do not know each other, and in this ignorance we accumulate resentments which can explode at any moment."

Mexicans summarize their own attitude in this proverbial statement: "*Poor Mexico, so far from God, and so close to the United States!*"

XXIII

SOME DIFFERENCES IN OUR CULTURES

To be strong is for the individual to integrate his total development: physical, intellectual, ethical and esthetic, in the determination of a character.

—JUSTO SIERRA

MANY North Americans who visit Mexico are taken in by the guidebooks, and they expect the impossible. They do not speak the language; they do not know the customs. They feel disgruntled and desperately alone in Mexico (as in any foreign country), so they seek each other out like birds of a feather, and every resort is full of them, all speaking English. A sizable proportion of them are disillusioned with Mexico and everything Mexican. I have often seen the sad and bewildered look on the faces of these people as they put aside their street smiles and return to the solitude of their hotels. They would be the first people in the United States to expect a foreign visitor here to learn our language and to understand our ways, but they would be the last people in the world to admit that any of their disappointment in Mexico may have raisen from their abysmal ignorance of the Mexican people.

Our cultures are not alike. There are certain surface resemblances, but even these are very deceptive. In broad terms Mexican culture has always been characterized by (*a*) the very cultured, literate few, on the one hand, and, on the other (*b*), the illiterate but not uncultured masses. The cultured few, reminiscent of the exceptional men of the Renaissance, are the great artists, the intellectual leaders, the writers. This small minority represents a summit of artistic achievement, and in these fields the cultivated Mexican is equal to the world's best.

On the other hand, there are the illiterate masses. Without education, without our newer techniques, these masses still have a deep intuitive feeling for cultural values. They have always produced a folk art which is strong and beautiful. They possess what one writer has called a kind of "literacy of the illiterate." They *feel* their way into cultural expressions: they extemporize their own art forms. When they speak, or dance, or sing, everyone takes part, the mass soul speaks; they are not spectators. And in that creativity tensions melt away, there is catharsis, there is peace, while we in the United States have become a nation of spectators. We observe, as others perform. We work at some small specialized labor, while others use the fruits of our labor. We feel a strong alienation of creativity, and also an alienation of productivity. We are often rootless, cut from the vine, cut from the community. We are no longer a part of our own culture. We have achieved a high average level of education, which has almost completely smothered our folk art and has made it increasingly difficult for the superior person to achieve a superior development. Our educational system, according to one well-known Latin-American writer, has become a vast leveling process, losing in profundity what it has gained in extension. Our schools are predicated on the principle that Simple Simon must never come to think that Socrates was the better man.

When the North American goes to Mexico he does not meet the masses, but he will see and admire and buy and use folk-inspired, even folk-made products. On the other hand, he does often meet and come to know many Mexicans of culture, but he is unable to find any bond or common ground on which to stand. In Mexico the individual, the person, one's own person, has an almost absolute value. Hence, the dominance of personal rule in the national life, the frequency of dictatorship. Even Mexican culture consists largely of that which can be expressed without the need to go beyond one's self. Therefore, "it is rich in such values as literature, art, personal dignity, heroism, religious feeling, richness of interior life expressed with beauty, distinction or grace," as the writer Américo Castro has pointed out.[4]

Mexican society, composed as it is of many of these personal islands, is lacking in social cohesion, solidarity, collective enterprise, collaboration, and human charity. In the United States the group is of supreme importance; democracy and education have both become group arts among us, and large-scale business enterprises have made things increasingly difficult for the small individual establishment. Loyalty to the group is a paramount concern; collective rather than personal values are transcendent.

Psychologically, this is one of the great rifts between the North American and the Mexican. The Mexican feels a necessity to speak and to write of himself as a person. Particularly in private conversation he likes to express his personal beliefs, his personal hopes and values, for in this way he feels important as an individual. What he says characterizes him as a self, not as a member of any group or collectivity. He therefore cannot understand the North American's reluctance to open his heart, and he regards his constant talking about business matters and commonplaces as indicative of a superficial character or mentality.

Another fundamental part of the difference between us, culturally speaking, is that the Mexican (like every Hispanic Latin) lets the heart rule the mind, while the North American lets the mind rule the heart. Our philosophy is scientific, his is poetic. Culture to the Mexican is an emotional quality, while to the North American it is an intellectual expression. The Mexican is ruled by sentiment, the North American by rational thinking. The Mexican accepts the reason of the heart, the North American invariably seeks to follow the reason of the mind. It is the difference between faith and intellect, which has nothing to do with religious dogma but is the result of a long historic tradition in both instances. Character, at least in part, is fashioned by the historic environment which has for centuries surrounded the person.

Is there, then, such a thing as a national character in the Mexican people? Something more concrete than the general cultural differences outlined above? A search for national characteristics is at best a tenuous thing, but sometimes it can be helpful in the understanding of a different race and culture. With this thought in mind the following paragraphs are written. Literature, after all, is what a people think of themselves, and I have been teaching Mexican literature for over thirty years. The following thoughts, therefore, represent the distillation of my readings. They are not personal reactions pure and simple. They are all thoughts which Mexicans themselves have expressed about themselves with a sufficient insistence for me to believe them. But unless personal experience has borne out the theoretical statements, I have not used them.

In the first place, Mexican character, like Mexican social reality, is in a state of flux. It has not yet jelled. This is one of the main things that one notices in reading Mexican literature. While the literature of Europe, and even of the United States, depicts character against the background of a known and stable social reality, Mexican literature does not. Rather, it places the emphasis on that very element of flux in Mexican society. Different Mexican writers and different Mexican books reveal various aspects of that reality in a state of ebb and flow, where change is constant. And it is primarily this state of flux which interests the Mexican author, not the character delineated upon it. Until the social reality has become stabilized, great character delineation is impossible. It will lack focus, it cannot be a vital symbol of the whole, for the whole is not one but multiple.

The Spaniard who conquered and settled Mexico was himself the result of many racial fusions. Bolívar exclaimed that "Africa begins at the Pyrenees, Spain ceases to be European by virtue of her Moorish blood." Then when the conquistador reached the New World he encountered not one but many tribal groups in Mexico. He mixed his blood with all of them. The result of this race mixing was what one Mexican writer refers to as *nuestro mestizaje inconcluso,* "our inconclusive racial mixture." Add to this the geographic barriers which divide Mexico into so many regions, and one can easily see that this lack of a geographic unity has perpetuated the initial heterogeneity of race and character.

The Pampa gives Argentina a great geographic and cultural unity, which is strongly reflected in the national culture and the national economy. Mexico has no such great prairie, but its Central Highlands come closest to this. This area, in the long run, will be the prime molder of the national character. The process of this molding is clearly noticeable in Mexico today.

What are the main attributes of character in these Central Highlands? First, as a result of the inconclusive race mixing the mestizo Mexican, who is in the great majority, feels within himself a lack of unity and cohesion. As one Mexican writer has put it, "The two bloods we carry within us have not yet reached a state of peaceful blending; they find themselves in perpetual conflict." [14]

During the colonial regime, when the white Spaniard was dominant in Mexico, the mestizo and the acculturated Indian, saw this conflict exteriorized; he put Cortés at one social pole and Las Casas at the other. The conqueror versus the defender of the Indians. But after independence, during the Reform years (with the Indian Juárez as president), the mestizo and the red man began to view the social organism (and his own mixed being) in terms of the poles of Cortés versus Cuautemoc, the last Aztec chieftain. The mestizo had now taken a dominant position in Mexico, and the government was no longer white. Juárez and the Reform had vindicated Indian blood. The Revolution went even further in revitalizing the indigenous element in the national life. The Indian was exalted above even the mestizo. In Mexico today, in many history books, the statement will be made that "here we defeated the Spaniards." [14] Cuautemoc became a symbol of Mexican feeling, he was honored by many statues, while Cortés had none. In Peru the opposite was true; there Pizarro was exalted and Atahualpa and his Indians were relegated to a secondary place in the national psychology.

In Mexico today the average mestizo feels closer to Cuautemoc than he does to Cortés, at least symbolically. On October 10, 1949, a national decree was proclaimed which states as follows: "Let it be categorically declared that the heroic figure of Cuautemoc is the symbol of our nationality, and therefore deserves the sincere devotion of the Mexican people."[14] The fact is, however, that Cortés is just as much a part of Mexico as Cuautemoc—more so, in my opinion. It is the language of Cortés that is spoken in Mexico today, and the institutions which rule that country are also largely Hispanic, with many Indian-North American admixtures. The Mexican Indian past is alive most noticeably in the emotional and in the cultural life of the nation. To draw it out of focus is to misinterpret the reality of Mexican life. The Mexican Revolution has unfortunately had this result. Perhaps it was the only way to destroy the myth of Hispanic superiority in a country which by blood was overwhelmingly Indian. But now the time has come to strike a proper perspective. The racial fusion of Mexico will not be complete until Cortés is accepted fully by the mestizo citizen as being just as worthy a forebear as the Indian Cuautemoc.

In their present inconclusive racial and social state the great mass of mestizo citizens of Mexico have a sense of inferiority, for which they must find supercompensations. This feeling "of lesser value," as the Mexicans call it, is the emotional result of many historic factors. First, the Mexican who knows anything about the rest of the world, and especially the United States, has a feeling that the Hispanic culture brought to him by the conquest was in itself inferior. Proximity to the more powerful and more wealthy United States emphasizes this point. Then, this very Hispanic civilization which is so much a part of him tried for four centuries to make the mestizo minimize and subordinate his own native cultural achievement. Besides this, his Indian part comes to him from a conquered race, and his mixed blood was brought about by violence rather than love. The Spaniard came to Mexico without women, and took whatever native women he could find, more often than not outside of marriage. Having satisfied his urgent biological instinct, the Spaniard took little or no responsibility for his offspring. Yet another cause for the Mexican sense of inferiority is the century-long nutritional deficiency of his diet, which had caused him to be of smaller size than the average of most other nations of Western civilization. As a kind of supercompensation for all these things the Mexican loves to make diminutive things, he stresses quality rather than size or quantity, he employs many diminutives in his language.

Daniel Cosío Villegas, one of today's leading Mexican writers, has said: "The North American, fabulously rich, is accustomed to counting what he has, what he makes and what he loses; from this arises his propensity to base many of his judgments on size and quantity. The Mexican, *pobre de solemnidad* miserably poor as he generally is, has in reality nothing, or almost nothing, to count, and, in consequence, the notion of size, of quantity, appears strange to him; from this his judgments are based or pretend to be based on the notion of quality." [35]

The Mexican makes many diminutive things with his hands, miniatures of bone or ivory, metal or stone; he will even carve the kernel of a peach, make a tiny picture of colored straws, dress fleas in microscopic clothes, make toys and candies of miniature proportions. Every Mexican loves flowers and little animals. It is natural that he who does not have the large should stress the small. The use of diminutives in ordinary Mexican speech is a further proof of this. The Mexican adds onto many words an *ito* ending which any other Hispanic person would never think of doing. This diminutive ending emphasizes both the smallness and the quality of the item referred to, and the *personal* tenderness one feels toward it.

Other results of this sense of inferiority in the Mexican are a frequently excessive timidity, a strong reserve, a frequent dissimulation of real feelings. His subordinate historic position for so many centuries has made this reserve an integral part of Mexican character. The Mexican is also a sad human being, whose gaiety is very loud (love of great noise is another supercompensation) and whose humor is biting and sharp. He makes fun even of death, and will eat miniature skeletons made of sweets with the greatest gusto. This is a kind of getting even with fate, a mocking laughter at destiny. The Mexican Indian carries this feeling still further; to him the wake is a fundamental social expression, a veritable fiesta around the corpse.

The Mexican does not immediately make friends with another person but, once the barrier has been lowered, he will cross it completely. He will trust everything in the hands of his friend. He will defend him against all comers, even against his own kind. Obviously, it is not easy for a foreigner to enter this intimate circle, but those who do never wish to leave it. In his private life the Mexican is very loving and tender to wife and children, but in his life as a social being he is often violent.

Mexico has a rate of violent crime almost ten times that of Great Britain. As a member of a group the Mexican very frequently does not function effectively; he is always on the lookout for his person. He carries a chip on his shoulder; if it is so much as touched, the conflict begins. He lacks the ability to collaborate completely; his society lacks cohesion and organization.

Cosío Villegas balances the above statements somewhat in the Mexican's favor with these words: "In few things are the North American and the Mexican so far apart as in the impression that each of them causes when he is outside his own country: the Mexican is seen to much better advantage, the North American puts his worst side forward. . . . The strength of the United States is the collectivity and not the individual; the best of Mexico is the individual person, not the social being."[35]

Therefore, in his public life and in his government the Mexican is often chaotic, even corrupt, while his private life may be honest, humble, exemplary. How could he revere public figures or impersonal law when the only law that he has known until our own generation has always tried to oppress and persecute him? Politics, therefore, is a profit-making business. Hence, the custom of the *mordida*, the "bite," a kind of payoff which one often has to make in Mexico in return for a public or a legal favor, even in return for justice. Partly due to the very low salary scales, partly due to a widespread acceptance of corruption in public life, the *mordida* has become one of the most evil of Mexican institutions. Until it has been controlled, integrity in government and in justice will have rough sledding. Fortunately, the present President of Mexico, Luis Echeverria Alvarez, ex-professor of the National University, is a man in whom absolute personal honesty is united with public honor and great executive ability.

In his religion the Mexican places the emphasis on dogma and on formalism, rather than on ethics or morality. He may become very emotional about it, but is seldom rational. He feels the same way about patriotism. A sense of heroic martyrdom pervades his patriotic thinking. Although he has no very clear notion of what the words *my country* mean, he is willing to give his life for them. Even in this, the heart rules his mind and his body.

The Mexican is a great imitator; he possesses the mimetic instinct developed to the last degree. Imitation of the Hispanic overlords has equipped him well to imitate today the civilization of the United States. Thirty or forty years ago people were writing that a Mexican Indian had no mechanical sense, could never learn to drive a car or run a tractor. Today this sense is taken for granted. The Mexican is a fine mechanic. His deft use of the hands in little things has been rapidly carried over into the technical skills.

The Mexican is not lazy. Anyone who knows even a modicum of the history of Mexico must regard the Mexican as one of the hardest working human beings on earth. The myth of Mexican laziness, propagated by the North Americans and even taken up by the Mexicans themselves, is symbolized by the peon sleeping under a huge sombrero beside a great cactus. The cactus is always on arid, unproductive land. Much of Mexico, of course, is arid, unproductive land, and the North American associates a lack of productivity with laziness. The two seem to go together, like winter and leafless trees. But this impression is wrong.

The Mexican has produced little because he has had so little with which to work. And having had so little for so long a time has reduced his wants, or at least has kept his wants at a constant minimal level. In spite of all this, the Mexican works as hard as any man. Given proper diet and proper conditions of work he will labor like a Trojan, as many forward-looking American business enterprises have now found out. The Mexican also has in his work a spirit which is frequently lacking in the North American. He takes a personal pride in it; he does not find it to be an impersonal Moloch. He tries to make his work more than a job; he tries to make it an expression. When the time comes to rest, the Mexican will rest, completely. He will not pace nervously about until the time to start working again has arrived he will relax and drowse and let his body recover. The American will wear himself out with impatient waiting.

The Mexican is a great improviser. After his independence was won he had to improvise everything: constitutions, government, a new social organism, a new economy, a new set of laws and customs. His lack of material wealth has emphasized this skill of improvisation. He can get by on almost nothing, he can make what he needs out of almost nothing. He can even repair a tractor or an automobile out of almost nothing. Give him an old watch spring and a couple of bolts and nuts and he can manufacture a precision instrument.

Among the many ethical and cultural values—goodness, justice, truth, beauty, charity—the Mexican will invariably choose beauty. Until the most recent times art was to him synonymous with beauty, and was the summit of human expression. The Mexican Francisco Bulnes has written: "The great Latin delusion is the belief that art is the highest, almost the only object of national life. Latins bend every effort to be artists in religion and turn out idolators; they strive to be artists in industry, and become improverished; even in science they want to be artists, and they fail to understand scientific method. . . . Latins set themselves to be the great artists of politics, and the result is that a republic becomes for them a perfectly impossible system of government."[7]

It is wise to remember that all the above statements are relative. Mexico is now in a state of flux, and this is the fundamental character of the national and the private life. The emotional qualities referred to in the preceding paragraphs occur perhaps more often in Mexican character than in the character of the North American. We had better not go much further than this. Yet these differences, slight though they may be, very often prove to be the great stumbling blocks of understanding and friendship among peoples. The North American, who seldom feels the divine frenzy of poem or picture, has no reason in the world to regard as inferior the less organized but more emotional culture of Mexico. The garden that is too well organized and laid out comes very quickly to resemble a cemetery. Culture is as alive in Mexico today as anywhere on earth. It is a brilliant, beautiful, powerful culture with roots that reach deep into the bottomless past. If this book has contributed one iota toward a further awareness of that culture, if it has opened one single door of understanding between us, it will have served its purpose. No one can doubt for a moment that Mexico today stands on the threshold of a magnificent achievement.

ADDITIONAL READINGS

The reader who wishes to keep up with Mexico today by readings in English will find accurate and fascinating reports in the magazine *Mexico This Month*. It is edited by Anita Brenner, one of the truly great authorities on Mexico, who has assembled a staff of outstanding specialists. The address is *Mexico This Month*, P.O. Box 6–767, Mexico 6, D. F.; the cost of a subscription is five dollars a year. The magazine contains articles on investments in Mexico, retirement there, travel, fiestas, places to eat, artistic life, schools and colleges, etc.

Books on Mexico in English which can be recommended are: Leslie Simpson's *Many Mexicos*, Charles Flandrau's *Viva Mexico*, and William Weber Johnson's *Mexico*. D. H. Lawrence is one of the many literary figures who have written excellent books on the country. H. B. Parkes has written a good *History of Mexico*, and Samuel Ramos is the author of a provocative *Profile of Man and Culture in Mexico*. Alfonso Reyes, Dean of Mexican letters, is known in English mainly for his *Mexico in a Nutshell*, a collection of essays. Octavio Paz, in *The Labyrinth of Solitude*, probes uncomfortably into Mexican psychology, and the contemporary novelists Carlos Fuentes, Juan Rulfo and Agustín Yáñez have converted this probing into a literary art form. Several of their novels available in English are listed at the beginning of this book under Acknowledgments. *Into the Mainstream*, by Luis Harss and Barbara Dohmann, contains penetrating essay-like interviews with Carlos Fuentes, Juan Rulfo, and several other Latin American writers, among them Borges, Cortázar, and Carpentier. *American Extremes*, by Daniel Cosío Villegas, Mexico's best historian, astutely compares our two Americas, and contains valuable insights into Mexican and Latin American character and culture.

INDEX

About the Author

John A. Crow received his M.A. and his Ph.D. from Columbia University He has taught at the University of North Carolina, Davidson College, New York University, and for many years at the University of California in Los Angeles, where he was for some years chairman of the Department of Spanish and Portuguese. He has traveled widely in Europe, especially Spain, Italy and Greece, and in Mexico, and has talked with many people from all walks of life. He is the author or co-author of more than a dozen books, about half of them in Spanish. He has also contributed to the best encyclopedias, and his college texts have sold widely.

72 73 74 75 10 9 8 7 6 5 4 3 2

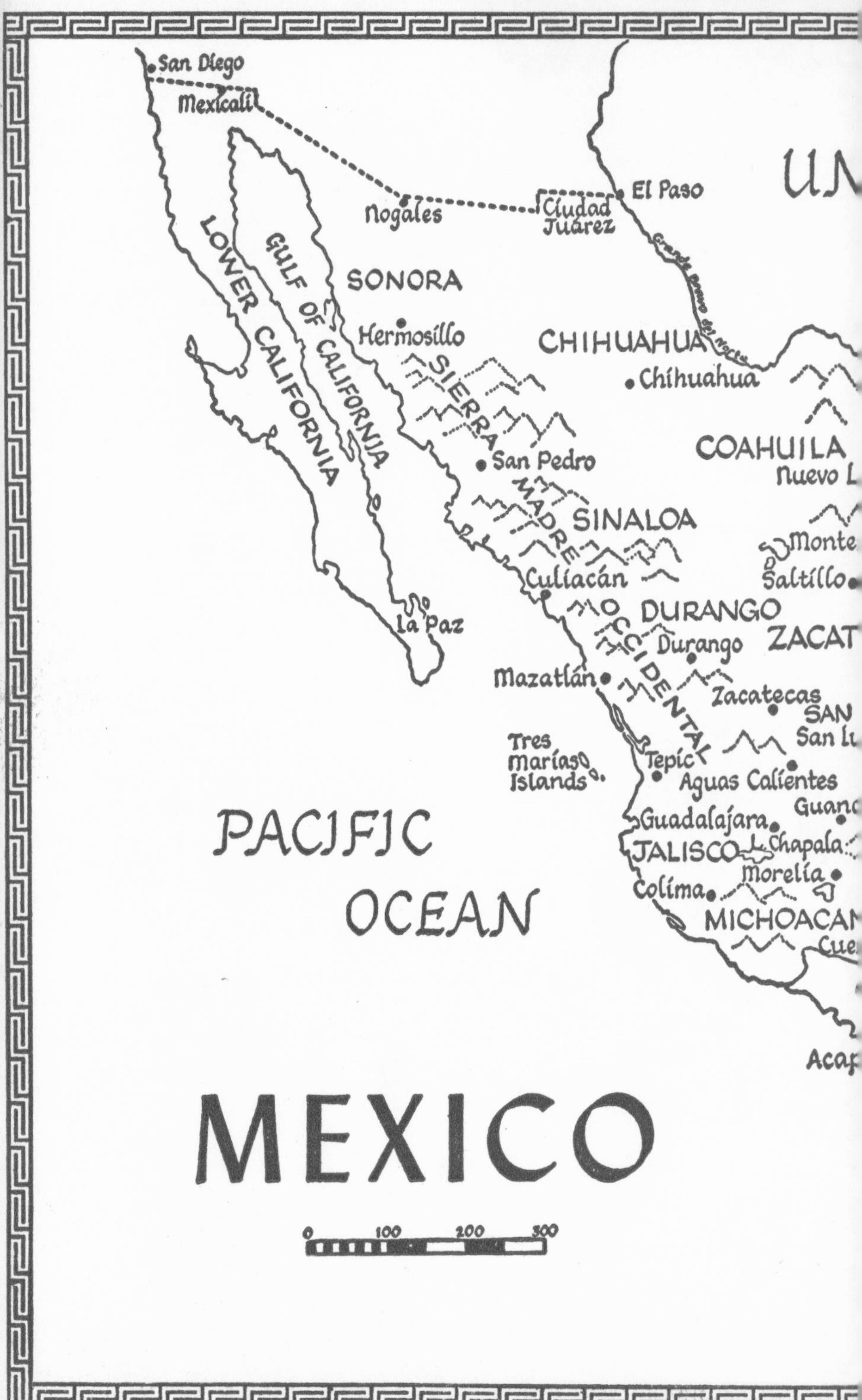

San Diego
Mexicali
Nogales
Ciudad Juarez
El Paso
SONORA
Hermosillo
LOWER CALIFORNIA
GULF OF CALIFORNIA
CHIHUAHUA
Chihuahua
SIERRA MADRE OCCIDENTAL
San Pedro
COAHUILA
SINALOA
Culiacán
Saltillo
DURANGO
Durango
La Paz
Mazatlán
Zacatecas
Tres Marías Islands
Tepic
Aguas Calientes
Guadalajara
JALISCO
Chapala
Morelia
Colima
PACIFIC
OCEAN
MEXICO
0
100
200
300